THE

OXYRHYNCHUS PAPYRI

VOLUME LXXVIII

THE OXYRHYNCHUS PAPYRI
VOLUME LXXVIII

EDITED WITH TRANSLATIONS AND NOTES BY

R.-L. CHANG   W. B. HENRY   P. J. PARSONS
and
A. BENAISSA

WITH CONTRIBUTIONS BY

M. J. ANDERSON   J. H. BRUSUELAS   L. CAPPONI   D. COLOMO
N. GONIS   N. KARAPANAGIOTI   W. LUPPE   M. MAEHLER   M. MALOUTA
F. MALTOMINI   Z. ÖTVÖS   P. M. PINTO   S. RISHØJ CHRISTENSEN
M. D. REEVE   PH. SCHMITZ   S. TROJAHN   M. VIERROS

Graeco-Roman Memoirs, No. 99

PUBLISHED BY
THE EGYPT EXPLORATION SOCIETY
3 DOUGHTY MEWS, LONDON WC1N 2PG

WITH THE SUPPORT OF
THE ARTS AND HUMANITIES RESEARCH COUNCIL
AND
THE BRITISH ACADEMY

2012

TYPESET BY
THE STINGRAY OFFICE, MANCHESTER
PRINTED IN GREAT BRITAIN BY
CHARLESWORTH PRESS, WAKEFIELD
AND PUBLISHED BY
THE EGYPT EXPLORATION SOCIETY
(REGISTERED CHARITY NO. 212384)
3 DOUGHTY MEWS, LONDON WC1N 2PG

Graeco-Roman Memoirs

ISSN 0306-9222

ISBN 978 0 85698 211 8

PREFACE

Section I of this volume offers fragments from three Christian texts. **5128** combines biblical excerpts within a larger text, perhaps a hymn. **5129** represents the first text of Justin Martyr to appear among the papyri. **5127** is a miniature parchment copy of Psalm CIX, a favourite text for amulets.

Section II has fragments of two lost classical works. **5130**, an excerpt from Alcidamas, the once famous sophist and rival of Isocrates, proves that he wrote, or was thought to have written, a paradoxical 'Praise of Poverty'. **5131** provides a central scene of Greek Tragedy, with a corpse borne onto the stage in the presence of Athamas: perhaps Euripides, *Ino*, possibly the corpse of Athamas' son Learchus, whom his own father had killed.

In section III, **5132** (from the same roll as **3840** and **4935**) adds an early witness to the tradition of Aristophanes, *Thesmophoriazusae*. There follow three groups of known prose texts. **5133–5147**, from speeches of Isocrates, exemplify various dates, formats and levels of production: textually, they show no tendency to side with one or other family of medieval MSS, so confirming the fluidity of the tradition at this early stage. (This part was made available to editors of the Isocrates OCT in advance of publication.) **5148–5152** contain fragments of speeches of the Demosthenic corpus rarely represented in papyri: note the final stichometric total in **5151**, and the quite unusual textual interest of **5148** and **5150**, both of relatively early date. **5153–5158** contain works from Plutarch's *Moralia*. These too add new readings and confirm old conjectures; and three of them have been dated to the second century, a further indication that works of Plutarch circulated at Oxyrhynchus within a generation of their author's death.

Section IV provides utilitarian literature. **5159** is a rare example of a metrical handbook. **5160** presents a commentary, learned and detailed notes on an Old Comedy, perhaps Eupolis, *Goats*. **5161–5163** belong to another uncommon type, glossaries for Greek-speakers learning Latin. This might be expected under the Tetrarchy and later (**5161**), much less expected in the first/second century AD (**5162–5163**, where the Latin is transliterated into Greek script).

Section V collects documentary texts of various types. **5164–5172** date from the earliest years of Roman rule in Egypt, when the new régime set out to increase revenue: for taxation see **5167** and **5172** (pig- and dike-tax), **5166** (slave-sales tax); for public sales of unproductive land see **5171**, where the Prefect excludes officials from such purchases (providing, that is, against insider trading). From the second century come letters sent to officials: **5178** raises questions about the lading of corn-transports at low Nile and on the Sabbath; **5179** shows that the internal customs had a post also at Ptolemais Hormou. Other items touch everyday crises. So **5168** employs a wet nurse for a foundling from the dung-hill; **5169** shows an under-age girl working as a servant, against a loan made to her father and brothers; and in **5182** Chenthonis complains to Petosiris (on the back of the Glossary **5161**) that her father and the local governor's guards had appeared at her door and exacted tax-money from her 'with insults'.

Most items in section V have benefitted from the comments and criticism of Professor Thomas. The industry and scholarship of Dr R.-L. Chang, Dr D. Colomo, and Dr W. B. Henry have been invaluable at every stage of the preparation of this volume. Dr Henry further read the penultimate version of all editions, compiled the indexes, and coordinated the correction of the proofs. The plates were produced from digital images created by Dr Chang.

Once again, we are grateful to Dr Jeffrey Dean for his deft copy-editing and typesetting, and to The Charlesworth Group for efficient production; and we remain in the debt of the Arts and Humanities Research Council and the British Academy for their very generous support.

October 2012   P. J. PARSONS / N. GONIS

CONTENTS

TEXTS

INDEXES

TABLE OF PAPYRI

IV. SUBLITERARY TEXTS

V. DOCUMENTARY TEXTS

FM = F. Maltomini   ZsÖ = Zs. Ötvös   PJP = P. J. Parsons   PMP = P. M. Pinto
MDR = M. D. Reeve   SRC = S. Rishøj Christensen   PhS = Ph. Schmitz   ST = S. Trojahn
MV = M. Vierros

LIST OF PLATES

I.	**5128, 5129, 5151, 5156**	VII.	**5162**
II.	**5130**	VIII.	**5166** (front)
III.	**5131**	IX.	**5166** (back)
IV.	**5153, 5157, 5167**	X.	**5178** (front)
V.	**5160**	XI.	**5178** (back)
VI.	**5161**	XII.	**5182**

NUMBERS AND PLATES

5128	I	**5160**	V
5129	I	**5161**	VI
5130	II	**5162**	VII
5131	III	**5166**	VIII–IX
5151	I	**5167**	IV
5153	IV	**5178**	X–XI
5156	I	**5182**	XII
5157	IV		

NOTE ON THE METHOD OF PUBLICATION AND ABBREVIATIONS

The basis of the method is the Leiden system of punctuation; see *CE* 7 (1932) 262–9. It may be summarized as follows:

αβγ̣	The letters are doubtful, either because of damage or because they are otherwise difficult to read
. . .	Approximately three letters remain unread by the editor
[αβγ]	The letters are lost, but restored from a parallel or by conjecture
[. . .]	Approximately three letters are lost
( )	Round brackets indicate the resolution of an abbreviation or a symbol, e.g. (ἀρτάβη) represents the symbol ⲧ, cτρ(ατηγόc) represents the abbreviation cτρ∫
⟦αβγ⟧	The letters are deleted in the papyrus
ʽαβγʼ	The letters are added above the line
⟨αβγ⟩	The letters are added by the editor
{αβγ}	The letters are regarded as mistaken and rejected by the editor

Bold arabic numerals refer to papyri printed in the volumes of *The Oxyrhynchus Papyri*.

The abbreviations used are in the main identical with those in J. F. Oates *et al.*, *Checklist of Editions of Greek Papyri and Ostraca* (*BASP* Suppl. no. 9, ⁵2001); for a more up-to-date version of the *Checklist*, see http://scriptorium.lib.duke.edu/papyrus/texts/clist.html.

I. THEOLOGICAL TEXTS

5127. LXX, Psalm xc 4–13 (Amulet)

95/74(a)   8.6 × 3.8 cm   Late fifth century

A small sheet of parchment forming two consecutive leaves which give the central portion of Psalm xc. When the sheet is open, the flesh side is uppermost. The page dimensions (4.3 × 3.8 cm) correspond to the smaller examples in Turner's group of 'miniature' parchment codices (*Typology* 29–30). The wild orthography, the small quantity of text per page, and the absence of stitching suggest that the sheet did not belong to a codex containing a Psalter: the original document probably consisted of only two sheets, **5127** and another, now lost, the latter providing the first leaf (with the beginning of the Psalm, 1–4[1] εν τοις) and the fourth leaf (with its end, from 13[2]) of the quire. The ratio of the space available to the number of letters is not incompatible with this reconstruction: the missing opening of the Psalm, not counting the heading, contains 186 letters in Rahlfs's edition, the final missing portion 213 letters, while the first and second leaves of **5127** contain about 254 (the uncertainty depends on the corrupt illegible text in 10–11) and 261 letters respectively. It would not be surprising if the original first page contained less text than the others.

The first three pages have ten lines each, the fourth page eleven. The number of letters per line is markedly variable (between 9 and 15). The majuscule writing, sloping slightly to the right, roughly bilinear, is clumsy and irregular, with inconsistency in letter shapes (ⲁ generally with rounded loop, often open at the top, but also in three strokes; ⲏ generally h-shaped, but also with crossbar ascending and linked to the top of the second vertical; v-shaped ⲩ alternating with y-shaped; central stroke of ⲛ both oblique and curved). It can be dated to the late fifth century: compare PSI inv. 535 (Cavallo–Maehler, *GBEBP* 19c). The verses are written continuously, without division, and punctuation and other lectional signs are lacking. There are many spelling mistakes, and the rules of word division are not observed. In fol. 1(a) the text is often extremely difficult to read, as the ink is faded and the surface damaged in many places.

Psalm xc, due to its content, was the Psalm most frequently used in protective amulets (for full information, see J. Chapa, in G. Bastianini and A. Casanova (edd.), *I papiri letterari cristiani* (2011) 59–90). **5127** is no doubt an example of that use, since, in addition to the medial fold, there are three further vertical folds running down both leaves: the sheet was evidently folded to form a small packet (*c.*1.1 × 3.8 cm), to be carried or fastened on the person, possibly inserted in a tubular capsule. Once the text had been written, cuts were made at mid-height through the central fold and through the innermost and the outermost of the three folds running down both leaves, so that five rhomboidal holes are visible when the sheet is opened, of which the outer four form two pairs, the outer pair smaller than the inner (similar cuts in VIII **1077** = PGM P4; Christian amulet, parchment, vi; cf. also P. Bingen 19). The cuts have resulted in the loss of some letters. The sheet was trimmed at top and bottom with a similar disregard for the text, causing the loss of the upper part of the first line and the lower part of the last line on each page. Such miniature 'codex amulets' are well known: cf. XVII **2065** (parchment, page 2.85 × 4 cm, Psalm xc 5^2–10^2, v or vi), P. Ant. II 54 (papyrus, page 2.6 × 4 cm, Pater Noster, iii), and the other references given in the introduction to P. Leid. Inst. 10; add MPER XVII 10 and, possibly, 1 (see M. J. Kruger, *JTS* 53 (2002) 81–94). See in general T. S. de Bruyn and J. H. F. Dijkstra, 'Greek Amulets and Formularies from Egypt Containing Christian Elements', *BASP* 48 (2011) 163–216.

The text of **5127** is highly corrupt: v. 8 of the Psalm is displaced, and v. 9 and part of v. 10 are omitted (see 22–8 n.); the expected text does not appear at 10–11; see also 1, 5, 6–7, 17, 28 nn. Two known variants are conflated at 12–15. There appears to be a unique reading at 18. Some errors shared with the contemporary XVI **1928** may be of interest: 24–5 οφθαλμοις ⟨c⟩ου, 33–4 οδαιc cου (**1928** οδε cου), 37–8 ποδον (also P. Ryl. I 3), 38–9 επι αcπιζα.

Collated against A. Rahlfs, *Psalmi cum Odis* (^{3}1979). In the notes, Rahlfs's sigla are employed for mediaeval manuscripts, but the usual abbreviations for papyri.

Fol. 1(a) (hair)

```
     μετ[αφρε]ν[οιc αυτου]        (4)
     επιcκιαc[ει c]οι και
     υπο ταc πτ[ερυγ]αc
     αυτου [ελπιει]c οπ-
  5  λω κυκλωc[ει cε] η αλ[η-
     θια αυτο[υ ου] φοβ-
     ........ [απ]ο φο-
     βου νυκτερινου
     απο βελο[υ]c πετου-
 10  ου ημερα[c..].[.]..
```

Fol. 1(b) (flesh)

```
     [.].[...]..[.]...
     ραγματοc εν              (6)
     cκοτι διαπορ-
     ευομενου εν
 15  cκ[ο]τι απο [c]υμ-
     π[τω]ματο[c] και
     δα[ι]μονιου
     πεcιται δε εκ            7
     του κ[λι]τουc cου
 20  χ[ιλιαc κ]αι μ..-
```

Fol. 2(a) (flesh)

```
     ριαc [εκ δεξιων]
     cου προc cε δε κακα        10
     και μαcτιξ ουκ ε-
     γει πλην θηc οφθ-          8
 25  αλμ[ο]ιc ου κατ[α-
```

Fol. 2(b) (hair)

```
     [ρι cου του] δ..
     ιαφαιλαξε cε              10
     ε παcαιc ταιc οδ-
     αιc cου επι χιρων          12
 35  αρουcιν cε μηπο-
```

νοη[c]εις και αντα-
ποδοσιν αμαρτω-
λος οψιν οτι της   11
ανγελης αυτου
  30 εντελειται [π]ε-

τε προσκοψ[η]ς πρ-
ος λιθον τον πο-
δον σου επι ασ-   13
πιζα και βασι-
  40 λισκος επιβυ
[ση και καταπ]ατ-

1 μετ[αφρε]ν[οις αυτου]. The reading is difficult, but ε is highly probable and τ possible. The transmitted text, as printed, appears about two or three letters too long for the available space, but this may be explained by miswritings, so numerous in our document. Note however that αυτου is omitted by LXXIII **4931**.

2 επισκιας[: a guess based on the expected text rather than a reading.

c]οι: so most of the witnesses; cε P. Oslo inv. 1644 (*SO* 24 (1945) 141–7), P. Laur. IV 141, P. Duke inv. 778 (*BASP* 41 (2004) 93–113). The reading is quite uncertain.

3 υπο with all MSS except 55 and P. Bodmer XXIV, which have επι.

5 The reading of the faint traces between λω and the internal lacuna is far from certain, and the distribution of the individual letters insecure. In any case spacing seems insufficient for the expected text, as printed above: possibly an iotacistic spelling of κυκλωσει was used, as in P. Laur. 141 and P. Duke inv. 778; more likely a major accident occurred.

5–6 l. αληθεια.

6–7 φοβ| . . . . [απ]ο. The traces are too faint to read, but spacing requires more than the φοβηθηςη of most MSS (Rahlfs's text). **5127** may have agreed with one of the witnesses that have here a longer text: ου φοβηθηςη και απο φοβου S Sa, P. Laur. 141; ου φοβηθηςεται α. φ. P. Bodm. XXIV; ου φ[ο]βηθηςομαι α. φ. P. Duke inv. 778; ου φοβηθηςαι (l. -ςη) οι ('possibly meant for οὐ or ἤ' ed. pr.) α. φ. **1928**.

8 νυκτερινου: only tiny faded traces of ink remain from the first seven letters. There is a space between ν and ου.

9 S Sa and P. Duke inv. 778 have και before απο.

9–10 πετον|ου (l. πετο⟨με⟩ν|ου) ημερα[ς. The reading is very difficult. No variants are attested; however, the space after πε accommodates only three letters; then the parchment breaks, but just at the point where the right-hand margin should fall (so that πετομ[εν] would be too long, even if μ were a plausible interpretation of the trace).

10–12 After ημερας all MSS have απο πραγματος. **5127** has ραγματος at the beginning of 12, but the traces at the end of 11 do not suit απο π-: see n. Apparently the second half of 10 and the whole of 11 contained an extraneous text (a dislocation as in 22–8?), but since the traces are largely illegible, it cannot be determined what it was.

11 The traces are extremely confusing and their distribution uncertain. After the last internal lacuna: a vertical with smudged ink; possibly a triangular letter (delta?); perhaps a vertical followed by a possible short cross-stroke.

12–15 εν σκοτι (l. -ει) διαπορ|ευομενου | εν σκ[ο]τι (l. -ει). **5127** appears to conflate the two readings between which MSS are divided: εν σκοτει διαπορευομενου (the word order of the Masoretic Text) *L*'' 1219, **1928**, **2065**, P. Ryl. I 3, P. Laur. 141, P. Bodm. XXIV and διαπορευομενου εν σκοτει B' R'' Ga A', P. Gen. 6, BKT VIII 12, BKT VIII 13, P. Vindob. G 348 (*Vig. Chr.* 37 (1983) 42), P. Duke inv. 778; as for **4931**, see n. Does the error derive from collating two exemplars?

13 There is ink above the ο of σκοτι. If not accidental, perhaps, as Dr Coles suggests, an attempt to insert ε?

17 After δα[ι]μονιου all other copies have μεσημβρινου.

18 l. πεϲειται.

δε: not attested elsewhere.

19 κ[λι]τουϲ: so Rahlfs and, among the papyri, only P. Gen. 6 and P. Bodmer XXIV; the other papyri have, in various spellings, κλιτου; see **4931** 6 n. for details.

20–21 μ. . |ριας: the scribe certainly did not write μυ-, nor do the two traces (a small round letter, it seems; the right end of a horizontal emerging from a lacuna) conform to any attested iotacistic spelling (cf. μηρ[ια]ς P. Duke inv. 778, μοιριας P. Leid. Inst. 10). Probably μου-: cf. 19]τους and 35 αρουϲιν for the second oblique of upsilon curving to right at top (for υ > ου, see Gignac, *Grammar* i 215).

22–8 The jumps from 7³ to 10¹, then backwards from 10² to 8¹, and finally from 8² to 11¹ may be explained as *sauts du même au même* (προϲ ϲε δε ~ προϲ ϲε, εγγιει~εγγιει, οτι~οτι). They have resulted in the omission of 9¹–10¹ οτι ϲυ . . . προϲ ϲε and 10² ουκ εγγιει τω ϲκηνωματι ϲου.

23–4 l. εγγιει.

24 l. τοιϲ.

25 ου: a haplography, ⟨ϲ⟩ου, as in **1928**, P. Ryl. I 3 and P. Duke inv. 778.

27–8 l. αμαρτωλων.

28 οψιν: it is uncertain (as in the case of οψι in **1928**) whether οψει of *L'* or οψη of all the other authorities was intended.

28–9 l. τοιϲ αγγελοιϲ.

31 δ. .: after δ ink for 1–2 letters, the first of which suggests λ and the second possibly a vertical. If, as is probable, this represents the beginning of διαφυλαξαι, a spelling mistake of an unexpected kind.

33 ε: l. εν.

παϲαιϲ with most witnesses; παϲιν R, om. B.

33–4 l. οδοιϲ.

34 l. χειρων.

37–8 l. ποδα.

38 επι with R *L*ᵈTHeSᶜ A´´, **1928**, BKT VIII 13, P. Ryl. 3, P. Gen. 6, P. Duke inv. 778 : επ᾽ (Rahlfs's text) B´ *L*ᵈ⁽ˢⁱˡ⁾´, P. Vindob. G 348, P. Bodm. XXIV.

38–9 l. αϲπιδα.

39–40 l. βαϲιλιϲκον.

40–41 l. επιβηϲη.

41 [ϲη και καταπ]α̣τ̣-: I waver between this and [ϲη και κατ]α̣π̣-.

F. MALTOMINI

5128. Christian Text with Biblical Excerpts

88/125 part   4.5 × 3.6 cm   Third/fourth century
                                                                Plate I

A fragment from a leaf of a papyrus codex with remains of 5 lines on each side. There are neither codicological nor internal elements to indicate which page comes first. On the → side the left-hand margin is preserved to a maximum of 1.7 cm. On the basis of the reconstruction of → 4 and ↓ 4 (see → 4 n.), we may reckon with an average of 20 letters per line and a written area approximately 10 cm wide; assuming that side margins were not less than 2 cm each, we obtain a width of about 14 cm.

The script looks professional and presents some standard features of the Severe Style, with the typical contrast between broad square letters and narrow rounded ones: м and ν are particularly large; ο is rather small; ω (↓ 2) presents a flat base without division into two lobes. Note also the contrast between ascending and descending diagonals of λ, of which the latter is slightly thicker, and the ligature between λ and ο in → 1. Two good parallels are PSI X 1169 (Pap. Flor. XXX, pl. LIII), of the end of the third century, and P. Herm. 4 (*GBEBP* 2a), written around 320 (but here μ is rather different). On this basis I have assigned **5128** to the third/fourth century.

There are no lectional signs. → 3 is written in *eisthesis*. ↓ 3 and 4 are line-ends (3 ends with a blank space; in 4 the cross-bar of the final epsilon is extended); ↓ 5 ends with a blank, but well to the left of 3, so that the space may indicate a short verse or a paragraph-end or simply punctuation. An interlinear addition by the same hand in a slightly smaller size occurs in ↓ 3 above the final blank: perhaps a carry-over from the line before. For an estimate of letters lost in lacuna, see → 4.

→ 2–5 contains parts of Exodus 34.6–7, and ↓ 4–5 parts of Susanna 35a of the Old Greek version (= 42 in Theodotion's). However, on both sides (→ 1, 3, ↓ 1–3) there are textual elements that do not match the known text of the LXX for the books of Exodus and Susanna. These unidentified textual elements may be explained in two ways:

(1) They are quotations, but unrecognizable because either (*a*) they have been garbled in quoting from the LXX or (*b*) they derive from a quite different version of the Greek translation. (*a*) Quotations within exegetical or homiletic texts, and generally in patristic literature, are often written by heart and therefore rather free: see N. Fernández Marcos, *The Septuagint in Context: Introduction to the Greek Versions of the Bible* (2000) 259–60, 265–6, 269–71. (*b*) In the case of Exodus, we can think of a revision of the LXX text from the Hebrew text: since it does not seem to be possible to trace back the putative revision in the Massoretic Text, we could assume a different Hebrew. For examples of revisions of Exodus, see van Haelst 34

(= Rahlfs–Fraenkel 885, pp. 280–81; ed. M. V. Spottorno, N. Fernández Marcos, *Emerita* 44 (1976) 385–95); and van Haelst 16 (Rahlfs–Fraenkel 886, pp. 183–4, 367; ed. A. Bülow-Jacobsen, J. Strange, *APF* 32 (1986) 15–21), which points to a Hebrew *Vorlage* different from the Massoretic Text.

(2) The fragment belongs to a larger text, in which quotations are inserted. On this view, the *eisthesis* in → 3 could be explained as a means of distinguishing quotations from the main text. Certainly the two passages quoted in **5128** are individually very popular in patristic literature (see → 1 ff. n., ↓ 4–5 n.); and the fact that quotations from two different books occur within a single leaf of a codex may encourage us to seek a thematic link between them. On the one hand, the Exodus excerpt outlines divine mercy and justice, and on the other, the quotation from Susanna focuses on the spatial and temporal omniscience of God; in other words, both passages concern the divine nature. But the two quotations appear to be even more closely connected by the concept of Justice: the former refers to God's δικαιοϲύνη (→ 5), in the latter God is invoked against the ἄνομοι. Moreover, ↓ 1 αληθεια echoes as a 'catchword' the word αληθινοϲ that we should probably supply in lacuna at → 4.

If we accept (2), we need to consider what genres of text might include these quotations. At least three suggest themselves: collection of *testimonia*; homily/exegesis; prose hymn/prayer.

Testimonia. The two quotations may form part of a testimony collection; see LXXIII **4933** introd. (pp. 11–12) for a general discussion and bibliography, to which add A. Delattre, *AnPap* 18–20 (2006–8) 119–23. In the case of **5128** the focus of the quotations is on divine qualities. Although their formulation appears at first rather general, they can easily be inserted into a 'messianic' context, which is what one expects in a testimonial collection: the attributes of clemency, justice, and omniscience could be related to the divine plan of the salvation of mankind through Christ's descent to the world. In the notes to → 1 ff. and ↓ 4–5 I offer a few examples of these quotations interpreted in a Christological direction within a 'messianic' context. Comparable examples of excerpts that despite their rather generic formulation are inserted in messianic contexts occur in Ps.-Epiphanius, *Testimonia ex divinis et sacris scripturis* 30.1 and 81.1. In such collections, deviations from the *textus receptus* and exegetical remarks are both frequent (cf. M. C. Albl, *And Scripture Cannot Be Broken: The Form and Function of the Early Christian* Testimonia *Collections* (1999) 100–101, 66): the unexplained elements in **5128** might belong to either strand.

Homily. Ps.-Athanasius, *Homilia de passione et cruce Domini*, PG 28.196 §28, in discussing divine omniscience and clemency, refers to the threatened destruction of Nineveh announced by Jonas (Jonas 3.4–4.11) and reinforces his theme with our quotation from Susanna and another from Jonas 4.2 (cf. Joel 2.13; see → 1 ff. n.) that is modelled on our Exodus 34.6–7. Here certainly the two quotations are juxtaposed on the basis of their thematic similarity. Thus Ps.-Athanasius and **5128** have something in common. In similar cases scholars have argued that both authors drew their material from the same book of *testimonia* (see Fernández Marcos, *Septuagint* 269 n. 53; Albl, *Scripture* 66–7; id., *Pseudo-Gregory of Nyssa: Testimonies against the Jews* (2004) pp. xiv–xv). However, in our case the argument would be hazardous: we do not know the order of the quotations in **5128**, or the size of the codex page that separated them. Nevertheless, the apparent 'coincidence' between **5128** and Ps.-Athanasius remains striking.

Hymn. A hymn or prayer might incorporate, not necessarily verbatim, well-known textual segments from the OT: the text of **5128** could be considered as a series of eulogistic phrases in the nominative, probably not extending beyond a single leaf. The mid-fourth-century prayer collection ascribed to Sarapion of Thmuis may offer an example for biblical quotations inserted in prayers (see M. E. Johnson, *The Prayers of Sarapion of Thmuis* (1995), esp. 88). As an example of Christian liturgy, **5128** would be very early: the comparable LX **4011** belongs to the sixth century. However, the layout on the ↓ side (see 2–3 n.), suggesting a text set out in verses like the Psalms, seems to offer some support for this possibility.

The text of Exodus has been collated with the edition of J. W. Wevers, *Exodus* (1991); I have also used Wevers's *Text History of the Greek Exodus* (1992). The text of Susanna has been collated with J. Ziegler, *Susanna, Daniel, Bel et Draco* (1954).

→

       .   .   .   .

    φιλο[ ] . [

    μακροθ[υμος

      νọ[

    πọλυελẹ[ος και αληθινος και

5   δικαιος[

       .   .   .   .   .

1 . [, slightly below line-level, two tiny traces very close to each other, the second higher than the first, both perhaps part of a gently rising diagonal

↓

       .   .   .   .

      ] . αληθεια[

      ]ς . [.]υν . χων[

               κος[

      ] . απο . [.]της

    ο ειδως τα π]αντα πριν γε-

5   νεσεως α]υτων [

       .   .   .   .   .

1] ., upright projecting below baseline   2 c ., blurred traces at mid-height   ν ., traces in horizontal alignment in upper part of writing space   3] ., right-hand arc   .[, two traces in diagonal alignment ascending from left to right at line-level and at top-line respectively   5 after α]υτων blank space equivalent to two letters

→

1 ff. In 2, 4 and 5 it is possible to identify elements contained in Ex. 34.6–7: καὶ παρῆλθε Κύριος πρὸ προσώπου αὐτοῦ καὶ ἐκάλεσε Κύριος ὁ Θεὸς οἰκτίρμων καὶ ἐλεήμων, **μακρόθυμος καὶ πολυέλεος** καὶ ἀληθινὸς καὶ **δικαιοσύνην** διατηρῶν καὶ ποιῶν ἔλεος. The passage is particularly striking since it contains the self-definition of the divine nature in the frame of the 'Covenant', which occurs with slight variations in other biblical passages (Num. 14.18.1, Esdras ii 19.17, Ps. lxxxv 15.1–2, cii 8, cxliv 8, Od. 12.7.2, Joel 2.13, Jonas 4.2) and with comparable textual variations in numerous patristic texts. Two relevant works based on testimony collections interpret the passage in a 'Christological/messianic' sense, as containing the revelation of the complex mystery of God beyond the God of the Old Testament: Eus. *DE* V 17, p. 239.20–21, and Ps.-Greg. Nyss. *Testimonia adversus Iudaeos* PG 46.197.37–200.26 (cf. Albl, *Pseudo-Gregory* 94–5); cf. Cyr. H. *Catech.* 1–18, 10.8–9. See also: Eus. *Generalis elementaria introductio* p. 45; Cyr. Alex. *Comm. in xii proph.*, i 380–81; Cyr. Alex. *Comm. in Iohannem I*, i 140–44; Bas. Caes. *Liturgia* PG 31.1649; Jo. Chrys. *In epistulam ad Hebraeos*, PG 63.223–4. In relation to the hypothesis that **5128** is a hymn, we should note that an echo of this passage, in the form ὁ ἐλεήμων καὶ οἰκτίρμων, ὁ μακρόθυμος καὶ πολυέλεος, occurs in *Constitutiones Apostolorum* 7.33.2 as a 'free-floating liturgical formula' inserted in a prayer with many originally Jewish elements (see P. W. van der Horst, J. H. Newman, *Early Jewish Prayers in Greek* (2008) 39 with n. 83, 89 with n. 259).

1 φιλο[] .[. Since the divine attributes in Ex. 34.6 begin with οἰκτίρμων, I am tempted here to suggest φιλο[ι]κ[τίρμων]: of κ there survive only two traces just below the base-line, which would suit its sloping upright. This adjective does not occur in the LXX, but is frequently attested as a qualification of God/Christ in the Church Fathers. Note especially Eus. *Comm. in Psalmos* PG 23.892.15–16 καὶ ἐπιλήσεται τοῦ οἰκτειρῆσαι ὁ μακρόθυμος καὶ πολυέλεος καὶ φιλοικτίρμων; This clearly paraphrases Ex. 34.6 (unless indeed it quotes a variant text which had φιλοικτίρμων instead of οἰκτίρμων, perhaps in a different word order); and it would support the supplement suggested here. Note also Cyr. Alex. *Expositio in Psalmos* PG 69.965–8 ὁ μὲν γάρ ἐστιν ἀγαθὸς καὶ φιλοικτίρμων καὶ θᾶττον μετανοῶν ἐπὶ ταῖς κακίαις, κατὰ τὴν Γραφήν, where μετανοῶν ἐπὶ ταῖς κακίαις appears to recall the slightly different formulation of our Ex. quotation found in Od. 12.7, Joel 2.13, and Jonas 4.2 (see → 1 ff. n. and introd.).

3 νο[in *eisthesis*. In theory, this might continue the quotation, μακρόθ[υμος καὶ πολυέλεος καὶ ἀληθι]|νὸ[ς καὶ δικαιοσύνην διατηρῶν, with the indentation marking the continuity, as sometimes in the lemmata of commentaries. However, that produces a line length substantially greater than the plausible restoration in ↓ 4–5. Otherwise, νο[does not match the LXX text, and the *eisthesis* may serve to distinguish the text (of a homily or of an exegetical commentary?) from a quotation.

4 I have supplied the lacuna *exempli gratia* from the last phrase of Ex. 34.6: the space would be enough if we assume a left-hand margin of at least 2 cm on the ↓ side and a smaller size of letters at line-end. Alternatively **5128** may have contained a slightly different text, for example without the first καί.

5 δικαιος[. The Ex. passage suggests the supplement δικαιος[υνην διατηρων. But note that in free quotations of the passage this phrase is often replaced with the simple adjective δίκαιος, which in theory cannot be ruled out in **5128**; see Jo. Damasc. *Sacra parallela* PG 96.392.38–40, and Ephr. Syr. *Sermones paraenetici ad monachos Aegypti* xxxii, lines 29–30.

↓

1 ff. There is more than one way to articulate the sequence] ̣ αληθεια[in 1, and relate it to what follows. (1) The word ἀλήθεια may be part of a commentary on the passage Susanna 35a (= 42 in Theodotion's version), which appears in 4–5: this is part of a direct speech of Susanna, in which she calls God the omniscient (ὁ εἰδὼς τὰ πάντα πρὶν γενέςεως αὐτῶν) as witness of the truth against the false accusations (ψευδῆ) of her enemies. Following this line of interpretation, the sequence in 3 can be articulated as απο ạ[υ]της and referred to Susanna (but see ↓ 3 n. for alternative articulations). (2) The trace in 1 before αληθεια is a descender, which would suit ρ. A possible supplement would be πατη]ρ̣ αληθεια[ς, an expression well attested in patristic literature: see 2 Clem. 3.1, Or. *Cels.* 8.12, Didym. Caec. *Comm. in Zachariam* III §1.1. Alternatively, we could consider τ]η[ς] αληθεια[ς (1 Esdras 4.40 εὐλογητὸς ὁ θεὸς τῆς ἀληθείας). But this is palaeographically not very satisfactory: the descender appears to be too long and curvilinear to suit the right upright of η, and the space would be very narrow for the putative ς.

2–3 In 3 we seem to have line-end, with a final blank of *c.*3 letter-spaces. The interlinear κος[stands above this blank, which suggests that it is not superscript to line 3, but subscript to line 2. If that is right, we cannot take κος[as the insertion of an omitted word, since we would expect it to be added above the line; we should assume instead that line 2 was unusually long and the last word had to be pushed down underneath. That in turn would suggest a text set out in verses (like the Psalms), i.e. with line-end coming at fixed places. Note the line-end in 4 and what may be a very short line in 5.

On this basis, a rather tentative supplement would be ọ [ς]υνεχων [τον] | κος[μον]. This assumes that [τον] was squeezed in at line-end, and that κος[continues the phrase. The expression so reconstructed refers to the divine entity in pagan philosophers: Xen. *Mem.* 4.3.13.7 ὁ τὸν ὅλον κόςμον ςυντάττων τε καὶ ςυνέχων, Porph. *De antro nympharum* 33.13 ὁ ςυνέχων τὸν κόςμον δημιουργός; cf. also *Scholia in Aratum (scholia vetera)* 1.41–2 καὶ αὐτὸς διὰ παντὸς ἔρχεται τοῦ κόςμου ςυνέχων αὐτόν, and Chrysipp. Stoic. *SVF* fr. 447.3–4. For the verb ςυνέχω applied to God/Christ, see Lampe s.v., Cyr. Alex. *Comm. in xii prophetas minores* ii 310.7 ςυνέχων τὰ πάντα πρὸς τὸ εὖ εἶναι καὶ ζῆν, and Bas. Caes. *De spiritu sancto* 5.7.35–6 οὗτός ἐςτιν ὁ ςυνέχων τὴν γῆν καὶ περιδεδραγμένος αὐτῆς.

3] ̣απο ̣[̣]της. The sequence may be restored in various ways. The remains of the first letter certainly point to a round letter, ο (but perhaps it would be too large in comparison to the other occurrences in this script) or θ; the diagonal traces at ο ̣[would allow λ, δ, α. Apart from] ̣ απο ạ[υ]της (see 1 ff. note) we could consider (1)] ọ απολ[υ]της, 'the liberator'; cf. Agathangelus, *Historia Armeniae* 25.6–7, where Christ is presented as τῆς φυλακῆς τῶν δεςμῶν ἀπολύτης. (2)] ọ αποδ[ο]της, 'the donor'; however, I have found no parallels. (3) μις]θαποδ[ο]της, in the sense of 'rewarder', applied to God/Christ; see *Ep. Hebr.* 11.6.3 and Lampe s.v.

4–5 ο ειδως τα π]αντα πριν γε|[νεςεως α]υτων. The precise calculation of the space available at line-beginning in 4 is difficult: after attempts to reconstruct the lost text through tracing, I cannot rule out the possibility that ο was omitted. The passage from Sus. restored here does not occur anywhere else in the LXX. It is very popular among Church Fathers, who sometimes quote it with slight variations. Particularly interesting are the following cases, where the quotation is inserted in a clearly Christological context: Eus. *PE* VI 11.20.5–7, Cyr. Alex. *Comm. in Iohannem IV*, i. 557.11–15; Or. *Comm. in Gen.*, PG 12.57.13–19 (all three passages focus on Jesus' omniscience in relation to Judas' betrayal); Or. *Selecta in Psalmos*, PG 12.1104.37–54 (related to the crucifixion).

D. COLOMO

5129. Justin Martyr, *First Apology* 50.12, 51.4–5

103/13(h)   6.3 × 3.4 cm   Fourth century
                                                       Plate I

A scrap from the foot of a parchment codex leaf. Inner and lower margins are preserved, the former to a width of about 0.9 cm on both sides, the latter to a depth of about 2.2 cm on both sides; the original margins are unlikely to have exceeded these figures by much. The hair side precedes the flesh side, which will have held approximately 25 lines. The dimensions of the written area will have been approximately 9.5 × 10.6 cm. If the outer margin was approximately as wide as the inner margin and the upper margin two-thirds as deep as the lower (cf. Turner, *Typology* 25), the original dimensions of the leaf will have been about 11.3 × 14.3 cm, and the codex will belong to Turner's Group XI (*Typology* 29).

The text is written in a medium-sized upright angular hand of the 'severe' type with small ε, ο, and ϲ hanging from the notional upper line. Letter formation is not perfectly consistent: for example, ϲ is fairly tall at the start of a line (hair side 3) but can be very short (as later in the same line). A fairly similar hand is that of XXXIV **2699** (*GMAW*² 49), which Turner dates to the fourth century, comparing P. Herm. 5 (*GMAW*² 70) of about 317–23. The only preserved lectional sign is an inorganic trema on an initial υ (flesh side 2), probably due to the original scribe.

This is the first published ancient copy of a work of Justin Martyr. The text is otherwise known only from the unreliable manuscript A (Parisinus graecus 450, of 1364). **5129** corresponds closely in the Isaiah quotation at 51.4–5, as was to be expected, but differs significantly at 50.12, where it has a shorter text. Collated with D. Minns and P. Parvis, *Justin, Philosopher and Martyr: Apologies* (2009).

Hair side

    ·   ·   ·   ·   ·

    προφητειαι̣[ϲ ε]ν̣ α[ιϲ παντα ταυτα   (50.12)
    προειρητο γενηϲ[ομενα πιϲτευ
    ϲαντεϲ και δυναμ[ιν

Flesh side

    ·   ·   ·   ·   ·

    ] δ[ικαιο]ν̣ ε̣υ̣ δ[ουλευ   (51.4)
οντα πολλοιϲ] κ̣α̣ι̣ τ̣α̣ϲ αμαρτιαϲ ϋ
μων αυτοϲ ανο]ιϲει δια τουτο αυτοϲ   51.5

Hair side

A's text of this sentence runs as follows:

ὕστερον δέ, ἐκ νεκρῶν ἀναστάντος καὶ ὀφθέντος αὐτοῖς καὶ ταῖς προφητείαις ἐντυχεῖν ἐν αἷς πάντα ταῦτα προείρητο γενησόμενα διδάξαντος, καὶ εἰς οὐρανὸν ἀνερχόμενον ἰδόντες καὶ πιστεύσαντες καὶ δύναμιν ἐκεῖθεν αὐτοῖς πεμφθεῖσαν παρ' αὐτοῦ λαβόντες καὶ εἰς πᾶν γένος ἀνθρώπων ἐλθόντες, ταῦτα ἐδίδαξαν, καὶ ἀπόστολοι προσηγορεύθησαν.

 εντυχειν was evidently not present in this copy following προφητειαι[ς (1), but ε]ν α[ις παντα ταυτα] may provisionally be accepted at the end of the line: it gives a line of suitable length, to judge from the other side, where the supplements (in a quotation from Isaiah) are not open to much doubt. The text of the following line must again have been shorter than that known from A. γενης[ομενα πιστευ]|σαντες, as printed above, appears to be of the right length, and it accounts for the case of προφητειαι[ς, now governed not by εντυχειν as in A but by πιστευ]|σαντες. The absence of εντυχειν before ε]ν α[ις (1) could by itself be explained by parablepsy, but no easy mechanical explanation is available for the apparent absence of διδαξαντος και εις ουρανον ανερχομενον ιδοντες και following γενης[ομενα (2). Perhaps the fuller form of the text known from A is the result of a later elaboration. Admittedly, the ἐκεῖθεν that follows δυναμ[ιν (3) in A would be deprived of its reference if εἰς οὐρανὸν ἀνερχόμενον ἰδόντες did not precede, but there is no way of telling whether the word (or the phrase to which it belongs) was present in this copy.

Flesh side

2–3 ὑ|[μων: A has ἡμῶν both here and in the quotation of the same passage (LXX Is. 53:11) at *Dial.* 13.11. The Septuagint has αὐτῶν with no variants recorded except in these quotations in Justin. It is not easy to choose between the readings of this copy and of A. ὑ|[μων may be due to the influence of the second-person-plural forms at 51.3 ἐὰν δῶτε περὶ ἁμαρτίας, ἡ ψυχὴ ὑμῶν ὄψεται σπέρμα μακρόβιον. But either reading could produce the other by itacism.

W. B. HENRY

II. NEW LITERARY TEXTS

5130. From Alcidamas, *Praise of Poverty*

88/197   Fr. 1 11.5 × 18 cm   Third century
                                                                                                 Plate II

The main fragment offers the end of a roll, with colophon. There are a few line-ends from one column, then an intercolumnium of 1.5 cm; then a second column to full width (6.5 cm, 20–24 letters), with a right-hand margin of at least 3 cm, and a lower margin of at least 4.3 cm below the colophon. Writing with the fibres; back blank. The vertical edge of a *kollesis* shows just to the right of the line-ends of col. ii. Eight scraps are assigned to the same item on the basis of the handwriting; backs all blank. Fr. 2 may have belonged in col. i, but I have not managed to join or place it precisely; on frr. 3+4 see note there.

The script is a rapid, practised semi-cursive, without abbreviations (except perhaps final eta suprascript, frr. 2.7, 6.3); it is assignable to the third century, compare for example XVII **2106** (Letter of Prefect, AD 306 or not much earlier). No lectional signs except paragraphos below fr. 1 ii 16 (and probably below frr. 3+4.6) and a final coronis whose top can be seen to the left of fr. 1 ii 21–2; short blanks mark clause-end in fr. 1 ii 19 (after ναις) and 20 (after εχει), cf. frr. 3+4.1 and 2. Unmarked elision fr. 1 ii 12?, 16. Iota adscript written correctly, fr. 1 ii 21–2. Corrections fr. 1 ii 5 (word added above line), 18 and 19 (both *currente calamo*).

The colophon describes this piece as ἐκ τοῦ Ἀλκιδάμαντος πενίας ἐγκωμίου. The ἐκ-formula typically introduces an excerpt, for example in Stobaeus. The script suggests that this was a private enterprise, not part of a tralatician anthology; of course, copying extracts, especially from rare books, is a normal part of ancient literate practice; see William A. Johnson, *Readers and Reading Culture in the High Roman Empire* (2010) 153–6. This copyist is literate, ending his work with a coronis and a formal end-title, spaced and centred; in the few surviving lines, his orthography is perfect, including iota adscript as needed; his one lapse from the professional is the syllable division between fr. 1 ii 12 and 13 (see note). We cannot exclude the possibility that he abridged or paraphrased his 'excerpt'. However, the lines fully preserved show no example of hiatus, and each clause has some form of cretic ending (‒ ‒ ‒ ◡ ‒ fr. 1 ii 15, 18–19, 19–20, 23–4, ‒ ◡ ‒ ◡ 16, ‒ ◡ ‒ ‒ ◡ 22–3); see on this M. Winterbottom in D. Obbink and R. Rutherford (edd.), *Culture in Pieces* (2011) 263–5. That speaks in favour of taking them as authentic Alcidamas, written μετ' ἀκριβείας καὶ ῥυθμοῦ (περὶ τῶν γραφόντων, *Artium scriptores* B XXII 15.16).

The work itself may be mentioned by Menander Rhetor 346.17 (p. 32 Russell and Wilson): παράδοξα δὲ (sc. ἐγκώμια) οἷον Ἀλκιδάμαντος τὸ τοῦ Θανάτου ἐγκώμιον ἢ τὸ τῆς Πενίας [ἢ τοῦ] Πρωτέως τοῦ κυνός. The bracketed words occur in only one of the three branches of the tradition (manuscripts MmW; the other representatives of the branch do not contain this passage: see Russell and Wilson pp. xli–xliii). Spengel printed them without comment in his edition of 1856 (*Rhetores graeci* iii 346), which was for long the standard version; Bursian in his edition of 1882 (pp. 23, 46), and Volkmann, *Die Rhetorik der Griechen und Römern* (²1885) 316, argued for their omission, and so R. Kassel, *Untersuchungen zur griechischen und römischen Konsolationsliteratur* (1958) 15 n. 3; Russell and Wilson omit them as 'clearly wrong'.

With this omission, Menander mentions only two works, the *Encomium of Death* by Alcidamas, and the *Encomium of Poverty* by Proteus the Cynic. Against this we could argue that no other source mentions any specific written work of Peregrinus Proteus; Lucian credits him with 'many books' (*de morte Peregrini* 11), but in the context of his alleged Christian phase, so that the information has not always been taken seriously.[1] In favour, we have the difficulty of explaining the longer text. Various editors have understood it as (*a*) '. . . or the encomium of poverty or (the encomium) of Proteus the Cynic; (*b*) '. . . or the encomium of poverty or Proteus the Cynic' (alternative titles of the same work); (*c*) '. . . or the encomium of poverty (by Alcidamas) or (the encomium of poverty) by Proteus the Cynic'. However, (*a*) and (*b*) have the disadvantage that they give no author-name to balance that of Alcidamas; (*c*) would work only if τοῦ were emended to τὸ or τὸ τοῦ. See the editions of Alcidamas by G. Avezzù (1982) 68–70 and J. V. Muir (2001) p. xxvii n. 58; M. Narcy in R. Goulet, *Dictionnaire des philosophes antiques* i (1989) 108.

The new papyrus shows that Alcidamas did leave (or was credited with) an *Encomium of Poverty*; Cornford argued from Aristotle, *Rhet.* 1401a that he left also an encomium of the dog/Cynic (*CQ* 3 (1909) 281–4). It would be neat if Menander cited three examples, all by Alcidamas; but in that case Πρωτέως must be eliminated, or the text is more seriously corrupt or interpolated. Russell and Wilson note the Πρωτεὺς κύων ἢ σοφιστής attributed in the *Suda* to the elder Philostratus; but it is also worth remembering that Alcidamas' contemporary Antisthenes wrote Περὶ Πρωτέως and Περὶ τοῦ Ὀδυσσέως καὶ Πηνελόπης καὶ [so P: καὶ om. B] περὶ τοῦ κυνός (DL 6.17–18), presumably the Odyssean Proteus and the dog Argos.

The papyrus gives us only the very end of Alcidamas' argument, which sets up a disjunction between 'praising those who have most despised wealth' and 'not thinking like them'. If fr. 1 ii 12–13 is rightly reconstructed, he will have condemned this situation: it is absurd to laud great examples of austerity in the past, yet not to

---

[1] See e.g. C. Heusch, *Gymnasium* 114 (2007) 458 with n. 80 (I owe the reference to Dr Henry). P. Ross. Georg. I 22 i 15 would provide concrete evidence, if we accept Crönert's Πε]ρεγρίνου ἀπ[ο]-λογίαι in place of Jernstedt's Νε]ιγρίνου ἀπ[ο]λογίαι (M–P³ 2089; see CPF I.1* (1989) no. 2 with IV.2 pl. 242; R. Otranto, *Antiche liste di libri su papiro* (2000) no. 15 with pl. XII); and indeed Lucian, *mort. Per.* 20, mentions an Olympic *apologia*. However, neither reading seems verifiable from the published photographs.

share their attitude in the present. For the subject matter in general, see W. Meyer, *Laudes inopiae* (diss. Göttingen, 1915); W. D. Desmond, *The Greek Praise of Poverty* (Notre Dame, 2006).

I am greatly indebted to Dr W. B. Henry for his amendments to the detail and to the overall interpretation of this text.

Fr. 1 col. i   col. ii

. . . . . .

1   ].[
                          ]η.με[
                          ].παρασκευ[
                          ].τωνμε.[
5   ].ᵈᵉτωνα
                          ].νδετων
                          ].ιανδε
                          ].ουτον
                          ].οσγι
10   ]ματων
                          ]φθειρει
                          ]ωσδουκ

. . .   α.ο.[].ν.νμ.[].[...]λαι..
]η   επαινειντουσπλ.[].[.]ουμα
]ζη 15 λιστακα.απεφρο[ ]ηκοτας
].   μηφρονεινδεκ.[..]οισομοια
. . .   εγωμενουνικ[..]ωσεβοη
         θησαταισανθρωπειοισπλα
         ναις ειδετισ⟦απιστει⟧δυσπει
20   στωσεχει τονισονχρονον
         τωιλογωιδιατριψασονκαι
    ≟   τηισυνηθειαιδεδουλευ
         ....]υτωποιεισθωτηνκρι
         ]
25   ]
         ].κτουαλκιδαμαντος
         ].ενιασεγκωμιου

col. ii

2]η., c rather than ε?   3]., horizontal tip joining π at mid-height   4]., point on edge above cross-bar of τ   .[, λ, м, possibly n   5]., upright element curving leftwards at base   6]., oblique element sloping down to join ν at mid-height   7]., right-hand elements of в?   8]., shallow oblique descending to join o at mid-height   9]., point at two-thirds height, then

upper part of upright (together, N?)   13 ạ., foot of vertical, then high horizontal joining o   o.[],
two verticals, with traces of high horizontal on the broken edge above, apparently π but narrow   ν,
lower arc   .ν, trace on line; then e.g. right-hand side of N or ω   μ.[]., lower hook e.g. of ϵ; foot
of sloping upright   14 .[, lower loop   ].[.], shadowy ink, vertical with horizontal crossing
at top; then patch of damaged surface, no ink visible   15 ạ., high horizontal, damage below
16 κ., in ligature with κ ink rising to right   18 θρ overwritten on ạ. (perhaps a diplography of
the preceding αν)   23 of τ the upright and higher up horizontal ink joining left-hand tip of ω
26]., ligature rising from mid-height to left-hand tip of κ   27]., upright

Fr. 2   Frr. 3+4

```
            · · · ·                          · · ·
            ].[                              ]..[ ] ϵ[
          ]...[                            ].ροπων [
        ]ναλλι.[                         ]μ[...].οδοκιμα[
        ]ντοιϲï.ρο[                      ]...[ ].ιμενϵ[
  5    ].τονπλουτο[ ] [                 ].αυξειδερ.[
       ].ναναιρων [                    ]δεκ[].τερ[
        ]μενουν..[                     ].[ ].[ ]...[
          ]..νατ[                         · · ·
          ]...[
            · · ·
```

Fr. 2

     3 ι, no diaeresis visible, but surface damaged   .[, upright, separate trace at mid-height to
right: N?   4 .ρ, high trace (tip of rising oblique?) above damaged patch   5]., trace on
edge just below left horizontal of τ   ] [, promontory of papyrus preserved to upper level, no trace of
ink   6]., point level with letter-tops above hole   ν [, after ν papyrus preserved to mid-height,
no trace of ink, probably line-end   7 ..[, upright, short horizontal at top left, π or perhaps τ;
to right lower arc, above line-level, cf. fr. 6.3   8–9 disordered fibres

Frr. 3+4

     These fragments show a common fibre-pattern; each provides half of omicron in 3 δοκ, and of
nu in 4 ϵνϵ[1 One letter-space blank before ϵ   2]., horizontal trace at two-thirds height
end, one letter-space blank after ων   3]., upright curving leftwards at top   4]...[, clear
but ambiguous ink, e.g.]π..[,]ϲπ.[   ].ι, apparently ι in ligature, e.g. ʌι   5]., perhaps
ink from left joining the upper junction of ʌ   .[, part of oblique loop, ʌ or ο?   6]., perhaps
the top overhang of ϵ or ϲ   7].[, horizontal ink in the interlinear space, rising to the right:
paragraphus rather than extended top e.g. of τ with or without ligature from left.

Fr. 5   Fr. 6   Fr. 7   Fr. 8   Fr. 9

```
   · · ·          · · ·          · · ·          · · ·          · ·
  ]φικ.[        ].ν            ].αν[          ]..[          ]ω[
  ].ϵ[          ].ιϲ           ]πω[           ]θο.[          · ·
   · · ·        ].ιμ^η         ].[            ]ωτο[
                 · · ·
```

Fr. 5

  1 .[, upright hooked to right at foot, ε?   2]., horizontal ink joining ε at mid-height cross-bar of ε extended but not joining next letter

Fr. 6

  Line-ends.   1]., foot of vertical well below the line, e.g. 1   2]., curving trace low in line, perhaps lower right of o   3]., oblique, rising from left to right, in upper part of line

Fr. 7

  1]., turned-over papyrus may conceal traces; otherwise perhaps line-beginning

Fr. 8

  Probably not the same hand.   2 ọ.[, from the apparent o a long vertical descends into the line below: original ρ corrected to o? After ọ, probably ν

Fr. 1

col. i   col. ii

                         .   .   .   .   .   .

                                              ].[
                                         ]η.με[
                                      ].παρασκευ[
                                      ].των με.[
                  5   ].ᵈᵉτωνα
                                      ].νδετων
                                      ].ιαν δε
                                      ].ουτον
                                      ].ος γι
                 10   ]ματων
                                      ]φθειρει
                                      ]ωϲδουκ
   .   .   .   α.ο.[].ν..νμ.[].[...]λαι..
  ]η   ἐπαινεῖν τοὺς πλ.[].[.]ου μά-
  ]ζη   15 λιϲτα καταπεφρο[ν]ηκότας
  ].   μὴ φρονεῖν δ' ἐκε[ίν]οιϲ ὅμοια.
   .   .   .   ἐγὼ μὲν οὖν ἱκ[αν]ῶϲ ἐβοή-
                 θηϲα ταῖϲ ἀνθρωπείοιϲ πλά-
                 ναιϲ· εἰ δέ τιϲ ⟦ἀπιϲτεῖ⟧ δυϲπεί-
                 20 ϲτωϲ ἔχει, τὸν ἴϲον χρόνον
                 τῶι λόγωι διατρίψαϲ ὃν καὶ
                 τῆι ϲυνηθείαι δεδούλευ-
                 κεν ο]ὕτω ποιείϲθω τὴν κρί-
                 ϲιν.]

]
] ἐ̣κ τοῦ Ἀλκιδάμαντος
] Π̣ενίας Ἐγκωμίου

'. . . *How is it not absurd* to praise those *of the ancients* who have the most contempt for wealth, but not to think like them?—Well, I for my part have done enough to rescue human error. If anyone finds himself incredulous, let him spend the same time on the argument as he has also spent enslaved to the customary view, and on that basis make his judgment.'

(End-title) 'From Alcidamas' *Praise of Poverty*'

col. i

14 actually ranges with the line-space between ii 14 and 15.

15 See below on frr. 3+4.6–7.

col. ii

7 βιαν?

8 π]λ̣ουτον?

10–11 E.g. χρη]μάτων (πλῆθος?) . . . δια]φθείρει.

12 ουκ: the kappa is very cursively written, but I see no clear alternative; and οὐκ | ἄτοπον seems likely as a phrase. However, the division over the line-end is then anomalous (ου|κατοπον would be the norm), a strange carelessness in an otherwise literate copy.

13 α̣ . ο . [] . ν: perhaps ἄτ̣οπ̣ο̣ν. οὐκ | ἄτ̣οπ̣ο̣ν by itself could introduce a positive assertion (in which case e.g. ὁμοί]ως); π]ῶς δ' οὐκ | ἄτοπ̣ο̣ν would, as often, introduce an incredulous question. The choice affects the interpretation of 14–16: 'to praise those who most despise wealth but not to think like them'—'that is not absurd', or 'how is that not absurd'?

]λ̣αι̣ . . : perhaps]λαιων. Dr Henry suggests e.g. τ̣ῶν μ̣ὲ̣ν̣ [πα]λαιῶ̣ν̣, commenting 'Perhaps A. has just been discussing famous persons of old who are generally praised but who (in his opinion) can be shown not to have thought highly of wealth. People revere these men but have failed to act on this reverence by adjusting their own attitude to the pursuit of wealth accordingly (or rather have simply failed to notice the problem).'

14 πλ . [ ] . . ου: presumably πλο̣[ύ]τ̣ου, with a space between τ̣ and ου to avoid a flaw in the surface.

15 Dr Henry notes the (intentional) jingle -φρονη- . . . φρονειν.

16 ἐκε̣[ίν]οις: the space looks tight for [ιν], but the typical ligature of ει helps. Not δὲ α̣[ὐτ]ο̣ῖς.

17–18 ἱκ̣[αν]ῶς ἐβόηθηςα: ἱκανῶς ἐβοήθηςεν Plato, *Phaedo* 88E (τῷ λόγῳ), *Euthyd.* 297D (helping a person).

18–19 ταῖς . . . πλά|ναις. Either the writer is wandering, or ἀνθρώπειος is here treated as two-termination. LSJ and DGE quote Lucian, *Asin.* 46 for this (ἀνθρωπείου τροφῆς all MSS, to judge from Macleod's silence); W. Kastner, *Die griechischen Adjektive zweier Endungen auf -OC* (1967) 69 n. 43, cites also SEG XI 922.20 (Gytheion, Laconia, AD 15) ταῖς μετριωτέραις τε καὶ ἀνθρωπείοις (sc. τιμαῖς).

19–20 δυςπείςτως ἔχει. The adverb is attested only in this phrase, and the phrase appears first in Isocrates (*Panegyricus* 18), then once each in Dion. Hal., Plutarch and Justin Martyr. It appears also once in [Plato], *Eryxias* 405B, a dialogue on the use of riches that might well have made use of Alcidamas.

The copyist first wrote the simple ἀπιςτεῖ, then crossed it out with a single horizontal stroke and carried on with the correct phrasing: his *dictée intérieure* comprehended the whole clause, but at this point lapsed momentarily into paraphrase.

20–21 τὸν ἴϲον χρόνον | τῶι λόγωι διατρίψαϲ: the plain dative, where we might expect e.g. ἐν τῶι λόγωι, by anticipated parallelism with τῆι ϲυνηθείαι?

21–2 τῶι λόγωι . . . τῆι ϲυνηθείαι: abstract, 'reason . . . convention', or particular, 'my reasoning . . . your conventional usage'? The use of the article might favour the latter, but compare e.g. Julian, Πρὸϲ Ἡράκλειον κυνικόν 4 . . . τῇ ϲυνηθείᾳ προϲέχειν οὐδαμῶϲ προϲήκει, τῷ λόγῳ δὲ αὐτῷ μόνῳ, καὶ τὸ ποιητέον εὑρίϲκειν οἴκοθεν, ἀλλ' οὐ μανθάνειν ἔξωθεν.

22–3 τῆι ϲυνηθείαι δεδούλευ|[κεν: for the image see e.g. Menander, *Samia* 624–5 ὅρκοϲ, πόθοϲ, / χρόνοϲ, ϲυνήθει', οἷϲ ἐδουλούμην ἐγώ (I owe the reference to Mr P. G. McC. Brown), Posidon. fr. 76 Theiler ἔρωτι καὶ τῇ προγεγενημένῃ ϲυνηθείᾳ δεδουλωμένον, Greg. Nyss. *Oratio Catechetica Magna* 18 ϲυνηθείᾳ μᾶλλον ἢ διανοίᾳ δουλεύοντεϲ (and commonly in the Church Fathers). In περὶ τῶν γραφόντων Alcidamas' picture of the chained prisoners expresses the idea much more picturesquely (*Artium scriptores* B XXII 15.17), cf. Plato, *Resp.* 514A–518D.

Fr. 2

```
                  ]. [
               ] . . . [
            ]ναλλι . [
            ]υτοιϲϊ . ρο[
      5   ] . τον πλουτο[ ] [
          ] . ναναιρων [
            ]μενουν . . [
               ] . . νατ[
               ] . . . [
```

The line-spacing suggests that this might belong to fr. 1 col. i, but not to col. ii as preserved. 5 and 6 probably line-ends.

3 E.g. ἀλλ' ἵν[α.

4 E.g. τοῖϲ ἱερο[ῖϲ.

5 (-)τον πλοῦτο[ν].

6 E.g. ἐ]ὰν ἀναιρῶν, ἀναιρῶν|[ται. The verb in similar contexts, Isocr. *Panath.* 19, 112.

7 E.g. μὲν οὖν. At the end, apparently a raised letter (cursive eta, as in fr. 6.3?): abbreviation?

Frr. 3+4

```
               ] . . [ ] ε[
               ] . ροπων [
          ]μ[ . . . ] . οδοκιμα[
          ] . . . [ ] . ιμενε[
      5   ] . αυξειδερ . [
          ]δεκ[ ] . τερ[
          ] . [ ] . [ ] . . . [
```

2]τροπων acceptable; small space (i.e. word- or phrase-end?) after ν.

3 ἀ]ποδοκιμα- acceptable.

5 E.g. αὔξει.

6–7 The paragraphos shows that these are line-beginnings; and that excludes an otherwise tempting join with fr. 1 i 15 to give α]ποδοκιμα|ζη, since the resulting line would be much shorter than those of fr. 1 col. ii. Alternatively, the 'paragraphos' might belong to one or two extended letter-tops, but the ink stands very high and no connecting traces are visible.

P. J. PARSONS

5131. TRAGEDY (EURIPIDES, *INO*?)

18 2B.66/F(2–3)d   12.5 × 20.5 cm   Third century
Plate III

Parts of two consecutive columns of a verse text written in a sloping book-hand not unlike that of XXVII **2458** (*GMAW*² 32; Eur. *Cresphontes*); for a datable parallel, compare LXXV **5046** (Xenophon), on whose verso is a document dated 286–305.

The style suggests an ascription to Euripides: see the notes on ii 5, 8–9, 10, 14. One of the two surviving speaker indications names Athamas (ii 8). A numeral, β, was added to the name on a second line, apparently at a later stage, perhaps to indicate that the lines are assigned to the deuteragonist. The fragmentary speaker indication at ii 12 seems also to have included a numeral on a second line, also perhaps added later. The indication of speakers by letters of the Greek alphabet is found elsewhere: see Turner on *GMAW*² 32; T. Gammacurta, *Papyrologica scaenica* (2006) 240–47. The combination of name and numeral however appears to be unusual. Of the corrections, those at ii 24 and 25 at any rate appear to be due to a second hand, while that at ii 16 may be due to the hand of the main text, as are the marks of elision at ii 8 and 10, these being the only lection-signs in the papyrus. Deletion is effected by oblique cancel strokes (ii 16, 25 (twice)). The back is blank.

Col. i is lost apart from two line-ends. Col. ii begins with two indented lines, perhaps in a lyric metre, followed by a paragraphus. There follow five anapaestic lines, from which we learn that a body is being borne aloft to the home of a ruler; τὴν βαρυδαίμονα[(5) might suggest that the body is female. The line of Cadmus is mentioned (6). These verses would naturally be assigned to the chorus-leader, and since there is no speaker indication at 3, one may suppose that the opening of the column forms the end of a passage of choral lyric. Following another paragraphus, Athamas is named as the speaker of four iambic trimeters (8–11), in which he instructs bystanders to lay the body gently in front of the palace and to uncover it. According to a probable supplement, their burden is said to be painful to him (9). At 12, there is a change of speaker; some at least, perhaps all, of the following lines are in lyric metres, and the vocalization of ψυχα at 12 is also indicative of sung verse if part of a singular form, as seems most likely. Little can be made of this part of the text, but the few recognizable words, including the repeated δύϲτηνοϲ (15, 19), are suggestive of a lament.

Athamas was a character in the two *Phrixus* plays of Euripides and in his *Ino*. For the plot of *Ino* we are dependent on Hyginus, *Fab.* 4:

> *Athamas in Thessalia rex cum Inonem uxorem, ex qua duos filios ⟨susceperat⟩, perisse putaret, duxit nymphae filiam Themistonem uxorem; ex ea geminos filios procreavit. Postea resciit Inonem in Parnaso esse, quam bacchationis causa eo pervenisse: misit qui eam adducerent; quam adductam celavit. Resciit Themisto eam inventam esse, sed quae esset nesciebat. coepit velle filios eius necare; rei consciam quam captivam esse credebat ipsam Inonem sumpsit, et ei dixit ut filios suos candidis vestimentis operiret, Inonis filios nigris. Ino suos candidis, Themistonis pullis operuit; tunc Themisto decepta suos filios occidit; id ubi rescïit, ipsa se necavit. Athamas autem in venatione per insaniam Learchum maiorem filium suum interfecit; at Ino cum minore filio Melicerte in mare se deiecit et dea est facta.*

Thus an ill-starred female mentioned in this play may be either Themisto or Ino. (i) If she is Themisto, newly dead by her own hand, then ii 12 ff. may be assigned to Ino. But Ino would not be expected to sing a lament for Themisto, who had plotted to kill her children; and Themisto is not likely to have killed herself away from home. (ii) Alternatively, she may be the grief-stricken Ino, whose son Learchus Athamas has killed while hunting: in that case, we are close to the end of the play. If she is dead, it will be necessary to suppose that she has left behind a corpse on becoming a goddess, and that this corpse has now been recovered and brought back to the palace; it is again not clear to whom ii 12 ff. are then to be assigned. It may be easier to suppose that she is still alive, and that she herself, once uncovered, sings at ii 12 ff. The reference to Cadmus's line at ii 6 is easier to account for if there is a reference to Ino; and Athamas's request that she be laid 'gently' in front of the palace may indicate that she is alive.

An alternative hypothesis, suggested by Professor Parsons, would make the body that of the boy Learchus himself. The bearers would be the hunting party, with Athamas (now recovered from his madness) at their head. Athamas orders the body to be uncovered; Ino laments over her son. Ino's flight and death and deification (announced by a *deus ex machina?*) will have occupied the rest of the play. This interpretation requires us to explain away the feminine article in ii 5 (see 5–6 n.). On the other hand, it would give a special point to ii 9 μικρὸν . . . ἄχθοϲ (a child's body); and it would be confirmed if we recognise a masculine participle in the damaged stretch of ii 11. See further on ii 12 ff.

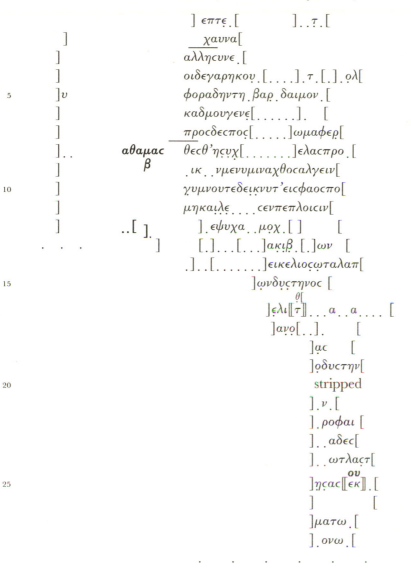

```
                          ] επτε . [          ] . . τ . [
          ]                    χαυνα[
          ]                 αλλησυνε . [
          ]               οιδεγαρηκου . [ . . . . ] . τ . [ . ] . ολ[
    5    ]υ              φοραδηντη . βαρ . δαιμον . [
          ]               καδμουγενε[ . . . . . . ] .   [
          ]               προσδεσποϲ[ . . . . . ]ωμαφερ[
    ] . .      αθαμας      θεϲθ'ηϲυχ[ . . . . . . ]ελαϲπρο . [
          ]         β      . ικ . . νμενυμιναχθοϲαλγειν[
   10    ]               γυμνουτεδεικνυτ'ειϲφαοϲπο[
          ]               μηκαιλε . . . . ϲενπεπλοιϲιν[
          ]       . . [ ] .    ] . εψυχα . . μοχ . [ ]        [
                      ]      [ . ] . . . [ . . . ]ακιβ . [ . ]ων   [
               .   .   .      . ] . . [ . . . . . . ]εικελιοϲωταλαπ[
   15                        ]ωνδυϲτηνοϲ [
                                         θ[
                             ]ελι[[τ]] . . . α . . α . . . . [
                             ]αυο[ . . ] .      [
                                ]αϲ     [
                                ]οδυϲτην[
   20                         stripped
                             ] . υ . [
                             ] . ροφαι [
                             ] . . αδεϲ[
                             ] . . ωτλαϲτ[
                                       ου
   25                        ]ηϲαϲ[[εκ]] . [
                             ]        [
                             ]ματω . [
                             ] . ονω . [
```

col. i   8 Traces of a tail joined to an upright

col. ii   1 ε . [, the upper left-hand arc of a circle with specks below and a trace suggesting the end of a cross-bar at mid-line level; the lower end of an upright on the line   ] . . τ . [, a cross-bar with a trace suggesting the top of an upright projecting above it at approximately its mid-point; an upright; traces suggesting the left-hand part of the cross-bar of τ joining its upright, to which a further trace lower down perhaps also belongs; to the right, a trace at a higher level   2 of the paragraphus, only specks   3 . [, a trace at mid-line level   4 υ, the left arm and ink in place for the foot   . [, the lower part of an upright   ] . , the top and bottom of an upright preceded by a trace high in the line   . [, on the lower layer, a short oblique ascending from the level of the cross-bar of τ　] ̣ọ, an upright; most of a small circle high in the line　　　5 ̣ (first), the upper part of an upright ̣ (second), the foot of an upright　 ̣[, at mid-line level, an oblique ascending from left to right　　6 of ϵ, the turn-up　] ̣[, a high trace; above, the edge of the upper right-hand arc of a circle, abraded on the left　　There are no further traces, although the cross-fibres continue to the right　　8 *mg.* 2 β written in a greyer ink than that of αθαμας above it　　8 of ς, the base and a trace of the left-hand side; of υ, most of the upper part and the tip of the tail; of χ, the upper part of the first oblique and specks compatible with the upper part of the second　 ̣[, level with the base of ο, the left-hand end of a cross-stroke　　9 ̣ ̣, two uprights connected by a cross-bar sagging very slightly in the middle, the second projecting slightly above the end of the cross-bar and with a hook serif to the right　 ̣ ̣, an upright descending below the line; an abraded trace, perhaps the edge of the lower right-hand arc of a circle　　10 γ, the lower part of a slightly concave upright　 ικ, an upright; a trace suiting the right-hand part of the upper branch of κ together with part of the upright and a speck in place for the end of the lower branch　　11 of ι, the lower part of an upright joined to α　 of λϵ, the lower parts　 ̣ ̣ ̣ ̣, first, the foot of a stroke sloping slightly to the right; second, the foot of an upright followed by abraded traces suggesting the end of a cross-stroke high in the line joining an upright; third, abraded traces suggesting a cross-bar at mid-line level crossed by another stroke perpendicular to it; fourth, perhaps the right-hand end of the base of ω with specks belonging to the left- and right-hand sides of the letter　　12 *mg.* ̣ ̣[, the lower part of an upright; at a slightly higher level, the foot of an upright, followed at a still higher level by a trace suggesting the base of a tiny circle or the junction of an oblique descending from left to right and an upright: ɴ seems possible　] ̣ ̣, in greyer ink and at a slightly lower level, the lower half of an oval with a stroke suggesting the tail of ᴀ or the like; above, the edge of an abraded stroke suggesting the upper left-hand arc of a circle　　12] ̣, low and high specks　 ̣ ̣, joined to the tail of ᴀ, perhaps the cap of ϲ or the like; specks　 ̣[, a high speck　　13] ̣ ̣ ̣[, a high trace; the upper parts of an upright and of an oblique descending from left to right　 of κ, which would be narrower than expected, traces suggesting the lower part of the upright and the lower branch　 ̣[, on the line, part of a stroke ascending from left to right　　14] ̣ ̣[, a shank crossing the lower left-hand arc of a circle, φ perhaps the likeliest, though the traces are not quite like any of the preserved examples; a speck　　16 The supralinear θ is abraded on the right; ϵ may also be possible　 ̣ ̣ ̣, a trace at mid-line level; an upright with a short cross-stroke emerging from its top, abraded on the right, closely followed by another upright: perhaps ɴ　 ̣ ̣, the lower parts of two uprights, the first with a leftward-pointing finial at the foot　 ̣ ̣ ̣ ̣, the foot of an upright close to the tail of ᴀ; low traces　　17] ̣, anomalous, perhaps the right-hand side of ω　　18]ạ, the tip of a tail close to ϲ　　21] ̣, specks　 ̣[, a speck　　22] ̣ ̣, the end of a cross-stroke touching ρ near the top　 ̩23] ̣ ̣, a trace suggesting an upright; traces of a stroke descending below the line　　24] ̣ ̣, an upright; in greyer ink, a large ʟ-shaped sign, its base extending below the line as far as the right-hand side of ω, with fainter traces suggesting a flat top extending above the letter-tops just beyond the upright of the following τ; more may be lost below the line on the left　　25 ̣[, a trace at mid-line level, not prima facie belonging to the oblique cancel stroke, perhaps the left-hand end of the cross-bar of τ, and a speck on the line, possibly casual　　27 above the first upright of μ, specks on the edge, perhaps casual　 ̣[, the top and lower part of a slightly concave upright on the edge　　28] ̣, a cross-stroke sloping upwards on the right to join the top of ο, perhaps ϵ or τ　 ̣[, a speck on the line

'... empty ...

'Another (disaster has struck?): here ... have arrived bearing aloft the ill-starred ... the line of Cadmus ... to the ruler's house.

'ATHAMAS Lay ... gently before (the palace?), bystanders (?), a small burden for you, but grievous to me. Uncover, display to the light ... so that ... wrapped in robes ... not ...

'[?] ... soul ... shameful, o much-suffering ... wretched ... wretched ...'

col. ii

2 The paragraphus is vestigial, but the horizontal alignment of the traces suggests that they are more than accidental.

3–7 Anapaests: 4–5 probably dimeters (5 with quasi-caesura between the two halves of a compound adjective: West, *Greek Metre* 95 n. 56), 6 monometer or (more probably) dimeter, 7 dimeter (not paroemiac, although it ends the system). Attic η 3, 5. The acatalectic dimeter in final place is anomalous. Perhaps something has dropped out after 7: for example, the scribe may have skipped ahead to a second instance of -ντες at line-end concluding the system.

3 cυνέκ[υρς(ε)? Cf. Eur. *Ion* 1446–8 πόθεν μοι cυνέκυρς' ἀδόκητος ἡδονά;, *IT* 875 τίς τύχα μοι cυγκυρήςει; Then e.g. ὀδύνη μελάθροις (*IT* 195–6 †ἄλλοις† δ' ἄλλα προςέβα χρυςέας ἀρνὸς μελάθροις ὀδύνα), or βαρεῖα τύχη. Or cυνέβ[η? Cf. Eur. fr. 963.3 μηδ' ἤν τι cυμβῇ δυςχερές. Then e.g. νῦν δυςτυχία.

4 ἤκους[ι: both the shape and the position of the trace suggest γ rather than ν (ἤκον).

5 φοράδην Eur. *And.* 1166, *Rhes.* 888; in a different sense at Soph. *OT* 1310.

βαρυδαίμων Eur. *Alc.* 865, *Tro.* 112 [and a conjecture at fr. 913.1]; not elsewhere in tragedy.

6]. [: the surface is stripped to the left of the trace, and though it is present to the right, further traces may have been lost to abrasion. If the trace is casual, we could treat the line as a monometer; if not, we need another dimeter.

5–6 If the reference is to Ino (or Themisto), restore e.g. τὴν βαρυδαίμονα [νύμφην | Κάδμου γενε̣[ᾶς or (in apposition) Κάδμου γενε̣[άν (monometer); or an equivalent dimeter. If the reference is to Learchus, Parsons suggests e.g. τὴν βαρυδαίμονα [θήραν | Κάδμου γενε̣[ᾶς γέννημα νέον (θήραν concrete, 'prey', as at Soph. *Phil.* 1146; cf. Eur. *Ba.* 1144 θήρᾳ δυςπότμῳ). Hyginus says simply *in venatione . . . interfecit*; more explicitly Apollod. 1.9.2 ἐτόξευςε, 3.4.3 ὡς ἔλαφον θηρεύςας.

7 δεςπόςυνος is found in Aeschylus (*Pers.* 587; *Cho.* 942 δεςποςύνων δόμων) and Euripides (*Hec.* 99, 1294, *IT* 439, *Pha.* 88 D. [fr. 773.44]), but not in Sophocles.

8–9 Eur. *Tro.* 1156–7 θέςθ' ἀμφίτορνον ἀςπίδ' Ἕκτορος πέδωι, | λυπρὸν θέαμα κοὐ φίλον λεύςςειν ἐμοί.

8 πρὸ δ[ωμάτων likely: cf. Eur. *Herc.* 525*, *Or.* 479, 1504*, 1541, *IA* 820* (* = in this place in the line); not elsewhere in tragedy.

π]έλας (]ε, though damaged, seems clear; not π]υλας) will have been preceded by the article. Otherwise the line would lack a regular caesura; and the precise πρὸ δ[ωμάτων is not likely to have been paired with the vague 'nearby'. We also expect a direct object to which the accusative in the following line may stand in apposition, as in Eur. *Tro.* 1156–7, quoted above. θέςθ' ἡςύχ[ως νιν οἱ π]έλας would fit the space and produce a line-beginning comparable to that of Eur. *Phoen.* 762 (in a suspect part of the play) τρέφ' ἀξίως νιν coῦ τε τὴν τ' ἐμὴν χάριν.

9 μικρὸν μὲν ὑμῖν ἄχθος, ἀλγειν[ὸν δ' ἐμοί. At the beginning, μικρον rather than πικρον: μ rather than π, since the top horizontal is (slightly) concave, and the word itself makes a better contrast with ἀλγειν[ὸν, all the more so if the body is a child's. Less likely ἀλγειν[ὸν δ' ὅμως (cf. Eur. *Hel.* 268 βαρὺ μέν, οἰςτέον δ' ὅμως, *Or.* 230 ἀνιαρὸν ὂν τὸ κτῆμ', ἀναγκαῖον δ' ὅμως) or ἀλγειν[όν θ' ἅμα (cf. Eur. *Hipp.* 348 ἥδιςτον, ὦ παῖ, ταὐτὸν ἀλγεινόν θ' ἅμα).

10 Eur. *Hec.* 679 cῶμα γυμνωθὲν νεκροῦ, *Hipp.* 714 ἐς φάος δείξειν.

End, perhaps πό[λει βλέπειν, with the infinitive as in Soph. *El.* 1458–9 κἀναδεικνύναι . . . ὁρᾶν, *OT* 791–2 (?), Pind. *Ol.* 9.74–5, *Nem.* 6.8. None of these contains εἰς φάος or a comparable qualification, but since δείκνυτ' εἰς φάος is hardly more than 'uncover', the objection is not a serious one. πο[θῶ βλέπειν preceded by punctuation is a theoretical possibility (cf. Eur. *Ion* 1432 ποθῶ μαθεῖν), but would make little contribution to the sense.

11 μὴ καὶ λεληθώς seems acceptable, and suitable to the theme of a shrouded body. It would confirm that the body is that of a male. At the end, πέπλοις or -λοιςι(ν), then a verb in the subjunctive, e.g. εὑρεθῇ, ἐγκρυφῇ, εἰςίῃ ('enter' the palace for the πρόθεςις).

11–12 A paragraphus marking a change of speaker may have been present. We should not expect any trace of it to survive as the surface is stripped.

12 *mg.* The traces on the right, at a lower level, could be taken as the lower loop and further remains of α, corresponding to β in 8 *mg.* and written in the same greyer ink. The higher traces to

the left should then offer a character indication. If so, ιν[ω or ιν̣(ω) is a possibility, though no more, consonant with α if that signifies 'protagonist'.

12 ff. If it is Ino who has just been brought on, who sings this lament? The dying Hippolytus laments his own fate (Eur. *Hipp.* 1347–88), but he walks on, supported by his servants; the victim in **5131** is carried shoulder high. ἡςυχ[(ii 8) might hint at the care due to a still-living person, but the general context, and the brusque stripping of ii 10, suggest the contrary. But if Ino has been brought on dead, we must find another character to sing these lines. On the other hand, if Ino is the singer, we must find another victim, and her son Learchus would fit the bill.

12 ψυχαϲεμοχθ[, however articulated, seems possible but cannot be confirmed. We have considered also ψυχαδ (ψυχὰ δ᾽, δέ), but if the trace represents the left-hand oblique of delta it seems too close to the alpha before it.

13 βα[λ]ών appears suitable. Before it, perhaps [κάμ]ακι, 'with a spear-shaft', with reference to the killing of Learchus, though in Apollod. 1.9.2 the fatal weapon is an arrow (5–6 n.). [κάμ]ακι βα[λ]ών could be the end of a dochmiac: cf. 14 n.

14 Eur. *And.* 131 δέμας αἰκέλιον καταλείβειν. The adjective is not found elsewhere in tragedy. It is seldom used of persons; Parsons proposes μόρος ἀ]εικέλιος.

ταλαπείριος is used for ταλαίπωρος by the tragedians according to the Et. Gen. and Photius (Trag. Adesp. 599). No other word beginning with these letters is attested for tragedy; ταλαπενθής only in epic and in Bacchylides. ὦ ταλαπ[είριε or ὦ ταλαπ[είριος may be considered; or ω may represent ὤ.

ἀ]εικέλιος ὦ ταλαπ[ειριχ may be the end of one dochmiac and the whole of the next.

15 If the metre is dochmiac, word-end is likely before ×]ων δύϲτηνος (West, *Greek Metre* 110). The first word may be a participle, e.g. θαν]ών.

16 Perhaps λιτον corrected to λιθον.

17 ἀνο[ϲί]ῳ?

22 (-)]τροφαι, (-)ϲ]τροφαι.

24 For the sequence ωτλαϲ, cf. perhaps Eur. *Alc.* 837 ὦ πολλὰ τλᾶϲα καρδία καὶ χεὶρ ἐμή, *Ion* 1497 ὦ δεινὰ τλᾶϲα, μῆτερ. The function of the sign placed after the first letter-trace is unclear. The thick upright might be a divider; its continuation, a thinner concave stroke extending horizontally below ω, suggests a ὑφ᾽ ἕν. The corrector may have intended to show that ωτλα- forms a unit (ὦ + ατλα- *in crasi*?), but if so we do not see how to continue. Perhaps two lines had mistakenly been run together (as in Bacchyl. 13.159–60) and the corrector simply wished to indicate the correct division.

W. LUPPE / W. B. HENRY

III. KNOWN LITERARY TEXTS

5132. Aristophanes, *Thesmophoriazusae* 1203–9
(Addendum to LVI 3840 + LXXIII 4935)

87/281(c)   2.2 × 4.5 cm   Second/third century

A newly identified fragment belonging to the right of **4935** fr. 2 and to the same column. **3840** (inv. 87/281(a)), taken from the same folder as the new piece, gives 1185–93, and will be from the previous column, but its level relative to **4935** fr. 2 + **5132** cannot be established as there is a *kollesis* on the right-hand side of **3840** and so no possibility of tracing the fibres across. Each of the fragments offers only a small quantity of writing for comparison, and some degree of variation may be observed, as was to be expected in a semi-cursive hand of this type, but I am confident that all four are the work of a single writer. The letters of Hippocrates in P. Berol. 7094 v. (BKT III 5–9) are copied in a similar informal style, assigned to the second/third century (BKT III pl. 1, CPF IV.2 pl. 26). **5132** contributes a second double dot signifying change of speaker (1209) to add to that at 1190 (**3840**). The cross-bar of final ϵ is greatly extended at 1206, as at 1190. The length of the longest iambic trimeter (1203) may be estimated at 10.5 cm; 1208, which extends to the right-hand edge of the new piece, was about 9.6 cm long. The back is blank.

There is no presumption in the case of this part of the collection that items placed in the same folder were found close together. Rather, it appears that **5132** and **3840** were put together as giving the ends of comic trimeters in the same hand, while the two fragments published as **4935** (inv. 88/287) were associated instead with the prose manuscript LXXVI **5084** (Plato, *Crito*, with the same inventory number), whose writing, though not identical in every respect, is probably due to the same hand.

The supplements printed are taken from C. Austin and S. D. Olson's edition of the play (2004). The manuscript is their Π₃, and P68 in N. G. Wilson's Oxford Classical Text (2007). There are no readings of interest.

	4935 fr. 2	**5132**
	Ερμ]η δολ[ιε ταυτι μεν ετι καλωϲ ποειϲ	
	ϲυ μ]εν ου[ν αποτρεχε παιδαριον το]υ[τι λαβων	
	εγω] δε λυ[ϲω τονδε ϲυ δ οπωϲ αν]δρ[ικωϲ	
1205	οταν λ]υθ[ηϲ ταχιϲτα φευξει και] τεν[ειϲ	
	ωϲ τη]ν̣ γ[υναικα και τα παιδι οικαδ]ε̣ [	
	εμοι με]λη[ϲει ταυτα γ ην απαξ λυθ]ω [	
	λελυϲο]· ϲο̣[ν εργον φευγε πριν τον] τ̣οξοτην [	

ηκοντα] κạ[ταλαβειν εγω δη τουτο δ]ρω: [

1210   ω γραδι] ως [καριεντο coι το τυγατριο]   [

κου δυcκολ αλλα πραο που το γραδιο]   [

·   ·   ·   ·   ·

1210–11 The space to the left of **5132** would also accommodate the transmitted -τριον] (1210), δύcκολλ' (1211).

W. B. HENRY

5133–5. Isocrates, *Ad Nicoclem*

This section includes fragments of a parchment codex and two papyrus rolls preserving sections from the first part, the second part, and near the end of the speech.

The primary mediaeval manuscripts are Γ, representing the first family, and the group of the second family ΛΠΝSVat. In addition, Δ, while basically a *descriptus* of Γ, may have in some cases independent value (see M. Fassino, in I. Andorlini et al., *Studi sulla tradizione del testo di Isocrate* (2003) 151–200, esp. 163–81; S. Martinelli Tempesta in CPF I.2*, p. xii). Sigla of MSS are based on the list in CPF I.2*, pp. xxxi–xxxii; sigla of papyri are those adopted in CPF I.2* and I.2**. As collation text I have used my forthcoming edition of *Ad Nicoclem*, which is part of the joint project to publish a new edition of Isocrates for the Oxford Classical Texts series. F. Seck, *Untersuchungen zum Isokratestext* (diss. Hamburg 1965) is cited as Seck, *Untersuchungen*.

Hitherto 21 papyri and parchments preserving parts of *Ad Nic.* have been published (p16–33, p119T, p120T, and P. Gen. IV 160, a sixth-century school exercise including *Ad Nic.* 42–43, 46, together with a passage of *Ad Dem.*), of which eight (p18, p19, p21, p26, p28, p29, p30, p32) come from Oxyrhynchus.

I am grateful to Dr Stefano Martinelli Tempesta and Dr Marco Fassino for helpful advice.

5133. Isocrates, *Ad Nicoclem* 4–5

105/219(b)   (*b*) 3.9 × 6.8 cm   Third/fourth century

Two fragments, (*a*) and (*b*), from a leaf of a parchment codex. Each page holds 11 lines. Upper and lower margins are preserved to 1.2 and 3 cm; preserved straight edges suggest that these are the original figures. The inner margin is about 0.8 cm wide (probably the original figure, since a straight edge is present) and the preserved outer margin about 1.7–2 cm wide. The original size of the page was 7.5 × 9.8 cm; the written area was 4.8 × 5.8 cm. Thus **5133** is a miniature codex, to be assigned to Turner's group XIV (*Typology* 29–30). Three other published parchment codices of Isocrates have similar dimensions: P. Ant. II 84 (p89; III/IV), LXIX **4717** (p18; IV) and VIII **1096** (p43 + p95; IV). Traces of ruling, extending into the outer margin, are visible on the flesh side above and below the first line. Page numbers are partially preserved above the outer edge of the column of writing, with the upper margin extending to a height of 0.3 cm above the tops of the numbers.

Of the codex we have the leaf representing pages 119 and 120. Assuming an average of 143 characters per page, we can calculate that *Ad Nic.*, which contains about 16,109 characters, occupied *c.*113 pages: it started on page 110 (probably in the second half of the page) and thus was preceded by another text (cf. VIII **1096**, which contains the end of *Panegyricus* and the beginning of *De Pace* on the same page).

We can try to reconstruct the original content of the codex with the help of the information available on the Isocratean *paradosis*: *Ad Nicoclem* is the second speech within the group of the so-called παραινέϲειϲ, the first being *Ad Demonicum* and the third *Nicocles*, and these three speeches could be transmitted as a *corpusculum* separate from the rest of Isocrates' works, as we see from P. Kell. III G 95 (see LXIX **4717**, introd.; CPF I.2*, p1, esp. pp. 256–7; M. Menchelli, 'Gli scritti d'apertura del "corpus" isocrateo tra tarda antichità e medioevo', in I. Andorlini et al., *Studi sulla tradizione del testo di Isocrate* 249–327, esp. 289–95. *Ad Dem.* (about 15,571 characters), copied in the same format, would have occupied about 109 pages. The initial paragraphs of *Ad Nic.* would then have occupied pages 110–118. The third speech, *Nic.*, at about 20,020 characters, would require a further 140 pages. Thus the whole *corpusculum*, in this format, would have reached about 362 pages. This seems to result in a rather bulky codex considering its miniature size. Compare the figures that have been calculated for the other miniature codices mentioned above: **1096** would have required 300 pages for *Panegyricus* and *De Pace*; P. Ant. II 84, 180 pages for *Panegyricus*; **4717**, 40 pages for *Ad Nic.*, but probably contained other texts (cf. S. Martinelli Tempesta, 'Dai rotoli al codice: tracce della formazione del *Corpus* Isocrateo nell'Urbinate greco 111', *Accademia Raffaello: atti e studi* 10/2 (2011) 73–88, esp. 83).

Alternatively the codex could have contained only the first two paraenetic speeches, making about 222 pages. Photius (*Bibliotheca* cod. 159) mentions *Ad Demonicum* and *Ad Nicoclem* as a pair, qualifying them as χρηϲίμουϲ παραινέϲειϲ περιέχονταϲ, while the anonymous βίοϲ Ἰϲοκράτουϲ clearly implies that the two speeches, sharing the paraenetic element, are complementary to each other: on the one hand, *Ad Dem.* is addressed to private individuals, on the other, *Ad Nic.* to kings (Mathieu–Brémond, *Isocrate: Discours* i p. xxxv 68–83). Moreover, P. Massil. of *Ad Nic.* (p17) contains the title λόγοϲ ΒΒ, which could be interpreted as 'of the two paraenetic speeches (i.e. the pair *Ad Dem.* and *Ad Nic.*) the second', and thus provide evidence for the transmission of the two παραινέϲειϲ *Ad Dem.* and *Ad Nic.* as a *corpusculum* (cf. Menchelli, 'Scritti d'apertura', 291–5).

The text is written in a now brown ink in a formal book-hand of medium size, of the mixed type with a very slight slant to the right. It is basically bilinear. An even right edge is produced by the use of smaller letters at line-end (p. 119.2, 3). Shading is not particularly emphasized, but cross-strokes tend to be thinner than uprights. Parallels for this hand are P. Flor. II 259 (*c*.260), especially the script of the two Homeric verses written in the left-hand margin perpendicular to the main text (Pap. Flor. XXX, tav. 126; Roberts, *GLH* 22d), and P. Herm. 4 and 5 (*c*.325) (*GBEBP* 2a and *GMAW*² 70). XI **1352** (= *GBEBP* 12a), assigned by Cavallo–Maehler to the early fourth century, is also comparable, but its hand is upright with alpha made in three strokes, while in **5133** alpha has an oval loop.

Elision is applied and marked by apostrophe, which has been added later apparently by the same hand (p. 120.3, 8). δέ is not elided at line-end (p. 120.10). Inorganic diaeresis occurs at p. 119.10.

5133 overlaps with p16 (P. Kell. III G 95), p17 (P. Massil.), p19 (PSI XI 1198) and p22 (PL II/40). One good reading is shared with the other papyri and the second family against Γ (p. 120.8–9), and another with the other papyri and Γ against the second family (p. 119.10–11).

Page 119

(a)   ρι]θ

Page 120

(a)   ρκ

```
              των ιδιωτ]ευον        (§4)
              των με]ν επιεικως
              δε πρατ]τοντων
              η τον των τ]υραν
(b)   5       νευο]ντ[ων οτα]ν       §5
              μ]εν γαρ [αποβλε
              ψωcιν ει[c τac τι
              μac και τουc [πλου
              τουc και τac [δυνα
      10      cτειac ϊcοθ[εουc α
              παντεc [νομιζουcι
```

```
              τουc [εν ταιc μοναρ
              χιαιc ον[ταc επει
              δαν δ’ ε[νθυμηθω
              cι του[c φοβουc και
(b)   5       τ[ουc κι]νδυ[νουc
              και διε]ξιοντ[εc
              . . . . .]ιν τουc μ[εν
              . .] ων ηκιc .’. ε
              χρ]ην διεφθαρ
      10      με]νουc τουc δε
              ειc του]c οικειο
```

Page 119

2–7 p17 omits μέ]ν (2) and γαρ (6) uniquely and [τον] (4) with Δ alone (but the error will have arisen independently there); it also offers the unique corruption αποβλεψουcιν for [αποβλε]|ψωcιν (6–7).

7–10 ει[c ταc τι]|μαc . . . τac [δυνα]|cτειαc with Γ^unc ΛΠΝSVat. In p19 and p22 this reading can be reconstructed on the basis of the space; p16 inserts αυτων after τιμαc, while p17 wrongly omits the preposition before τac | [τιμ]αc; Γ has πρὸc τοὺc τὰc τιμὰc . . . τὰc δυναcτείαc ἔχονταc (interpolated from §8).

10–11 a]|παντεc with p16 p17 p22 Γ: ἅπανταc ΛΠΝSVat: π[αντεc *vel* π[ανταc p19. On the (inferior) reading of the second family, see Seck, *Untersuchungen* 41–2 n. 14; CPF I.2* on p17 III 8 (p. 402). Of course one cannot rule out the possibility that **5133** offered παντες, not α]‖παντες; the space would allow either. On Isocratean usage, see Seck, *Untersuchungen* 78 n. 89; LXIX **4721** 5–6 n.; CPF I.2* on p17 XIV 3–4 (pp. 433–4).

Page 120

2–3 επει]‖δαν δ’ with the rest of the witnesses, apart from p16, which omits δὲ and transmits επειδ’ αν.

7 . . . . .]ιν: ὁρῶcι p17 (ορωcιν) Γ: εὕρωcι p16 (ευρωcιν) ΛΠΙΝSVat. The former seems too short here. (It is not clear which p19 had.) For a detailed discussion of the two readings, see Seck, *Untersuchungen* 42 n. 15, who states that εὕρωcι gives better sense, especially in relation to the preceding participle διεξιόντεc, and is supported by Isocratean usage; cf. also CPF I.2* on p17 III 11 (p. 402).

8 . .]: restore υφ] (p16 Γ), εφ] (ΛΠSⁱᵗVat), or αφ] (NSˢˡ). υφ] gives the best sense: see CPF I.2* on p17 III 12 (pp. 402–3).

8–9 ηκιc . ’. ε|[χρ]ην: ἤκιcτα χρῆν Γ: ἤκιcτα ἐχρῆν p16 p17 p22 Δ ΛΠΙΝSVat, inserted in Γ² as a correction. Only tiny vestiges of the letters represented by sublinear dots are preserved. Perhaps the scribe wrote ηκιcτα in full and then cancelled the final α and substituted an apostrophe. The variation χρῆν/ἐχρῆν represents an interesting problem in the textual tradition of Isocrates; see recently (on this passage) CPF I.2* p. 403. We have no reliable evidence for normal prose usage in the fourth century BC (Attic inscriptions provide scattered examples of both forms, but all in verse texts of Hellenistic and Roman date; see Threatte, *Grammar* ii 499); the form with syllabic augment is that normally attested in documentary papyri of the Roman and Byzantine periods (Gignac, *Grammar* ii 226). M. Fassino, *L'Encomio di Elena e il* Plataico *di Isocrate* (diss. Milan 2011; available at http://air.unimi.it/handle/2434/158082), comm. ad *Plat.* 21, pp. 271–2, argues that ἐχρῆν should be preferred except where hiatus would result.

10–11 δε | [εic. The scribe seems to have written δε | [εic with *scriptio plena*: there was no room for δ’ εic in 10, but without δε, the line would have been too short.

D. COLOMO

5134. Isocrates, *Ad Nicoclem* 39–41

104/117(c)   fr. 1 3.2 × 6 cm   Early third century

Two fragments of a papyrus roll, possibly from the same column. Intercolumnium is preserved to *c*.1.5 cm on the right-hand side of fr. 1. The column width was about 7 cm. The back is blank.

The text is written in a small hand of the Severe Style, slightly sloping to the right; cf. II **223** (Roberts, *GLH* 21a), assigned to the early third century on the basis of the document on its front (II **237**, a petition of 186). High stop is found at fr. 1.9.

5134 overlaps with p16 (P. Kell. III G 95). It presents one certain agreement with Γ (fr. 1.8–9) and one very probable agreement with the MSS of the second family (and partially with p16; see fr. 2.3–5 n.). Moreover, **5134** partially preserves the section of §39 quoted in the *Antidosis* in an abbreviated form, a section which, together with other parts of the same oration, has been considered by several scholars as a later interpolation; see fr. 1.1–7 n.; P. M. Pinto, *Per la storia del testo di*

Isocrate (2003) 172–6; S. De Leo, 'La citazione della "De Pace" nell'"Antidosis"', in I. Andorlini et al., *Studi sulla tradizione del testo di Isocrate* 215–22, esp. 217. p33 (P. Lips. inv. 1456), assigned to the late third century BC, provides comparable textual evidence for §§33–4.

Fr. 1

. . . . .

```
     τοιϲ πραγμαϲιν και τοιϲ] α[ν                      (§39)
     θρωποιϲ δυναμενουϲ κα]ι μη
     διαταραττομενουϲ εν τ]αιϲ τοῦ
     βιου μεταβολαιϲ αλλ]α κα
5    λωϲ και μετριωϲ και τ]αϲ ϲυμ
     φοραϲ και ταϲ ευτυχι]αϲ φε
     ρειν επιϲταμενουϲ κα]ι μη              §40
     θαυμαϲηϲ ει πολλα των] λεγο
     μενων εϲτιν α και ϲυ γιγνω]ϲκειϲ·
10   ουδε γαρ εμε τουτο παρ]ελα
     θεν αλλ ηπιϲταμην οτι] το
```

. . . . .

(*c*.5 lines missing)

Fr. 2

. . . . .

```
          ] αυτοι τ[υγχανου
     ϲιν επιτη]δευοντ[εϲ αλλα γαρ
     ουκ εν το]ιϲ λογοιϲ [χρη τοιϲ πε
     ρι των επ]ιτηδευ[ματων              §41
5    ζητειν ταϲ κα]ινοτ[ηταϲ
```

. . . . .

Fr. 1

1–7 **5134** does not support the view that part of §39 is a later interpolation, a view based on the fact that the corresponding extract quoted in *Antid.* is shorter and contains variations. γ and θ transmit two short sections of *Ad Nic.*, χρῶ . . . τούτων (end of §38) and ϲοφοὺϲ . . . λέγονταϲ (beginning of §39), in inverse order, a transposition very probably made by Isocrates himself, possibly for the sake of the rhythm; see Pinto, *Per la storia del testo di Isocrate* 176 n. 54.

3 The supplement printed may be slightly too long for the gap.

8–9 λεγο|[μενων with Γ: εἰρημένων p16 ΛΠΝSVat. Seck, *Untersuchungen* 88–9 n. 135, expresses a slight preference for the second reading: he notes Isocrates' tendency to use the participle εἰρημένα to indicate 'vorhergehende Darlegungen' and λεγόμενα to indicate statements that follow in his speech.

9 The supplement printed seems about two letters too long.

10–11 I have restored e. g. παρ]ελα|[θεν with Γ against διέλαθεν transmitted by p16 and the MSS of the second family, but the space would allow either reading. Seck, *Untersuchungen* 89 n. 136, defends the reading of Γ on the basis of Isocrates' usage.

Fr. 2

3–5 In the supplemented parts, for τοιc περι (p16 ΛΠΝSVat; suggested here by the spacing, and preferred by Seck, *Untersuchungen* 89–90 n. 139), Γ has τουτοιc; and p16 has χρη after ζητειν rather than after λογοιc. Note that the supplement printed seems about 2 letters too short to fill the space available between επ]ịτηδευ[ματων (4) and κα]ινοτ̣[ητας (5).

D. COLOMO

5135. Isocrates, *Ad Nicoclem* 48–9, 51–2

105/77(c)   4.8 × 10.8 cm   Third century

A fragment of a roll containing parts of two columns, written along the fibres. The back is blank. The upper margin is preserved to 1.3 cm; intercolumnium of *c.*1 cm. Of col. i, only line-ends survive; of col. ii, beginnings of 22 lines. Col. i appears to have held about 38 lines. Ten lines of col. ii occupy an area about 4.5 cm high. The height of col. i will then have been about 17.1 cm. Column width can be calculated at *c.*8–8.5 cm. Col. ii will be the penultimate column of the work. The entire *Ad Nicoclem* in this format would have required a roll about 1.85 m long. However, it is possible that **5135** belonged to a larger roll including the *corpusculum Ad Demonicum*, *Ad Nicoclem*, and *Nicocles* (for which see **5133** introd.). Such a roll would have been about 6 m long. For comparable 'reconstructed' cases, see D. Colomo, *Segno e testo* 6 (2008) 27–30.

The script is a medium-sized hand of the Severe Style, slightly sloping to the right. Contrast is rather emphasized: horizontals and rising obliques are thinner and sometimes delimited by finial dots. A good parallel is VII **1012** (pl. IV; CPF IV.2, pll. 152–3), written on the back of a tax-register of *c.*205 (VII **1045**). I am inclined to assign **5135** to the mid third century, but I do not rule out a date in the second half of the same century.

A thick paragraphus, written in lighter ink apparently by a second hand, occurs below ii 5, very probably to mark pause within the line, where a new clause begins. In the intercolumnium there are remains of an annotation (or correction?) to the left of ii 3, written cursively and at small size by another hand (perhaps the same that wrote the paragraphus, judging from the colour of the ink).

5135 overlaps with p16 (P. Kell. III G 95), but shares none of its unique readings and idiosyncrasies. It agrees with the MSS of the second family in an inferior reading (ii 12–14) and in a superior reading (ii 9, reading supported by p16 also); the deviation in ii 5–6 is merely a slip.

Col. i

Col. ii

```
                                          οι μεν δ[ια των εριϲτικων        (§51)
                                          λογων ο[ι δε δια των πολι
                                          τικων οι δ[ε δι αλλων τινων
        ποιηϲι]ν κ̣[αι] (§48)    ].ạ.     φρονιμῳ[τερουϲ εϲεϲθαι τουϲ
  5  τουϲ πρωτουϲ ευρονταϲ] τρα          5  αυτοι̣ϲ π̣[ληϲιαζονταϲ εκει
     γωδιαν αξιον θαυμαζει]ν              νοι δε πα[ντεϲ ομολογουϲιν
     οτι κατιδοντεϲ την φυϲι]ν            οτι δει το[ν καλωϲ πεπαιδευ
     την των ανθρωπων αμ]φ̣ο              μενον ε̣[ξ εκαϲτου τουτων
     τεραιϲ ταιϲ ιδεαιϲ ταυταιϲ κ]ạ       γεν[εϲθαι βουλευεϲθαι δυνα
  10 τεχρηϲαντο προϲ την ποι]η        10  μεν[ον χρη τοινυν αφε        §52
     ϲιν ο μεν γαρ τουϲ αγωνα]ϲ   §49     μεν[ον των αμφιϲβη
     και τουϲ πολεμουϲ τουϲ τω]ν̣         τουμ̣[ενων επι το ομολογου
     ημιθεων εμυθολογηϲεν οι]            μενο[ν ελθοντα λαμβα
     δε τουϲ μυθουϲ ειϲ αγωναϲ]          νειν [αυτων τον ελεγχον
  15 και πραξειϲ κατεϲτηϲαν]        15   και μ̣[αλιϲτα μεν επι των
     ωϲτε μη μονον ακουϲτο]υ̣ϲ            καιρ[ων θεωρειν ϲυμβου
     ημιν αλλα και θεατουϲ γεν]ε̣         λευ[ονταϲ ει δε μη και καθ ο
     ϲθαι τοιουτων ουν παραδει]          λων̣ [των πραγματων λε
     γματων υπαρχοντω]ν                  γον[ταϲ και τουϲ μεν μηδεν
  20 δεδεικται τοιϲ επιθυμου]       20   γι̣[γνωϲκονταϲ των δεον
     ϲιν τουϲ ακροωμενου]ϲ              τ[ων αποδοκιμαζε δηλον
                                        γ̣[αρ ωϲ ο μηδεν ων αυτοϲ
```

Col. i

The above reconstruction is proposed *exempli gratia* and cannot be confirmed in detail.

1 At the level of line 1, on the edge, 0.7 cm from col. ii (i.e. clearly within the intercolumnium), there is a short stroke, 1 mm long, more or less horizontal, in the same ink as the main text: remains of annotation or correction?

21 The supplement printed may be slightly too short to fill the space.

Col. ii

2–3 ο[ι δε δια των πολι]|τικων οι δ[ε δι αλλων τινων with Γ ΛΠΝSVat: οι δε δια των αλλων τινων p16 (apparently *saut du même au même* rather than a genuine variant; cf. K. A. Worp, A. Rijksbaron, *The Kellis Isocrates Codex* (1997) 41).

3–4 To the left of these lines, in the intercolumnium, we see]. ạ.., apparently written by the same hand as the paragraphus below 5. After what looks like a cursive alpha comes a long descending oblique ligatured to it, possibly iota or perhaps the sign of abbreviation. Before the alpha, an upright whose top seems to carry the right-hand end of a cross-bar projecting slightly to the right; this would fit pi (rather than tau), but pi in a much less cursive hand and without ligature to the next letter. Alternatively, one could see the putative pi as the end of another abbreviated word (e.g. iota with horizontal bar above); the intercolumnar space to the left would hardly have room for more than two letters. Since the meaning of the annotation is obscure, we cannot know whether it referred to line 3 of col. i (now lost) or to line 3 of col. ii. Textual variants and textual annotations are usually written to the left of a column, while explanatory annotations are accommodated to its right; see K. McNamee, *Annotations in Greek and Latin Texts from Egypt* (2007) 15–16.

4–5 τουϲ] | αυτοιϲ with all MSS, except p16, which has τοιϲ αυτοι, apparently a mere slip.

5–6 εκει]|νοι: ἐκεῖνο p16 Γ ΛΠΝSVat. This apparently unique variant is in fact a mere slip, produced by a sort of homoearchon within the kola between lines 2 and 6 (οἱ δὲ . . . οἱ δὲ . . . ἐκεῖνο δὲ) and probably also by the fact that ἐκεῖνο δέ is followed by another nominative plural, πάντες.

6 ομολογουϲιν suits the space. p16 alone has ανομολογουϲιν, a compound that does not occur elsewhere in Isocrates.

8 ε[ξ with all MSS apart from p16 (αφ). The traces in **5135** are clearly compatible with epsilon, but not with alpha.

9 γεν[εϲθαι with ΠΝSVat: γίγνεϲθαι p16 Λ (γίνεϲθαι): φαίνεϲθαι Γ. For discussion of these variants cf. Seck, *Untersuchungen* 97 n. 165, who defends γίγνεϲθαι as giving better sense after ἐξ ἑκάϲτου τούτων; compare *Antid.* 187 and 293.

10 Line slightly shorter than the average: perhaps blank space after [δυνα]|μεν[ον to mark the start of a new section/new paragraph?

11 If we reconstruct this line according to the text transmitted by all witnesses, it would contain 14.5 letters, i.e. the line would be too short, even taking into consideration the fact that in the lacuna broad square letters predominate. Therefore I am tempted to assume a different text or a case of dittography of some elements.

12–14 [επι το ομολογου]|μενο[ν ελθοντα restored with ΛΠΝ^pc(τὸν N^ac ν induct.)SVat on the basis of the space. Γ transmits ἐπὶ τοῦ ϲυνομολογουμένου (preferred by Seck, *Untersuchungen* 97–8 n. 166). p16 transmits επι τουϲ ομολογουμενουϲ ελθοντα, where ομολογουμενουϲ can perhaps be referred to λόγουϲ (so, doubtfully, Worp–Rijksbaron, *The Kellis Isocrates Codex* 209).

16–17 ϲυμβου]|λευ[οντας: so Γ: τοὺς ϲυμβουλεύοντας p16 and MSS of the second family. The shorter reading seems to fit the space better; and in any case, as Seck, *Untersuchungen* 98 n. 167, points out, the participle here has a predicative function and therefore does not need the article.

17–18 The paradosis is divided: καὶ καθ᾽ ὅλων Γ: τοὺς καθ᾽ ὅλων p16 N^pc: τοὺς καθ᾽ ὅλον N^ac: τοὺς καὶ καθ᾽ ὅλων S^acVat: τοὺς καὶ καθ᾽ ὅλον S^pc: τοὺς καθ᾽ ὅλου Λ: τοὺς καὶ καθ᾽ ὅλου Π. καθ᾽ ὅλων (p16 ΓN^pcS^acVat) is certainly right; see CPF I.2* on p17 IV 9 (p. 404). Before this phrase, to judge by the space, **5135** may have had καὶ (Γ) or τουϲ (p16 N) but not both. Seck, *Untersuchungen* 98 n. 168, rejects both καὶ and τουϲ, but the former gives good sense ('even') and should be adopted.

D. COLOMO

5136–9. Isocrates, *Nicocles*

Four newly identified papyri are edited here, one from the beginning and three from near the end of the text. All except the first include parts not otherwise preserved in ancient copies: of these, twelve have been published so far (p1, p68–77, p125T), including four from Oxyrhynchus. The primary manuscripts are Γ and, from the second family, ΛΠΝSVat (and for the opening sections also Auct = Bodl. Auct. T.1.11). Collations have been kindly provided by Dr Mariella Menchelli. The collation text is E. Drerup, *Isocratis Opera omnia* i (1906) 131–46.

5136. Isocrates, *Nicocles* 1–2

A. 10^D B4/7(H)1–2   3.2 × 3.4 cm   Second/third century

A fragment of a roll. On the back, written across the fibres, six lines of third-century semi-cursive. A line of the Isocrates text was about 7 cm long and held about 21 letters. The speech probably began at the top of the column to which this fragment belonged. The column will then have had at least 21 lines and been at least 12.3 cm high. If the speech had begun at the top of a preceding column, that column could be no more than 9.4 cm high, which seems excluded: see Johnson, *Bookrolls and Scribes* 119–25. The gently sloping hand is an example of the 'Severe Style,' comparable to that of LX **4045** + **4053** (Aeschines).

The papyrus offers a new but probably false variant (1).

This part of the text is also transmitted in p1 (P. Kellis III 95; iv).

```
        .   .   .        .   .
      ε]υρησουσι γιγ[νομε            (§1)
   νας επε]ιτα κακειν [ατοπον        §2
   ει λελη]θεν αυτους [οτι τα
   περι του]ς θεους ευς[εβουμεν
5  και την] δικαιοσυν[ην
        .   .   .   .        .
```

1 ε]υρησουσι: εὑρήσομεν is given by the other sources, including p1. The third person plural verb makes sense but is probably a corruption due to the influence of the preceding third person plural forms in -ουσι(ν).

2 επε]ιτα: επειτα δε p1, wrongly: see the editors' note.
κακειν [(as Γ) or -ν[o (as p1 ΛΠΝSVat Auct).

W. B. HENRY

5137. Isocrates, *Nicocles* 55, 57

67 6B.11/F(2)a   7 × 4.4 cm   Sixth century

A fragment of the inner edge of a papyrus codex leaf. The inner margin is about 1.7 cm wide. If the reconstruction printed is more or less correct, a line will have been about 14 cm long and contained about 28 letters on average. A column will have held 24 lines and occupied an area about 15 cm high. The written area will then have been approximately square, and the codex will perhaps have belonged among Turner's 'aberrants of Group 5' (*Typology* 18).

The 'Biblical Majuscule' hand displays an exaggerated contrast of thick and thin strokes: the latter can now sometimes scarcely be made out. ⲁ has a very

narrow loop joining the back of the letter low in the line. There is some resemblance to the second hand of the Vienna Genesis (cod. theol. gr. 31; *GBEBP*
29b; VI).

There are no new variants. Textual uncertainties make the reconstruction
of the missing parts rather complicated: for the procedure followed, see the commentary.

The papyrus briefly overlaps with p75 (P. Vindob. G 29797 = P. Rain. Cent. 22;
III?) in §57 (up to τὴν παιδευϲιν τὴν τοιαυτ[ην).

→

. . . .

.[

[χαλε   (§55)

που[ϲ] η πραο[τερουϲ ειναι τουϲ τυραν

νουϲ αλλα κα[ι τον τροπον τον των

5   πολιτων πο[λλοι

..]......[

..]..[

...].[

↓

. . . .

].[

παιδ]ευϲι[ν την] ε[ι   (§57)

ρημενην εθιζετ αυτουϲ] ωϲ μα[λ]ιϲτα

διατριβειν ην γαρ καλωϲ αρ]χεϲθαι μαθω

5   ϲιν πολλω μαλλον αρχειν] δυνηϲον

ται   ].[

                        ].[

. . . .

Choice among the transmitted variants is constrained by the need to ensure a perpendicular
left-hand margin on the ↓ side. For the stretches of text to be supplied in ↓ 4 and 5, apart from minor
variants, a longer and a shorter form are known from the later manuscripts: but if the lines are to
begin on the same alignment as ↓ 3, the longer versions must be adopted in both places, in conjunc-
tion with the shorter of the two possible verbs in ↓ 3. There is then a similar choice between shorter
and longer versions to be made in → 3 and 4; again, if the lines are to be of about the same length
as those previously reconstructed on the ↓ side, the longer versions must be adopted. But no certainty
can be claimed for the reconstruction, since the papyrus may have had in some places readings not
found in the later tradition.

→

2–5 These sentences are transmitted by Stob. 4.6.18.

3 πρᾳο[τερουϲ: so Γ, followed by Drerup. ΛΠΝΣVat Stob. have πράουϲ.

4 The second τον is present in Γ Stob. (followed by Drerup), but not in ΛΠΝΣVat.

↓

2–3 την] ε[ιρημενην: so Γ, followed by Drerup. Λ has τὴν τοιαύτην, as did p75 (την τοιαυτ[ην), while ΠΝΣVat have τῆϲ τοιαύτηϲ ἀρετῆϲ.

3 I have supplied εθιζετ with ΛΠΝΣVat (-ετε). Γ, followed by Drerup, has διδάϲκετ᾽, repeated from the beginning of the sentence.

4 I have supplied ην (Γ: ἐὰν ΛΠΝΣVat) and καλωϲ (Γ: om. ΛΠΝΣVat), following Drerup.

5 πολλω μαλλον supplied from ΛΠΝΣVat. Γ, followed by Drerup, has πολλῶν, which has been doubted (F. K. Hertlein, *Neue Jahrbücher* 109 (1874) 18). But Isocrates always has πολὺ μᾶλλον rather than πολλῶι μᾶλλον (Preuss, *Index Isocrateus* 65), though he uses οὐ πολλῶι with ὕϲτερον (*Paneg.* 72, *Hel.* 26).

W. B. HENRY

5138. Isocrates, *Nicocles* 59–60

23 3B.13/L(1–4)　　　　　　　3.9 × 3.2 cm　　　　　　　Fourth century

The upper outer corner of a miniature codex leaf. A line will have been about 5.6 cm long and held about 15 letters. The → page will have had about 10 lines, occupying an area about 6.3 cm high. The upper margin is about 0.3 cm deep, and the outer margin 0.3 cm wide on the → side and 0.9 cm wide on the ↓ side.

The hand is crude, with considerable variation in letter size and formation. It has some resemblance to the only slightly more skilfully executed hand of II **209** (Romans 1; *GBEBP* 1a; R. Cribiore, *Writing, Teachers, and Students in Graeco-Roman Egypt* (1996), no. 302), 'no doubt a schoolboy's exercise,' which 'was found tied up with a contract dated in 316 AD, and other documents of the same period.' (The contract in question has been identified as I **103**: see further A. Luijendijk, *JBL* 129 (2010) 575–96.) No doubt **5138** is also a school exercise. The format has no good parallels in papyrus codices of classical texts (Turner, *Typology* 22, 25), but closely resembles that of the schoolbook P. Vindob. G 29274 (*MPER* NS IV 24; Cribiore, *Writing, Teachers, and Students*, no. 403; IV–V), which is preserved complete in four sheets of papyrus measuring 9.5 × 5 cm. The book to which **5138** belonged may have had about the same number of pages. There is no way of telling how much of it was occupied by this extract.

The text appears to have been fundamentally a good one, but it is marred, as expected, by poor spelling (η for ε: → 2; ι for ει: ↓ 4, 5(?)). The frequency and nature of the errors suggest that the text may have been copied from dictation. The same is plausibly suggested in the case of the other published student's exercise consisting of an extract from the *Nicocles*, P. Vindob. G 39977 (§19; p125T; first edition: J. Lundon and G. Messeri, *ZPE* 132 (2000) 125–31; VI). In general on the use of the *Cyprian Orations* in education, see R. Cribiore in R. S. Bagnall (ed.), *The Oxford Handbook of Papyrology* (2009) 329–30.

The papyrus overlaps with **5139**.

→   ↓

	νοματω]ν εκαϲτον των	(§59)	μαϲ αυτου[ϲ παρεχον	(§60)
	πραγματω]ν τητυ		τεϲ εξι[ϲου	
	χηκεν τ]οιαυταϲ η		ϲθαι τοιϲ [προεχου	
	γειϲθε κα]ι ταϲ δυνα[		ϲι]ν φιλιν [οιεϲθε	
5	μειϲ αυτ]ων ε[ιναι	5	διν κ]α[ι	

.   .   .   .

→

This sentence is transmitted by Stob. 3.1.69.

1 εκαϲτον. So Γ (followed by Drerup): ἕκαϲτα ΛΠΝΣVat Stob. (Tr.: ἕκαϲτον Stob. cod. Par. 1985 according to Gaisford, apparently an emendation).

2–3 τητυ[χηκεν: l. τε-. ΛΠΝΣVat Stob. omit the ν.

3–5 τ]οιαυταϲ . . . ταϲ δυνα[μειϲ: a unique corruption (singular for plural) is offered by **5139** 1–2.

3–4 η[γειϲθε. So Γ ΛΠΣVat Stob. (followed by Drerup): ἡγεῖϲθαι (Π^ac ΝΣ^ac) not excluded.

↓

The first sentence (up to 3–4 [προεχουϲι]ν) is transmitted by Stob. 3.38.40.

1–2 παρεχον]τεϲ. So **5139** Γ Λ^pc Stob. (followed by Drerup): -ταϲ Λ^ac ΠΝΣVat.

2–3 εξι[ϲου]ϲθαι. So **5139** ΛΠΝΣVat Stob. (MABr: καὶ ἐξιϲοῦϲθε S Tr.) Γ⁴ in mg. (followed by Drerup): ἀξιοῦϲθαι Γ. The supplement is uncertain, since line 2 could easily have accommodated the whole of the infinitive. Perhaps the writer committed an error of some kind.

3 τοιϲ om. Vat.

3–4 [προεχουϲι]ν. So Γ S: προέχουϲι ΛΠ (-έ-) ΝVat.

4–5 φιλιν and [διν]: l. φιλεῖν and δεῖν. [διν] is not quite certain but suggested by the space available.

W. B. HENRY

5139. Isocrates, *Nicocles* 59–61

15 2B.42/C(e)   2.6 × 7.6 cm   Second/third century

The foot of a column of a papyrus roll, blank on the back, with a lower margin 1.4 cm deep. The column was wide: a line held about 31 letters and was about 9.5 cm long. Johnson, *Bookrolls and Scribes* 206, notes only two rolls from Oxyrhynchus containing prose texts whose columns fall in this 'aberrantly wide' group, XVIII **2181** (Plato, *Phd.*) and LII **3667** ([Plato], *Alc.* ii): in both cases, the column width is estimated to be 10.1 cm, while the column heights are estimated to be 21.7

cm (**2181**) and 23.25 cm (**3667**). Ten lines of **5139** occupy a space about 5 cm high. Since the text from the end of this column to the end of the work would occupy only about 26 lines, this is almost certainly the penultimate column.

The text is written in a small informal and rather irregular round hand with numerous ligatures. The upright of τ has a right-pointing hook at its foot, as do both uprights of η and sometimes ι. ξ is cursive and descends below the line; ρ also descends, as does ι when ligatured to a preceding α. α and υ may be looped at the apex (α) or base (υ), but the loop and tail of α are usually made separately. The only lection sign is a trema on εξϊc̣[ουcθαι (5), presumably added by the scribe. Among Isocrates papyri, the hands of LXIX **4722** (*Ad Nic.*; p30; ii) and **5141** (*De pace*; ii/iii), which was found together with this papyrus, are similar, but in some respects the semi-cursive hand of LXX **4760** (Antonius Diogenes; ii/iii) is closer. Cf. also SPP XXII 1 (Harrauer, *Paläographie* Abb. 143; ii/iii), especially its αι and ξ.

The papyrus offers a new corruption (1). There are three instances of -αι for -ε in verbal endings (-cθαι for -cθε: 4, 6; -ται for -τε: 9), but φρονει]τ̣ε (10) is spelt correctly.

5139 overlaps with **5138** at the beginning (1–6) and with p76 (P. Erl. 10; iii) at the end (7–12). The latter has a similarly pronounced tendency to substitute -αι for -ε in verbal endings (3, 6, 11, 12 (×2), 22), and in the one place where it is possible to check, the papyri agree in offering the false spelling (**5139** 9, p76.3).

. . . .

] τοιαυτην̣ [ηγειcθαι (§59)
και την δυναμιν αυ]τ̣ων ειναι̣ [μη φθο §60
νειτε τοιc παρ εμοι] π̣ρωτευου̣[cιν αλ
λ αμιλλαcθαι και πει]ραcθαι χρ̣[ηcτουc
υμαc αυτουc παρεχο]ντεc εξϊc̣[ουcθαι
τοιc προεχουcιν φιλει]ν οιεcθαι̣ [δειν
και τιμαν ουcπερ αν κ]αι ο βαcιλευ̣[c ινα και
παρ εμου τυγχανητε] των αυτων̣ τ̣[ουτων
οια περ παροντοc μο]υ̣ λεγεται τ̣[ο]ι̣[αυτα
και αποντοc φρονει]τ̣ε την ευν̣[οιαν §61
την προc ημαc εν τοιc ε]ρ̣γοιc ενδε̣[ικνυ
cθαι μαλλον η εν τοιc λο]γοιc̣ α̣ π̣αcχ[οντεc

1–2] τοιαυτην̣ [. . . την δυναμιν: other copies (including **5138**) correctly give the plural τοιαύτας . . . τὰς δυνάμεις. The corruption may be due to the influence of the preceding singular ἕκαστον (v.l. ἕκαστα: see on **5138** → 1).

1, 4, 12 -cθαι supplied for -cθε: cf. 4, 6, and 9 for the scribe's practice; **5138** → 3–4 n.

2–6 μη φθονειτε . . . προεχουcιν is transmitted by Stob. 3.38.40.

4 και πει]ραcθαι (l. πειρᾶcθε) om. Stob.

5 παρεχο]ντεc εξϊc̣[ουcθαι: for transmitted variants, see on **5138** ↓ 1–3.

6 οιεϲθαι: l. οἴεϲθε.

9–10 As no margins are preserved, it is not possible to determine reliably on the basis of the space available whether **5139** had περ (Γ² ΛΠΝSVat) . . . και (ΛΠΝSVat), as given above, or περι . . . και περι, with Γ (followed by Drerup), but I have tentatively preferred the former. For discussion, see CPF I.2** on p76.2 (p. 685).

9 λεγεται: l. λέγετε. The same error in p76.

12 In the supplement, I have tentatively preferred η εν (Γ² [p76]: μὲν Γᵖʳ), printed by Drerup, to η (ΛΠΝSVat) on grounds of space. For discussion, see CPF I.2** on p76.5 (p. 685).

W. B. HENRY

5140–43. Isocrates, *De Pace*

Four further papyri of this work are presented here, of which **5140** is the most extensively preserved ancient copy of the work except p46 (P. Lond. Lit. 131). The others, though small, shed interesting light on the ancient transmission. **5141** presents in its short compass two unique deviations from the word order as known from other manuscripts. **5142** and **5143**, the earliest copy published to date, demonstrate the ancient circulation of corruptions hitherto unique to p46: for a comparable case, cf. p59 (LXIX **4737**) ii 10–11 n.

18 other ancient manuscripts have been published, of which 15 are from Oxyrhynchus. All four of the new papyri overlap with p46; **5140** alone also overlaps with p48 (LXIX **4728**), p49 (LXIX **4729**), p50 (P. Heid. I 208), p51 (P. Oxy. Hels. 7), p53 (LXIX **4731**), p55 (LXIX **4733**), and p58 (LXIX **4736**; possibly part of an extended quotation in *Antid.*). The later manuscript tradition is represented by Γ and, from the second family, ΛΠΝ; in the passages cited in *Antid.*, (γ)θλ are used. The collation text is the Budé edition of G. Mathieu (1942). Information about manuscript readings is drawn from B. Mandilaras, Ὁ περὶ εἰρήνης λόγος τοῦ Ἰσοκράτους ἐκ τοῦ παπύρου τοῦ Βρεταννικοῦ Μουσείου (1975), and E. Drerup, *De codicum Isocrateorum auctoritate* (Leipziger Studien xvii/1, 1895) 136–60, and from CPF where available. N has been collated from digital images. For the quotations in Dionysius of Halicarnassus (*Dem.* and *Isoc.*), the Budé edition of G. Aujac (1978–88) has been used. Variants in the restored portions are only mentioned where considerations of spacing seem decisive, and minor variations in such matters as use of elision or *scriptio plena* and presence or absence of optional final *ν* are not generally mentioned. Poorly attested corruptions in other manuscripts are recorded only selectively.

W. B. HENRY

5140. Isocrates, *De Pace* 13–14, 16, 22–3, 25–7, 31, 35–6, 40–44,
46–7, 49–50, 58–63, 70–73, 76–9, 88–91, 99,
102–3, 112–13, 124–5, 136–7, 142

87/53(a) + 88/242   Fr. 8 9.2 × 14.5 cm   Second century

Numerous fragments of a papyrus roll, written along the fibres. (Not included below are several unplaced fragments and scraps.) The back is blank. The fragments represent about 24 columns scattered throughout the text of the speech. No complete line is preserved, and none of the columns is preserved to its original height. Fr. 8, the largest, contains the lower portions of two adjacent columns, the second of which had about 48 lines. Frr. 25 and 29 preserve the top and foot of a single column also of about 48 lines. Apart from frr. 8 + 9, 14–16, 17–18, and 25–9, the arrangement of fragments in columns is uncertain, but each of the following groups is likely to have belonged to a single column: frr. 4–5, 19–21, and 23–4. The height of each column was about 29 cm (one of the highest figures attested for a roll from Oxyrhynchus: see Johnson, *Bookrolls and Scribes* 121–5), the width was about 6.5 cm, and lines contained between 18 and 22 letters. Fr. 17 preserves the upper margin to a depth of 2 cm. Fr. 8 preserves the lower margin to a depth of 2.5 cm and an intercolumnium 1 cm wide. The height of the roll was therefore at least 32.5 cm. A rough letter count suggests that fr. 1 is to be assigned to col. 4 of the roll, fr. 2 to col. 5, fr. 3 to col. 7, fr. 4 to col. 8, fr. 5 to col. 9, fr. 6 to col. 10, fr. 7 to col. 11, frr. 8 + 9 to cols. 13–14, fr. 10 to col. 15, frr. 11–12 to col. 16, fr. 13 to col. 18, frr. 14–16 to col. 19, frr. 17–18 to col. 20, frr. 19–21 to col. 22, fr. 22 to col. 23, frr. 23–4 to col. 24, and frr. 25–9 to col. 27. The reconstruction of the end of the roll, where no column tops or bottoms survive, is more uncertain. If we assume that each column in this stretch of the text contained on average about 1,080 letters (the approximate figure for the column represented by frr. 25–9), then fr. 30 will belong to col. 30, frr. 31 and 32 to col. 31, fr. 33 to col. 34, fr. 34 to col. 37, fr. 35 to col. 40, and fr. 36 to col. 42; the work will have ended in col. 43. If a lower average letter count is assumed for the final columns, the work may have occupied 44 or possibly 45 columns. 43 columns would give a short total length of about 3.25 m for the roll (not including initial or final titles). *Kolleseis* can be recognized in frr. 11, 14, 16, and 25.

The text is written in a roughly bilinear medium-sized informal round hand. α, δ, and λ extend above the line, and φ both above and below the line. π and τ are often shorter than adjacent letters, and ω is sometimes shallow. c, θ, o, and ρ are narrow; μ, π, and ω are broad. There is no shading and little ornamentation. The top of φ carries a hook to the left or a serif. The top of δ occasionally bears a hook to the left. ι sometimes has a half-serif to the left at the top and/or to the right at the foot. β has a short descending oblique joining its upright on the line from the left. The right leg of π curves and sometimes hooks to the right. α is usually rounded but sometimes angular. ε and c are tall and angular at the top; o and the loop of θ are tall and oval, slightly pointed at the top; μ is rounded, and the bowl of φ is triangular. The writing is often careless and letter forms are not consistent. Letters occasionally slant to the left and sometimes touch. Comparable hands include those of P. Mich. inv. 3690 (Aristophanes, *Heroes*; *CLGP* I.1.4, pl. 8) and the letter LXXIII **4959**; see further the introduction to the latter.

Lectional signs are rare. A strong pause is occasionally marked by a paragraphus or high stop. A space filler (>) ends the line at frr. 1.3, 8 + 9 ii 22, 17.5, and 17.9. Elision is effected but not marked; *scriptio plena* at fr. 27.23. Crasis is not effected at frr. 8 + 9 ii 21. Iota adscript is not written (frr. 1.12, 16.31, and 19.2). ει is substituted for ι at frr. 1.4, 17.4, 36.3, and probably at 5.9 and 34.4, and ι for ει at fr. 22.7. Corrections are made by striking out letters or with additions above the line (frr. 8 + 9 ii 43 and 48, 18.13, and 19.3); at least some of the corrections are made with a thin pen by a different hand. There are uncorrected errors at frr. 2.3 and 19.2. There is a marginal addition (perhaps a variant reading or correction) at fr. 16.27.

As a witness to the text, **5140** is of value chiefly as providing for the first time ancient evidence for known good readings in places where the tradition is divided. In most of the passages in question, where its text can be determined with a reasonable degree of certainty, it sides with all other witnesses (if trivial errors are excluded) against p46 alone (frr. 3.5, 8 + 9 ii 21–2, 16.36, 22.3–4, 8, 25.2, 35.4) or p46 and Dionysius (fr. 1.12); in a few, the mediaeval manuscripts are divided and the papyrus agrees with Γ alone (frr. 8 + 9 ii 45, 17.3, 33.9–11) or ΓΠΝ (fr. 19.1–2). It presents four new readings: an apparent inversion of word order at fr. 5.9; perhaps ποιήϲουϲιν for ποιοῦϲιν at fr. 14.8; perhaps ἐκπείπτονταϲ for ἐκπεπτωκόταϲ at fr. 34.4; ἐπ' for ἐξ (v.l. ἀπ') at fr. 36.7. The first of these is at least possible, but the others seem inferior.

For the identification of some of the smaller fragments we are grateful to Ms D. Bafa and Dr W. B. Henry.

Fr. 1   Fr. 2

. . . .

α]ξιον θαυμαζε[ιν   (§13)   μεναιϲ με[ν προϲ βαϲιλεα   (§16)
ει τιϲ ελ]πιζει την πολιν τοι[ου   και Λακεδαιμονιο[υϲ προϲ
τοιϲ cυ]μβουλοιϲ χρωμε>   τατουϲαιϲ δε τουϲ Ελ[ληναϲ
νην επι] το βελτειον επιδω   αυτονομουϲ ειναι κ[αι ταϲ
5 cειν εγ]ω δ οιδα μεν οτι προϲ   §14   5 φρουραϲ εκ των αλλοτ[ριων πο
αντεϲ εϲ]τιν εναντιουϲθαι   λεων εξιεναι και τ[ην αυ
ταιϲ υμε]τεραιϲ διαν[οι]αιϲ και   των εχειν εκαϲτουϲ [του
οτι δημο]κρατιαϲ ουϲηϲ ουκ ε   των γαρ ουτε δικαιοτ[εραϲ
cτι παρρ]η[ϲι]α πλην ενθα   ευρηϲ[ομεν
10 δε μεν τοιϲ α]φρονεϲτατοιϲ   . . . . .

και μηδεν υμ]ων φροντιζου
cιν εν δε τω θε]ατρω τοιc κω
μωδοδιδαc]καλοι[c ο και παν
των εcτι δει]νοτατ[ον οτι τοιc
15 μεν εκφερ]ουcι[ν ειc τουc αλ
λουc Ελληναc] τα τη[c πολεωc α
μαρτηματα] τοcα[υτην εχε
τε χαριν οcη]ν ουδ[ε

Fr. 3   Fr. 4

.   .   .   .   .   .

μηδ]ενο[c των αλλοτριων ε   (§22)   ταραχαc] μηδ α[ναβολην αλλ α (§25)
φιε]μεν[ουc νυν μεν γαρ ει   παλλαγ]ην ευ[ρηcομεν τινα
κο]τωc φο[βουνται γειτονα
π]οιηcαcθ[αι την πολιν   *c.*3 lines missing
5 τ]αιc α[υτων δυναcτειαιc
ορ]ωcι γ[αρ ημαc ου cτεργον   §23
τ]αc εφ [οιc αν εχωμεν αλ

.   .   .

Fr. 5

.   .   .   .

].[.].[
μ]ωτερα[ν και κερδαλεωτεραν   (§26)
ει]ναι τ[ηc πολυπραγμοcυνηc
τ]ην δε δ[ικαιοcυνην τηc αδι
5 κι]αc την [δε των ιδιων επι
μ]ελειαν [τηc των αλλοτρι
ω]ν επιθ[υμιαc περι ων ουδειc
π]ωποτε [των ρητορων εν υ
μ]ειν ειπ[ειν ετολμηcεν εγω
10 δε] περι αυ[των τουτων τουc
πλ]ειcτου[c των λογων μελ
λ]ω ποιει[cθαι προc υμαc ορω
γ]αρ την ε[υδαιμονιαν εν
το]υτοιc ε[νουcαν αλλ ουκ εν
15 οι]c νυν τυ[γχανομεν πρατ
τ]οντεc α[ναγκη δε τον εξω   §27
τω]ν ειθι[cμενων επιχει

ρου]ντα δ[ημηγορειν και
τας υμ]ετ[ερας γνωμας

.   .   .

Fr. 6   Fr. 7

.   .   .   .

το]ν βιον [τον καθ ημερ]αν συμ (§31)   αδικιας χ]ειρον δ οιο[νται (§35)
φ]ερουσαν [την δε δικ]αιοσυ   βιωσεσθαι] τους ταυτη [χρω
ν]ην ευδοκ[ιμον μεν] αλυσι   μενους τ]ων την π[ονη
τε]λη δε και [μαλλον δυ]να[ριαν προηρημε]νω[ν ηβου   §36
                                         5   λομην   c.8   ].[

.   .   .   .

Frr. 8+9
Col. i   Col. ii

                                      *c.*20 lines missing

(Fr. 9)

                                      .   .   .

                                21   ] και τα ε   (§42)
                                        ναντια τοις τοτε] πρατ>
                                        τοντες αγανακτου]μεν ει
(Fr. 8)   μη την αυτην τι]μην ε
                                        25 κεινοις   ].[

.   .   .   .   .   3 lines missing

τιν τας με]ν κ[αυ]σε[ις] κ[α]ι (§40)   χρο[νον γενομενων ο   (§43)
τας τομ]ας των ιατρων [υ]πο   30 σον [οι μεν υπερ της των
με]νειν ινα πλειόνων αλ   Ελλ[ηνων σωτηριας την
γη]δονων απαλλαγωμεν   τε π[ατριδα την αυτων εκ
5 το]υς δε λο[γους αποδοκιμα   λιπε[ιν ετολμησαν και
ζειν πριν ει]δεναι σαφως   μαχ[ομενοι και ναυμαχουν
ει τοιαυτην ε]χουσι την δυ   35 τες τ[ους βαρβαρους ενι
ναμιν ωστ ω]φελησαι το[υ]ς   κης[αν ημεις δ ουδ υπερ
ακουοντας του]του 'δ' ενεκα   §41   τη[ς ημετερας αυτων πλε
10 ταυτα προειπον] οτι περι   ο[νεξιας κινδυνευειν α
των λοιπων ου]δεν υπος   ξι[ουμεν αλλ αρχειν μεν   §44
τειλαμενος αλλ]α παντα   40 απ[αντ]ω[ν ζητουμεν στρα
πασιν ανειμεν]ως μελ   τευεσθα[ι δ ουκ εθελομεν
     1 line missing   και πολεμ[ον μεν μικρου
15   ].[δειν' προς [απαντας ανθρω
                                         πους [αναιρουμεθα προς δε

*c.*4   ] . ελθω[ν και μηπ]ω ϲ[υ]ν
δι]εφθαρμενος ημιν αλλ ε
ξαι]φνης επιστας τοις γιγν[ο
με]νοις ουκ αν μαινεσθαι

45 τουτοις ο[υχ ημας αυτους
ασκουμε[ν αλλ ανθρωπους
τους μεν [απολιδας τους
δ αυτο[[ν]]ʼμ̣ο̣[λους

Fr. 10

ρο]υ̣ς αυ[των ιδια λυμαινο   (§46)
μεθα κ[αι δασμολογουμεν
ι]να το[ις απαντων κοινοις
εχ]θ̣ρο̣ι̣[ς τον μισθον εκπορι
5 ζ]ωμε[ν τοσουτω δε χειρους   §47
εϲ]μ̣εν̣ [

Fr. 11

και την] πολιν τα[υτην προτε (§49)
ραν οι]κιϲθηνα[ι των αλλων
πρ]οσηκον δ ημᾳ̣[ς απασιν
ειναι παραδειγμα τ[ου καλως
5 και τεταγμεν[ω]ς πο[λιτευε
σθαι χειρον και ταρ[αχωδεσ
τερο̣ν την ημετε[ραν αυ
των διοικουμεν τ[ων αρ
τι τας πολεις οικιζον[των
10 κ̣αι σεμνυνομεθα [μεν   §50
και] μεγα φρονου[μεν

5 lines missing

Fr. 12

δυ]ϲγε[νειας   (§50)
πλειστους δε τι]θεμ[ενοι
νομους ουτως ολ]ι̣γο̣ν̣ [

Fr. 13

ην] εν[ικηϲαν Θηβαιοι Λακε (§58)
δ]αιμο̣[νιους εκεινοι μεν ε
λ]ευθε[ρωϲαντες την Πελο
π]ονν̣[ηϲον

*c.*14 lines missing

Frr. 14–16

(Fr. 14) ημι]ν ποι̣ο̣[υϲιν ημεις δ εκει
ν]οις ωστ ει ν̣[ουν εχοιμεν
α]λληλοις αν [εις τας εκκληϲι
ας αργυριον π[αρεχοιμεν ο
5 ποτερο̣[ι] γαρ α[ν πλεονακις ϲυλ
λεγωϲ̣[ι]ν̣ ο̣υτ̣[οι τους εναντι
ους αμε̣[ινον πραττειν ποι

(§59)

ησου[cιν χρη δε τους και μικρα λο   §60

γι]ζεϲθα[ι δυναμενους ουκ

10   εν τοιϲ των ε[χθρων αμαρτη

μαϲιν ταϲ ελπ[ιδαϲ εχειν

τηϲ ϲωτηρ[ιαϲ αλλ εν τοιϲ αυ

των πρα[γμαϲιν και ταιϲ αυ

των δια[νοιαιϲ

15   1 line missing

(Fr. 15)   ϲυμβαιν]ον [ημιν αγαθον

τυχον α]ν παυ[ϲαιτο και λαβοι

μεταβο]λην [το δε δι ημαϲ

αυτους γ]ιν[ο]μ[ενον

      3 lines missing

(Fr. 16)   λημ[ψειϲ ποιουμενους ου χα   (§61)

λεπ[ον αντειπειν ει δε δη

25   τιϲ μο[ι παραϲταϲ των επιει

κεϲτ[ερον διακειμενων α

    ].. ληθη [μεν λεγειν με προϲομο

λογηϲ[ειεν και προϲηκοντωϲ

επιτι[μαν τοιϲ γιγνομενοιϲ

30   δικαι[ον δ ειναι φαιη τουϲ ε

π ευν[οι]α νου[θετουνταϲ μη

μονον κατη[γορειν των πε

πραγμενων α[λλα και ϲυμβου   §62

λευειν τινων [απεχομε

35   νοι και ποιων [ορεγομενοι

πα[υ]ϲαιμεθ αν [ταυτην ε

χον]τεϲ την γν[ωμην και τοι

αυτα] εξαμαρτα[νοντεϲ ουτοϲ

Frr. 17–18

(Fr. 17)   ο λογοϲ απορειν α]ν με

ποιηϲειεν απο]κριϲεωϲ

ουκ αληθουϲ κ]αι ϲυμφερουϲ[ηϲ

αλλ αρεϲκου]ϲηϲ υμειν· ου

5   μην αλλ επει]δη περ απο>

κεκαλυμμενω]ϲ ωρμημαι

λεγειν ουκ απ]οκνητεον
αποφηνασθαι] και περι του
των α μεν ουν υ]παρχειν>   §63
10   1 line missing
(Fr. 18)   μονησειν την ευσεβε]ιαν και
την cωφροσυνην και] την αλ
λην αρετην ολι]γ[[ον]]ʿωʾ προ
τερον ειρηκαμ]εν ως δ αν
15   ταχιστα προς το τοι]ουτοι γε

.   .   .   .   .   .

Frr. 19–21

(Fr. 19)   ω]ς τοινυν [ουδ]ε δεξας[θαι δι   (§70)
δο]νμενη[ν τ]η πολε[ι συμ
φε]ρει[[ν]] δοκ[ειτε μοι ταχιστ αν
ε]κειθε[ν
c.17 lines missing
(Fr. 20)   βαιως] και τη[ν πολιν και τους   (§71)
αλλο]υς Ελλην[ας αγαγειν α   §72
ναγκ]η δε τους [νουθετουν
25   τας και] το[υς
c.17 lines missing
(Fr. 21)   τ]ας συμφορ[ας τας   (§73)
44   απ αυτ]ων γινομεν[ας

.   .   .   .   .

Fr. 22

.   .   .   .

Ελλ]αδος [κινδυνοις ουτω   (§76)
δε] πιστε[υομενον ωστε τας
π]λειστας [αυτω των πολε
ω]ν εκο[υσας εγχειρισαι
5   c]φας αυτ[ας τουτων δ υπαρ   §77
χο]ντων [αντι μεν της πο
λι]τιας τ[ης παρα πασιν ευδο
κι]μουση[ς επι τοιαυτην α
κο]λασιαν [η δυναμις ημας
10   αυ]τη προ[ηγαγεν ην ουδεις
α]ν ανθρω[πων επαινεςει

ε]ν αντ[ι δε του νικαν τους
ε]πιστρατ[ευοντας ουτω
του]ς πολι[τας επαιδευσεν
15   ως]τε μη[δε προ των τει
χω]ν τολ[μαν επεξιεναι
τοι]ς πολ[εμιοις αντι δε   §78
τη]ς ευ[νοιας

    .   .   .   .

Frr. 23–4

    .   .   .   .

(Fr. 23)   ασελγε]ιαν των [(§79)
πατερων των η]μετερων [
οι συναγοντες] εξ απασῃ[ς
      *c.*4 lines missing
(Fr. 24)   τ]ας τρι[ηρεις απηχθα
νοντο τοι]ς Ελλησιν [και τους
10   μεν βελ]τιστους τω[ν εν ταις
αλλαις] πολεσιν εξ[εβαλλον
τοις δε] πονηροτατ[οις

    .   .   .   .

Frr. 25–9

(Fr. 25) μον δι]εφυγον ευρη[σομεν επι   (§88)
της αρχ]ης ης επιθυμ[ουμεν ανα
στατου]ς γεγενημεν[ους ωστ ει   §89
τις σκοπεισθαι] βου[λοιτο περι
5   των αλλων] ωσπερ π[ρος δειγμα
τουτ αναφ]ερων [
      *c.*9 lines missing
(Fr. 26) τυραννιδας κ]ατεχ[οντας μη
17   δε τους μει]ζω δ[υναστειαν
του δικαιου] κεκτ[ημενους
αλλα τους αξι]ους [μεν οντας
20   [της μεγιστης τιμης στεργον]
(Fr. 27) τας δ ε]πι τα[ις υπο του πλη
θους] διδομε[ναις ταυτης   §90
γαρ εξ]ιν ουτε [ανηρ ουτε πολις
λαβει]ν αν δυ[ναιτο σπουδαιο
25   τεραν]· ουδ ασ[φαλεστεραν ουδε

πλειο]νος αξια[ν
    *c.*6 lines missing
(Fr. 28) κα̣[κοις καθεστωτες αλλα
    πε[ρι μεν την τροφην την
35   καθ [
    *c.*11 lines missing
(Fr. 29) εστιν τους αρχο]μ̣εν̣ο̣[υς ταις   (§91)
48   αυτων ε]π̣ιμελειαι̣ς̣ [ποιειν

Fr. 30

   ·   ·   ·   ·   ·

τας νησο]υς ανη[ρουν δε τας   (§99)
εν Ιταλια κ]αι Σικε[λια πολιτει
ας και τυ]ραννου[ς] κ̣[αθιστα
σαν ελυμαιν]ο̣ντο δε τη[ν

   ·   ·   ·   ·   ·

Fr. 31   Fr. 32

   ·   ·   ·   ·   ·   ·

        τη]ς α[ρχης (§102)   εστι]ν· ουδ̣ [ως (§103)
αυτοις εγγενομεν]ην [ταχε   παραφρονειν ποιει] τους α[γαπων
ως κακεινης της η]γεμ[ονι   τας αυτην ουδ οτ]ι̣ την [φυσιν
ας απεστερηθησαν ο]υ γ[αρ   ομοιαν εχει ταις ετ]αιρα̣[ις

   ·   ·   ·   ·

        *c.*11 lines missing

Fr. 33   Fr. 34

   ·   ·   ·   ·   ·   ·

ειδον μηδεν δ η]ττον φ[οβει (§112)   ραχ]ας ας ουτο[ι πεποιηκασιν (§124)
σθαι τους φυλαττο]ντας η τ̣[ους   τω]ν μεν αλ[λων πολιτων
επιβουλευοντας]· ουτω [δ υπο   πο]λλους εκ τ[ων πατρωων
πτως προς απ]αντα[ς εχειν   εκ]πειπτον̣[τας τουτους δ εκ
5 ωστε μηδε το]ι̣ς ο[ικειοτα   5 πε]νητ[ω]ν π[λουσιους γεγε
τοις θαρρειν π]λη[σιαζοντας   νη]μεν[ου]ς ο[υκ αγανακτου
εικοτως σ]υνι̣ς[ασι γαρ τους   §113   με]ν̣ ουδ̣ε φθ[ονουμεν ταις ευ
προ αυ]των τ̣[ετυραννευ   πραγι]αις α[υτων αλλ υπο §125
κοτας του]ς με[ν υπο των   μενομε]ν̣ τ̣[ην
10 γονεων α]νηρ̣[ημενους τους
δ υπο τω]ν πα[ιδων τους
    ].[

   ·   ·   ·   ·   ·   ·   ·

Fr. 35   Fr. 36

. . . .

την την πολ]ιν αλ[λα και τους (§136)	κτησασθαι] δε [τη πολει την (§142)
αλλους Ελ]ληνας α[παντας ου §137	ηγεμονια]ν εις [τον απαν
δε γαρ α]λλη των π[ολεων	τα χρ]ον[ο]ν· μεισῃ[σαι μεν
ουδεμι]α τολμησε[ι περι	α]πασας τας τυρα[ννικας
5 αυτους] εξαμαρταν[ειν αλλ ο	5 αρ]χας και τας δυ[ναστειας
κνησο]υσιν καὶ πολλη[ν ησυ	α]ναλογισαμε[νους τας συμ
χιαν αξο]υσιν ὁταν [ειδωσιν	φο]ρας τας επ αυ[των γεγε
εφεδρευου]σαν [	νημ]ενας· ζη[λωσαι δε και μι
].[	μη]σασθαι τ[ας εν Λακεδαιμο

. . . .

Fr. 1

    5 *οτι* with p46 codd. Dion. *Isoc.* 16.

    8 In the lacuna, *οτι* (codd.) rather than *διοτι* (p46 Dion.).

    8–10 *ουκ εστι παρρησια* precedes *πλην ενθαδε μεν* as in p46 codd.: in Dion., the order of the two phrases is reversed.

    12 *τω θε]ατρω* with codd.: *τοῖς θεάτροις* p46 Dion. For discussion, see CPF I.2** on p46.35 (p. 551).

    12–13 *κω[μωδοδιδας]καλοι[c*: so p46ᵖᶜ Γ Λ⁺: *κωμωδιδασκάλοις* ΛΠΝ Dion.

    15–16 *αλλους* restored with codd. Dion.; om. p46. For discussion, see CPF I.2** on p46.40 (p. 552).

    16–17 *τα . . . [αμαρτηματα]*: Dion. alone omits the article and has the singular *ἁμάρτημα*.

    18 *ουδ[ε*: om. ΠΝ.

Fr. 2

    1 *με[ν*: om. Dion.

    3 *-τατ-*: l. *-ταττ-*. The error appears to be due to confusion of *προστάττω* and *προστατέω* (WBH). On *-τ-* for *-ττ-*, cf. Gignac, *Grammar* i 161.

    6 *εξιεναι*: so p46ᵖᶜ codd.: *εξεινια* p46ᵃᶜ Dion.

    6–7 *τ[ην αυ]των*: Dion. offers *τὴν αὐτὴν* (FAV) or *αὐτὴν* (TB).

Fr. 3

    5 *α[υτων δυναστειαις*: p46 alone offers *δ[υναστειαις αυ]των*. Against, see CPF I.2** on p46.191–2 (p. 556).

    7 *εφ* with Γ (and p46 to judge from the space): om. ΛΠΝ.

Fr. 5

    3 *τ[ης* om. p46 (to judge from the space).

    8–9 *εν υμ]ειν ειπ[ειν*: l. *ἐν ὑμῖν εἰπεῖν. εἰπεῖν ἐν ὑμῖν* Γ ΠΙΝ (and p46 to judge by the gap): *εἰπεῖν ὑμῖν* Λ. As often, it is hard to be sure of the original word order: *Archid.* 2 *τῶν εἰθισμένων ἐν ὑμῖν ἀγορεύειν* does not point clearly in either direction. See in general CPF I.2** on p46, pp. 549–50 (WBH).

    10 *τουτων* seems likely to have been present in the gap. It is omitted by Γᵖʳ (ins. Γ²) and p46 (to judge by the space).

14 Spacing strongly favours το]υτοις with Γ ΛΠΝ (and p46 to judge by the space) rather than τοις τοιο]υτοις with θλ. See CPF I.2** on p46.262 (p. 558).

15 νυν τυ[γχανομεν: ἐτυγχάνομεν ΛΝ.

Fr. 7

1 οιο[νται: only feet preserved: οιε[(for Γ's οἴεϲθαι) not excluded.

5].[: a high horizontal; the spacing suggests that it is the upper portion of π in προχειρον.

Frr. 8+9
Col. i

3 πλεʹίονων: the ι intersects the cross-bar of ε and is presumably a later addition. On the evidence for πλε- and πλει- in this word, cf. CPF I.2* on p17 X 9 (p. 422).

7 There is an upright on the edge extending from the upper left-hand corner to the lower left-hand corner of]χ: apparently the scribe began by writing another letter.

την om. θ.

11–12 ου]δεν υποϲ[τειλαμενοϲ: reversed in θ.

15–16 τι]ϲ [γαρ αν αλλο|θεν ε]πελθων suits the traces (that in 15 suggests the lower part of ϲ) and spaces. αν was present in p46 (to judge by the space) ΛΠ θλ, Dion. *Isoc.*, Dion. *Dem.* 17, and Dion. *Dem.* 19 (AVJBT), but omitted by Γ N with Dion. *Dem.* 19 (I). Then at the end for ε]πελθων p46 has ελθων. See CPF I.2** on p46.466–7 (pp. 562–3).

16–17 μηπ]ω ϲ[υ]ν[δι]εφθαρμενοϲ: variants are known from Dion. (μὴ ϲυνδιαφθειρόμενοϲ *Isoc.*: μὴ ϲυνδιεφθαρμένοϲ *Dem.* 17 and 19).

17 ημιν: ὑμῖν ΛΠΝ.

18–19 γιγν[ομε]νοιϲ. The first ν is unusually small, extending from the top to only the middle of the line. In place of the present, Dion. *Isoc.* alone has γενομένοιϲ.

Col. ii

21–2 και τα ε[ναντια: so θ: καὶ τἀναντία Γ ΛΠΝ λ Dion.: τ[α δε εν]αντια p46 (so Bell: see Mandilaras (1975) 223 on lines 486–92).

22–3 πρατ[τοντεϲ: πραττομένοιϲ ποιοῦντεϲ λ.

24–5 τι]μην ε[[κεινοιϲ] with p46 p49 Γ θλ Dion.: ἐκείνοιϲ τιμὴν ΛΠΝ.

25 The trace looks like the top of an upright or oblique with a half serif to the left, surrounded by a circle, all in a thin pen. This may be a correction or punctuation.

29 For the supplied γενομενων, θλ alone have γεγενημένων. See S. De Leo in *Studi sulla tradizione del testo di Isocrate* (2003) 228.

31 Ελλ[ηνων with p46 p49 ΛΠΝ Dion. *Dem.* 17 and 19: ἄλλων p48 Γ θλ. For discussion, see CPF I.2** on p46.501 (p. 563).

32 τε with p48 p49 codd. Dion. *Dem.* 17 and 19: om. p46. See CPF I.2** on p46.502 (p. 563).

την is uniquely omitted by p48, but is likely to have been present here to judge by the space. After it, p46 and Dion. *Dem.* have ἑαυτῶν in place of αὐτῶν: either is possible here.

32–3 εκ]]λιπε[ιν ετολμηϲαν with p48 p49 codd. Dion. *Dem.* 17 and 19: ετολμ[ηϲαν] ε[κλ]ιπειν p46. See CPF I.2** on p46.503–4 (p. 564).

37 Spacing favours restoring αυτων with p46 (to judge by the space) p48 p49 Γ ΛΠΝ λ: om. p50 (to judge by the space) θ Dion. *Dem.* 17. See CPF I.2** on p46.507 (pp. 564–5), p50.A2 (pp. 609–10).

39 The supplied μεν is uniquely omitted by p49.

40–41 ϲτρα]τευεϲθα[ι with p46 [p49] [p50] codd.: ϲτρατεύειν Dion. *Dem.* 17.

43 Manuscripts have either δειν (Γ² ΛΠΝ θλ Dion. *Dem.* 17) or δει (p46 Γᵖʳ). Here a correction reflects this disagreement; a second hand has added a shallow ν above the line between ι and π.

45 τουτοιc with Γ: τοῦτον [p46] ΛΠΝ θλ Dion. *Dem.* 17.

46 After the supplied ανθρωπουc, Γ⁵ mg. θλ add αἱρούμεθα.

48 Originally no doubt αυτονο[μουc as in Dion. *Dem.* 17 (I); a second hand has crossed out ν and inserted a shallow μ above the line.

The letters in this line (and the interlinear space above) seem vertically compressed: apparently the scribe was making an effort not to let the column of writing extend into the lower margin.

Fr. 10

1–2 ιδια λυμαινο]μεθα restored with p46 Dion. *Dem.* 17: δι᾽ οὓς λυμαινόμεθα Γ⁵ mg. θλ: λυμαινόμεθα Γᵖʳ ΛΠΝ. See CPF I.2** on p46.537–8 (pp. 565–6).

3 απαντων κοινοιc supplied with p46 p51 ΛΠΝ: ἁπάντων ἀνθρώπων κοινοῖc Γ θλ, ἁπάντων κοινοῖc ἀνθρώπων Dion. *Dem.* 17. See CPF I.2** on p51.2–3 (p. 615).

4 μιcθον restored with all witnesses but p51, which gives βιον (on which see CPF I.2** on p51.3). (There is no need to assume that τον was not written at the lost end of P. Oxy. Hels. 7 (p51) 2. [NG])

5 After the supplied δε, Dion. *Dem.* 17 (but not *Dem.* 20) uniquely has και, for which there is not room here.

Fr. 11

3–4 απαcιν] ειναι: in Dion. *Dem.* 17, ἅπαcιν is omitted and AVJ have τῶν ἄλλων after εἶναι.

4 After the supplied καλωc, Dion. *Dem.* 17 has τε.

7–8 αυ]των om. θ.

11 μεγα φρονου[μεν: μεγαλοφρονοῦμεν Dion. *Dem.* 17.

Fr. 13

3 A letter count suggests that the papyrus did not have the τε presented by Γ alone after την: so too [p46] [p50] ΛΠΝ. See CPF I.2** on p50 B II 2 (p. 610).

Frr. 14–16

1–2 ημι]ν . . . [εκειν]οιc with Γ: ἡμᾶc . . . ἐκείνουc ΛΠΝ. p50 had the dative in the first and presumably also the second place. See CPF I.2** on p50 B II 13–14 (pp. 611–12).

7–8 Probably ποι]ηcου[cιν for the ποιοῦcιν of the other witnesses. Cf. for the corruption *Nic.* 50 ὁπότερον ἂν ἐν καιρῷ καὶ μετ᾽ ἀρετῆc γίγνηται, τοῦτ᾽ ὠφελεῖ τοὺc ποιοῦντας, where for ὠφελεῖ (Γ Stob.), p1 [p73] ΛΠΝSVat have the future ὠφελήcει. (WBH)

8 The supplement printed may be over-long. Perhaps the papyrus had τοὺc μικρὰ (ΠΝ) rather than τοὺc καὶ μικρὰ (Γ Λ) or και τουc μικρα (p46 p50). See CPF I.2** on p46.695 (p. 572).

9–10 The presumed division ουκ|εν (instead of ου|κεν) seems irregular, but P. Kell. III 95 (p1) has ουκ᾽ at line-end at *Nic.* 28 (line 171); cf. also **5130** fr. 1 ii 12 n. (WBH)

23 -]λημ[ψειc: l. -λήψειc.

27 Above and to the left of λ, the remains of two lines in a small cursive hand, perhaps a variant or correction. (Annotations are extremely rare in papyri of oratory: see K. McNamee, *Annotations in Greek and Latin Texts from Egypt* (2007) 117–18.)

In the supplement, προc- appears to have been omitted by p46 alone; so too τοιc γιγνομενοιc (29).

34–5 τινων . . . ποιων with Γ: ποίων . . . τίνων ΛΠΝ. (p46 has πο[ιων in the second place and presumably had τινων in the first.)

36 πα[υ]caιμεθ αν: p46 uniquely has παυcω[μεθα corrected to παυco[μεθα.

Frr. 17–18

3 κ]αι with Γ: οὐδὲ [p46] ΛΠΝ.

5 απο-: variants in Λ alone (ἐπι- Λ^pr, ὑπο- Λ¹ mg., ἀπο- Λ⁴).

12 After cωφροcύνην, ΛΠΝ have καὶ τὴν δικαιοcύνην, but spacing indicates that it was omitted here as in p46 Γ. See CPF I.2** on p46.739–40 (p. 573).

13]χ[[ον]]: only letter-tops preserved, apparently with an expunction stroke on the edge.

Frr. 19–21

1–2 δεξαc[θαι διδο]νμενη[ν (l. διδομένην) τ]η πολε[ι with Γ ΠΝ: διδ- δέξ- τ. π. Λ: δεξ- τ. π. διδ- p46. For the inserted nu, cf. Gignac, *Grammar* i 118.

22–3 τουc αλλο]υc Ελλην[αc with p46 Γ ΠΝ: τοὺc Ἕλληναc τοὺc ἄλλουc Λ.

44 The traces favour γινομεν[αc with p46: γιγνομέναc p53 codd.

Fr. 22

3–4 αυτω των πολεω]ν with codd.: των πολεων αυτω p46. See CPF I.2** on p46.924–5 (p. 575).

8 ευδοκι]μουcη[c with codd.: ευδοκουcηc p46.

11 α]ν om. ΠΝ.

Frr. 23–4

3 A letter count suggests that the papyrus had cυναγοντεc (p46 ΛΠΝ) rather than cυναγαγοντεc (p46² Γ). See CPF I.2** on p46.963–4 (p. 576).

Frr. 25–9

2 επιθυμ[ουμεν with codd.: επεθυμουμεν p46.

5 Spacing favours π[ροc δειγμα with Γ rather than π[ροc παραδειγμα with p46 ΠΝ, though it does not exclude π[αραδειγμα with Λ. For discussion see CPF I.2** on p46.1119 (p. 581).

22 Spacing favours διδομε[ναιc with p46 Γ rather than διδομέναιc δωρεαῖc with ΛΠΝ.

23 εξ]ιν (]ι: an upright on the edge) with p46 Γ: ἐξουcίαν ΛΠΝ.

ουτε [ανηρ with p46² (ουτε corrected from ουτ αν) Γ (οὔτ' ἀνὴρ): οὐδεὶc οὔτε ἀνὴρ ΛΠΝ.

34 πε[ρι μεν: μεν om. p46.

Fr. 30

3 τυ]ραννου[c] with p46 Γ ΠΝ: τυραννίδαc Λ.

Fr. 31

4 [απεcτερηθηcαν] supplied with p46² Γ: επεcτ- p46: εcτ- ΛΠΝ. The spacing is of little help in determining which the papyrus had when so much is lost.

Fr. 33

9–11 [των γονεων] . . . τω]ν πα[ιδων with Γ: γονέων . . . παῖδων ΛΠΝ.

Fr. 34

1 ουτο[ι with p46 Γ: αὐτοὶ ΛΠΝ.

4 The letters do not accord with the transmitted ἐκπεπτωκόταc. The left end of a high horizontal is preserved after ι, probably π. Following ο there is the left edge of a short upright curving to the right at the base with a slight projection to the left at the top. It is unlikely that the scribe made an ungrammatical error as there is no sign of correction. A plausible reconstruction would therefore be εκ]πειπτον[ταc (l. -πίπτονταc), present for perfect. But the perfect provides a better balance for γεγενη]μεν[ου]c below (5–6).

In the supplement, for τουτουc p46² alone has τουc.

7 ουδε: of δ, the top of the descending oblique: not τ (ουτε p46²).

Fr. 35

2 Spacing favours [αλλουc] as in p46 Γ θλ over its omission (cett.).

4 ουδεμι]α τολμηcε[ι: reversed in p46.

5–6 Spacing favours οκνηco]υcιν with p46 Γᵖʳ (-cι ΛΠΝ) rather than ὁμονοήcουcιν with Γ⁵ mg. θλ (-cι).

8 εφεδρευου]cαν: placed here in the primary tradition, where it is followed by τὴν δύναμιν τὴν ἡμετέραν (p46 Γ) or τὴν ἡμετέραν πόλιν (ΛΠΝ); θλ have instead τὴν δύναμιν τὴν ἡμετέραν followed by ἐφεδρεύουcαν. See S. De Leo in *Studi sulla tradizione del testo di Isocrate* (2003) 232–3.

Fr. 36

1 Spacing indicates that [τη πολει] was written as in p46 p58 Γ θλ rather than omitted (ΛΠΝ).

3–4 μεν α]παcαc with p46 Γ ΛΠΝ rather than δὲ πάcαc as p58 θλ.

5 τας δυ[ναcτειαc with p46 Γ ΛΠΝ: δυναcτειαc p46² p58 ut vid. θλ. See CPF I.2** on p46.1802 (p. 595).

6 α]ναλογιcαμε[νους with p46² Γ θλ: -λογιζομένουc p46 (*prima manus*) ΛΠΝ.

7 επ: a new but inferior variant. ἐξ p46 Γ θλ: ἀπ' ΛΠΝ. Cf. *Phil.* 122 εξ αυτων **5145** Γ ΛΠΝ: ἐπ' αὐτῶν Θ.

7–8 γεγενημεν]αc supplied with p46² Γ: γενηcομέναc ΛΠΝ: γιγνομέναc θλ. See CPF I.2** on p46.1803–4 (pp. 595–6). The spacing here does not point decisively to any one of the attested variants.

M. J. ANDERSON

5141. Isocrates, *De Pace* 38–9

15 2B.42/C(i)   2 × 9.2 cm   Second/third century

The top of a column of a papyrus roll, with parts of 13 lines and upper margin preserved to a height of 2.2 cm. A line contained 20–25 letters. The column will have been *c.*6 cm wide. The back is blank.

The text is written along the fibres, in an elegant, semi-cursive hand, with serifs and small hooks regularly added to uprights and obliques. The letters are medium-sized and upright. ε is narrow. ρ descends below the line, and the upright of φ is very tall, almost filling the interlinear spaces above and below, and contrasting with the letter's flattened oval loop. Other distinctive forms are θ with a broad cross-bar extending beyond its body in both directions, κ with upright and upper branch made in a single movement, looped at the foot, and cursive ξ. This hand can be placed alongside others affiliated to the Chancery Style, such as those of **5139** (Isoc. *Nic.*; II/III), with which it was found, and LXVI **4505** (pl. XIV; II/III).

There are no lectional signs, but a possible example of blank space used as punctuation (10).

The papyrus has a different word order from that of all other witnesses at 6–7 and 8–10.

```
       ·        ·              ·      ·

       προϲ υμαϲ απεχθει]αν δοκ̣[ει              (§38)
       μεν γαρ μοι βελτιο]ν ειναι δι̣[α
       λεχθηναι περι αυ]των ορω [δ υ
       μαϲ χαλεπωτερον] διατιθεμ̣[ε
   5   νουϲ προϲ τουϲ επι]τιμωντ[αϲ
       η προϲ τουϲ αιτιουϲ] γεγενημε̣[
       νουϲ των κακων ο]υ̣ μην αλλ α̣[ιϲ      §39
       χυνθειην αν ει μαλ]λον φροντι[
       ζων τηϲ εμαυτου] δοξηϲ η τη[ϲ
  10   κοινηϲ ϲωτηριαϲ φ]ανειην ε̣[
       μον μεν ουν εργο]ν̣ εϲτιν κ[αι
       των αλλων των κηδ]ο̣μενω[ν
       τηϲ πολεωϲ προαιρειϲ]θαι τ̣[ων

       ·        ·        ·      ·      ·
```

2 μεν restored with p46 Γ θλ on grounds of space: om. ΛΠΝ.

3–4 In the lacuna, δ υμαϲ (with p46 Γ θλ) or δε υμαϲ (with ΛΠΝ).

5 A short cross-stroke touches ι on the left near the foot.

6 προϲ om. p46.

6–7 γεγενημε[νουϲ των κακων: τῶν κακῶν γεγενημένουϲ p46 codd. 'The usual word order is defended by *De bigis* 14 τοῖϲ αἰτίοιϲ τῶν ϲυμφορῶν γεγενημένοιϲ; cf. also *Plat.* 32 τοὺϲ ἅπαϲι τοῖϲ Ἕλληϲιν αἰτίουϲ τῆϲ ϲωτηρίαϲ γενομένουϲ. In such expressions, we expect γεγενημένοϲ to come at the end: see CPF I.2** on p46.1344–5 (pp. 587–8).' (WBH)

8–10 φ]ανειην is here uniquely placed at the end of the sentence. p46 and the primary mediaeval manuscripts have it before μαλ]λον (8). Dr Henry notes: 'φανείην belongs immediately after εἰ: cf. *Panath.* 22 εἰ φανείην ϲπουδάζων κτλ. The text as given in the papyrus would be in danger of being understood as meaning "if, being more concerned (i.e. inasmuch as I am more concerned) . . .": cf. *Antid.* 44 εἰ, πολλάκιϲ εἰρηκὼϲ ὅτι κτλ. Isocrates could not reasonably expect a reader to go back and reassess the construction on reaching φανείην at the end of the sentence. If the undesirable ambiguity is to be avoided, φανείην must come first.'

9 The high speck at the right-hand edge cannot belong to ϲ. Its function is not clear.

10 The short blank space after φ]ανειην may have been intended as punctuation.

10–11 ε̣[μον μεν restored with [p46] Γ (ἐμοὶ μὲν θ): ἐμὸν ΛΠΝ λ.

11 εϲτιν with Γ: ἐϲτὶ p46 ΛΠΝ θλ.

12 κηδ]ο̣μενω[ν with Γ ΛΠΝ: κηδεμόνων θλ.

R.-L. CHANG

5142. Isocrates, *De Pace* 127, 130

38 3B.84/G(1–3)c   3 × 3.5 cm   Fourth century

A fragment of a papyrus codex leaf with six line-ends on the → side and seven line-beginnings on the ↓ side. The papyrus breaks off just before the right-hand margin on the → side except at 6, where a little of the margin is preserved, while the line-beginning is indicated at ↓ 3–7 by the presence of oblique strokes in the margin. On average, the line-length will have been about 13 cm, with about 29 letters per line. A page will have contained 30–31 lines. Five lines and the interlinear space underneath occupy an area about 3 cm high. The written area will thus have been approximately 13 × 19 cm. Of the codices listed by Turner in *Typology*, those with similar dimensions (written area only) and date are XIII **1599** and IX **1170**, classified under Group 4 and among the aberrants of Group 6 respectively (*Typology* 16, 18).

The text is written in an informal, upright, basically bilinear hand related to Biblical Majuscule. There is considerable irregularity in letter formation: e.g. ο can be vertically compressed (e.g. → 4) or fill the space between the notional upper and lower lines (→ 5); a similar variation is seen in ε (→ 5, ↓ 3). Cross-strokes and the oblique of ν are thinner than other strokes. The descender of γ may curve slightly to the left at the foot. ∧ is triangular with a more or less horizontal crossbar. The upright of τ joins its crossbar rather to the right of its mid-point. There is some resemblance to the hands of the parchment codices P. Ant. II 82 (pl. iv; Isoc. *Hel.* [p66]) and XIII **1621** (pl. v; *GBEBP* 13b), both assigned to the fourth century.

There are no lectional signs. A supralinear bar replaces *ν* at line-end (→ 4). Single oblique strokes are found to the left of most, perhaps all, lines on the ↓ side. Their precise function here is impossible to determine: see K. McNamee, *Sigla and Select Marginalia in Greek Literary Papyri* (1992) 17–18.

There is a correction at → 6, and a supralinear addition, perhaps another correction, at ↓ 2. The latter involves a variant found only here and in p46.

→

· · · · · · ·
τοcουτον εκεινου διενηνο]χαcιν [(§127)
ωcτε λεγειν μεν τολμωcιν ω]c δια την [
των κοινων επιμελειαν ου] δυνανται [
τοιc αυτων ιδιοιc προcεχει]ν τον νοῡ [
5   φαινεται δε τα μεν αμελου]μενα τοcαυ[
την ειληφοτα την επιδοcιν] ⟦ˬˑ⟧cην ου [
· · · · · · ·

↓

.   .   .   .   ‾

c]ιων [και των εντευθεν λημματων υ   (§130)

] φ αυτούς [δια την ενδειαν ηναγκασμε

], νους ειν[αι και πολλην χαριν εχον

], τας ταις ε[ιcαγγελιαις και ταις γραφαις

5   ], και ταις α[λλαις cυκοφαντιαις ταις δι

], αυτων χ[ιγνομεναις εν ουν ταις απο   §131

], [ριαις εν αις δυναcτευουcιν εν ταυταις

.   .   .   .

→

2 τολμωcιν (codd.) suits the space better than τολμωcι (p46).

4 αυτων: om. p46.

νοῡ: i.e., νου(ν).

6 ⟦°⟧cην: the letter on the line (possibly ɴ) is crossed out. Although ο is small, the shape and ink suggest that there is no change of hand.

↓

1–2 Oblique strokes may have stood at the beginnings of these lines too.

2 αυτούς. The mediaeval manuscripts have the dative (αὐτοῖc Γ, αὐτοῖc ΛΠΝ), while p46 has αυτοιc corrected to αυτουc. The superscript ι in our papyrus seems to have been added by the original scribe. As the upsilon on the line is not deleted (contrast the correction in → 6), this may be either a correction or an indication of an alternative reading. The latter may be more plausible, since both ὑφ' αὑτοῖc and ὑφ' αὑτούc may signify subjection, though Isocrates uses the dative in this sense, especially when the prepositional phrase is governed by εἶναι or γίγνεcθαι. There is a similar variant at *Panath.* 166 (ὑφ' αὑτοῖc] ὑπ' αὑτούc Θ, ὑφ' αὑτούc Λ).

6–7 Restored *exempli gratia.*

R.-L. CHANG

5143. Isocrates, *De Pace* 127–8

22 3B.20/H(d)   2.5 × 4 cm   First century ʙᴄ/first century ᴀᴅ

A fragment of a papyrus roll, with the ends of seven lines written along the fibres. There are between 19 and 27 letters in each line. The column will have been roughly 7 cm wide. On the back, against the fibres and in a different cursive hand, there are three line-ends.

The hand is an untidy semi-cursive. It resembles that of XIV **1635** (pl. ɪɪ; also Schubart, *Griechische Paläographie* Abb. 21, p. 45; Cavallo–Maehler, *Hellenistic Bookhands* 85), which dates from 44–30 ʙᴄ (see BL VII 140), though **1635** has a more polished appearance, and some of its letter forms are different (in particular ᴍ and ᴛ). These papyri share a distinctive cursive form of ᴀ, found again in **5166** (*c.*20s

BC), but recurring in e.g. XXIII **2367** (commentary on Bacchylides) and LXV **4443** (LXX Esther), both plausibly assigned to the late first or second century. A date in the second half of the first century BC or the earlier first century AD will not be far off the mark.

No lectional signs are present. A blank space is used as punctuation (2).

There is a case of haplography (shared with p46) in 7. The assimilation of *ν* to *γ* before the velar stop *γ* in 2–3 is rather characteristic of Hellenistic papyri; see **5148** I 9–10 n.

Among published papyri of Isocrates, only p33 (P. Lips. inv. 1456; late III BC), p65/p98 (P. Yale II 103; both early III BC, on either side of the same roll), and P. Toronto inv. F4107 (*APF* 54 (2008) 153–60; III BC) certainly predate **5143**.

. . . . . .

```
      ραθυμως αλλ οδυρμω]ν με              (§127)
      cτην ειναι την πολι]ν   οι μεγ        §128
      γαρ τας πενιας και τα]ς ενδειας
      αναγκαζονται διεξιε]ναι και θρη
5     νειν προς cφας αυτου]ς οι δε το
      πληθος των προσταγ]ματων
      και των λειτουργιων και] τα κα τα
```

. . . . . .

6 προσταγ]ματων restored with p46 ΛΠ by reason of space: πραγμάτων Γ N, 'an error due to a misunderstood abbreviation; cf. *Ad Nic.* 17 with CPF I.2* on p17 IX 1 (p. 418)' (WBH).

The curved stroke in the lower part of N looks more like an accidental extension of the right-hand upright than a correction.

7 των restored with p46 Γ on grounds of space: om. ΛΠN.

τα κα, l. τὰ κακά. The phrase is omitted in ΛΠN. The haplography found here occurs also in p46. The sequence κακατα could be mistaken for the preposition κατα.

R.-L. CHANG

5144–6. ISOCRATES, *PHILIPPUS*

This section presents three papyri of this work, the first to appear from Oxyrhynchus. Only three other ancient manuscripts have been published: P. Toronto inv. F4107 (ed. *APF* 54 (2008) 153–60; M–P³ 1268.11), a cartonnage fragment of unknown provenance assigned to the third century BC and containing §§1–2; P. Rain. III 40 (p96 in CPF I.2**; M–P³ 1269), from the Fayum, remains of a leaf of a fourth-century parchment codex containing §§38–9, 40–42; and *MPER* II 74–6 (p97; M–P³ 1270), also from the Fayum, a fragment of a book-roll of the second century containing §§114–17; cf. also IV **683** (p126T; M–P³ 2194.1), a second-century fragment of an unknown historiographical work quoting §97.

The primary mediaeval manuscripts are Γ and four manuscripts of the second family, ΘΛΠΝ; see the discussion of the manuscript tradition in CPF I.2* pp. xviii–xxxiv. Collations of ΓΘΛΠ were published by H. Buermann, *Die handschriftliche Überlieferung des Isokrates* i (1885) 16–28; see also A. Martin, *RPh* 19 (1895) 191 (for Γ); E. Drerup, *De codicum Isocrateorum auctoritate* (Leipziger Studien xvii/1, 1895) 40–46, and *Philol.* 55 (1896) 660–66 (for Λ). Θ (Laur. Plut. 87.14) and N (Laur. Plut. 58.5) have been collated afresh from the digital images on the library's website. Dr Pinto has provided collations of the remaining primary manuscripts for the parts represented in the new fragments. Minor orthographical variants are not always reported. C. Muenscher (i.e. K. Münscher), *Quaestiones Isocrateae* (diss. Göttingen 1895), is cited as 'Münscher'.

5144. Isocrates, *Philippus* 70–77, 79–80, 101–5

Frr. 1 and 3: 38 3B.86/N(4–5)a	Fr. 1 4.9 × 25.8 cm	Fourth century
Fr. 2: 38 3B.85/K(1–2)a	Fr. 2 4.6 × 5.8 cm; Fr. 3 12.8 × 21 cm	

Three fragments from a single-column papyrus codex. Fr. 1 is a tall strip preserving about half the width of a column and its full height (36/7 lines = *c.*18 cm), with an upper margin of *c.*2.8 cm and a lower margin of *c.*5.2 cm. Fr. 2 is relatively small and preserves parts of 11/12 lines on each side. It belongs to the leaf following that represented by fr. 1 and begins eight lines down the column. Fr. 3 preserves parts of the first 29 lines of a column, up to full width (*c.*6.5 cm) in places, but a good portion of its upper half has been destroyed. Calculation indicates that it belongs to the fifth leaf after that represented by fr. 2. Its inner margin measures *c.*4 cm, its outer one *c.*1.3 cm. Each line holds about 22 letters.

The dimensions of the codex fit Turner's Group 8 ('B half H, B14/12 × H30/25' cm), most of whose representatives belong to the third and fourth centuries; see E. G. Turner, *The Typology of the Early Codex* (1977) 20–21, 24. It was probably a single-quire codex, like most codices in this group (Turner, *Typology* 24, 58). If it contained only the *Philippus*, letter count suggests that the speech would have covered 60 pages = 30 leaves = 15 sheets. In that case fr. 2 would come from the exact middle of the codex (leaf 15), and the alternation of fibres from ↓→↓→ in the first 'half' (i.e. frr. 1 and 2 = leaves 14 and 15) to →↓ in the second 'half' (i.e. fr. 3 = leaf 20) would strengthen the hypothesis that this was a single-quire codex; cf. Turner, *Typology* 57, 65.

The hand is small, rapid, and leans heavily to the right. Bilinearity is minimal. The letters are very densely crowded, with occasional ligatures (e.g. η and β in fr. 1 → 9; π and o in fr. 1 → 31), and are so rapidly executed that they often approach informality. ⲁ is in one movement, narrow, and with an oval-shaped loop; в is tall, with its two loops separate from each other; ⲇ is so oval that its two sides often do not meet in an apex; ⲉ ⲑ ⲟ ⲥ are narrow (but ⲥ often has an extended cap); z is in two strokes, sometimes with detached upper horizontal; н is h-shaped; λ's second leg stops at mid-height; м is deep and broad; the oblique of ɴ and the arms of κ sometimes approach the horizontal; ʒ is cursive; π is broad, with its horizontal projecting in both directions; τ sometimes has a split top; ω is broad, with a pronounced central cusp. Some letters have hooked serifs (e.g. в, н, ı, κ). The hand is generally similar to that of P. Mich. inv. 1570 (*GBEBP* 4b, from a codex of Matthew), which is assigned to the first half of the fourth century on the basis of comparable documentary scripts.

The right and left margins are not very even, as letters at line beginning and end are often enlarged and their horizontals (especially at line end) prolonged beyond the notional margin. One can observe in fr. 1 ↓ that the beginnings of lines make a progressive shift to the left ('Maas's Law').

The scribe does not write iota adscript, accents, or punctuation. An inorganic diaeresis appears over initial υ in fr. 1 → 8, fr. 2 ↓ 10. Nu is sometimes written as a suprascript bar at line end. Line-fillers in fr. 1 → 13, 20. In most cases elisions are tacitly effected, but there are two exceptions (fr. 2 → 11 τε εταιρους; fr. 3 → 16 ωϲτε εκεινω). Orthographical mistakes are mainly limited to iotacistic confusion of ει and ι, especially in the aorist optative.

Besides the usual mixture of readings known from the two main families of medieval manuscripts (including agreements in possible error with ΘΛΠΝ in fr. 1 ↓ 5–6, 10–11, 12, → 28, and with Γ in fr. 1 → 2–3), **5144** offers a number of new readings. That at fr. 1 ↓ 20 is uncertain due to the state of the papyrus but is likely to be corrupt. Two variants are viable but not necessarily improvements on the familiar text: fr. 1 → 32 ἔτι δὲ καί for ἔτι δέ; fr. 3 → 27–8 ϲυνκαταλῦϲαι for καταλελῦϲθαι. The rest are indefensible or obvious corruptions: fr. 1 ↓ 16 θ' ὑπερβαλλούϲαϲ omitted; fr. 1 ↓ 17–18 οἱ προειρημένοι for τὰ προειρημένα; fr. 2 ↓ 11 προϲείλετο for προείλετο; fr. 3 → 20–21 μὴ νὴ Δία γε τὸν ευρωπατατον for μὴν Ἰδριέα γε τὸν εὐπορώτατον; fr. 3 → 28 second article omitted; fr. 3 ↓ 6 τε τ' ἄλλων for τ(ε) ἄλλων; fr. 3 ↓ 2–3 διαβαίνοιϲ for διαβαίηϲ; fr. 3 ↓ 23 καὶ μέγιϲτα omitted. Three of these cases involve dittography (fr. 1 ↓ 20, fr. 3 → 21, fr. 3 ↓ 6).

I am much obliged to Dr W. Benjamin Henry for several helpful suggestions and to Dr Daniela Colomo for her restoration work on fr. 3.

Fr. 1 ↓

δ]ιωςι μη προτ[ερον τι πα   (§70)
θης πριν τελο[ς επιθειναι
τοις πραττο[μενοις ων γι   §71
γνομενων π[ως ουκ αν εικο
5   τως μεγα φρο[νοιης πως δε
ουχι περιχαρη[ς ων τον βιον
διατελοιης τηλ[ικουτων ςε
αυτον ειδως π[ραγματων
επιστατην γεγ[ενημενον τις
10   δ ουκ αν των κα[ι μετριως λογι
ζεςθαι δυναμε[νων ταυτας
αν ςοι μαλιστα [παραινεςειε
προαιρειςθαι τ[ων πραξεων
τας αμφοτερα[(.) φερειν αμα
15   δυναμενας ω[ςπερ καρπους
ηδονας και τειμ[ας μεγιςτας
απεχρη δ αν μ[οι οι προειρη   §72
μενοι περι τ[ουτων ει μη πα
ραλελοιπως η[ν τινα λογον
20   ουκ αναγαμ[c.9   αλ
λ οκνηςας ειπ[ειν ον ηδη μοι
δοκω δηλωςειν [οιμαι γαρ ςοι
τε ςυμφερειν [ακουςαι περι αυ
των εμοι τε προ[ςηκειν μετα
25   παρρηςιας ωςπ[ερ ειθιςμαι ποι
ειςθαι τους λογου[ς αιςθανομαι   §73
γαρ ςε διαβαλλο[μενον υπο
των ςοι μεν φ[θονουντων
τας δε πολεις τ[ας αυτων ει
30   θ[ις]μενων εις τ[αραχας καθι
ς[τα]ναι και την [ειρηνην
τ[η]ν τοις αλλοις κ[οινην πο
λεμον τοις αυτω[ν ιδιοις ειναι
νομιζοντων οι [παντων των
35   αλλων αμεληςα[ντες περι
της ςης δυναμ[εως λεγουςιν ως

Fr. 1 →

ουχ υπερ τη]ς Ελλαδος αλλ ε
πι ταυτην αυ]ξανεται και συ
　　c.5　χρονο]ν ηδη πασιν η
μιν επιβουλε]υεις και λογω με(ν)　　　§74
5　μελλεις Μεσσ]ηνιοις βοηθειν
εαν τα περι Φω]κεας διοικησης
εργω δ υπο σεαυ]τω ποιεισθαι Πε
λοποννησο]ν υπαρχουσι δε σοι
Θετταλοι μεν] και Θηβαιοι και
10　παντες οι τη]ς Αμφικτυονιας
μετεχοντες] ετοιμοι συνακο
λουθειν Αργειο]ι δε και Μεσση
νιοι και Μεγαλ]οπολειται και <
των αλλων πο]λλοι συνπολεμι(ν)
15　και ποιειν αν]αστατους Λακεδαι
μονιους ην δε] ταυτα πραξης
ως και των αλλ]ων Ελληνων
ραδιως κρατης]εις ταυτα φλυα　　　§75
ρουντες και φα]σκοντες ακριβως
20　ειδεναι και τα]χεως απαντα <
τω λογω κατας]τρεφομενοι
πολλους πειθ]ουσιν και μαλις
τα μεν τους] των αυτων κα
κων επιθυμο]υντας ωνπερ οι
25　λογοποιουν]τες επειτα δε και
τους ουδενι λο]γισμω χρωμε
νους υπερ τ]ων κοινων αλλα
πανταπασι]ν ανοητως δια
κειμενους κ]αι πολλην χαριν
30　εχοντας τοις] υπ[ε]ρ αυτων φο
βεισθαι και δεδιεναι] προσποι
ουμενοις ετι] δε και τους ουκ α
ποδοκιμαζο]ντας το δοκειν
σε επιβουλευ]ειν τοις Ελλησιν
35　αλλα την αιτια]ν ταυτην αξιαν
επιθυμιας ει]ναι νομιζοντας
οι τοσουτον α]φεστασι του νουν　　　§76

Fr. 2 ↓

.   .   .   .   .

δρωδεστερον αυτον και] πλει
ονος αξιον δοκειν ειναι π]οιηϲι
εν ει δε των αφ Ηρακλεουϲ] τινι
πεφυκοτων οϲ απαϲηϲ κα]τεϲ
5   τη τηϲ Ελλαδοϲ ευεργετη]ϲ επι
φεροι την αιτιαν] ταυτην ειϲ τη(ν)
μεγιϲτην αιϲχ]υνην αν αυτον
καταϲτηϲειεν] τιϲ γαρ ουκ αν αγα   §77
νακτηϲειε και] μειϲηϲιεν ει φαινοι
10 το τουτοιϲ επι]βουλευων ϋπερ ω(ν)
ο προγονοϲ αυτ]ου προϲειλετο κι(ν)

.   .   .   .   .

Fr. 2 →

.   .   .   .   .

δε[(?) παρα μικρον ηγειϲθαι το   (§79)
παρ[α(?) παϲιν ευδοκιμειν
αλ[λα τοτε νομιζειν καλην ε
χειν [και μεγαλην την δοξαν
5   και π[ρεπουϲαν ϲοι και τοιϲ ϲοιϲ
προ[γονοιϲ και τοιϲ υφ υμων
πεπραγμε[νοιϲ οταν ουτω   §80
διαθηϲ τουϲ Ε[λληναϲ ωϲπερ
οραϲ Λακεδαιμον[ιουϲ τε προϲ
10 τουϲ εαυτων βαϲιλ[εαϲ εχον
ταϲ τουϲ τε εταιρουϲ [τουϲ ϲουϲ
προϲ ϲε διακειμ[ενουϲ

.   .   .   .   .

Fr. 3 →

τουϲ τ]ου δερ[υϲ τουτο]υ ϲυν   (§101)
αγαγων] γαρ δ[υναμιν] οϲην
οιοϲ τ ην πλειϲτην και] ϲτρα
τευϲαϲ επ αυτουϲ απηλ]θεν ε
5   κειθεν ου μονον ηττη]θειϲ
αλλα και καταγελαϲθει]ϲ και
δοξαϲ ουτε βαϲιλευειν ο]υτε

ϲ]τρατ[ηγειν α]ξιο[ϲ ειναι] τα   §102
τοι[νυν περ]ι Κυπ[ρον και] Φοι

10 νικην και Κιλι[κιαν κ]αι το(ν)
τοπ[ον] εκεινον οθε[ν ε]χρων
το ναυ[τι]κω τοτε μ[ε]ν ην με
τα βαϲιλεωϲ νυν δε τα μεν α
φεϲτηκεν τα δ εν πολεμω

15 και κακοιϲ τοϲουτο[ιϲ] εϲτιν
ωϲτε εκεινω μεν μηδεν
ειναι τουτων των [εθ]νων
χρηϲιμον ϲοι δ ην πολεμει(ν)
προϲ αυτον βουληθηϲ ϲυμ

20 φορωϲ εξειν και μη νη Δια   §103
γ]ε [τ]ον ευρωπατατον των
ν]υν περι την ηπειρον προϲ
ηκε]ι δ[υϲ]μενεϲτερον ειναι
τοιϲ βα]ϲιλεωϲ πραγμαϲι

25 των π]ολεμουντων η παν
τω]ν γ αν ειη ϲχετλιωτατοϲ
ει μ]η βουλοιτο ϲυνκαταλυ
ϲαι] ταυτην την αρχην αικι
ϲαμε]νην μεν τ[ο]ν α[δελ]φ[ο](ν)

    .   .   .   .   .

Fr. 3 ↓

καθ ε[καϲτον] ενια[υτον α   (§104)
ναπ[εμπει]ν ει δ[ε ϲυ διαβαι
νοιϲ [ειϲ την] ηπε[ιρον εκει
νοϲ [τ αν αϲμενοϲ ιδοι βοη

5 θον η[κειν αυτω ϲε νομιζων τω(ν)
τε {τ} α[λλων ϲατραπων πολ
λουϲ [αποϲτηϲειϲ ην υπο
ϲχη τ[ην ελευθεριαν αυτοιϲ
και το[υνο]μα τ[ουτο] διαϲπ[ει

10 ρη[ϲ ε]ιϲ [τη]ν Αϲιαν οπερ [ει]ϲ
τουϲ Ελ[λ]ηναϲ ειϲπεϲον
και την ημετεραν και τη(ν)
Λακεδαιμονιων αρχην κα
τελυϲ[εν] ετι δ αν πλειω λεγει(ν)   §105

15 επεχ[ει]ρουν̣ ον τρο̣πον πο
    λεμων ταχιϲτ α̣ν περιγε
    νοιο τ̣ηϲ του βαϲιλεωϲ δυ
    ναμ̣εωϲ νυν δε φοβουμα̣ι̣
    μη τι[ν]εϲ επιτειμηϲωϲιν
20 ημι̣ν̣ [ει] μηδεν πωποτε
    μεταχειριϲαμενοϲ των̣ ϲ[τρ]α
    τιωτικων ϲο̣ι τολμωη[ν
    παραινειν τω πλ̣[ειϲ]τ̣[α δι]α̣
    πεπραγμενω κα̣[τα πολ]ε̣
25 μον ωϲτε περι μ[εν του
    των ουδεν οιμα̣ι δε̣ιν [π]λ̣ε̣ι
    ω λεγειν περ̣ι δε των αλλω(ν)
    ηγουμαι τον τε πατε[ρα ϲου
    .[. . . .] . [. . .] . [c.10   ] .

        ·   ·   ·   ·   ·   ·

Fr. 1 ↓

  1 δεδ]ι̣ωϲι rightly with Γ (-ίωϲιν) Θ (-ιῶϲι): δεδίαϲιν Λ, δεδίαϲι ΠΝ.

  3–4 ων γι]γνομενων rightly with ΓΘ: οἷϲ γινομένοιϲ ΛΠΝ.

  5–6 δε] ο̣υχι with ΘΛΠΝ (δ᾿ Ν): δ᾿ οὐκ ἄν Γ. ἄν, necessary with the potential optative διατε-
λοίηϲ, could be understood from the previous sentence (cf. K.–G. i 248–9), but the anaphoric style
here favours its repetition with πῶϲ οὐκ. Isocrates, moreover, does not seem to use οὐχί elsewhere.
One may compare p1's πωϲ ουχι in place of ὅπωϲ οὐ καί at *Nic.* 3, which Worp–Rijksbaron, *The Kellis
Isocrates Codex* (1997) 251, consider a corruption.

  7–8 ϲε]αυτον ειδωϲ: ϲαυτὸν (ϲαὐτὸν) εἰδώϲ ΘΛΠΝ: εἰδὼϲ ϲαυτόν Γ. The rules of syllabification
necessitate the restoration of the trisyllabic, uncontracted form of the reflexive pronoun, for which
compare fr. 2 → 10 εαυτων; cf. LXIX **4717** p. 11.12 n. and CPF I.2** on p80 I 8 (pp. 706–7). Münscher
43 argues for Γ's word order.

  10–11 λογι]ζεϲθαι δυναμε[νων with ΘΛΠΝ: λογιζομένων Γ. The reading here was perhaps
influenced by φέρειν . . . δυναμέναϲ a little further on in the same sentence, or arose as a gloss on
λογιζομένων. Γ's reading is better as it avoids the close repetition of the participle.

  12 μα̣λιϲτα [παραινεϲειε with ΘΛΠΝ (παραινέϲειεν ΠΝ): παραινέϲειεν μάλιϲτα Γ. The latter
word order is undoubtedly the correct one, for μάλιϲτα is to be taken with both προαιρεῖϲθαι and
παραινέϲειε (so Münscher 43).

  14 αμφοτερα[(.): ἀμφότερα ΓΘ: ἀμφοτέραϲ ΛᵖʳΠΝ: ἀμφότερά ϲοι Λ⁴. Because of the break it is
impossible to determine what the papyrus had (ἀμφοτέραϲ, at any rate, is wrong).

  15 δυναμεναϲ rightly with ΓˢΘΛΠΝ: δυνάμειϲ Γᵖʳ.
  ω[ϲπερ καρπουϲ: ὥϲπερ *vac.* πουϲ Λᵖʳ: ὥϲπερ καρπούϲ Λ²: ὥϲπερ ἄρα καρπούϲ Λ⁴ (conjecture).

  16 ηδοναϲ και τειμ̣[αϲ (l. τιμάϲ) μεγιϲταϲ. The primary MSS at this point have ἡδονάϲ θ᾿ (τε
ΘΛΠΝ) ὑπερβαλλούϲαϲ (-βαλούϲαϲ Θ) καὶ τιμὰϲ μεγίϲταϲ (μεγίϲταϲ om. Λᵖʳ in lac.: ἀνεξαλείπτουϲ
Λ⁴ (conjecture)). θ᾿ ὑπερβαλλούϲαϲ will have been left out by a *saut du même au même* as a result of the
succession of feminine plural accusative endings in -αϲ.

  17 απεχρη with ΓΠΝ: ἀπέχρην Θ: ἀπόχρη Λ.

δ ạν μ[οι with ΛΠΝ, δ' ὁ δ' ἄν μοι Θ: δ' ἄν ἤδη μοι Γ. The last preserved trace is too exiguous to guarantee either н or м, but η[δη μοι would be too long for the available space. Γ's addition was perhaps a copying mistake resulting from the influence of ὄν ἤδη μοι a little further on in the same sentence (cf. Blass, *Praefatio editionis alterius* p. vi), but for a defence of such repetitions see Drerup's edition, pp. lxxvi–lxxix (especially p. lxxix for the reading here).

17–18 οι προειρη]μενοι: new reading. All primary MSS have τὰ προειρημένα (except that Θ omits προ-). The variant οἱ προειρημένοι (sc. λόγοι) is impossible with singular ἀπέχρη and perhaps arose from the influence of the immediately preceding μοι and the anticipation of τινα λόγον in the following clause (cf. also ποιεῖcθαι τοὺc λόγουc further on in the same paragraph). For the corruption to the masculine, cf. *Ad Nic.* 52, where the reading of the second family (and apparently of **5135** ii 12–13) ἐπὶ τὸ ὁμολογούμενον ἐλθόντα has become επι τουc ομολογουμενουc ελθοντα in p1 and Worp–Rijksbaron, *The Kellis Isocrates Codex* 209, wonder whether λόγουc is to be understood from the context.

18 περι τ[ουτων: om. Λ^pr in lac.: πάντωc Λ⁴ (conjecture).

20 ουκ αναναμ[*c.*9: οὐκ ἀμνημονήcαc ΓΘΛ²ΠΝ: οὐ *vac.* μονήcαc Λ^pr: οὔκουν μὲν ἀμνημονήcαc Λ⁴ (conjecture). There is room for the expected αμ[νημονηcαc αλ at the end of the line. αναν before it may be a product of confusion with ἀναμνη- combined with dittography; for a similar dittography, cf. p1's ανα{να}βαλεcθαι at *Nic.* 33. Possibly the end of the word was also corrupted and the scribe intended the rare ἀναμνημονεύcαc 'having remembered', a verb that is unattested in the Classical period and would give the wrong sense: the opposition οὐκ . . . ἀλλ' ὀκνήcαc implies that Isocrates' failure to mention the point under discussion was due to his hesitation rather than forgetfulness.

20–21 αλ]λ οκνηcαc: omitted by ΠΝ.

25–6 ποι]ειcθαι: cοι ποιῆcθαι ΠΝ.

28 μεν: omitted by Λ.

31–3 την [ειρηνην] τ[η]ν τοιc αλλοιc κ[οινην πο]λεμον τοιc αυτω[ν ιδιοιc with ΓΘ: τῆc εἰρήνηc τοῖc ἄλλοιc κοινῆc τὸν πόλεμον αὐτῶν ἴδιω Λ^pr (οὔcηc inserted after εἰρήνηc by Λ⁴), τῆc εἰρήνηc τῆc τοῖc ἄλλοιc κοινῆc τὸν πόλεμον τῶν αὐτῶν ἰδίω ΠΝ. The paraphrase of the passage in Arist. *Rh.* 3.10, 1410b29–31 and the allusion to it by [Dem.] 12.19 support the reading of the papyrus and ΓΘ.

Fr. 1 →

2–3 cυ[*c.*5 χρονο]ν ηδη παcιν: cὺ πολὺν χρόνον ἤδη πᾶcιν Γ: πολὺν ἤδη χρόνον ἄπαcιν Θ, cυχνὸν ἤδη χρόνον ἄπαcιν ΛΠΝ. The papyrus probably agreed with Γ in the lacuna, though cυ[χνον (a word not used by Isocrates) is not excluded. Isocrates is more likely to have written πολὺν ἤδη χρόνον (as at *Paneg.* 162, *De pace* 30, 36, *Hel.* 4, *Antid.* 285, *Epist.* 9.11) than πολὺν χρόνον ἤδη (cf. Münscher 32).

3–4 η[μιν: omitted by Θ.

4 επιβουλε]υειc with ΓΘ: ἐπιβουλεύοιc ΛΠΝ.

με(ν): omitted by ΛΠΝ.

6 Φω]κεαc with ΘΛΠΝ: Φωκεῖc Γ. See L. Threatte, *The Grammar of Attic Inscriptions* ii (1996) 247, and Seck, *Untersuchungen* 81–2.

6–7 διοικηςηc [εργω δ υπο ςεαυ]τω restored with ΓΘ (which have the form cαυτῷ; for the restoration of trisyllabic cεαυ]τω, see on fr. 1 ↓ 7–8): ἔργῳ διοικήcηc ὑπὸ cαυτῷ δέ Λ, ἔργῳ διοικήcειc ὑπὸ cαυτῷ (cαυτὸν Ν) δέ ΠΝ.

8 ΛΠΝ have διανοῇ after Πελοπόννεcον (needed following the loss of the λόγῳ μέν . . . , ἔργῳ δέ . . . contrast). The papyrus agrees with ΓΘ in construing ποιεῖcθαι with μέλλειc from the preceding clause.

13 Μεγαλ]οπολειται: l. Μεγαλοπολῖται.

14 cυνπολεμι(ν): l. cυμπολεμεῖν.

17 ὡc (Γ) omitted by ΘΛΠΝ but required here to fill the space. The repeated ὡc (cf. §73) is needed as an indication that Isocrates himself is not of this opinion (Münscher 43).

22 πειθ]ουϲιν with Γ: πείθουϲι ΘΛΠΝ.

23 μέν after μάλιϲτα is omitted by ΛΠΝ, but the available space indicates that the papyrus had it; it is necessary for the contrast with ἔπειτα δὲ κτλ.

αυτων: only specks of ink on a heavily abraded surface.

25 δε with ΓˢΘΛΠΝ: om. Γᵖʳ. Münscher 21 argues that δέ is an interpolation, comparing *Ad Nic.* 2–3 μάλιϲτα μέν . . . ἔπειθ' . . . ἔτι δ' . . . , but μάλιϲτα μέν . . . ἔπειτα δὲ καί . . . is found at *Paneg.* 175 and *Plat.* 63: cf. CPF I.2* on p17 I B 20–21 (pp. 398–9).

26 λο]γιϲμω with ΓΘ: λόγῳ ΛΠΝ. λόγῳ has been used earlier in the sentence (but in the sense of 'speech'), so that λογιϲμῷ is preferable here. The same choice of variants recurs a few lines later in §76 (not preserved in **5144**), but with the readings differently distributed among the manuscripts (λόγοιϲ Γ: λογιϲμοῖϲ ΘΛΠΝ, sc. χρώμενοϲ); there, however, the meaning 'speeches, words', i.e. λόγοιϲ, is more appropriate.

28 πανταπαϲι]ν with ΓΘΠΝ: παντάπαϲι Λ (hiatus).

ανοητωϲ with ΘΛΠΝ: ἀναιϲθήτωϲ Γ⁴: ἀναιϲθήτουϲ Γᵖʳ. ἀναιϲθήτωϲ is perhaps better supported by *C. soph.* 9 ἀναιϲθήτωϲ . . . διάκεινται, *Panath.* 85 ἀναιϲθήτωϲ διεκείμην. Münscher 43 suggests that ἀνοήτωϲ (which recurs in *Panath.* 155, 232, *Epist.* 5.4) is a gloss on the less familiar ἀναιϲθήτωϲ.

32 ετι] δε και: new reading. The primary MSS have simply ἔτι δέ. The phrase ἔτι δὲ καί is well attested in Isocrates (*C. Loch.* 20, *Nic.* 33, 40, *Panath.* 154, *Epist.* 4.11), but in *Trap.* 40 one finds the comparable sequence πρῶτον μέν . . . ἔπειτα δέ . . . ἔτι δέ (cf. also *Antid.* 151, *In Call.* 8). ετι] δε και is likely to be due to the influence of επειτα δε και (25). Cf. for a similar variant *C. Soph.* 16 (discussed in CPF I.2** on p42 I 5 (p. 531)); in general on the formulae used in such sequences, see S. Ljungdahl, *De transeundi generibus quibus utitur Isocrates commentatio* (1871) 43–7.

34 ϲε επιβουλευ]ειν restored with ΘΛΠΝ: ἐπιβουλεύειν ϲε Γ. While the papyrus agrees with ΘΛΠΝ in word order, it is impossible to decide whether it elided ϲε or not (like ΘΛΠΝ), since it is not consistent in this respect (see introd.). Münscher 43 prefers the reading of Γ, as it avoids the need for elision.

35 αιτια]ν restored *exempli gratia* with ΓΛ: ἀρχήν ΘΠΝ.

35–6 αξιαν [επιθυμιαϲ ει]ναι restored with ΓΘΠΝ: ἀξίαν εἶναι ἐπιθυμίαϲ εἶναι Λ.

Fr. 2 ↓

1–2 πλει[ονοϲ with ΛΠΝ: πλέονοϲ ΓΘ. See Threatte, *Grammar* ii 321, Seck, *Untersuchungen* 67–8, CPF I.2* on p17 X 9 (p. 422), and cf. fr. 3 ↓ 14 πλειω.

2 [δοκειν] restored with Γ: δοκεῖν ἄν ΘΛΠΝ. There does not seem to be sufficient space for the particle in the lacuna. Münscher 44 argues in favour of its omission.

2–3 π]οιηϲι[εν: l. ποιήϲειεν.

8–9 ΠΝ accidentally omit the apodosis τίϲ . . . μιϲήϲειεν.

8 αν: omitted by Γ and inserted by Γˢ above the line.

9 μειϲηϲιεν: l. μιϲήϲειεν.

11 ο προγονοϲ αυτ]ου restored with ΓΘΠΝ: αὐτοῦ ὁ πρόγονοϲ Λ (hiatus).

προϲειλετο: new reading. All primary MSS have προείλετο. προϲαιρέομαι, however, has the sense of 'choose and associate with', 'take for one's companion/ally' (as in, for example, *Aegin.* 38, where προϲείλετο is the reading of Γ, while Λ has προείλετο) or 'choose in addition' (see LSJ s.v.); it would not be appropriate here, where only the simple meaning 'choose' is required.

Fr. 2 →

5 Considerations of space suggest that the papyrus omitted either καί before ϲοι (with Γᵖʳ; καί added in the margin by Γ³) or ϲοῖϲ following τοῖϲ (with ΘΛΠΝ). *Exempli gratia* I have opted for the former possibility in the supplemented text.

10 εαυτων with ΓΛΠΝ: αὐτῶν Θ.

11 τε εταιρους with ΓΘ (both θ᾽) ΛΝ^{sl}: τε ἑτέρους ΠΝ^{pr}.

Fr. 3 →

1–9 Some scattered and indeterminate traces on damaged or displaced fibres here and at ↓ 1–9 are not taken into account in the transcription.

1–2 cυν[αγαγων: so Γ⁵ΘΛΠΝ. cυμπαρασκευασάμενος (Γ^{pr}) cannot be accommodated in the available space. The middle voice of this compound verb, also found in a variant at *C. soph.* 21 (cυμπαρασκευάcαcθαι ΘΛ: cυμπαρακελεύcαcθαι Γ), has only a few late attestations, but it has been favoured by modern editors (Benseler–Blass excepted), perhaps as a *lectio difficilior.* cυνάγω, however, is quite common in Isocrates, e.g. *Panath.* 49 τριήρεις μὲν cυναγαγόντος κτλ., 104 cτρατόπεδον . . . cυναγαγόντες. Γ᾽s reading may have been influenced by παρασκευῆς in the previous line; cf. Blass, *Praefatio editionis alterius* p. vi. Münscher 14 suggests that it originated as a gloss.

2 γαρ: omitted by ΘΛΠΝ. Λ⁴ attempted to heal the asyndeton by conjecture, inserting ὥcτε before cυναγαγών (Münscher 47).

3 [πλειcτην] restored with Γ: transposed after δύναμιν by ΘΛΠΝ, wrongly (Münscher 47).

12 Λ⁴ adds τῷ before ναυτικῷ.

12–13 μετα βαcιλεως with ΘΛΠΝ: βαcιλέως Γ.

13–14 αφεcτηκεν with Γ: ἀφέcτηκε ΘΛΠΝ.

16 ωcτε εκεινω: likewise unelided in Θ.

17 τουτων των [εθ]νων with Γ: τῶν ἐθνῶν τούτων ΘΛΠΝ^{pc} (τουτον Ν^{ac}). Isocrates' tendency to avoid ending one word and beginning the next with the same syllable does not appear to apply to the article; cf. Drerup's edition, p. lxvi, and S. Martinelli Tempesta, *Gnomon* 78 (2006) 595.

18 cοι rightly with ΓΠΝ: cύ ΘΛ.

19–20 cυμφορῶc with ΓΘΛ^{pr}ΠΝ: cυμμάχους Λ², apparently a conjecture (E. Drerup, *De codicum Isocrateorum auctoritate* (Leipziger Studien XVII/1, 1895) 43; id., *Philol.* 55 (1896) 661).

20–21 μη νη Δια [γ]ε [τ]ον ευρωπατατον: μὴν Ἰδριέα (so Γ, Harpocrat. ι 2: Ἰδρέα ΘΛΠΝ) γε τὸν εὐπορώτατον MSS. The corruption of the unusual sequence μηνιδριεαγε to μηνηδιαγε will be due to confusion with a phrase familiar in later Greek, νὴ Δία γε: cf. Drerup's edition, p. lxxx (errors arising 'scriptura continua male disiuncta'). ευρωπ- for ευπορωτ- may be due to confusion with 'Europe' in this geographical context. The dittography of -ατ- in the superlative is a corruption paralleled in p1 (*Ad Nic.* 20 οικειοτα{τα}τους, 41 χαριεπα{τα}τον for χαριέcτατον); cf. Worp–Rijksbaron, *The Kellis Isocrates Codex* 40, and fr. 1 ↓ 20 n.

26 γ: omitted by ΠΝ.

27–8 cυνκαταλυ[cαι: new reading. The primary MSS have the perfect passive καταλελύcθαι. The restoration cυνκαταλυ[ειν is theoretically also possible, but -λῦcαι is more likely to occur in a variant for -λελύcθαι. The active compound with cυν- conveys the notion that Idrieus would collaborate with Philip in undoing the King's empire, implying a greater role for Idrieus than Isocrates appears to envisage in §104 (merely ἐκεῖνός τ᾽ ἂν ἄcμενος ἴδοι βοηθὸν ἥκειν αὐτῷ cε νομίζων). It is easier, moreover, to envisage a corruption of καταλελύcθαι to (cυν)καταλῦcαι than vice versa, since one at first expects the subject of the infinitive to be the same as the subject of βούλοιτο.

28–9 την αρχην αικι[cαμε]νην. Γ omitted τήν before ἀρχήν, but Γ² added it above the line. The papyrus omits τήν before αἰκιcαμένην, which all primary MSS have. The omission is probably due to parablepsy (αρχ**ην**τ**ην**αικιcαμενην).

Fr. 3 ↓

1–9 See above, fr. 3 → 1–9 n.

1 καθ ε[καcτον] ενια[υτον: so ΘΛΠΝ. Γ has τόν before ἐνιαυτόν (likewise in §51), but spacing would not allow it here; cf. above, fr. 3 → 17 n.

2–3 διαβαι]νοιϲ: new reading. All primary MSS have διαβαίηϲ. Aspectually, the aorist is required. διαβαίνοιϲ is probably an intrusive gloss on διαβαίηϲ. Isocrates does not employ the present optative of (-)βαίνω elsewhere.

5 The supplement here is rather longer than those of neighbouring lines. No variants are reported for this part of the text.

10 ε]ιϲ: omitted by ΠΝ.

11 τουϲ Ελ[λ]ηναϲ: *vac. vac* Λ^{pr}, τοὺϲ ἕλλη suppl. Λ².

12–13 την ημετεραν και τη(ν) Λακεδαιμονιων αρχην with Γ: τὴν ἡμετέραν ἀρχὴν καὶ τὴν Λακεδαιμονίων ΘΛΠΝ. Münscher 47 argues for Γ's reading.

14 πλειω with ΓΘΠΝ: πλείονα Λ. See Threatte, *Grammar* ii 311, and cf. above, fr. 2 ↓ 1–2 n.

17–18 δυναμεωϲ with ΓΘΛΝ: δύναμιν Π.

19 τι[ν]εϲ with ΓΘΛ¹ΠΝ: τιϲ Λ^{pr}.
επιτειμηϲωϲιν: l. ἐπιτιμήϲωϲιν.

21 μεταχειριϲαμενοϲ with Γ: μεταχειριϲάμενοι ΘΛΠΝ. The plural will be due to the influence of ἡμῖν in the preceding clause (cf. Münscher 47).

21–2 των ϲ[τρ]ατιωτικων with Γ: τῶν ϲτρατηγικῶν ΘΠΝ: ϲτρατηγικόν Λ.

22 ϲοι τολμωη[ν: νῦν τολμώην ϲοί Γ: ϲοὶ τολμῶμεν ΘΛΠΝ. The final trace is too slight to guarantee either η or μ, but the first person singular form is restored because of μεταχειριϲαμενοϲ in 21 (see n. ad loc.). The papyrus agrees with Γ in the use of the singular rather than the plural, but with ΘΛΠΝ in word order and the omission of νῦν. Münscher 47 argues that the dative should not be separated from παραινεῖν.

23 πλ[ειϲ]τ[α: all primary MSS have πλεῖϲτα καὶ μέγιϲτα, but καὶ μέγιϲτα would not be possible within the available space. Its omission here is unjustifiable and is probably a copying error arising from the two identical endings in -ιϲτα.

24–5 πολ]εμον restored with ΓΘΠΝ: τὸν πόλεμον Λ. Considerations of space suggest lack of the article in 24.

28 του om. Λ^{pr} in lac., ἀρκεῖν πρὸϲ παράδειγμα τόν add. Λ⁴ (conjecture).

A. BENAISSA

5145. Iꜱᴏᴄʀᴀᴛᴇꜱ, *Pʜɪʟɪᴘᴘᴜꜱ* 117–19, 121–3, 126–7

9 1B.181/H(a)   15.5 × 18.3 cm   Second century

A fragment of a roll giving the lower parts of three consecutive columns and the lower margin. The text is written along the fibres. On the back are remains of a documentary text, written in a hand of the late second or early third century. Col. i preserves ends only from a stretch of 25 lines, occupying a space about 12 cm high; col. ii (about 13.6 cm high and 6 cm wide) preserves 28 lines, some to their full length; col. iii (about 6 cm high) preserves 13 line-beginnings. Lines will have held between 17 and 24 letters. A column will have contained *c*.50 lines and been about 25 cm high. The lower margin is about 4.5 cm deep. Each intercolumnium measures approximately 1.2 cm. Traces of ink are visible in the intercolumnium between cols. ii and iii: there is an upright trace at about the level of iii 4 and a few horizontal traces at about the level of iii 10. Possibly these are the remains of sigla or marginalia.

The text is written with a thick pen in a medium-sized informal round hand with some ligatures. There is some inconsistency in letter formation. ⲁ is tall, sometimes ascending well above the line; ⲅ, ⲡ, and ⲧ are flattened; ⲙ is broad and rounded; ⲟ is often very small; ⲩ is v-shaped, sometimes with a nearly upright left-hand branch; ⲱ has a flat or nearly flat base. A comparable hand is that of the astrological(?) text P. Tebt. Tait 45 (pl. 10), assigned to the second century, and written on the back of a document in a hand also possibly of the second century.

Paragraphus with high point is used for punctuation at ii 22 and 26 (the high point being misplaced in the second case). Iota adscript is not written. A supralinear bar replaces *ν* at line-end at i 23.

The papyrus agrees with the MSS of the second family against Γ in a true reading at ii 22; cf. also i 7, 8–9. It has a unique reading in ii 6–7. There is a clear agreement in genuine reading with Γ and Θ, against the remaining primary MSS of the second family, at ii 20.

There is a small overlap with p97.

Col. i

    *c.*23 lines missing

                       ].   (§117)

    τας και τας πολεις και νε]ως

    και βωμους ιδρυμεν]ọ[υς]

    τους δ ουτ εν ταις ευχα]ịς

5   ουτ εν ταις θυσιαις τιμω]με

    νους αλλ αποπομπα]ς ạυ

    των ημας ποιουμενους]...

    ενθυμουμενον εθιζειν] ce   §118

    αυτον χρη και μελεταν] οπως

10   ετι μαλλον η νυν τοιαυ]τ̣ην

    απαντες περι coυ την γ]ν̣ω

                     ].

                     ].

    μουντας περιβαλ]λ̣ε̣c̣θαι

15   μεν τη διανοια τας πρ]ạξεις

    δυνατας μεν ευχη δ] ọμọι

    ας εξεργαζεcθαι δε ζη]τ̣ειν̣

    αυτας οπως αν οι και]ρọι πα

    ραδιδωcιν εκ πολλων δ] αν̣ κ[α]   §119

20   τανοηcειας οτι δ]ει τουτ[ο]ν

    τον τροπον πραττ]ε̣ιν̣ μ̣ạ

λιςτα δ εκ των Ιαςο]νι ϲυμ
βαντων εκεινος γαρ ουδ]ε̄
τοιουτον οιον ϲυ κατεργα]
25   ϲαμενος μεγιϲτης δοξη]ϲ
          2 lines missing

Col. ii

          *c.*22 lines missing
          ω[ϲτε μηδεν ηττον αυτους   (§121)
          ειν̣[αι φοβερους τοις Ελληϲιν
          η το̣[ις βαρβαροις ων ουδεμιαν
          ποιο̣[υμεθα προνοιαν αλλ α
5   γνοο̣[υμεν κοινον φοβον και
          κιν̣δ[υνον απαϲιν ημιν αυ
          ξομε̣[νον εϲτιν ουν ανδρος   §122
          μ]ε̣γ̣[α φρονουντος και φιλελ
          λ]η̣[νος και πορρωτερω των αλ
10   λω[ν τη διανοια καθορωντος
          απο̣[χρηϲαμενον τοις τοιου
          [τοις προς τους βαρβαρους
          και [χωραν αποτεμομενον
          τ̣[οϲαυτην οϲην ολιγω προτε
15   ρον̣ ειρ[ηκαμεν απαλλα
          ξαι τε το̣[υς ξενιτευομενου]ς
          των κ̣ακω̣[ν ω]ν̣ [αυτοι τ εχ̣]ου
          ϲι και το̣ις αλλοις παρεχο̣υϲι
          και πολεις εξ αυτων ϲυϲτη
20   ϲαι και ταυταις οριϲαι την
          Ελλαδα και πρ̣[ο]β̣α̣λεϲθαι
          προ απαντων ημων· ταυ   §123
          τα γαρ πραξας ου μο̣νον εκει
          νους ευδαιμονας ποιηϲεις
25   αλλα και παντας ημα̣ς εις
          α̣ϲφ̣α̣λειαν καταϲτηϲει·ϲ ην
          δ ουν τουτων δια[μαρ]τ̣ης
          αλ̣λ̣ εκεινο γε ρ̣[αδ]ι̣ω[ϲ π]ο

Col. iii

　　　　　*c.*37 lines missing

　　　　.].[

　　　ειν [ωcτ εξον ημιν τακεινων　　　　　　(§126)

　　　αδεω[c εχειν προc ημαc

　　　αυτου[c περι μικρων πολε

5　　μουμ[εν και τουc αφιcταμε

　　　νουc [τηc αρχηc τηc βαcιλε

　　　ωc cυγ[καταcτρεφομεθα

　　　και λελη[θαμεν ημαc αυτουc

　　　ενιοτε με̣τ̣α̣ [των πατρικων

10　εχθρων τουc τηc̣ αυτ̣[ηc cυγ

　　　γενειαc με[τεχονταc απολ

　　　λυναι ζητο[υντεc διο και cοι　　　　　§127

　　　ν̣[ο]μιζω cυμ[φερειν ουτωc

Col. i

　　7 [ημαc] om. Γ^pr, add. Γ^5.

　　The traces after the break are hard to interpret: first two low specks; then the right-hand part of a circle with a dot above; finally a supralinear cross-bar and on the line traces suggesting a flattened N. ων is expected but would be written in an anomalous way and leave ink unaccounted for.

　　8–9 cε[αυτον with ΘΝ (cεαυτὸν) Λ (cὲ αὐτὸν) Π (cὲ αὐτὸν): cαυτὸν Γ. Cf. **5144** fr. 1 ↓ 7–8 n.

　　12–13 There are confused traces in 13, perhaps partly offset, and further ink in 12, again perhaps partly offset. If the papyrus offered no new reading here, the text written in these two lines would be [μην εξουcιν χρη δε τουc μειζονοc δοξηc των αλλων επιθυ].

　　14 περιβαλ]λε̣c̣θαι restored *exempli gratia* with Γ. ΘΛΠΝ have περιβαλέcθαι.

Col. ii

　　6–7 αυ]ξομε[νον against all the primary MSS, which have αὐξανόμενον. The fluctuation between the two equivalent forms is found in §38 (αὐξομένηc Γ: αὐξανομένηc ΘΛΠΝ), but otherwise αὐξαν- is the preferred form; cf. §73 (**5144** fr. 1 → 2), *Paneg.* 104, *De pace* 51, *Panath.* 47, 115. Inscriptional evidence is inconclusive (Threatte, *Grammar* ii 509). Münscher 29 (on §38) argues for αὐξαν-.

　　16 ξενιτευομενου]c̣ restored with ΘΛΠΝ and Harpocrat. ξ 3. Γ has πολιτευομένουc.

　　17 [αυτοι τ εχ]ο̣υ restored with ΓΘΛΠ: τ om. N.

　　19 εξ αυτων with ΓΛΠΝ: ἐπ' αὐτῶν Θ.

　　20 οριcαι with ΓΘ: ἐχυρῶcαι ΛΠΝ.

　　22 προ with ΘΛΠΝ: πρὸc Γ.

　　26 Through an oversight, the high stop was inserted after καταcτηcει instead of after καταcτηcειc where it belongs.

　　28 π]ο, i.e. π]ο|[ηcειc: ποιήcειc ΓΘΛΠΝ.

　　　　　　　　　　　　　　　　　　　　　P. M. PINTO

5146. Isocrates, *Philippus* 120, 123–4

93/Dec. 28/G.2   3.4 × 7.7 cm   Fourth century

The lower inner corner of a papyrus codex leaf with remains of 8 lines (→)
and 9 lines (↓). The lower margin is about 3.4 cm deep at its shortest. The inner
margin is about 0.3 cm wide at its narrowest on the → side and about 0.6 cm wide
at its narrowest on the ↓ side. Each line held about 21–4 letters, and the maximum
line length seems to have been about 12–12.5 cm. Five lines and the interlinear
space following them occupy an area about 2.7 cm high. Approximately 39 lines
are missing at the top of the ↓ side. The height of the written area will have been
about 26 cm, and that of a page about 31 cm (allowing for an upper margin about
two-thirds the depth of the lower margin: cf. Turner, *Typology* 25). For codices with
similar dimensions (the first class of aberrants, 'much higher than broad', from
Turner's Group 8), see Turner, *Typology* 21.

The text is written in a medium-sized decorated formal upright hand. Broad
letters (Δ Η Κ Μ Ν Π Τ Υ Φ) contrast with tiny ε θ ο ϲ. Uprights and descending
obliques are thick, cross-strokes and ascending obliques thin. The tails of Ρ Υ Φ
descend well below the line; the oval-bowled Φ extends also well above the line. Μ
is rounded and deep in the middle. LXVI **4507** (Anubion?) is written in a hand
of a similar type; the slightly slanting hand of the letter P. Herm. 5 (*GMAW*² 70;
about 317–23) may also be compared.

There are new but unappealing or impossible variants at → 5–6 and 8 and ↓ 2.

→

     ·   ·   ·   ·   ·

     τα πρ[αξηϲ και μαλιϲτα μεν πει   (§120)
     ραθη[ϲ οληντην βαϲιλειαν ανε
     λειν [ει δε μη χωραν οτι πλειϲτην α
     φοριϲα[ϲθαι και διαλαβειν την
5   Αϲιαν ω[ϲ λεγουϲι τινεϲ απο Κι
     κιλιαϲ [μεχρι ϲινωπηϲ προϲ δε
     τουτοι[ϲ κτιϲαι πολειϲ επι τω
     π[ο]ντ[ω

↓

     ·   ·   ·   ·   ·

            ].[
     ευδοκιμηϲ]ειϲ δι   (§123)
  καιωϲ ηνπερ αυτοϲ τ] επι ταυ
  θ ορμηϲηϲ και τουϲ Ε]λλη

5   ναϲ προτρεψηϲ επε]ι νυν   §124
        γε τιϲ ουκ αν εικοτωϲ] τα ϲυμ
        βεβηκοτα θαυμαϲειε]ν και κα
        ταφρονηϲειεν ημων ο]που πα
        ρα μεν τοιϲ βαρβαροιϲ ο]υϲ υπει

→

2–3 ανε]λειν: so Γ: ἑλεῖν ΘΛΠΝ. Line 2 would be too short without the prefix.

3 The supplement seems two or three letters too long. Perhaps οτι was not present, but that is not the only possibility.

5 *Αϲιαν*: so ΓΘΛ. Π has the corruption οὐϲίαν (and διαβαλεῖν where the other manuscripts have διαλαβεῖν), while Ν has οὐϲίαν in the text with ἀϲίαν added above the line.

ω[ϲ: so Γ. ΘΛΠΝ have ἦν, wrongly (Münscher 48).

5–6 *Κι]κιλιαϲ*: an anagrammatic corruption, for *Κιλικίαϲ*. I have considered the possibility that *Κι*] is not to be supplied at the end of the preceding line, the variant being instead merely *Κιλιαϲ*, but this would leave 5 too short, even if λεγουϲιν (Γ) was written where I have restored λεγουϲι (ΘΛΠΝ).

7–8 επι τω] π[ο]ντ[ω: a new false variant. The later manuscripts have ἐπὶ τούτωι τῶι τόπωι (Γ) and ἐν τῷ τόπῳ τούτῳ (ΘΛΠΝ). As Sinope is a city on the Pontus, πόντωι could easily make its way into the text. Cf. *De pace* 86, where for ἐν Δάτῳ δὲ (Γ), ΛΠΝ give ἐν δὲ τῷ Πόντῳ, apparently a gloss (M. L. W. Laistner, *CQ* 15 (1921) 81; CPF I.2** on p46.1073–4 (pp. 579–80)).

↓

1]ֹ.[, on the line, a stroke descending from left to right. μαλ]λ[ον] | [των αλλων ευδοκιμηϲ]ειϲ seems possible. In Γ, μόνον, repeated from earlier in the sentence, has replaced the correct reading μᾶλλον (ΘΛΠΝ).

2 ευδοκιμηϲ]ειϲ: -ϲηϲ ΠΝˢˡ.

The papyrus omits the καὶ otherwise transmitted before δικαίωϲ. Though not essential, the particle seems desirable for clarity.

3–4 αυτοϲ τ] επι ταυ[θ: so ΓΘ (αὐτὸϲ τὲ ἐπὶ ταῦτα). ΛΠΝ give ἐπὶ ταῦτα αὐτόϲ τε.

5 προτρεψηϲ seems compatible with the space available. ΘΠΝ have προτρέψῃ.

7 θαυμαϲειε]ν: so Γ. ΘΛΠΝ omit the ν.

W. B. HENRY

5147. Isocrates, *Antidosis* 2–4

5 1B.44/D(f)   11 × 9.2 cm   Second century

A fragment containing the lower part of the first two columns of a papyrus roll. The writing runs along the fibres and the back is blank. The lower margin is 3.2 cm deep; the intercolumnium is between 1.7 and 2.1 cm wide. Col. i preserves ten lines, and col. ii ten line-beginnings. About 22 lines are missing at the top of col. ii and the lost opening will have occupied about 21 lines. The original column height will have been about 19 cm. There are 12–16 letters to a line, and the maximum preserved line length is 5.6 cm.

The small formal round hand resembles those of **LII 3685** (Plutarch), assigned to the first half of the second century, and XVII **2099** (Herodotus), also assigned to the early second century. Bilinearity is breached only by φ. There are no lection signs except for a filler at the end of i 10.

Collated with the primary manuscripts (ΓΘΛ). There are no points of textual interest.

The papyrus does not overlap with any of the other known papyri of this speech, all of which come from rolls (see CPF I.2** pp. 497–513). These are p34 (P. Princ. III 113), p35 (PL inv. III/273E), p36 (XLV **3233**), p37 (I **27** + PL inv. II/870), P. Köln XI 435 (possibly part of the same roll as p34), and the unpublished p33 *ter* (P. Mich. inv. 1592); there is also p58 (LXIX **4736**), which contains a part of *De pace* quoted in *Antidosis* and may belong to a copy of either work.

Col. i   Col. ii

	*c.*21 lines lost			*c.*22 lines lost	
	δως [εν]ιο[υς] τω[ν	(§2)		κ[ο]υτω[ν το μεγε	(§3)
	cοφιcτων βλαcφη			θος και τ[οιουτων	
	μουντας περι της			πραγμα[των υπερ	
	εμης διατριβης			ων ουδε[ις αν αλλος	
5	καὶ λεγοντας ως		5	επιχειρη[cειε πλην	
	εcτιν περι δικο			των εμο[ι πεπλη	
	γραφιαν και παρα			cιακ[ο]τω[ν η των	
	πλησιον ποιουν			τουτους [μιμει	
	τας ωσπερ αν ει τις			cθαι βου[λομενων	
10	Φ[ει]διαν τον το ⟩		10	μεχρι μ[εν ουν πορ	§4

Col. i

6 εcτιν with Γ: ἔcτι ΘΛ.

10 The angular line filler might also be read as part of λ: the upper part of the left-hand oblique and the extension of the right-hand oblique above the apex. In that case, we would have to reckon with an omission, τὸν ⟨τὸ τῆς Ἀθηνᾶς ἕδος ἐργαcάμενον⟩ τολμῴη, which could be explained as a case of *homoeoteleuton* (-ον . . . -ον).

Col. ii

5 επιχειρη[cειε restored e.g. with ΘΛ. Γ has -cειεν.

P. M. PINTO

5148–52. Demosthenes

This group contains papyri of Demosthenes XXV, XXX and XXXIV. In collating them, we have based ourselves on the critical text of M. R. Dilts, *Demosthenis Orationes* iii (Oxford 2008). Where the papyrus provides, or suggests, a unique variant, we have consulted also the editions of Dindorf (Oxford 1846) and Dindorf–Blass (Leipzig 1907); for speech XXV also Butcher (Oxford 1907), Sykutris (Leipzig 1937), and Mathieu (*Démosthène, Plaidoyers politiques* iv, Paris 1947); for speeches XXX and XXXIV also Rennie (Oxford 1921) and Gernet (*Démosthène, Plaidoyers civils* i, Paris 1954). The readings of S have been verified from the printed facsimile, and those of A from the images available on the website of the Bayerische Staatsbibliothek, by Dr W. B. Henry.

5148–5150. [Demosthenes] XXV (*in Aristogitonem I*)

This speech, which most editors follow Dionysius of Halicarnassus (*Dem.* 57) in thinking spurious, has been poorly represented in the finds from Egypt. Here we publish three more witnesses. The total coverage is now:

6–8, 10–11	**5148**	papyrus roll	I/I
26, 31–2	**5149**	parchment codex	V
47–8	VI **882** (P. Yale I 23)	papyrus roll	II
50–51, 68–71	**5150**	papyrus roll	I
63–7	P. Lond. Lit. 125	parchment codex	V

All these come from Oxyrhynchus, except P. Lond. Lit. 125, whose provenance is uncertain.

5148. [Demosthenes] XXV 6–8, 10–11

21 3B.27/E(3–6)e   7.5 × 9 cm   First cent. BC/first cent. AD

A fragment from the bottom of two columns. The back is blank, but shows a repair patch (3.2 × 7.8 cm) roughly corresponding to the second column, with the outer layer of fibres parallel to the writing on the front; underneath, on its upper part, some traces of ink are visible (either accidental or due to contact with writing). Remains of a similar patch can also be seen on the right, in correspondence with the first column of the recto. The lines had an average of 22 letters; the columns, of about 47 lines, measured about 7 × 25 cm and were 1 cm apart, with a margin of at least 1.2 cm at the foot. The speech will have begun at the top of the column preceding col. i; the whole work would have taken up about 2.6 m (9 feet). The hand, smallish, upright and serifed in absurd fashion, resembles those of XXI **2303** (pl. XI) and XXXI **2545** (pl. IV), assigned to the late Ptolemaic or early Roman period; earlier examples like P. Lond. Lit. 134 probably date from the second century BC (Cavallo–Maehler, *HB* no. 46, pp. 80–81; Cavallo, *Scrittura* pp. 47–9). The serifs, sometimes straight and sometimes curved, often connect one letter with the next, emphasizing the baseline. The only mark of punctuation is a paragraphos (ii 6); wider spaces are sometimes left between words (ii 7 after αγαπωσαν, 9 after πολεις, 11 after δικην, 14 after θρονον), but it seems that the only ones to which any significance attaches are the widest (i 9; ii 6, with paragraphos). Iota adscript written correctly in i 10. Note μεγ|γαρ (i 9–10). ει for ι i 14, ii 11–12.

The text is of considerable interest, not least by reason of its date.

Col. i

```
           νομ]ων εις
ελ ηλυθεναι] ει δ ετερον τι              §7
τουτων περι]εσται ο μηδεις
μεν αν αυτος πε]ποιηκεναι φη
```
5
```
σειεν εν δε ταις ψη]φοις ευρεθη
σεται δεδοικα] μη δοξητε τι
σιν τον αει βο]υλομενον πο
νηρον ειναι τ]ων εν τ[η]ι πολει
παιδοτριβειν]  ασθεν[η]ς μεγ
```
10
```
γαρ πας πονηρος] καθ εαυ[το]ν ωι
δ αν υμεις πρ]οσθησθε ουτος
ισχυρος γιγνε]ται εσ[τι δ]ε του
το τωι μεν c.3 ].[.].. πα[ρ υ]μων
εργασια και δυ]ναστεια [υ]μειν
```
15
```
δε τοις δουσι]ν ονει[δο]ς βου          §8
```

Col. ii

```
π[ολυ]ν ηδη [χρονον αισχρως
και κ[α]κως υ[πο τουτων δια
κειμενα βελ[τιω ποιησαι
παντα τα τοια[υτα εθη παρι
```
5
```
δοντας τημερο[ν ορθως δει δι
κασαι   και τ[ην τα δικαια α          §11
γαπωσαν ευν[ομιαν περι πλει
στου ποιησομε[νους η πασας
και πολεις κα[ι χωρας σωζει
```

10   και την απαραιτ[ητον και cεμνην

         δικην ην ο τα[c αγιωτατας η

         μειν τελετας [καταδειξας ορ

         φευc παρα τον [του διος φηcι

         θρονον καθη[μενην παντα

15   τα των ανθρ[ωπων

Col. i

2 δ ετε̣ρο̣ν̣: so SFY: δὲ πρότερον A.

3 τουτων περι]εcται: so AF: περιέcται τούτων SY, in contravention of Blass' Law (τῐ πε̆ρῐ-), which the author of the speech observes as strictly as Demosthenes himself.

6 δοξητε: so SFY: δόξετε A.

7–8 πο||[νηρον ειναι: εἶναι πονηρόν codd., in unanimous contravention of Blass' Law (-λŏμε̆νŏν). If Blass or anyone else had conjectured πονηρὸν εἶναι, the air would have been thick with accusations of temerity, but that is precisely what **5148** now reads. On the general issue, see LXX **4769** ii 5–6 n.

9–10 μεγ||[γαρ. Such assimilations, normal in inscriptions of the Classical period, disappear from documentary papyri in the second century BC (Mayser, *Grammatik* i.1² 206) and occur only rarely in literary papyri of the Roman period; for examples in the Herculaneum papyri, see W. Crönert, *Memoria graeca herculanensis* (1903) 61. Cf. **5143** 2.

10 παc πονηροc]: ἐcτιν ἅπαc ὁ πονηρόc SFY (ὁ om. Yᶜ): πᾶc ἐcτιν ὁ πονηρόc A. The previous line and the next suggest that about 12 letters are missing from this. As no reading in any of the manuscripts has less than 17, **5148** must have omitted something. Though it is always possible that it accidentally omitted πονηρόc, the likeliest supposition is that it read γὰρ πᾶc πονηρόc. That the manuscripts disagree over the position of ἐcτι(ν) proves nothing, because such disagreements occur in places where no word is dispensable; but a later hand is more likely to have added it than to have omitted it. For the omission compare **5150** fr. 2 ii 4.

13 The surface is so badly worn before α̣ (π represented only by a speck at line-level) that only one or two minute traces remain, but there is no reason to doubt that **5148** had λαβόντι.

15 The upper trace before β may be a high point rather than part of the c.

Col. ii

4–5 παρι]||δονταc: so Fᵃ: παριδόνταc ὑμᾶc SAYFʸʳ.

5 δεῖ om. hic A.

6 και: om. codd.: 'fort. τὴν ⟨δὲ⟩' Sykutris. The mediaeval manuscripts provide no satisfactory way of articulating the clause that begins in 4. S reads ὀρθῶc δεῖ δικάcαι, τὴν τὰ δίκαι' ἀγαπῶcαν Εὐνομίαν περὶ πλείcτου ποιηcαμένουc, ἢ . . . cώζει, καὶ τὴν ἀπαραίτητον καὶ cεμνὴν Δίκην, ἣν . . . ἐφορᾶν, εἰc αὐτὸν ἕκαcτον νομίcαντα βλέπειν οὕτω ψηφίζεcθαι; editors make syntactical sense of this by printing a colon after cώζει, but the chiasmus is unnatural and without the colon any reader would go astray. FY agree for the most part with S but repeat ἣν before εἰc αὐτόν; so too A, which also inserts ἄν after νομίcαντα and restores before ψηφίζεcθαι the δεῖ that it had omitted before δικάcαι. Sykutris' conjecture ὀρθῶc δεῖ δικάcαι, τὴν ⟨δὲ⟩ was commended by C. Rüger, *Phil.² Woch.* 58 (1938) 1148—not without justification, as it turns out, since **5148** now has ορθωc δει δι]||καcαι και τ[ην κτλ. The space before και, wide enough for three letters, is presumably not a sign of trouble but a partner to the paragraphos; the space in i 9 before αcθενηc, which begins a sentence, is wide enough for more than one letter and may have been wider.

8 ποιηcομε[νουc: -cαμένουc codd.

10 Unless **5148** disagreed with the mediaeval manuscripts, this line had 14 letters where the lines on either side had 11. It is hard to imagine that any difference was an improvement.

12 τελετας here in SFY, before ἡμῖν in A.

13–14 φησι‖ θρονον: θρόνον φησί codd., which in view of the attraction exerted on enclitics by the beginning of their phrase may well be thought an easier but less idiomatic order.

M. D. REEVE

5149. [Demosthenes] XXV 26, 31–2

6 1B.17/IV(a)   4.8 × 8.2 cm   Fifth century

A portion of the upper part of a leaf of a parchment codex with remains of 10 lines and upper and inner margins on each side. The line length was about 8.5 cm, and a line held about 20 letters on average. The text from the top of the column preserved on the front to the top of the column preserved on the back was about 2,242 letters long and will have taken up about 112 lines. Five lines and the interlinear space beneath the fifth occupy an area about 4.5 cm high. 112 lines will then have occupied a space about 50.4 cm high, too much for a single column, and it is safe to assume that this was a double-column codex, with each column holding about 37 lines and occupying an area about 16.7 cm high. The upper margin is preserved to a depth of 3.6 cm, and the depth of the lower margin may be estimated as 5.4 cm (if it is assumed that it was one-and-a-half times as deep as the upper: cf. Turner, *Typology* 25), so that the total height of the leaf will have been about 25.7 cm. The inner margin is preserved to a width of 0.9 cm on both sides. If we assume a similar figure for the outer margin and for the space between the columns, the total width of the leaf will have been 19.7 cm. For parchment codices with comparable dimensions, see Turner, *Typology* 27 (Groups IV and V). The speech, being of about 33,655 letters in length, will have occupied about 46 columns or 23 pages. The approximately 8,172 letters that preceded the top of the first column on this leaf will have taken up 11 columns.

The hand is a well-executed example of the 'Sloping Pointed Majuscule' (Cavallo–Maehler, *GBEBP* p. 4). ο is consistently small, an oval loop closed at the right by a short heavy oblique; ρ, τ, γ, and χ regularly descend below the line. Obliques descending from left to right are very thick; uprights and descenders are of medium thickness and often taper towards the base; horizontals, and obliques descending from right to left, thin to the point of invisibility and sometimes delimited by heavy finials. This emphatic shading indicates a date not earlier than the fifth century, and possibly of the sixth, a fairly late stage in the development represented by *GBEBP* 15a, 17b, 41c. Punctuation sparse: high stop, front 4. Iota adscript omitted in the only place that requires it (front 1).

There are no readings of particular interest.

Front (flesh side)

    λαχων τω λ[αχοντι και ο μη   (§26)
    χειροτονη[θεις τω χειρο
    τ[ο]νηθεντι [εξ ισου ζητοι
    η ειναι· και τ[ων αυτων με
5   τεχειν και ολ[ως μη νεος
    μη πρεϲβυτ[ερος τα προς
    ηκοντα πρ[αττοι αλλα παν
    το τεταγμεν[ον εξελασας ε
    καστος εκ τ[ου βιου την εαυ
10 του βουλ[ηϲιν νομον αρχην

    ·   ·   ·

Back (hair side)

    χεϲθαι τοις θε]οις μη γ[ε]νε   (§31)
    ϲθαι δει ει δ α]ρα ϲυμβαιη [ ]
    μειζον εϲτι]ν εϲτυχημα
    τη πολει απορ]ηϲαι τους βου
5   λομενους εξ]αμαρτειν δι
    ου τουτο ποι]ηϲουϲιν ει του
    τον αφειμεν]ον αυ[τ]οις
    ετοιμον υπ]αρξαι τι γαρ   §32
    ουτος οκνηϲειε]ν αν ω (ανδρες α)θ(ηναιοι) τ[ω(ν)
10 ανηκεϲτων η δει]νων α.

    ·   ·   ·   ·   ·   ·

Front (flesh side)

    2 In the left-hand margin, *c.*5 mm to the left of the line-beginning, a horizontal trace: accidental?

    9–10 εαυ]|του: with SAFY^c: ἑαυτῶν Y^a.

Back (hair side)

    2–3 ϲυμβαιη [ ]: ϲυμβαίη τι S^γρ. The lacuna at the end of 2 would accommodate only one letter, and there is no room for τι at the start of 3.

    3 εϲτυχημα: l. εὐτύχημα. The first syllable has been falsely assimilated to that of the preceding εϲτι]ν.

    6 ει with S^aY^a: ἤ S^cAFY^c. ει is probably an iotacistic spelling, not an indicative variant from a particular tradition.

    9 ω (ανδρες α)θ(ηναιοι): omega with theta written above it; the crossbar of theta extends well to either side of the roundel, and its ends are marked with heavy finials. See K. McNamee, *Abbreviations in Greek Literary Papyri and Ostraca* (1981) 113 (+ supplement in *BASP* 22 (1985) 220) for various abbreviations of this phrase. For this exact form she refers to P. Ant. I 27.52, P. Rainer Cent. 21 (P. Mich. inv.

1359), P. Ryl. I 58.92, 118, and P. Lit. Lenaerts 11, all Demosthenes; and P. Gen. 2.1 (inv. 256; see M–P³ 5), Aeschines. [Parsons notes that $\overset{\theta}{\omega}$ and its companion $\overset{\delta}{\omega}$ continue to appear in the mediaeval tradition of Demosthenes, e.g. in cod. A (D. M. MacDowell, *Demosthenes Against Meidias* (1990) 71–2); see in general M. R. Dilts, *Aeschinis Orationes* (1997) p. xx with n. 17. $\overset{\delta}{\omega}$ clearly represents $\hat{\omega}$ δ(ικαςταί), $\overset{\theta}{\omega}$ presumably ὠθηναῖοι: ἄνδρες is bypassed as common to both.]

αθηναιοι ποιηcαι S$^{\gamma\rho}$, but the verb was not present here.

τ[ω(ν): τ[ων would extend further to the right than any other line, and we guess that it was written as τῶ, a typical abbreviation though not one attested elsewhere in **5149**. However, the line ends in general exhibit a fair range of irregularity.

N. KARAPANAGIOTI / P. J. PARSONS

5150. [DEMOSTHENES] XXV 50–51, 68–71

fr. 1 34 4B.78/D(4–7)a	4.4 × 8.7 cm	First century
fr. 2 33 4B.79/G(1–2)a	10 × 10.7 cm	

Two fragments from the same season, boxed separately but presumably from the same roll, since the hand, the letter-size, the line-spacing, and the column-width are all very similar. Fr. 1 consists of two pieces from a single column; (*a*) provides the first three words of line 9, and (*b*) the remains of the last surviving letters of the same line. Fr. 2 contains the lower part of a column, with one trace of that preceding and some line-beginnings from that following. The edge of a *kollesis* can be seen *c*.3.5 cm from the left-hand edge; the overlap was of *c*.2.5 cm. The backs are blank.

There were between 24 and 28 letters to a line, with a column-width of *c*.6 cm. The intercolumnium measures *c*.1 cm, the lower margin *c*.2 cm. If the beginnings of fr. 2 col. iii are rightly identified, 8 or 9 lines are lost at its top, making a column height of 23 or 24 lines or *c*.14 cm, roll height 18 cm if the top margin equalled the lower.

The hand is a small neat example of the gawky type assignable to the first century AD (compare P. Lond. II 354 = *GLH* 9a, Cavallo–Maehler, *Hellenistic Bookhands* 88, of 7–4 BC; II **246** = *GLH* 10c, *HB* 96, of AD 66). The letters are roughly 2–3 mm square; the interlinear spaces measure about 4 mm. ᴀ sometimes sharp-nosed, sometimes rounded; ʙ bean-shaped; ε with cross-bar detached; κ once as a vertical followed by a c-shaped curve. Some ligatures: note especially ων, where a single stroke serves as both the final curve of ω and the first upright of ɴ; μαν fr. 2 ii 7, where the back oblique of ᴀ serves as the first upright of ɴ.

There are no signs of punctuation, accents or corrections (correction *currente calamo* fr. 2 ii 2). Iota adscript is written correctly where needed (fr. 1.10). ει for ι fr.1.13, fr. 2 ii 6 (γεινομενα), 11. Unmarked elision in fr. 2 ii 6 (and in fr. 1.9 if rightly reconstructed); *scriptio plena* in fr. 2 ii 4, 8.

Substantial new variants in fr. 2 ii 5–7, 14, iii 6.

Fr. 1 was first identified and edited by Dr M. Maehler; since then the original has been re-examined and its two constituent fragments realigned. Fr. 2 was identi-

fied as part of the same roll by Dr W. B. Henry. The combined version here printed
is the responsibility of Prof. P. J. Parsons.

Fr. 1

   . . . .

(*a*)   ].[

   πα]ντων κ[ακωι π]ε[φ]υκω[ς και προδη

   λος] ων οτι τοιου[τ]ος εστ[ι τωι βιωι

   σκο]πειτ[ε] γαρ εισιν ομου [δισμυριοι   §51

 5 παντε]ς αθηναιοι τουτ[ων εκαστος

   . . . . πρατ]των κατα την α[γοραν

   περιερχετα]ι ητοι νη τον [ηρακλεα

   των κοινων η] των ιδιω[ν αλλ ουχ

(*b*) ουτος ουδεν ουδ αν [εχοι δειξαι

 10 προς οτωι τον βιο[ν εστι των με

   τρι]ων η των καλω[ν ουχι των πολι

   τικων αγαθων ε[π ουδενι την

   ψυ]χην διατρειβ[ει ου τεχνης ου γε

   ωρ]γιας ουκ αλλης [εργασιας ουδεμι

 15 ας] ε[πι]μελ[ει]ται ο[υ φιλανθρωπιας

   . . . .

Fr. 2
Col. i   Col. ii

         . . . . . .

      ...[*c.*2].[*c.*8]......[(§68)

      των απαλλαγηνα[ι] αλλα ⟦τ⟧δια τι υμιν

      ουτος ευνους εστιν οτι φησιν αναι

      δης ο δε αναιδης εκ τινος ωνομασθη

  5   προς διος και των αλλων θεων ουκ εκ του

      καν τα μητ οντα μητε γεινομενα

      μητε γενησομενα τολμαν λεγειν

      δια αναισχυντιαν οπερ ουτος ποιει

      ηγουμαι τοινυν και περι της ενδει   §69

 10   ξεως α μοι παραλιπειν εδοξ..

      λυκουργος βελτειον ειναι προς

      υμας ειπειν εγω γαρ οιμαι δειν υμας

      ως[π]ερ αν ει χρεος εσκοπειτο ιδιον

      ουτως εξ]ετασαι τουτον και.....

 15].   τουτουι του αγωνος δικαια [..]

Col. iii

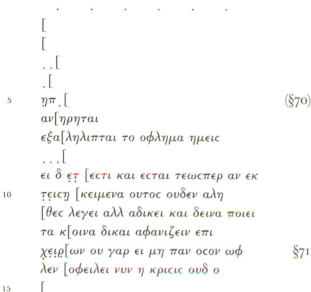

· · · · · ·

```
          [
          [
        . . [
        . [
5       ηπ . [                                    (§70)
        αν[ηρηται
        εξα[ληλιπται το οφλημα ημεις
        . . . [
        ει δ ετ [εcτι και εcται τεωcπερ αν εκ
10      τειcη [κειμενα ουτοc ουδεν αλη
        [θεc λεγει αλλ αδικει και δεινα ποιει
        τα κ[οινα δικαι αφανιζειν επι
        χειρ[ων ου γαρ ει μη παν οcον ωφ        §71
        λεν [οφειλει νυν η κριcιc ουδ ο
15      [
```

Fr. 1

6 ἕν γέ τι πράττων codd. εν γε τι is quite a tight fit at the beginning of the line, but possible. Alternatively the scribe may have written εν at the end of 5, or omitted γε.

8–9 αλλ ουχ] | ουτοc: this division seems unavoidable, if the lineation is rightly reconstructed, but normal orthography would require αλλ ου|χ ουτοc. Perhaps the scribe wrote ουχι, but that too (before a vowel) would be anomalous.

9 οὐδ' ἄν om. S.

11 των καλω[ν: καλῶν codd. (except that O has τῶν καλῶν, with the papyrus, according to Dindorf 1846).

12–13 [την | ψυ]χην: so AFY^c: τῇ ψυχῇ SY^a, with which compare e.g. Isocr. *Archid.* 85 ταῖc ψυ-χαῖc διατρίβειν. The corrupt accusative could be the result of an expectation that the verb following should have a direct object.

Fr. 2
Col. i

15]., curving trace like the right-hand side of omega.

Col. ii

2 [[τ]] with a deletion dot above, and partly covered by the replacement δ. The scribe apparently skipped δια (by parablepsy, or as unnecessary to the sense) and began to write τι, but caught himself in time.

2–3 υμιν ουτοc ευνουc εcτιν: so SY: εὔνουc οὗτόc ἐcτιν ὑμῖν A: ὑμῖν οὗτόc ἐcτιν εὔνουc F. Weil deleted the whole phrase.

3–4 αναιδηc: ἀναιδήc ἐcτιν codd. ἐcτιν would be easily omitted, or easily interpolated. Compare **5148** i 10 n.

4–7 The manuscripts have ἐκ τίνοc ὠνομάcθη τῶν ἄλλων ἀλλ' ἢ ὅταν τὰ (τὰ om. Y^c) μήτ' ὄντα μήτ' ἂν γενόμενα (μήτ' ἂν γενηcόμενα add. AY), ταῦτα τολμᾷ λέγειν δι' ἀναιcχυντίαν ὅπερ οὗτοc ποιεῖ; As a parallel for the construction, Schaefer cited XXIII 62 τί γὰρ ἄλλ' ἐcτὶν τὸ μεταποιεῖν ἢ ὅταν . . . ; τί δ' ἄλλο τὸ cυγχεῖν ἢ ὅταν . . . ; That however does not explain τῶν ἄλλων, which presumably means 'from what cause other than when . . .'.

The papyrus offers a quite different structure: ἐκ τίνος ὠνομάcθη, πρὸς Διὸς καὶ τῶν ἄλλων θεῶν; οὐκ ἐκ τοῦ κᾶν τὰ μήτ' ὄντα μήτε γεινόμενα μήτε γενηcόμενα τολμᾶν λέγειν δι' ἀναιcχυντίαν, ὅπερ οὗτος ποιεῖ;

Of the elements here, TLG produces no example of πρὸς Διὸς καὶ τῶν ἄλλων θεῶν; πρὸς τοῦ Διὸς καὶ τῶν ἄλλων θεῶν Aeschin. *In Tim.* 70, *In Ctes.* 156. This speech has νὴ τὸν Δία καὶ θεοὺς at §65; Demosthenes himself uses μὰ τὸν Δία καὶ τοὺς ἄλλους θεούς (IX 54), and elsewhere νὴ τὸν Δία καὶ πάντας θεοὺς / θεοὺς ἄπαντας. Syntactically, the oath might reinforce the initial question ἐκ τίνος ὠνομάcθη, or the answer (itself a rhetorical question) which follows. Dr Henry argues convincingly for the former, since in similar structures the answering question tends to begin with the negative: he compares Dem. XVIII 119, with Wankel ad loc., and LV 18, where πρὸς θεῶν can only belong to the preceding clause.

μήτ' ὄντα μήτε γεινόμενα μήτε γενηcόμενα as it stands produces an unexpected asymmetry of terms, 'what is', 'what is coming to be', 'what will be'. The expected triad of present, past and future would require γενόμενα, and perhaps the scribe intended this (the same form of words Ps.-Archytas p. 32.13); γ(ε)ινόμενα for γιγνόμενα would represent a really vulgar spelling.

The version of the papyrus is simpler and clearer than that of the MSS. If this long version is original, the shorter perhaps arose from damage to a common archetype; if the shorter is original, the longer may represent an attempt to clarify τῶν ἄλλων ἀλλ' ἢ ὅταν.

10 παραλιπειν: so FᶜY: παραλείπειν SA: περιλιπεῖν Fᵃ (misprinted παρα- in Dilts's OCT).

εδοξ . . : perhaps εδοξεν (the traces are spaced too widely for εδοξε alone), but there is unexplained ink on what should be the right-hand upright of nu.

12 εγω: so SAY: ἐγὼ μὲν F.

13 χρεος: so SFᶜY: χρέως AFᵃ. Later grammarians regard -ως as the Attic form (Phryn. 371 etc). εσκοπειτο: ἐσκοπεῖτε codd., rightly.

14 εξ]ετασαι: so SYF: ἐξετάζειν A.

και . . . . . : καὶ τὰ codd., but the papyrus had more letters. Perhaps ταυτα, i.e. ταὐτὰ, if that could mean anything suitable to the context.

15 δικαια [. .]: the final alpha is large, and perhaps its extended tail filled the rest of the line. Alternatively there might just be room for the next word, [ει].

Col. iii

Supplements from the standard text simply to test line-length.

5 ηπ . [: we expect η πα[ρα τη θεω κειμενη ει μεν ουν, but the trace does not suit ⋏.

6 ἀνήρηται ταῦτα καὶ codd., which leaves *c*.10 letters unaccounted for. One possibility: the papyrus added a noun to ταῦτα, e.g. τὰ γράμματα, τὰ cυνθέματα.

7 εξα[ληλιπται: so S: ἐξήλειπται F.

8 We expect ληρουμεν μαλλον δε ψευδομεθα, but I cannot find a fit in the traces.

13–14 ωφ]|λεν: this division of syllables runs against the normal assumption that *muta cum liquida* (especially such combinations as can begin a word) cohere, so that ω|φλεν would be expected. There are occasional apparent exceptions, but probably the papyrus actually wrote ωφει]|λεν.

M. MAEHLER / P. J. PARSONS

5151. Demosthenes XXX (*contra Onetorem I*) 39

6153/7(lit.)   4.7 × 5.2 cm   Second century
                                                                              Plate I

A scrap of a roll giving the end of the speech and, centred underneath, the title with stichometric total. The hand is that of LXI **4107** (Thucydides VII), and as expected, a line is of approximately the same length (4.9 cm in **4107**, about 5.0–5.1 cm in **5151**) and holds approximately the same number of characters (17–19 in **4107**, 16–18 in **5151**) in both rolls: see Johnson, *Bookrolls and Scribes* 33–4. A nearly perpendicular right-hand margin is obtained by the use of smaller letters at line-end (3) and of >-shaped fillers (2, 4 (supplied)); the latter also appear in **4107** (ii 4, 6, 8). A diaeresis is applied to an initial ι, and a low point marks a minor pause (3); both are due to the scribe. The column is the last of the speech, but the second speech against Onetor may well have followed (cf. 6–7 n.): the blank space to the right of the column was at least 1 cm wide, while the intercolumnium in **4107** is 1.6–1.7 cm wide.

The appearance of a final stichometric count in a copy of a prose text from Egypt appears to be a novelty, but many examples are already known from the Herculaneum papyri: see e.g. D. Obbink, *Philodemus On Piety: Part 1* (1996) 62–3; R. Janko, *Philodemus On Poems: Books 3–4* (2011) 198–207.

Only one other papyrus of this speech has been published, P. Berol. 17067, a third-century papyrus codex leaf from Hermopolis containing XXIX 60 and XXX 1 (ed. W. Brashear, *APF* 40 (1994) 25–7).

```
           ·      ·    ·
        απο]δουναι το αρ
      γυριον κα]ι εκ των αλ>
      λων απα]ντων· ϊκανως [
      αποδ]εδ[ε]ιχθαι μοι νο[>
   5  μιζ]ω
        π]ρος ονητορα
          εξο]υλης· ā
             ]ΔΔΔ[
             ] [
       ·      ·    ·
```

1–2 *το αρ[γυριον* as in S and A. Dilts prints τἀργύριον.

4 *μοι* om. S.

6–7 The subscription is given as in S. F has *KATA ONHTOPOC EΞOYΛHC A'*; A does not have the subscription. The decoration preserved in this copy appears to be limited to a short stroke under the final letter of the first line and a dot above the c in the second.

The absence of the author's name, as in **5152**, may be an indication that the roll held more than one speech of Demosthenes: cf. Johnson, *Bookrolls and Scribes* 143; F. Schironi, τὸ μέγα βιβλίον: *Book-Ends, End-Titles, and* Coronides *in Papyri with Hexameter Poetry* (2010) 65–8.

8 No stichometry is otherwise preserved for this speech. The stichometric indications presented by the mediaeval manuscripts in the other private speeches imply in nearly all cases an average stichos-length of 34–5 letters, though there are exceptions, not clearly relevant to the present speech: the figure for XLVIII is about 28.6, and that for LIX about 32. (The transmitted stichometric total for XLIII would imply a higher figure, about 35.6, but has been suspected.) The letter-count for this speech is approximately 12,340. If we assume as the basis for the stichometric count a stichos between 34 and 35 letters long, the stichometric total will lie between 352 and 363; but the preserved sequence of three deltas will not accommodate a figure in this range. If we take the basis to have been a stichos 32 letters long, the total will be 385. *HHHΓ*]*ΔΔΔ*[*Π* is compatible with the preserved letters, but it would not be perfectly centred, even if up to four iotas were added on the right (for 386–9). A better solution is to assume a stichos of *c*.36 letters (= *c*.2 lines of **5151**), such as we regularly find in the public speeches. 12,340 letters will then occupy about 343 stichoi. If written as *HHH*]*ΔΔΔ*[*ΔΙΙΙ*, the figure will have been centred in the column.

The set of copies to which the stichometric indications in the mediaeval manuscripts go back is unlikely to have employed in this speech a different stichometric basis from that used in the other private speeches (including XXXI), and it seems safe to assume that the stichometric total given there was approximately 352–63. But there may not have been only one stichometry in use in ancient manuscripts of Demosthenes. In XIX, SFQ all give the same figure for the stichometric total, but the marginal stichometric figures in FQ imply a shorter stichos-length than those in S and may go back to a copy where a different stichometric basis was applied: see D. M. MacDowell, *Demosthenes On the False Embassy* (2000) 36–8. On the stichometry in Demosthenes manuscripts, cf. Fr. Burger, *Stichometrische Untersuchungen zu Demosthenes und Herodot* (1892); E. Drerup, *JKPh* Supp. 24 (1898) 235–7; id., *Philol.* Supp. 7 (1899) 536 n. 1; in general on stichometry, F. G. Lang, *NT* 41 (1999) 40–57.

W. B. HENRY

5152. [DEMOSTHENES] XXXIV (*CONTRA PHORMIONEM*) 49–END

57/122/1   24 × 16 cm   Second/third century

This fragment contains, on the verso of accounts and upside down in relation to them, the last two columns of the speech, very badly rubbed, and 7.5 cm of blank papyrus to their right (11 cm if the lower right-hand corner is included). The lines had an average of 20 letters; the columns, of 23 lines, measured 6.5 × 12.5 cm and were 1.5 cm apart, with a margin of 1.5 cm at the head and 1.5 cm at the foot. The whole speech would have occupied about 3 m of papyrus.

The hand resembles that of XXXI **2539** (pl. II, Dictys); for dated parallels see *GLH* 17a (Commentary on Thucydides, mid-II AD), 18b (Favorinus, later than AD 191), 20b (Edict, AD 206). Punctuation and iota adscript are lacking. ει for ι ii 10.

5152 is the third known papyrus of speech XXXIV, which is also transmitted by P. Köln IV 184 (of the first half of the 3rd cent.), §§3–5, and P. Grenf. II 10 (= Hausmann XL, of the 2nd cent.), §§5–7.

Col. i

παρ υμιν μ[ηδα]μως ω αν   §50
δρες δικαστ[αι] υμεις γαρ ες
θ] οι αυτοι οι τ[ον] επ[ι]δανεισα
μενον εκ τ[ου] εμποριου πολ
5   λ]α χρηματα κ[α]ι τοις δανεισ
ταις παρασχοντα τας υπο
θηκας θανατω ζημιωσαν
τες εισαγγελθεντα εν τω
δημω και ταυτα πολιτην
10   υμε[τ]ερον οντα και πατρος
ε[c]τρ[α]τη⟨γη⟩κοτος ηγεισθε γαρ   §51
τους τοιουτους ου μονον
τ]ους εντυγχανοντας [α
δικειν αλλα και κοινη βλα
15   πτε[ι]ν το εμποριον υμων
εικοτως [α]ι γ[α]ρ [ε.]ποριαι τοις
ε[ρ]γαζομενο[ι]ς ουκ απο των
δανειζομενων αλλ απο των
δαν]ειζοντ[ω]ν εισ[ι]ν και
20   ουτε] ναυν ο⟨υ⟩τ[ε] ναυ[κ]λ[η]ρον
ουτ επ]ιβατη[ν] εστιν [αν]α
χθην]α[ι] το των δα[νε]ι
ζοντων] μερος εαν [α]φαι

Col. ii

ρεθη εν μεν ουν τοις νομοις   §52
πολλ[αι] και καλαι βοηθ[ε]ι[αι
εισιν [α]υτοις υμας δε [δει] cυν
επανορθουντας φαινεcθαι
5   και μη cυνχωρουντας
τοις πομηροις ιν υμιν ως
πλειστη εμπορια π[ε]ρι το
εμποριον η εσται δ[ε] εαν
διαφυλατ[τ]ητε τους τα ε
10   αυτων προειεμενους και
μη ε[π]ιτρεπητε αδικε[ι]cθαι
υ]πο τοιουτων θηρι[ω]ν ε
γ]ω μεν ουν οcαπε[ρ] οιος .

   ην ειρ[η]κα{ι} καλω δε και λα

15 λον τινα των φιλω[ν

   εα[ν] κελευητε

    ‾προς την‾

    ‾παραγραφην‾

    ‾την φορμ[ι]ωνος‾

As will be evident from the transcript, much less could be made of the text if it were unknown.

Col. i

  3 οἱ αὐτοί Π SF: om. A, del. Blass: οἱ del. Rennie.

  3–4 ἐπιδανεισάμενον Π A: ἐπιδεδανεισμένον SF.

  6 παρασχοντα Π: οὐ παρασχόντα codd.

  15 ὑμῶν Π SF: ἡμῶν A.

  16 [ε.]ποριαι Π: εὐπορίαι A: ἐμπορίαι SF. Cf. ii 7.

  17 An unprejudiced eye would have read γαζ as νοι.

Col. ii

  1 -ρεθῆ Π AF: -ρῆτε S.

  5–6 cυγχωροῦντας τοῖς πονηροῖς Π (-μη- apparently a simple mistake for νη) SF: τοῖς πονηροῖς cυγχωροῦντας A.

  7 εμπορια Π: εὐπορία A: ὠφέλεια SF. The reading of Π is not necessarily an anticipation of ἐμπόριον in the next line: cf. the variants at i 16.

   περί Π SAF: παρά edd. (corr. Aldina).

  8 εμποριον: ριον apparently in thicker ink, or re-inked, with a short blank before and after. The blanks perhaps avoid flaws in the writing surface (similarly in 12, between ο and υ of τοιουτων).

  9 διαφυλάττητε Π SA: φυλάττητε F.

  12 τοιούτων Π A: τῶν τοιούτων SF.

  13 οιος does not account for all the traces at the line-end, one of which may belong to something superscript: οἱός τ(ε) codd.

  14–15 λα|λον: ἄλλον codd., no doubt rightly, though λάλον would give the sentence a frankness and informality all too rare in forensic speeches.

  17–19 The end title is given differently in the mediaeval tradition: ΥΠΕΡ ΧΡΥCΙΠΠΟΥ ΠΡΟC ΤΗΝ ΦΟΡΜΙΩΝΟC ΠΑΡΑΓΡΑΦΗ S (misreported in Dilts's OCT): ΠΡΟC ΦΟΡΜΙΩΝΑ ΥΠΕΡ ΔΑΝΕΙΟΥ AF. The author's name is omitted: see **5151** 6–7 n.

Alongside the subscription remains of an unpretentious coronis, which may have continued above if its mid-point marked the end of the text proper, as expected. Another ornament of uncertain design appears to have descended from the right of 19 to a point level with the bottom of the previous column. The end-title was set off by horizontal strokes (some now obliterated) above and below the line-beginnings and line-ends.

M. D. REEVE

5153–8. Plutarch, *Moralia*

These six items, all dated on palaeographical grounds to the second or third centuries, offer primary evidence of the circulation of Plutarch's works in Graeco-Roman Egypt, a province which indeed he himself once visited (*Mor.* 678c shows him leaving Alexandria). If we omit works conjecturally attributed to Plutarch (XXXIV **2688–9**, P. Lond. Lit. 175), we have now fourteen witnesses, of which eight certainly (and one probably) come from Oxyrhynchus:

Moralia

5153	75A–C	*de profectibus in virtute*	II papyrus roll	Oxyrhynchus
5154	139E–140D	*coniugalia praecepta*	III papyrus roll	Oxyrhynchus
LII **3685** M–P³ 1431.1	155C–D	*septem sapientium convivium*	II, first half papyrus roll	Oxyrhynchus
5155	191E–F	*regum et imperatorum apophthegmata*	III/IV papyrus roll	Oxyrhynchus
PSI inv. 565 M–P³ 1432.001	452F	*de cohibenda ira*	II, first half papyrus roll	?
P. Harrauer 1 M–P³ 1432.01	456F–457B	*de cohibenda ira*	V parchment codex	?
PSI inv. 2055 (probably same roll as **5156**) M–P³ 1431.11	660D, 661D	*quaestiones convivales* iv	II papyrus roll	Oxyrhynchus?
5156 (probably same roll as PSI inv. 2055)	660C, 661B–C	*quaestiones convivales* iv	II papyrus roll	Oxyrhynchus
P. Laur. inv. III/543A M–P³ 1431.12	715D	*quaestiones convivales* vii	II papyrus roll	Oxyrhynchus?
5157	732E–F	*quaestiones convivales* viii	II papyrus roll	Oxyrhynchus

| P. Ant. II 85 + III 213 M–P³ 1432 | 890E etc. | *epitome de placitis philosophorum* | III papyrus codex | Antinoe |
| **5158** | 963D | *de sollertia animalium* | III papyrus roll | Oxyrhynchus |

VITAE

LII **3684** M–P³ 1429.1	*Lycurgus* 31		III papyrus roll	Oxyrhynchus
P. Heid. I 209 M–P³ 1430	*Pelopidas* 7		II papyrus roll	?
P. Köln I 47 etc. M–P³ 1431	*Caesar*		III papyrus roll	Panopolis?

Palaeographical datings must always be taken with a pinch of salt. Nevertheless, it is interesting that 12 out of 14 published papyri are assigned to the second and third centuries AD (and another to the third/fourth), and five of them (**5153**, PSI inv. 2055 + **5156**, **5157**, PSI inv. 565, **3685**) not long after the author's death. This suggests an early popularity, continuing into the third century, and then a slump more distinct even than what would be expected from the general survival rate. The works attested include two normally thought spurious (*regum et imperatorum apophthegmata*, *epitome de placitis philosophorum*); and two not included in the 'Catalogue' of Lamprias (*de cohibenda ira*; *quaestiones convivales*). For a general account of the early reception of Plutarch, see R. Hirzel, *Plutarch* (1912) 74–82.

The new pieces offer points of textual interest. (*a*) New readings, all right or plausible: **5153** i 4–5 adds εκα[cτην, 10 reads περικειμενη (confirming conjecture), ii 5–10 [ει] . . . γιγνώc[κ]ουcιν for ἄν . . . γιγνώcκωcι; **5155** ii 14 perhaps -ιτ- (confirming conjecture), 25 αυτα for αὐτόc (confirming conjecture); **5156** fr. 1.3 τηρε[ι for ποιεῖ, PSI inv. 2055 fr. 1.2–3 γευομενον for δεόμενον, fr. 2.2–3 cυνκαταθεcιc for κατάθεcιc (confirming conjecture), 5 ινα δε μη for εἰ δὲ μὴ (emended to εἰ δὲ δή). By contrast, **5154** fr. 4.5 κοινωc looks like simple error. (*b*) Agreements with the indirect tradition: **5154** fr. 4.3 το ουκ εμ[ον (Stobaeus) for οὐκ ἐμόν (codd.); **5158** two agreements with Porphyry against the MSS. The new variants in **5156** and PSI inv. 2055 have a special interest, since the mediaeval manuscript transmission of *Quaestiones convivales* can be traced back to a distinct archetype: Vindobonensis phil. gr. 148 (designated T), of the first half of the eleventh century.

The new papyri have been collated with the most recent Teubner editions. We have also consulted the Budé and Loeb editions; the two editions of G. N. Bernardakis (*editio minor*, Teubner 1888–96; *editio maior* brought to publication by P. D. Bernardakis and H. G. Ingenkamp, Academy of Athens, 2008–); and the individual editions in the Corpus Plutarchi Moralium series (for **5153–4** and **5156**: *De profectibus* ed. E. Valgiglio, 1989; *Coniugalia praecepta* ed. G. Martano and A. Tirelli, 1990; *Quaest. conv. IV* ed. A. M. Scarcella, 2001).

J. H. BRUSUELAS / P. J. PARSONS

5153. PLUTARCH, *MORALIA* 75A–C (*DE PROFECTIBUS IN VIRTUTE*)

112/48   13.0 × 11.8 cm   Second century
                                                                        Plate IV

Tops of two columns, with an upper margin of *c.*5.5 cm and intercolumnium of *c.*2.5 cm. Lines of 15–18 letters (*c.*5.5 cm), columns of *c.*28 lines (*c.*14 cm). The back is blank.

The copyist writes an elegant script of the 'Roman Uncial' type, bilinear except for φ, the base-line emphasised by regular serifs, the upper line by occasional ligatures; he maintains a certain regularity of line-ends by writing the last letter small (i 1, 7, 12) or by adding space-fillers (double, ii 10). No lectional signs except diaeresis (i 8); *scriptio plena* i 8, elision unmarked ii 4; iota adscript as required in i 9?, ii 12.

The text of *de profectibus* begins with the first line of col. i. There is no sign of a title above that; any such will have come at the end of the work, and possibly also to the left of col. i. The whole treatise would have taken *c.*60 columns in this format, *c.*4.8 m. of papyrus.

5153 offers unique variants in i 4–5, in i 10 (confirming a conjecture), and in ii 10.

Col. i   Col. ii

```
     τι]ς των λογων ω coc              τιαν εξιν εγγενεςθα[ι
     ci]ε cενεκιων cωcει               πανταπαcι του cωμ[α
     τη]ν αυτου βελτιουμε      75B     τος αναρρωςθεν[τος
     . . .] προς αρετην εκα            αλλ ωςπερ εν το[υτοις      75C
5    . . . .] ςυναιςθη[ς]ιν ει     5   ου προκοπτουςιν [ει προ
     μηδ]εμιαν αι πρ[ο]κο             κοπτοντες ανε[ςει
     παι] ποιουςι της αφρο            του βαρυνοντος οι[ον
     cυ]νης ανεcιν α[λ]λα ï           επι ζυγ[ο]υ προς τουνα[ν
     cωι] cταθμωι παcιν               τιον αναφερο[μ]ενο[ι μη
10   η κακ]ια περικειμενη     10      γιγνωс[κ]ουςιν την 〉〉
     μολυβ]διc ωcτε [δι]κτυ           μεταβολην ουτωc εν [
     ον κατ]εcπαcεν [ο]υδε            τ]ωι φιλοcοφειν ουτε
     γαρ ε]ν μουcικ[οιc               τινα πρ]οκοπην ουτε
```

].[προκο]πης [αις]θηςιν
    15   υποληπ]τεο[ν ει] μηθεν
                                  η ψυχη] με[θιηςι]ν μη
                                  δε απο]καθ[αιρεται τ]ης
                                  αβελτερι]ας α[λλ αχρι τ]ου
                                  λαβειν τ]ο.[
                                      .   .   .   .

Col. i

3–5 τη]ν αυτου βελτιουμε|[...] προς αρετην εκα|[....] ϲυναιϲθη[ϲ]ιν: τὴν αὑτοῦ βελτιουμένου πρὸς ἀρετὴν ϲυναίϲθηϲιν codd., except βελτιουμένου τινός Κ¹, βελτιουμένην τινός Κ² J. **5153** apparently had βελτιουμε|[νην or -|[νου in 3–4, and then uniquely added εκα|[ϲτην or εκα|[ϲτου before ϲυναίϲθηϲιν. Sense seems to require βελτιουμενου; then εκα|[ϲτην would add a practical touch, since improvement in each virtue separately is certainly easier to monitor than improvement in virtue as a totality.

10 περικειμενη: περιθεμένη codd. **5153** confirms the conjecture of Babbitt, where most editors print περι⟨τι⟩θεμένη (Emperius).

Col. ii

10 Unexplained ink in the left-hand margin.

γιγνωϲ[κ]ουϲιν: γιγνώϲκωϲι codd. The indicative requires us to supply ει in 5, replacing ἄν of codd.

11–12 εν | [τ]ωι φιλοϲοφειν: so GxC²D: ἐν τοῖϲ φιλοϲοφεῖν cett. (ἐν τοῖϲ φιλοϲοφεῖν ἐπαγγελλομένοιϲ FqM mg. a²AΘN mg. S).

15 υποληπ]τεο[ν: so xC²D: ἀποληπτέον W: ἀπολειπτέον cett. The last seems less well suited to the space.

17 δε (*scriptio plena*) suggested by the spacing.

19 τ]ο.[: τὸ ἄκρον codd., except ἄκρατον τὸ D. Of]ο we have only the upper right-hand arc; the next trace is indeterminate. But it seems likely that **5153** shared the majority reading.

                                          P. J. PARSONS / W. B. HENRY

5154. PLUTARCH, *MORALIA* 139E–140D (*CONIUGALIA PRAECEPTA*)

88/187(a)   fr. 1 3.5 × 5.5 cm   Third century

Four fragments from a roll (back blank). Upper margin preserved to 2.5 cm, intercolumnium 2 cm. Frr. 2, 3 and 4 all have upper margins; if they represent successive columns, the column had *c.*32 lines, with a width of *c.*8.5 cm and a height of *c.*17.5 cm. In this format the whole treatise would occupy *c.*30 columns, 3 m. of papyrus. The hand is a well-executed Severe Style, of classic type, comparable with II **223** (*GLH* 21a) and assignable to the third century. No lectional signs, except the diaeresis in fr. 2.4 and the circumflex on fr. 2.5 παιδιᾶϲ; punctuation by paragraphus (fr. 1 ii 7/8), and stops high above the line, i.e. added later (frr. 2.3, 3.5). No evidence for the treatment of elision or iota adscript.

Substantial corrections, perhaps by the first hand, at fr. 1 ii 8 and fr. 2.4. The unique variant κοινως for κοινοῖϲ (fr. 4.5) will be another error of copying, by false anticipation of the following ὡϲ. At fr. 4.3 the papyrus preserves a correct reading known only from the indirect tradition.

Fr. 1

Col. i   Col. ii

       .   .   .   .   .   .

```
                         .].[
                         οφ[ελοϲ ουδεν εϲτιν ει μη
                         δε[ικνυϲι την μορφην ο
                         μο[ιαν ουτωϲ ουδε πλουϲιαϲ      139F
  5      ]ρ.        5    γα[μετηϲ ονηϲιϲ ει μη παρε
         ].ι             χο[ι τον βιον ομοιον τω αν
         ].[]α           δρ[ι και ϲυμφωνον το ηθοϲ
         ]..             ει χαιρ[οντοϲ μεν εικονα ϲκυθρω
                         πη[ν
```

       .   .   .   .   .   .

Fr. 2

```
     ϲαϲ μετ [αυτων διδαϲκουϲιν               (140A)
     ενπιμπ[λαϲθαι μοναϲ γενο
     μεναϲ· ο[υτωϲ οι μη ϲυνοντεϲ
     [[ε]]ϊλαρωϲ τ[αιϲ γυναιξι μηδε
  5  παιδιᾶϲ κ[οινωνουντεϲ αυταιϲ
     και γελω[τοϲ ιδιαϲ ηδοναϲ χω
     ριϲ αυτω[ν ζητειν διδαϲκουϲιν
     το]ιϲ [των Περϲων βαϲιλευ
```

       .   .   .   .   .   .

Fr. 3

```
      φιλαθλ]ηται γυμν[αϲτικουϲ            140C
      ουτωϲ ανη]ρ φιλοϲωμα[τοϲ καλ
      λωπιϲτρι]αν γυναικ[α ποι
      ει φιληδο]νοϲ εταιρικ[ην και
  5   ακολαϲτο]ν· φιλαγαθοϲ [και
      φιλοκαλο]ϲ ϲωφρονα κα[ι κοϲ
      μιαν Λακαινα] παιδιϲκη [πυνθανο
      μενου τινοϲ ει] ηδη αν[δρι προϲ
```

       .   .   .   .   .

Fr. 4

$\qquad$ ευδαι]μο̣ν̣[α και μα $\qquad$ (140D)

καρια]ν̣ [ει]ναι πολ[ιν εν η το

εμο]ν̣ και το ουκ εμ̣[ον ηκιϲτα

φθε]γγομενων α̣[κουουϲι

5   δια το] κοινωϲ ωϲ ε[νι μαλι

ϲτα χρ]ηϲθαι τοιϲ αξ̣[ιοιϲ ϲπου

δηϲ τουϲ] πολιτα[ϲ πολυ δε

μαλλον εκ] γαμου δ̣[ει

.   .   .   .   .

Fr. 1 Col. i

We have not managed to place these line-ends. In 8] ̣ ̣, the first trace is part of a rising oblique or arc at upper level, the second the top of an upright,]ε̣ι̣ acceptable.

Col. ii

1 Calculation shows that this is near the top of the column next before fr. 2.

2 ἐϲτιν om. vΠ, according to Martano–Tirelli.

5–6 παρε]|χο[ι: so OJΘ and Stob. 4.22.135: παρέχει cett.

8 ει χαιρ[οντοϲ: so codd. Thus the new sentence, which elaborates the simile of the mirror, begins in asyndeton. Some editors have found this objectionable, and the Teubner prints εἰ ⟨γάρ⟩ (Sieveking). In **5154** the copyist began with χαρ; later ι was squeezed in after α, and ει added in the left margin, slightly out of alignment.

Fr. 2

1 In the left-hand margin a dot, too heavy to be accidental: to help alignment, or mark a difficulty?

με̣τ̣ [αυτων: Π has καὶ πινούϲαϲ before this phrase, and Zb after, where the papyrus has no room for it.

4 The scribe first wrote ειγαρωϲ, then crossed out ε, added diaeresis on ι, and converted γ to λ by adding the right-hand oblique.

5 παιδιᾶϲ: the accent distinguishes the genitive of παιδιά from that of παιδ(ε)ία.

Fr. 3

4 εταιρικ[ην: so codd., Apostol. 12.53g: ἐρωτικήν Stob. 4.28.10, Apostol. 2.100c.

6 φιλοκαλο]ϲ: after]ϲ unexplained ink, a short oblique trace at line-level. Perhaps a separator to mark the pause between the double subject and the double object, but nothing similar can be seen in 4.

7 These supplements from the transmitted text make a rather long line. It may be that the papyrus had a shorter version, e.g. [πυθο-.

8 α̣ν̣[δρι: the traces would not fit Platt's conjecture τἀνδρί.

Fr. 4

3 το ουκ: so rightly Stob. 4.23.43, Apostol. 12.97g: τὸ om. codd.

5 κοινωϲ: κοινοῖϲ codd. Stob (κοινῆϲ compend. A) Apostol.

8 εκ] γαμου: so rightly codd.: ἐν γάμῳ Stob. Apostol.

P. J. PARSONS / W. B. HENRY

5155. Plutarch, *Moralia* 191e–f (*regum et imperatorum apophthegmata*)

104/6(f)   6.4 × 19 cm   Third/fourth century

Two fragments and a scrap from a book-roll; writing with the fibres, back blank. The fragments join to give the upper part of a single column, with parts of 25 lines; top margin preserved to 4 cm, left-hand margin (intercolumnium) to 2 cm. The line originally measured *c*.6.5–7.0 cm (*c*.20 letters); if the suggested reconstruction of col. i is correct, the column originally measured *c*.19.5 cm (31 lines). On this scale, the whole work would have occupied 145 columns, a length of 12.5 m. To the left a heavy *kollesis*, and a few line-ends from the preceding column. The scribe writes a rather slack Severe Style, assignable to the third century or even later. Iota adscript correctly in ii 7 and 16; diaeresis on initial iota and upsilon (ii 23, 24). No lectional signs except a divider-mark below the beginnings of ii 2, 7, 14 and 21. This divider takes the form of a wide shallow curve, like a hyphen, joining an oblique that slopes sharply down into the left-hand margin: apparently a florid variant of the diple obelismene, for which see R. Barbis, *Pap. Congr. XVIII* (1988) ii 473–6; K. McNamee, *Sigla and Select Marginalia* (1992) 24–5 and Table 2c; and (for Herculaneum papyri) G. Del Mastro, *CErc* 31 (2001) 110. In some examples this sign serves to separate sections or blocks of text, rather than individual sentences. In **5155** this distinction does not apply, since each new sentence is in fact a new anecdote: individual anecdotes end with the divider, and where the end occurs in mid-line, the scribe leaves a blank of *c*.5 letters (ii 21, and by inference also 14).

Col. i   Col. ii

```
     ].                    των πολ[εμιων τοις ξιφε          (191E)
     ].οϲ                  ϲιν εφ[ικνουνται τωι δε
     ].θαι                 προ[δ]οτ[ηι παραδουναι
     ].α                   ϲτρατ[ιωταϲ των εφορων
5    ]..                5  κελευ[οντων ουκ εφη πι
     ].                    ϲτευε[ιν τουϲ αλλοτριουϲ
     ]α                    τωι π[ροδοντι τουϲ ιδιουϲ
     ].                    κλεο[μενηϲ προϲ τον υπι
     ].                    ϲχνου[μενον αυτωι δωϲειν
10   ].               10  αλεκτρ[υοναϲ αποθνηϲκον
                          τ]αϲ ε[ν τωι μαχεϲθαι μη ϲυ
                          γε ειπεν αλ[λ]α δοϲ [μοι τουϲ κα
                          ταϰτεινοντα[ϲ] ε[ν τωι μαχε
                          __ c.12  ....[                    191F
                      15  κριθειϲ ειϲ τουϲ τρ[ιακοϲιουϲ
                          ητιϲ ην εν τηι π[ολει πρω
```

τε]υους[α τιμ]η τη[ι ταξει

ιλαρος και μειδ]ιων [απηει

χ]α[ι]ρε[ιν λεγ]ων ει [τριακοσιους

20   η πο[λις ε]χει πολιτα[ς εαυτου

βελτιονας   (*vac.*)   δαμ[ωνιδας

δε ταχθεις εις την τελ[ευται

αν του χορου ταξιν ϋ[πο του τον

χορον ϊςταντος ευγε [ειπεν

25   εξευ]ρε[ς πως] και αυτα [εντι

.   .   .   .

Col. i

The slight traces of line-ends would fit the following reconstruction, which we owe to Dr D. Colomo: (191C–D) στρατοπεδον κελευσαν]τος | [επεξιεναι και διαμαχε]ςθαι | [του βασιλεως ουκ εφη δ]ια |⁵ [κωλυςειν τους πολεμιο]υς | [ιςους αυτοις γενεςθαι βο]υ | [λομενους ετι δε μικρον] α | [πολειπουςης της ταφρο]υ | [ςυναψαι κατα τουτο παρατ]α |¹⁰ [ξας το διαλειπον και προς] ι | [ςους. The ending] ος stands rather lower than line 1 of col. ii, and we have assumed that it belongs to line 2 of col. i; but the trace attributed to line 1 is very dubious and may be delusory.

Col. ii

11–14 μη ςυ]‖ γε ειπεν αλ[λ]α δος [μοι τους κα]‖τακτεινοντα[ς] ε[ν τωι μαχε]‖[ςθαι: so codd. (for the spelling of the participle see next note), except οὐ τούτων, εἶπε, δέομαι, ἀλλὰ μᾶλλον τῶν φονευόντων ἐν τῷ μάχεςθαι Σ g (the Teubner apparatus implies that the last three words are omitted, but that is not true at least for Σ).

13 κα]‖τακτεινοντα[ς: the medieval MSS have either -κτένν- or -κτέν-. ἀποκτέν(ν)ειν has a wide undisputed currency in LXX, NT and the Christian Fathers, and in later Byzantine usage; see TLG and Trapp, *Lexikon zur byzantinischen Gräzität* s.v. It appears also in MSS of secular writers of the Roman period, often as a variant and generally in danger of normalization: W. Crönert, *Memoria Graeca Herculanensis* (1903) 266 n. 1 collects some examples. The grammarians list κτέννω as Aeolic (Herodian III ii 303, 539), and that may have given the form some prestige, but most often it keeps vulgar company (Psaltes, *Grammatik der byzantinischen Chroniken* (1913) 241, argues that it actually represents a back formation from ἔκτεινα, by analogy with μένω/ἔμεινα): **5155** now gives a reason to remove it from our passage of Plutarch.

14 *c*.12 . . . . [. The surface is badly damaged. The space needs to accommodate -ςθαι, if line 13 is correctly reconstructed; then a space of *c*.5 letters before the next anecdote (as in ii 21); then what appears in the MSS as Παιδάρετος οὐκ ἐγ-. The same Laconic Spartan recurs at *Apophthegmata Laconica* 231A, 241D–E, in various spellings (παιδαρευτ-, παιδαρητ-, παιδαριτ-); also *Lycurg.* 25.6 (παιδάρητος). Editors have corrected all examples to Πεδαριτ-, the name of a Spartan harmost frequently mentioned in Thucydides VIII (Poralla, *A Prosopography of Lacedaemonians* (²1985) no. 599; Παιδαριτ-Suda s.v.), see Gomme, Andrewes and Dover on Thuc. 8.28. Of the variants, only Πεδαριτ- can be paralleled from inscriptions, see LGPN IIIA (three examples from Arcadia, IV–III BC); and Wackernagel, *Philologus* 86 (1931) 140–41 = *Kleine Schriften* i 752–3, argued conclusively that Παιδάρητος represents just an itacistic corruption. In **5155** the final traces would suit ιτ[, perhaps even ριτ[, but those before remain intractable; the clearest so high in the line that it might be suprascript.

19 πολιτα[ς: om. E.

25 πως: ὅπως Σ g. Here the shorter form suits the spacing.

ᾳυτα (i.e. αὗτα), rightly: αὐτός all MSS. In the same anecdote at 149A all MSS have αὐτὰ (αὗτα Wilamowitz); at 219E αὕτη (αὐτὴ ΦΠ) ἡ χώρα. Hertlein restored αὕτη here, but the Doric form, as at 149A, suits the Spartan Damonidas.

P. J. PARSONS / W. B. HENRY

5156. PLUTARCH, *MORALIA* 660C, 661B–C (*QUAESTIONES CONVIVALES* IV PR., 1.2)

112/60(b, c)	fr.1 3.7 × 9.8 cm	Second century
		Plate I

Two fragments from a roll, written along the fibres. Fr. 1 preserves a right margin of 1.3 cm and an upper margin of 5 cm (if indeed line 1 is the top of the column). The average number of letters per line is 12, suggesting a column width of about 4–5 cm. The backs are blank.

The text is written in a small informal round hand. Letters are upright and generally fairly well spaced, with a tendency toward cursive forms: ᴀ is quickly written in two movements, showing some variation in the size of its loop; ᴍ is deep and in three strokes; ʏ is V-shaped; and ω is very rounded with a high middle. The feet of the uprights of π, τ, and κ are ornamented with ticks or back-hooks. The cross bar of τ sometimes extends far to the left, and the mid-stroke of ε often extends to the right. The hand is generally bilinear, only the upright of φ extending above and below the line. Little attempt is made to justify the right-hand margin. *GMAW*^{2} 17 (X **1231**), assigned to the second century, is fairly similar. No lectional signs are present, and there is no evidence for the scribe's practice in respect of iota adscript or elision.

PSI inv. 2055, edited by I. Andorlini in ὁδοὶ διζήcιος: *le vie della ricerca: studi in onore di Francesco Adorno* (1996) 3–10, comes from the same stretch of text as **5156**, yet does not overlap it; and, to judge from the published image, its second-century hand is similar, particularly in respect of ᴀ, ʏ, ᴍ, ʜ, with further examples of unjustified line-end. Note also that both items show the same line-spacing and approximately the same line-length (*c*.13 letters occupying *c*.4.5 cm). Thus a strong case can be made for the claim that PSI inv. 2055 and **5156** come from the same roll.

5156 offers one unique variant (fr. 1.3), which appears very plausible.

These fragments and their connection to PSI inv. 2055 were identified by David Danbeck through the 'Ancient Lives' project.

Fr. 1

υγροτ]η[τ]ᾳ	(660c)
και ρυcι]ν̣ αφαιρων	
ευτον]ον τηρε[ι τ]ο	
μαλαcc]ομενον	
5 αυτου κ]ᾳι τυπ[ου	

μενον] ουτως ο
cυμπο]τικος λο
γος ουκ εαι δι]αφορει
cθαι παντα]πα̣
10   cιν υπο του οι]νο[υ
τους πινον]τα̣[c

      ·   ·   ·

Fr. 2

  ·   ·   ·   ·

].[
μ]ε̣ταβα [(661B)
λειν] κ̣[ρατ]ηθεισαν [
υπ]ο των εν η ·
5   μειν] δυ̣ν̣α̣μ̣[εων   661C
κρατ]ει δε και β[α

  ·   ·   ·   ·

Fr.1

    1 Perhaps the first line of the column, but the surface is stripped immediately above it.

    3 τηρε[ι τ]ο: ποιεῖ τὸ T. Chiara Meccariello had suggested this reading, and a later conservation of the papyrus has confirmed it. For this use of τηρεῖν, cf. e.g. 725B δηλοῦcιν αἱ χιόνες, τὰ κρέα δύccηπτα τηροῦcαι πολὺν χρόνον.

Fr. 2

    1].[. Only a small trace; then enough papyrus for about three letters, but the ink is now gone.

    2–4 In 2 the tail of final alpha is so extended as to suggest line-end. In that case 3 too probably ends with cαν, though there is no margin to prove it. 4 is short: after the final η a blank with a heavy dot, which I have taken as a space-filler.

    4–5 η|[μειν rather than -[μιν suggested by the spacing.

J. H. BRUSUELAS

5157. PLUTARCH, *MORALIA* 732E–F (*QUAESTIONES CONVIVALES* VIII 9.3)

57/15(e)   4.5 × 3.8 cm   Second century
                                                                   Plate IV

    A scrap of a roll with line beginnings, written along the fibres. Left-hand and lower margins are preserved to 1 cm and 0.8 cm. There is an average of 15 letters per line, suggesting a column width of about 5 cm. The back is blank.

    The text is written in a small informal and rather variable round hand. Letters sometimes touch. ω is rounded and looped at the centre. γ is v-shaped or looped at the base. χ at line-beginning (2) has on the left a curved stroke ascending from mid-line level connected to the descending oblique. The right-hand upright of ɴ may be raised. ᴀ may have a pointed or rounded loop. With the exception of ᴘ extending below the line, the hand is generally more or less bilinear. The hand of **XLIX 3435**, assigned to the second century, is similar.

Punctuation is by paragraphus in two forms (see 2 n.). There is no opportunity to observe the scribe's treatment of iota adscript or elision.

The papyrus does not come from the same roll as **5156**. It yields no surprises, but offers yet another text produced within a generation of the author's lifetime.

> ·   ·   ·   ·
> αρμ[ονιαι λογουϲ ε   (732ᴇ)
> χουϲι̣[ν α δε πλημμε
> λουϲιν ανθρω[ποι πε
> ρι λυραν και ω[ιδην και
> 5   ορχηϲιν ο[υκ αν τιϲ πε   732ꜰ
> ριλαβ̣[οι

2 The paragraphus apparently forks at its right-hand end: i.e. it is not the normal 'forked paragraphus' or *diple obelismene*; for similar types Dr Henry refers to IX **1175** fr. 6.9 (pl. ɪᴠ; Soph. fr. ******211), PSI XI 1212 fr. a.1, 21 (pl. ᴠɪɪ; Cratin. fr. 171). Does the difference of form indicate a difference of function? The paragraphus here seems to mark a minor pause, while the standard paragraphus at 6 indicates a full stop after πε]|ριλαβ[οι.

χουϲι̣[ν. The ι is badly damaged, and there is an exiguous trace of suprascript ink that I cannot explain.

J. H. BRUSUELAS

5158. Pʟᴜᴛᴀʀᴄʜ, *Mᴏʀᴀʟɪᴀ* 963ᴅ (*ᴅᴇ sᴏʟʟᴇʀᴛɪᴀ ᴀɴɪᴍᴀʟɪᴜᴍ*)

24 3B.72/C(d)   2.8 × 3.7 cm   Third century

A scrap with parts of eight lines written along the fibres. No margins are preserved. Line length ranges from 21 to 24 letters (about 7.3 cm). The back is blank.

The small hand, slightly sloping to the right, is a regular version of the Severe Style, assignable to the third century. The letters are angular and precisely formed, with the cross-bar of ᴛ sometimes touching the following letter. ɴ and ʜ display their typical broadness in comparison with narrower ᴇ and ᴄ, though these are not as narrow as one might expect in every instance. Bilinearity is breached by the descenders of ᴘ and ʏ. A similar hand is that of *GLH* 21a (II **223**), of the early third century. There are no lectional signs and no evidence for the scribe's treatment of iota adscript or elision.

This part of the text is quoted by Porphyry, *De abstinentia* 3.24.3–4. In two places, the papyrus has acceptable readings hitherto attested only by Porphyry (1 ἐν πα]θει, 4 ἐϲ[τιν), confirming the value of his quotations for the establishment of the text: see in general J. Bouffartigue and M. Patillon, *Porphyre De l'abstinence* i (1977) p. lxxxiv. In the one place where Porphyry can be seen to have made a deliberate change, the papyrus agrees with the remainder of the direct tradition, as expected (6 ἐγω). A collation of Plutarch's text in this passage and the quotation in Porphyry, with commentary, is given by W. Pötscher, *Theophrastos περὶ εὐϲεβείαϲ* (1964) 5–12.

The papyrus is collated with the Teubner edition of K. Hubert (*Moralia* vi.1, ²1959), but for the quotation in Porphyry, the Budé edition of Bouffartigue–Patillon, *Porphyre De l'abstinence* ii (1979), has been used.

<pre>
          .   .   .   .   .

        εϲτιν εν πα]θει γεν[εϲθαι μη   (963D)
        κεκτημ]ενον δυνα[μιν ηϲ το
        παθοϲ η ϲ]τερηϲιϲ η π[ηρωϲιϲ η
        τιϲ αλλη] κακωϲιϲ εϲ[τιν αλ
   5   λα μην εν]τετυχηκα[ϲ γε λυτ
        τωϲαιϲ κυϲι]ν εγω δε [και ιπποιϲ
                    ].[
        αλω]πη̣κ[αϲ

          .   .   .   .   .
</pre>

1 ἐν πα]θει with Porph.: ἐμπαθὲϲ MSS. Although only the bottom half of ι is preserved, the turn-up of ϲ was clearly not present. Bernardakis and Helmbold accept ἐν πάθει, while Hubert, Bouffartigue, and Pötscher 11 prefer ἐμπαθέϲ.

4 ἐϲ[τιν with Porph.: ἦν MSS. Either tense is possible: cf. Pötscher 11, who suggests that the present may be a corruption due to the influence of ἐϲτίν earlier in the sentence.

5 μην εν]τετυχηκα[ϲ restored with MSS: μὴ ἐντετύχηκα transmitted for Porphyry, whose Budé editors print μὴν ἐντετύχηκα, noting that the change to the first person will be due to his effort to remove evidence of the original dialogue form.

5–6 λυττω|ϲαιϲ: restored *exempli gratia* with the manuscripts (except Ψ, which give γλώϲϲαιϲ (γελώϲαιϲ g)) and Porph.

6 εγω with MSS. Porphyry's ἔτι does not suit the space. This further alteration was necessary following his change of ἐντετύχηκαϲ to ἐντετύχηκα, which eliminated the contrast of persons. Cf. Pötscher 11.

7–8 The surface is stripped in line 7 except for a few shadowy traces. One may reconstruct the text *exempli gratia* as [ενιοι δε φαϲι και βουϲ μαι]|νεϲθαι και αλω]πηκ[αϲ.

8 αλω]πηκ[αϲ: ἀλώπεκαϲ MSS Porph. The rare spelling with -η- outside the nominative singular is found in a fourth-century letter (LIX **3998** 37) and metrically guaranteed at Opp. *Cyn.* 1.433 and [Apolin.] *Metaphr. Ps.* 62.21; here it may be due to analogy with nom. ἀλώπηξ or to the phonetic interchange ε/η common in papyri of the Roman period; cf. Gignac, *Grammar* i 242–9. Above the eta there is further ink: some of it might be interpreted as the lower arc and cross-bar of a correcting ε, but if so it is due to a different hand (the mid-stroke is longer and more pronounced, with a sharp downward slope), and in any case some ink remains unexplained.

J. H. BRUSUELAS / W. B. HENRY

IV. SUBLITERARY TEXTS

5159. Chapter on Tetrasyllabic Feet

102/89(b)	Fr. 1 5.8 × 4 cm Fr. 2 6.5 × 6.6 cm	Second half of third century

Two fragments from a leaf of a papyrus codex containing definitions and examples of tetrasyllabic feet, probably part of a metrical treatise or schoolbook. Fr. 1 is from the top of the leaf with an upper margin of at least 1.2 cm. Reconstruction of the text on the basis of the order of feet in parallel works (see below) shows that ↓ must precede →, and suggests that only one line separates fr. 2 from fr. 1. This proximity is supported by the continuity of the fibre patterns between the two fragments on the ↓ side. A left margin of 4 mm is preserved in ↓ fr. 2. The full width of the column can be estimated at *c.*7.5 cm.

The writing is in an informal hand of medium size that is hardly bilinear and sometimes leans slightly to the right. It shows some kinship to the 'Severe' or 'Formal Mixed' style; cf. small and raised o, ⲁ sometimes with pointed nose, narrow ⲉ with protruding midstroke. Other noteworthy letters are ⲁ with a long base extending beyond its sides (especially on the left) and a looped apex, ⲥ with straight back, y-shaped ⲩ with a short left-hand arm attached to a right-leaning vertical, ⲫ with a compressed, oval-shaped loop, and relatively small, flat-bottomed ⲱ with rounded extremities. The hand may be placed in the later third century; compare LII **3662**, a papyrus of the *Iliad* assignable to the second half of the third century because written on the back of a house-property register from the first half of that century, and P. Flor. II 259 (*GLH* 22d), a letter from *c.*260. The scribe does not write any punctuation or accents, but he places a forked paragraphus (or *diple obelismene*; see *GMAW*² p. 12) before the indented heading of the present chapter in ↓ fr. 1.3, and fills the blank space at the end of the preceding section (↓ fr. 1.2) with the same sign. The contents of ↓ fr. 1.1–2 are uncertain as a result of heavy abrasion and small lacunae; groups of letters, separated by small blank spaces, are surmounted by horizontal strokes, such as are found in grammatical papyri to emphasize special terms and examples or to mark syllables under discussion.

The greater part of the papyrus consists of a list of tetrasyllabic feet with definitions and examples in the following format: (1) name of foot; (2) number and length of syllables constituting the foot, introduced by ἐκ (see ↓ fr. 1.5–6 n.); (3) number of its χρόνοι or time-units (see ↓ fr. 2.2 n.); and (4) a one-word example introduced by οἷον. The third chapter of Hephaestion's *Enchiridion* (second century AD) is our earliest attestation and systematic exposition of the sixteen tetrasyllabic feet (cύνθετοι πόδεc), which were considered to be composed out of the shorter feet (ἁπλοῖ πόδες) and some of which (e.g. the dispondeus) were mere theoretical possibilities rather than units actually used and recognized in ancient metrical analysis (cύνθετοι πόδες are first mentioned by Aristoxenus, *Elementa rhythmica* 2.22, 26, pp. 14–16 Pearson).

The format of presentation of feet in **5159** (name of foot ἐκ . . . *n*-χρονος οἷον . . .) recurs in a number of περὶ ποδῶν sections in Greek and Latin metrical and grammatical treatises, compendia, and appendices of the late Roman and Byzantine periods. Notable examples in this specific format are the so-called *Appendix Dionysiaca* (Suppl. III to the τέχνη γραμματική that goes under the name of Dionysius Thrax, ed. G. Uhlig, *Grammatici graeci* i.1 117–21) and *Appendix Rhetorica* (Parisinus gr. 1983 fol. 3–4), both printed in M. Consbruch, *Hephaestionis Enchiridion cum commentariis veteribus* (1906) 307–9 and 337–9 respectively; for a similar format in Latin (name of foot *ex . . . temporum* n *ut . . .*), cf. Diomedes (fourth century) in H. Keil, *Grammatici latini* i 480–81, Donatus (fourth century), *GL* IV 370 = L. Holtz, *Donat et la tradition de l'enseignement grammatical* (1981) 608, and the *Breviatio pedum*, *GL* VI 307–8. The papyrus is now probably our earliest example of this schema. The fact that it also appears in two school papyri from late antique Egypt (see below) suggests that it was originally devised as a pedagogical *aide-mémoire* to provide students with a handy and succinct summary of the names and shapes of metrical feet; cf. Diomedes, *GL* I 481: *hos omnes* (sc. *pedes*), *cum de metri tractatu aliquid legimus, diligentius considerare et in memoria habere debemus, ut singuli quique versus quibus pedibus constent scire possimus.* Knowledge of these feet was essential because some of them are the basis of the μέτρα πρωτότυπα with which poetry was analysed according to the predominant metrical theory in antiquity; cf. Aristides Quintilianus, *De musica* i 23 ed. Winnington-Ingram ἐκ δὴ τῶν ποδῶν cυνίcτανται τὰ μέτρα, and see R. Pretagostini in *Lo spazio letterario della Grecia antica* i.2 (1992–6) 372–81. On sections about metrical feet in metrical, grammatical, and rhetorical treatises, cf. in general J. Luque Moreno, *De pedibus, de metris: las unidades de medida en la rítmica y en la métrica antiguas* (1995).

The sequence of feet in such works varies considerably; see W. Hoerschelmann, *Ein griechisches Lehrbuch der Metrik: literarhistorische Studien* (1888) ch. VI, and Luque Moreno, *De pedibus* ch. 7. In its arrangement of tetrasyllabic feet the papyrus is broadly in agreement with the following works:

α) Aristides Quintilianus I 22 (second or third century).

β) A number of Latin grammatical and metrical treatises from the late second/ early third century onwards: Terentianus Maurus (second/third century), *GL* VI 369–72 = C. Cignolo, *Terentiani Mauri De litteris, de syllabis, de metris* (2002) i 105–13; Marius Plotius Sacerdos (third century), *GL* VI 499; Diomedes (fourth century), *GL* I 480–81; Donatus (fourth century), *GL* IV 370; Aphthonius (fourth century), *GL* VI 47–8 (transmitted with the *Ars grammatica* of Marius Victorinus); *Ars Palaemonis de metrica institutione*, *GL* VI 207–8 (~ *GL* VII 335); *Breviatio pedum*, *GL* VI 307–8; *De pedibus*, *GL* VI 646.

γ) A group of related sections of Byzantine handbooks and compendia: Book V of the 'Scholia B' to Hephaestion in Consbruch, *Hephaestionis Enchiridion* 298–303; Isaac Monachus (fourteenth century), Περὶ μέτρων ποιητικῶν, in L. Bachmann, *Anecdota graeca* (1828) ii 174–7 (on foot names), 177–9 (foot list); Pseudo-Draco in J. G. Hermann, *Draconis Stratonicensis Liber de metris poeticis* (1812) 127–33 (the author was in fact a sixteenth-century writer by the name of Jacob Diassorinos, and the second section of his work is virtually a copy of Isaac; see L. Cohn in *Philologische Abhandlungen, Martin Hertz . . . dargebracht* (1888) 133–43); Pseudo-Hephaestion §1ᵇ, in H. zur Jacobsmuehlen, *Pseudo-Hephaestion De metris* (1886) 33–5 = *Dissertationes philologicae Argentoratenses* 10: 219–21; Pseudo-Moschopulus (after thirteenth century), in F. N. Titze, *Manuelis Moschopuli cretensis Opuscula grammatica* (1822) 49–50. Add now Georgius Gemistus (four-teenth/fifteenth century), Περὶ παιδείας, in M. Scialuga, *AAT* 129 (1995) 3–34 at 19. For a general overview of some of these Byzantine compilations, see K. Krumbacher, *Geschichte der byzantinischen Litteratur* (²1897) 594–8. Isaac's foot list alone displays the same schematic format of presentation as **5159**.

Hephaestion ch. III, the *Appendix Dionysiaca*, the *Appendix Rhetorica* (with one excep-tion), and related works follow a strictly quantitative ordering principle and present the tetrasyllabic feet in ascending order according to number of χρόνοι or time-units (the main difference between them being the arrangement of the ἑξάχρονοι feet). The above-cited works and **5159**, however, belong to a different tradition that was evidently more widespread in late Roman and early Byzantine times. They place the longest foot (the dispondeus of eight time-units) in second position following directly after the shortest foot (the proceleumatic of four time-units). Moreover, they group the paeones (five time-units) and epitrites (seven time-units) together because of their formal resemblance, while the ἑξάχρονοι are moved from their quantitatively intermediary position between paeones and epitrites to stand before the paeones (except in Diomedes and Ps.-Moschopulus, who move them after the epitrites). There is some variation in the order of the ἑξάχρονοι feet within this collection of works (see Hoerschelmann, *Lehrbuch* 38), and it is their arrange-ment by Isaac and Ps.-Hephaestion that happens to correspond to the papyrus' specific presentation of these feet. The full arrangement of tetrasyllabic feet in **5159**, therefore, would have been as follows (feet between square brackets have not been preserved):

1 προκελευματικός (˘ ˘ ˘ ˘)
2 διςπόνδειος (– – – –)

3 διτρόχαιος (– ˘ – ˘)
4 διίαμβος (˘ – ˘ –)
5 χορίαμβος (– ˘ ˘ –)
6 [ἀντίςπαςτος (˘ – – ˘)]

7 (or 8) [ἰωνικὸϲ ἀπὸ μείζονοϲ (– – ⌣ ⌣)]
8 (or 7) [ἰωνικὸϲ ἀπ' ἐλάττονοϲ (⌣ ⌣ – –)]

9 [παίων πρῶτοϲ (– ⌣ ⌣ ⌣)]
10 [παίων δεύτεροϲ (⌣ – ⌣ ⌣)]
11 παίων τρίτοϲ (⌣ ⌣ – ⌣)
12 παίων τέταρτοϲ (⌣ ⌣ ⌣ –)

13 πρῶτοϲ ἐπίτριτοϲ (⌣ – – –)
14 δεύτεροϲ ἐπίτριτοϲ (– ⌣ – –)
15 τρίτοϲ ἐπίτριτοϲ (– – ⌣ –)
16 τέταρτοϲ ἐπίτριτοϲ (– – – ⌣)

As to the one-word examples illustrating the feet, one is common to all works that have examples (↓ fr. 2.3 Ἡρακλείδηϲ), while two partly damaged ones are potentially reconcilable with attested examples (see → fr. 1.2, 5 nn.). The papyrus, however, also offers at least four new examples not previously attested in any work, and its use of δόχμιοϲ as an alternative name of ἐπίτριτοϲ is rare among metricians (see → fr. 1.5 n.).

The uncertain content of the top of ↓ fr. 1, which does not seem to be a similar exposition of feet, is problematic. We can either suppose that a discussion of some kind intervened between the exposition of trisyllabic feet and that of tetrasyllabic feet, or that the list of tetrasyllabic feet was not part of a comprehensive presentation of feet, but was introduced at this point for some other purpose or was a self-standing section.

The appearance of new examples not paralleled elsewhere in the tradition is a characteristic of two similar lists of feet found on papyri. The fifth-century PSI I 18 (M–P³ 344 = 5 Wouters = 405 Cribiore) contains an early version of the *Appendix Dionysiaca* preserving only the last two trisyllabic feet and coming before the τέχνη of 'Dionysius Thrax' rather than after it as in the medieval manuscripts (like the fifth-century Armenian translation of the τέχνη and its supplements, it omits the tetrasyllabic feet). For the last foot (the molossus) two examples rather than the usual single example are given, and the second of them (Ἡρακλῆϲ) is unattested in the other lists. P. IFAO inv. 320 (M–P³ 2644 = 406 Cribiore), a miscellaneous schoolbook of the late fifth or early sixth century, contains a paragraph listing disyllabic feet (fols. III^v and IV^r). Two of its examples are different from those in other lists, one occurs only in one medieval manuscript, and another is common to almost all the other lists. (The small and fragmentary P. Giss. Univ. IV 43 i 5–7 (M–P³ 2171; first or second century BC) has ἐϲ]τὶν ὁρ[ιϲ]μόϲ [. . . τρ]εῖϲ ϲυλλαβαί εἰϲιν [. . .] ἐϲτὶ βραχεῖα; but it is unclear whether this was a systematic discussion of feet.) The occurrence of the rather technical tetrasyllabic feet does not suggest that **5159** was an elementary school text like PSI 18 and P. IFAO inv. 320, although there is nothing to rule out its use by a more advanced student under a γραμματικός. For a brief survey of the relatively few papyri discussing metre, see T. Renner, *Pap. Congr. XXIII* 600–601.

The notes focus on some metrical terms and examples of particular interest, and collate the examples of feet with the other works that have them. It will be useful to divide these works into three groups, following and supplementing Hoerschelmann, *Lehrbuch* ch. VII:

Group I = Ps.-Hephaestion §2 (supra cit.); Isaac Monachus (supra cit.); sometimes Ioannes Siculus in C. Walz, *Rhetores graeci* vi (1834) 237–40.

Group II = *Appendix Dionysiaca* (supra cit.); *Anonymi commentarium in Hermogenem* in Walz, *Rhetores graeci* vii.2 (1834) 988–90; Nicetas Serrarum (eleventh century) in W. J. W. Koster, *Tractatus graeci de re metrica inediti* (1922) 103–5; Ps.-Moschopulus (supra cit.); *Tractatus Harleianus* in T. Gaisford, *Hephaestionis Alexandrini Enchiridion* (1855) i 317–18; Ps.-Hephaestion §20 (supra cit.).

Group III = *Appendix Rhetorica* (supra cit.); *Tractatus de pedibus* (a. 1451) in Koster, *Tractatus graeci* 121–3.

When individual works or manuscripts within a group differ from their relatives, they are cited separately. I also cite the Latin grammarians and metricians who occasionally use Greek examples to illustrate the relevant feet (Terentianus Maurus, Donatus, Aphthonius). Parisinus gr. 2676 fol. 2ᵛ is a particularly poor version of the foot list and does not follow any particular tradition. For its unique and sometimes peculiar examples (not cited in the notes), see Hoerschelmann, *Lehrbuch* 43–4 (cf. also 40).

I am grateful to Dr Martin L. West for kindly reading and commenting on a final draft of this edition.

↓ Fr. 1

```
     ‾υ‾ .[ .]‾ ‾αρα‾ αρ‾.[
   ⟩.‾ε‾. .‾ερ‾ τ[‾.‾]⟩—[
     πε .[ .].οδωντ[
     .ο .ε .[ .].ϲ .τε .[
5    .π . . .[
```

→ Fr. 1

```
   ]κραϲκαιβ . . . . .αϲπ .[
   ] .[ .]ι . . .[ .] .δωροϲπα[
   ] .τοϲ .κτριωνβραχει
   ] .κρ[ .] .πεν .αχρονοϲ
5  ] .η[ . . .] .[ . . .] . .κ .[
```

↓ Fr. 2

```
           ] .[
   .]αρ . .μακρω .οκτα[
   .]ιο .ηρακλει .ηϲδι[
   εκμακραϲ . . .βραχει[
```

→ Fr. 2

```
   ]ω .μα[ .] .[
   ]νκ .βερνητ . .δ[
   ] .πιτριτοϲδευτερ .[
   ]μακραϲκαιβραχειαϲκα[
```

5   κρασκαιβραχειασε . . [5   ]μακρωνεπταχρονος

οιονμηνο . . ρο . δ . [   ] . φρ . δειτηδοχμιος

εκβραχειασκαιμα[   ]επιτριτοστρι . οcεκδ̣ . [

βραχειασκ . [.] . . κρ . [   ] . . . κ . ιβραχειασκαι

χρονοcο . ο . [   ]χρον . . . ιον . [

10   . .] . . κ . . κ . [10   ] . δηcδοχ . [

.   .   .   .

↓ Fr. 1

1 . . , three tiny dots at about two-thirds height (space could accommodate two letters); part of an upper arc or small circle (e.g. ᴀ, ϵ, θ, ο)   . [(first), lower arc at bottom of lacuna (ᴀ? θ? ο?)] . , upright leaning slightly to the right with join at top, or apex of triangular letter, then after small lacuna dot level with letter tops   . [(second), lower semicircle at line level, then further to the right thick trace of descending oblique at two-thirds height (bottom and tail of ᴀ?)   2 . ϵ, τ or (less likely) ɼ   . . , horizontal at two-thirds height, then dot at line level (foot of upright?): traces compatible with τ; after abraded surface, apparently an upright, perhaps with a join at top   τ[, left half 3 π, horizontal bar and second leg   . [, descender (like ρ)   ] . ο, π or ɼɪ; left half of small raised circle   τ[, top left perpendicular junction   4 . , upright, then after small abraded surface dot at mid-height   ο . , long horizontal at line level extending slightly below ο (like base of ᴧ)   . [(first), short upright with apparent horizontal join from top right   ] . , thick trace like upper half of upright ᴄ . , foot of upright(?), then thick dot at line level (displaced?)   . [(second), thick trace at two-thirds height   5 . . . [, thick trace level with letter tops resembling the upper part of an arc or circle; dot level with letter tops; top of thick upright

↓ Fr. 2

1] . [, foot of upright leaning to the right with a small hooked serif   2 . . , small right-facing semicircle at line level (ᴀ, ο, ω); upright slanting to the right, then dot at line level   ω . , descending oblique (κ, ɴ)   3 ο . , ᴧ, ᴍ, or ɴ   ι . , long base (as of ᴧ)   4 . . . , tall upright then two dots equidistant from it (one near line level, the other higher); apex composed of junction of two obliques (ᴀ, ᴧ, λ); two vertically aligned dots suggesting an upright   5 . . [, dot at mid-height, then at top short horizontal bar with raised extremities; very short vertical trace near line level 6 ο . . , long base (as of ᴧ); ο or ω   ο . , displaced high dot   . [, traces of upright leaning to the right   8 . [, thick trace level with letter tops   ] . . , top of upright; upper tip of thick upright or apex   . [, specks on edge   9 ο . , foot of upright slightly below line level   . [, tall upright on edge   10] . . , upper arc (ϵ, ᴄ, ʙ?); short horizontal or upper arc level with letter tops, below it another horizontal extending further to the right (compatible with top and midstroke of ϵ)   κ . . , two parallel uprights; thick ascending oblique or juncture of two obliques (as in nose of ᴧ), then flattened end of descending oblique   . [, ο or ρ

→ Fr. 1

1]κ, arms only   . . . . . , first, descender; second, ᴀ, λ, or (less likely) ᴧ; third, x or κ; fourth and fifth, ϵɪ or ʜ   . [, upper part of upright with joins from the right at top and two-thirds height Above β there are some traces of ink, but they are exiguous and indistinct, and seem too close to the first line to be a page number   2] . , short upright (perhaps displaced)   . . . [, first, thick trace at around mid-height; second, after small hole top of upright leaning to the right; third, thick and confused trace slightly below line level; above it to the right two short, parallel horizontals a short distance apart (slightly displaced?); the last two sets of traces may belong to separate letters   ] . ,

upper arc above extended base of ⅄   3] ., small upper arc (o, ρ)   c ., dot at line level and short horizontal at mid-height   4] ., thin horizontal almost touching foot of κ   ] ., right-hand tip of horizontal or upper arc level with letter tops   ν ., г or т   5] ., small trace of descending oblique then upright (perhaps with join at foot): most likely и   ] .[, broad upper arc (compatible with top-left arm of х)   ] . ., trace of short upright with perpendicular join at top (c?); o or ρ   .[, ⅄ or ⅄

→ Fr. 2

   1]ω . μ, second half of ω; dot at line level, then after small lacuna another dot; second half of м   ] .[, foot of long descender   2]ν, parts of oblique and second upright   κ ., foot of upright at line level   . ., upright; part of upper arc at mid-height   3] ., speck level with let-ter tops   .[, dot at mid-height   6] ., thick trace at line level touching loop of φ   ρ ., speck at mid-height   7 ι ., left-hand tip of thick horizontal level with letter tops, then faint trace of upright   κδ .[, somewhat confused traces on dirty surface, but it is possible to make out κ and ⅄ then the foot of an upright   8] . ., small loop (o or ρ); short horizontal then left-facing arc (ω?); slight trace of an upright leaning slightly to the right   κ ., apex of ⅄, ⅄, or ⅄   9 . . ., small trace of horizontal or lower arc at line level; dot at line level and another above it at around mid-height; damaged surface with confused traces at mid-height, but small loop discernible   .[, top of upright or apex slightly above letter tops   10] ., dot level with letter tops on edge   .[, м or (less likely) и

↓

Fr. 1   . ‾υ .[.]‾ ‾αρα‾ αρ‾[

          > ‾ε . . ‾ερ‾ τ[‾ .‾]>—[

          περ[ὶ] ποδῶν τ[

          πόδες [ε]ἰςὶ τετ[ρασύλλαβοι ι͞ϛ·]

    5   προκ[ελευματικὸς ἐκ τεσσάρων]

          [βραχειῶν, τετράχρονος, οἷον]

Fr. 2   [˘ ˘ ˘ ˘ . . δ]ι[cπόνδειος ἐκ τεc-]

          [c]άρων μακρῶν, ὀκτά[χρονος,]

          [ο]ἷον Ἡρακλείδης. δι[τρόχαιος]

          ἐκ μακρᾶς καὶ βραχεί[ας καὶ μα-]

    5   κρᾶς καὶ βραχείας, ἑξά[χρονος,]

          οἷον Μηνόδωρος. δι[ίαμβος]

          ἐκ βραχείας καὶ μα[κρᾶς καὶ]

          βραχείας κα[ὶ] μακρᾶ[ς, ἑξά-]

          χρονος, οἷον [˘ ‾ ˘ ‾ . χορίαμ-]

   10   [βο]ς ἐκ μακρ[ᾶς καὶ δύο βραχει-]

                .   .   .   .   .

→

Fr. 1   [καὶ μα]κρᾶς καὶ βραχείας, πε[ν-]

          [τάχρονο]ς, [ο]ἷον . [.]όδωρος. πα[ί-]

          [ων τέτα]ρτος ἐκ τριῶν βραχει-

          [ῶν καὶ μ]ακρ[ᾶ]ς, πεντάχρονος,

5   [οἷον ⏑ ⏓ ⏑]νη[.. δό]χ[μιο]ς ὁ κạ[ὶ]

        [ἐπίτριτος πρῶτος ἐκ βραχείας]

Fr. 2   [καὶ τρι]ῶṇ μα[κ]ρ̣[ῶν, ἑπτάχρο-]

        [νος, οἷο]ν κụβερνήτης. δ[όχμι-]

        [ος ὁ καὶ] ἐπίτριτος δεύτερọ[ς]

        [ἐκ] μακρᾶς καὶ βραχείας κα[ὶ]

5   [δύο] μακρῶν, ἑπτάχρονος,

        [οἷον] Ἀφροδείτη. δόχμιος

        [ὁ καὶ] ἐπίτριτος τρίτọς ἐκ δụ́[ο]

        [μακ]ρ̣ῶṇ κạὶ βραχείας καὶ

        [μακρᾶς, ἑπτά]χρονọς, οἷον̣ [.]

10   [*c*.9   ]̣δης. δόχμ̣[ιος]

.   .   .   .   .   .

'(↓) . . . On tetrasyllabic (?) feet. There are 16 tetrasyllabic feet: Proceleumaticus, out of four shorts, four time-units, such as . . . Dispondeus, out of four longs, eight time-units, such as "Heracleides". Ditrochaeus, out of a long, a short, a long, and a short, six time-units, such as "Menodorus". Diiambus, out of a short, a long, a short, and a long, six time-units, such as . . . Choriambus, out of a long, two shorts, (and a long, six time-units, such as . . .) . . . (Third paeon, out of two shorts,) (→) a long, and a short, five time-units, such as "—odorus". Fourth paeon, out of three shorts and a long, five time-units, such as . . . First dochmius or epitrite, out of a short and three longs, seven time-units, such as "*kubernetes*" ("helmsman"). Second dochmius or epitrite, out of a long, a short, and two longs, seven time-units, such as "Aphrodite". Third dochmius or epitrite, out of two longs, a short, and a long, seven time-units, such as "—des". (Fourth) dochmius . . .'

↓ Fr. 1

3 περ[ὶ] π̣ọδῶν τ̣[. Probably restore τ̣[ετρασυλλάβων.

4 πόδες [ε]ἰ̣c̣ὶ τε̣τ̣[ρασύλλαβοι ιϛ·]. The reading and restoration of what follows πόδες is based on a suggestion by Dr W. Benjamin Henry.

5–6 [ἐκ . . . βραχειῶν]: a compressed expression for cυγκείμενος (*vel sim.*) ἐκ τεccάρων βραχειῶν cυλλαβῶν.

↓ Fr. 2

2 ὀκτά[χρονος. A (πρῶτος) χρόνος was considered the smallest time-unit and was equated with the length of a short syllable, with two χρόνοι naturally corresponding to a long syllable. It is equivalent to what rhythmicians called a cημεῖον; see Aristides Quintilianus I 14 and J. M. van Ophuijsen, *Hephaestion on Metre: A Translation and Commentary* (1987) 55–6. For more complex ancient definitions of χρόνοι, see the brief description and references in M. L. West, *Greek Metre* (1982) 193.

3 Ἡρακλείδης. This example is universal among Greek lists. Aphthonius has *Calliclides*.

6 Μηνόδωρος: a new example and a common name. Groups I and II have Ἀρχέδημος (Ἀρχίδαμος in Ps.-Moschopulus). The *App. Rhet.* of Group III has Παιδαγώρας, but as Hoerschelmann, *Lehrbuch* 42, notes, this is probably a mistake for παιδαγωγός, which is the reading of *Tractatus de pedibus*. Other manuscripts have Ἑκτόρειος and Νικόλαος; see Hoerschelmann, *Lehrbuch* 42–3. *Zenodorus* in Aphthonius is the closest to the papyrus' example, but cannot be read here.

9 οἶọν [⏑ – ⏑ –. Most Greek lists have Ἀνακρέων as the example for the diiambus, but given

the papyrus' new examples for many other feet, it would be imprudent to assume that this name stood here. *Tract. de ped.* has Ἀθηνίων, Aphthonius *Simonides*, Diomedes *Cleonides*, and Terentianus Maurus *Corinthios*.

→ Fr. 1

2 . [ ]όδωρος. The small raised upper arc before δ is almost certainly ο, but the preceding space is damaged by a hole, and the initial traces, which could represent either one or two letters, are rather puzzling (see palaeographical apparatus). Θεόδωρος of Group I and Διόδωρος are difficult to reconcile with the traces. Group II has Κλεόβουλος, Group III Φιλόδημος, Aphthonius *Epicurus*, Terentianus Maurus *Menelaus*, while Donatus, the *Breviatio pedum* (*GL* VI 308), and *De pedibus* (*GL* VI 646) give *Menedemus*.

5 ᵛ ᵛ ᵛ]νη[.. Ν is the letter most likely to fit the traces before η, so that Θεοφάνης of Group I, Ἐπιγένης of Groups II and III, and Aphthonius' *Diogenes* would all be suitable. Terentianus Maurus has Πελοπίδαι (cf. Πελοπίδης in Parisinus gr. 2676 fol. 2ʳ).

δό]χ[μιο]ς. The use of the term δόχμιος as an alternative to ἐπίτριτος is rare in the writings of metricians and similar lists of feet. Only the commentary of Choeroboscus (eighth century) on chapter III of Hephaestion (p. 219 Consbruch) and the *Anonymi Ambrosiani De re metrica* (in G. Studemund, *Anecdota varia graeca, musica, metrica, grammatica* (1886) 229) offer it for the first and second epitrites (ᵛ – – – and – ᵛ – –), and Book V of the Scholia B to Hephaestion (p. 303 Consbruch) for the first epitrite. **5159**, in contrast, gives the term δόχμιος as an alternative to ἐπίτριτος for all four epitrites and even presents it first, whereas the above works cite it among other alternative names of the epitrite (ἵππειος, καρικός). Ancient theories of the dochmiac are far from unanimous and clear, but the δόχμιος or δοχμιακός was generally considered a ῥυθμός or metron (or a species of a metron like the antispast) constituted by smaller feet rather than a foot in its own right; cf. Choeroboscus' statement at p. 239 Consbruch: (τὸ δοχμιακὸν) κατὰ πόδα μετρεῖται (cf. similarly Quint. *Inst.* 9.4.79–80). For an overview of ancient views, see C. Del Grande in *La lingua greca nei mezzi della sua espressione* ii (1960) 368–9, and J. W. White, *The Verse of Greek Comedy* (1912) 295 §624. Among the few writers who admit and name pentasyllabic 'feet', namely Diomedes (*GL* I 481–2) and the *Anonymi Ambrosiani De re metrica* (in Studemund, *Anecdota varia* 232–5; cf. *Anonymus Berolinensis*, ibid. 295–6), a seven-time-unit δόχμιος ἢ προανάπαιστος is cited with the scheme ᵛ ᵛ – – ᵛ –, which can be viewed as a version of the third epitrite with resolution of the first long; otherwise the ὑποδόχμιος (– ᵛ – ᵛ –) and the δόχμιος κατὰ συζυγίαν (ᵛ – – ᵛ –) in these lists are ὀκτάχρονοι.

In tragedy, the sequence ᵛ – – – (= 'first epitrite') is sometimes interpreted as a syncopated or catalectic dochmiac (U. von Wilamowitz, *Griechische Verskunst* (1921) 407; W. S. Barrett on Eur. *Hi.* 811–16; West, *Greek Metre* 111; against, N. C. Conomis, *Hermes* 92 (1964) 34–5; J. Diggle, *Euripidea* (1994) 107, 395; C. W. Willink, *ICS* 27–8 (2002–3) 36–7 (= *Collected Papers on Greek Tragedy* (2010) 575) with n. 34); but in view of its rarity it is unlikely that its detection was the origin of the use of δόχμιος for ἐπίτριτος. Moreover, this phenomenon would not explain why δόχμιος is applied to the first two epitrites by Choeroboscus and the Anonymus Ambrosianus and to all four epitrites by the papyrus (only Book V of the Scholia B to Hephaestion limits it to the first epitrite), unless we assume that they applied the term mechanically to the other epitrites in analogy with the first epitrite.

Another possibility is that this rare use of δόχμιος as an alternative name of ἐπίτριτος implies an analysis of the dochmiac metron as an epitrite plus one syllable, i.e. as a hypercatalectic epitrite. Since many metra took their names from their main constituent foot (e.g. ἴαμβος > ἰαμβικόν; cf. van Ophuijsen, *Hephaestion* 15–16), some ancient metricians may have started applying the term δόχμιος (πούς) to the ἐπίτριτος by analogy, because this foot was interpreted as constituting the δοχμιακὸν μέτρον. In other words, this would be the reverse of the way metra are usually named after feet; in this case, the foot (ἐπίτριτος) would derive its second name (δόχμιος) from the metron (δοχμιακόν).

Two passages can be adduced as evidence for such an analysis of the dochmiac, although both are late. First, there is a statement in Choeroboscus' commentary on Hephaestion (p. 240 Consbruch) that (ἐν . . . τῷ δοχμίῳ) ἐπίτριτός ἐστι καὶ cυλλαβή. Consbruch brackets this sentence because it clearly breaks the flow of the passage and does not make sense at this point. But whatever its original placement in Choeroboscus' discussion (cf. Consbruch's note on p. 239 lines 17–18), it betrays perhaps the existence of a metrical theory in antiquity that considered the dochmiac metron to be composed out of one or more of the four epitrite feet. The forms that would be obtained through this definition are: ⏑ – – – –, – ⏑ – – –, – – – ⏑ –, and – – – ⏑ –. The first and last of these are possible dochmiacs, but not the third and probably not the second (cf. West, *Greek Metre* 110 n. 92; Diggle, *Euripidea* 150). Another passage that suggests a similar view of the dochmiac is found in the Scholia A to Hephaestion (p. 142 Consbruch), where the scholiast analyses Hephaestion's first example of his 'antispastic penthemimer called dochmiac' (κλύειν μαίεται, p. 32 Consbruch) as a fourth epitrite plus a syllable, because he (wrongly) considers κλυ- a long syllable. From such an analysis of the δοχμιακόν as an epitrite plus one syllable, it is not a big step to call its constituent epitrite foot a δόχμιος. If this definition of the dochmiac was voiced in antiquity, and if it is the explanation of the use here of δόχμιος for ἐπίτριτος, it evidently did not gain wide currency. Its main weakness and the probable reason for its limited diffusion is that it does not allow the derivation of the typical and most common form of the dochmiac ⏑ – – ⏑ –, recognized by both ancient and modern metricians.

→ Fr. 2

   2 κυβερνήτης: a new example. Ἀριστείδης is the example given by virtually all Greek lists. Ioannes Siculus has Ἰωάννης and Aphthonius *Aristocles*. The papyrus' example is a rare exception to the general tendency of such lists to offer personal names as examples, especially for tetrasyllabic feet. Common personal names or those of famous individuals must have been considered an effective means of illustrating and retaining the syllabic patterns of feet. Students will already have been familiar with lists of names from elementary reading exercises; cf. lines 67–114 of the *Livre d'écolier* (III BC) published by Guéraud and Jouguet (M–P³ 2642) with its list of mostly personal names from two to five syllables, and R. Cribiore, *Writing, Teachers, and Students in Graeco-Roman Egypt* (1996) 43 and nos. 101, 105, 106, 109, 112, 113, 118, 124 in her catalogue of school exercises.

   6 Ἀφροδείτη: read Ἀφροδίτη (the spelling with ει is perhaps chosen to mark unequivocally a long iota). Another new example. Names of Greek gods and goddesses are virtually absent from other lists. Εὐρυμήδης is the example of Groups I and II and *Tract. de ped.*, Ἀρχιμήδης that of *App. Rhet.*, Terentianus Maurus, and Aphthonius, and *Nicomedes* that of the *Breviatio pedum* (*GL* VI 308). Ioannes Siculus gives erroneously Ἡρακλείδης, while *Tract. de ped.* adds the unintelligible example cτηcιγήδης.

   9–10 . [.][*c*.9] . δης. Whatever the beginning of the word, this is again a new example, for Δημοcθένης is the example of almost all Greek and Latin lists (with the exception of *Tract. de ped.*, which has Ἡρωδίων). The ending suggests that the example is a personal name with a patronymic termination. The last trace in 9 is compatible with the tip of a tall upright or the apex of ⲁ, ⲇ, or perhaps λ; no more than one letter can be missing after it on that line. The lacuna in the following line can accommodate 8–10 letters, and the high dot at the edge of the papyrus before δ could be the upper tip of an upright, e.g. ι. It is difficult to think of a suitable personal name that is long enough for the large lacuna in 10 (Ἀντανδρίδης, Ἀρχανδρίδης, Δεξανδρίδης, Λυcανδρίδης, Λυcιππίδης, obtained through an online search of the *LGPN*, would be too short and were in any case too uncommon to have served as memorable examples). Perhaps the trace after ν in 9 is a mere stray mark and the example began in 10.

A. BENAISSA

5160. COMMENTARY ON EUPOLIS' *GOATS* (?)

101/175(a)   12.8 × 23.5 cm   Second/third century
                                                                                Plate V

Extensive stretches of two columns of a roll, together with a single line-beginning from a third at the level of ii 36. The back is blank. The text is written in a medium-sized upright 'severe' hand comparable to those of XXXVII **2804** (Sophocles?, later II) and XVII **2098** (Herodotus, II/III; *GLH* 19b), which has on its back a land survey assigned to the reign of Gallienus. The lower margin is preserved at the foot of col. ii to a depth of 1.7 cm. A line of text was about 5.1 cm wide and held about 17 letters. The intercolumnium is generally about 1.6 cm wide, but narrower (about 1.2 cm wide) to the left of ii 13, which projects slightly. The 40 preserved lines of col. ii occupy an area 21.7 cm high.

Corrections have been executed in several places. There are supralinear additions at i 10 and ii 28, and changes made on the line at i 16 and ii 35, all of which may be due to a second hand. Lection signs include, besides the high point added at i 16, an apostrophe (ii 15) and tremas on ι, organic (i 5, ii 39) and inorganic (i 14), all probably due to the original scribe. Except at ii 15, elision is unmarked. A short blank space at ii 12 may be intended as punctuation, and there may be another such at ii 28 (see n.). There is one probable instance of the paragraphus, apparently misplaced (ii 36 n.). A single possible case of ἔκθεϲιϲ (ii 13) may not be significant. Iota adscript is present wherever required. There is a possible example of ει for long ι at i 25.

The text is a learned commentary, with references to scholars including Seleucus Homericus, one Dionysius, Aristophanes of Byzantium, Callistratus, and Aristarchus (i 7, ii 11, 25, 27–8, 29–30; cf. ii 4). Quotations from the comic poet Aristomenes' *Dionysus in Training* and from Aeschylus' *Danaids*, introduced by the titles in the genitive case, are used to illustrate grammatical points (ii 32–6, 39–40). The work under discussion is a comedy: cf. ii 17–19 κωμ]ωιδεῖ δ' αὐτο.[. . . . .]ϲ εἰϲ μαλα[κίαν. It mentioned the Athenian general Nicias (i 4–6), and appears to have made use of a Euripidean phrase (i 30, ii 7–8). The characters included a female innkeeper (i 15, 24) and a goatherd (i 17, 31–2, ii 11). The apparent prominence of the latter suggests an identification of the play as Eupolis' *Goats*, in one fragment of which (9) a female innkeeper is mentioned. The statement in a lemma that 'Nicias is of the Aegeis' (i 4) could then be explained as a pun. Apart from this lemma and the Euripidean phrase mentioned above, there is little that can be ascribed with certainty to the poetic text rather than to the commentary on it: i 14 seems to be quoted, but it is not clear how far the quotation extends. To judge by the leisurely pace of the commentary at the foot of col. ii, we should not expect lemmas to form a large proportion of the text. For a recent discussion of the play, see I. C. Storey, *Eupolis: Poet of Old Comedy* (2003) 67–74; also his *Fragments of Old Comedy* ii (2011) 54–63.

Commentaries on plays of Eupolis are preserved in XXXV **2741** (*Maricas*), XXXVII **2813** (*Prospaltioi*), and XXXV **2740** (*Taxiarchoi*(?)), frr. 192, 259, and 268 in *PCG*.

A preliminary edition of this papyrus was prepared by Dr Trojahn, who received advice from Prof. W. Luppe; a brief description appeared in her monograph *Die auf Papyri erhaltenen Kommentare zur Alten Komödie* (2002) 205. Dr Rea made further contributions. The edition presented here is the work of Dr Henry. Fragments of comedy and tragedy are cited according to the numerations of *PCG* (followed by Storey) and *TrGF*.

Col. i

· · ·
|].[   ].[
|]προ̣τοαναλα
|]του̣βουλομενουϲ
|]α̣ϲταιγηιδοϲεϲτι̣ν̣
5 |]ϲγαραιγηϊδ[
|]ν̣ικιαϲο̣νικ̣[..].[
|]ελευκοϲδ̣ πο.[.].
|]τοιϲυμ̣αχο̣ϲ̣[
|]ωρ[..]εξαμενο̣ϲ̣.
10 |]α̣....[.]....
|]..ιν....[.].[.].
|]̣.ιϲμο....ρ...η
|]̣.λε̣ταιειϲαγοραν
|]δ̣ευρειϲιωνπροϲ
15 |]νδοκευτριαν
|]ηϲυντυχια·εν
|]οιμηναιπολω̣ι
|].̣ωνμιμειτα̣ι
|].̣ικουϲεψων
20 |].̣αρτιωϲτατ..
|].[.].κ̣....ενϲε
|]....ν...εταιοτιο
|]...μ̣.[.].ικτα.τηι
|]νδοκευτριαικαλει
25 |]..κεινηϲαι
|]δ̣...οδετου̣
|].τ[.]..διατο
|]..α̣.εντωιεργωι
|]....τ̣ειχυτραϲ
30 |]̣.ϲι̣.ιϲτυχαιϲ
|]̣.προϲτο̣ναιπο
|].̣ωνατρεα
|]ηναυτου
· · ·

· · ·
|].[   ].[
| ......] πρὸϲ τὸ ἀναλα-
| βεῖν] τοὺϲ βουλομένουϲ.
| Νικ]ίαϲ τ' Αἰγηΐδόϲ ἐϲτιν·
5 | τῆ]ϲ γὰρ Αἰγηΐδ[οϲ....
| ..] Νικίαϲ ὁ Νικη[ρά]τ̣[ου.
| ὁ δὲ C]έλευκοϲ διαπορ[ε]ῖ̣
| ....]τοι ϲύμμαχο̣ϲ̣[
| ....]ωρ[..]εξαμενο̣ϲ̣.
10 | ....]α̣....[.]....
| ....]..ιν....[.].[.].
| ....]̣.ιϲμο...ρ...η
| ....]̣.λεται εἰϲ ἀγοραν
| ...] δεῦρ' εἰϲιὼν προϲ
15 | ...πα]νδοκεύτριαν
| .....]η ϲυντυχία· εν
| ....π]οιμὴν αἰπόλωι
| ....].̣ων μιμεῖται
| ....].̣ικουϲ ἔψων
20 | .....].̣αρτιωϲτατε̣
| ...].[.].κ̣....ενϲε
| .].̣.. αἰνίττεται ὅτι ο
| ...].̣..μέ[μ]εικται τῆι
| πα]νδοκευτρίαι· καλει
25 | .....].̣.κεινηϲαι
| ....]δ̣...οδετου̣
| .....].τ[.]..διατο
| ...].̣.α̣. ἐν τῶι ἔργωι
| ....]....τ̣ει χύτραϲ
30 | ... ἀνα]ρϲίοιϲ τύχαιϲ
| ......].̣ πρὸϲ τὸν αἰπό-
| λον....].̣ων Ἀτρέα
| ....]ην αυτου
· · ·

Col. ii

```
           . . .                          . . .
        ]. [                           ]. [
        ]. . νε[                 . . . .]. . νε[. . . . . .
     προϲουδεν[                  πρὸϲ οὐδεν[. . . . . . .
     δετοιϲαριϲ[                 δὲ τοῖϲ Ἀριϲ[τ . . . .
5    παρ[                     5  παρ[
     τειδομων[                   τει δόμων [. . . . . .
     αναρϲιοιϲτυ.[               ἀναρϲίοιϲ τύχ[αιϲ Εὐρι-
     πιδε[.].νεϲτ.[              πίδε[ι]όν ἐϲτι[. . . . . .
     .πε..νη...ε..[             .πε..νη...ε..[. . . .
10   ..υ.εϲτινγ.[          10   ..υ.εϲτιν γ.[. . . . . .
     αιπολουωϲφη[               αἰπόλου ὥϲ φη[ϲι Διονύ-
     ϲιοϲ τηναρχε[              ϲιοϲ τὴν Ἀρχε[. . . . .
     λακηνουκο[                 λακην ουκο[. . . . .
     τραπταιουδε[               τραπται οὐδε[. . . .
15   ποϲταχαδ᾽.[.].[       15   ποϲ· τάχα δ᾽.[.].[. . . .
     .]τιν.[.]. . . .πα[        .]τι ὐ.[.]. . . .πα[. . . .
     .].ολελειμμ[               .]πολελειμμ[έν.. κω-
     .]ωιδειδαυ.ο.[             μ]ωιδεῖ δ᾽ αὐτο.[. . . . .
     . . .]ϲειϲμαλα[            . . .]ϲ εἰϲ μαλα[κίαν..
20   .]. . . .[.]τηνͺ[     20   .]. . . [.]τηνͺ[. . . . . .
     ..]δ[..].. [               ..]δ[..]. [. . . .
     . . . . .]. . . .τε[       . . . . .]. . . .τε[. . . .
     κτα..η.[..].υ[            κτα..η.[..].υ[. . . .
     καιαϲτρα..[                καιαϲτρα..[. . . . .
25   τοιϲαριϲτοφαν[        25   τοῖϲ Ἀριϲτοφαν[είοιϲ·
     λεγουϲιγαρπερ[            λέγουϲι γὰρ περ[ὶ . . . . .
     ενδετοιϲκαλλ.[..].[       ἐν δὲ τοῖϲ Καλλι[ϲτ]ρ[α-
             .[.]ͭ                       .[.]ͭ
     τει[.]ͺι. . . . .τιντηνϲυ.  τεί[ο]ιϲ . . ἐϲτιν τὴν ϲυν-
     τ. . .νενδετοιϲαρι         τόμων. ἐν δὲ τοῖϲ Ἀρι-
30   ϲταρχειοιϲαντιτο.    30   ϲταρχείοιϲ· ἀντὶ τοῦ
     π.[.]ιαυτουοεϲτι.ου        πε[ρ]ὶ αὐτοῦ, ὅ ἐϲτιν οὐ-
     χυπεραλλ..αρι.[...]ε       χ ὑπὲρ ἄλλου. Ἀριϲ[τομ]έ-
     νουϲδιονυϲουαϲκη          νουϲ Διονύϲου ἀϲκη-
     τουτουτιτουγκωμι          τοῦ· τουτὶ τοὐγκώμι-
35   ονω[.]ατυρο[.]περικον 35  ον, ὦ [Ϲ]άτυρο[ι], περὶ κον-
     δυλ[.]υηπερ[.]αυτων        δύλ[ο]υ ἢ περ[ὶ] αὐτῶν.
```

ο̣τιτ̣ωιαυ . . υχρων
ται[.]ντιτ . [.]ς̣αυτου
αισχυλουδ[.] . αϊδων
40   ςτυγηιδετοιο̣υτο̣[.] .

ὅτι τῶι αὑτο̣ῦ χρῶν-
ται [ἀ]ντὶ το̣[ῦ] ςαυτοῦ.
Αἰσχύλου Δ[α]ναΐδων·
40   ςτυγῆι δὲ τοιουτο̣[.] .

Col. iii

. .

φ[

. .

Col. i

1   ] . [(first), the tip of a stroke descending below the line   ] . [(second), a low speck   2   ]τ̣,
the second upright with a suggestion of the cross-bar extending to the right   ., a heavy trace on the
line   τ, a shank   3   ., a speck on the line   4   ] ., an upright   ο̣, lower parts   ς (first),
upper part   ε, tips of cap and cross-bar   ς (second), upper part   τ, both ends of cross-bar   ι,
top   ν, upper left-hand corner   6   . [, upright   ] . [, end of shank descending below the line
7   . ., upright; low specks   . [, end of shank descending below the line   ] ., upright   8   . ,
a trace at mid-line level suiting the bridge of Μ   . [, a faint trace at letter-top level on scoured surface
9   ρ, the middle part of the upright and the upper right-hand corner of the loop   ] . ., an abraded
trace at letter-top level, perhaps Α, Δ, or λ   . ., specks on abraded surface; the number of letters
represented is uncertain   10   . . . . [, an upright; a low speck; an oblique descending from left to
right; specks on abraded surface   at the end of the line, the base of ς or ε; specks at mid-line level;
a speck on the line; above the tops of the letters, a steeply descending stroke with a further speck to
the right; on the line, an upright and the left-hand edge of the lower part of another upright, abraded
on the right   11   ] . ., a trace at letter-top level; the base and top of ς, ε, or ο   . . . . [, a trace on
the line; the upper left-hand arc of a circle; scattered abraded traces; an upright   ] . [.] ., abraded
traces   12   ] . ., a shank descending below the line, abraded at the top and with a further trace to
the left at letter-top level   . . . ., two uprights; scattered traces   . . ., abraded traces, the second
set suiting the left-hand tip and foot of Υ   13   ] ., scattered traces including a suggestion of an
ascending oblique in the upper half of the line: perhaps Υ   14   ]δ̣, the lower right-hand corner
16   ·εν due to the second hand: the first hand wrote λι, which the second hand made into Ν, adding
a high stop and cursive ε in the narrow space preceding   17   ι̣, the right-hand edge of an upright
18   ] ., a descending oblique   19   ] . ., the end of a cross-bar at letter-top level   20   ] ., a speck
at mid-line level followed by a low speck and the top of an upright: Ν possible   . ., a trace suggesting the lower part of ε or ς, followed by specks and an upright on abraded surface   21   ] . [.] .,
abraded traces   . . . ., abraded traces, the first suggesting an upright, the last the right-hand side
of κ or χ   22   ] . . . ., specks   . . ., an abraded upright; the left-hand end of a cross-bar just
below letter-top level followed by a trace of an upright at mid-line level; a trace on the line followed
by a speck at letter-top level   23   ] . . ., a high abraded trace; the upper right-hand arc of a circle;
an upright with traces suggesting the upper left-hand arc of a circle extending from its top, followed
by a trace on the line suggesting the base of a circle on a displaced piece of papyrus   . [, abraded
traces, perhaps the cap, cross-bar, and turn-up of ε   ] ., abraded traces at letter-top and mid-line
levels   ., abraded traces, perhaps an upright   25   ] ., a low flat trace on abraded surface;
perhaps the cap of ς or ε   26   . . ., a trace in the lower half of the line suggesting an upright;
the upper edge of a cross-bar at mid-line level; specks   27   ] ., high and low specks   ] . ., a high
trace; a low trace followed by a short cross-bar at mid-line level   28   ] . ., a short low upright;
a high trace followed by a low trace suggesting an upright   ., an upright, ι or ρ   29   ] . . . .,

a high speck; the base and part of the left-hand side of ∈ or c; a trace on the line; the tail and specks belonging to the left-hand side of ʌ or ʌ   30] ., abraded traces at letter-top level, perhaps the loop of ρ   ., scattered specks   31]., a trace suggesting the base of c or ∈   32]., perhaps the lower part of the stem and the top of the loop of ρ

Col. ii

1].[, a low trace   2]..., the turn-up of c or ∈; the lower part of an upright   7 .[, a speck on the line   8 [.].., a narrow gap followed by the base of a circle   .[, a low trace 9 ., abraded traces   .., a tail turning to the left at the foot, with a further trace just above letter-top level; a trace on the line; an upright   ..., the lower parts of two uprights; an upright   ..[, an upright; the lower part of an upright   10 .., in damaged context, a trace now suggesting the top of a descending oblique; high traces   ., a high cross-bar: τ acceptable   .[, the left-hand arc of a circle attached to the cross-bar of the preceding г   11 η[, the top of the first upright and traces of the cross-bar   14 τ, rubbed traces at letter-top level: τ rather than г   15 .[, a low trace   ].[, a low stroke descending from left to right   16 .[, the top of an upright   ]...., traces at mid-line level; the lower parts of two uprights; a low dot; the turn-up of ∈ or c   17]., the foot of an upright   18 ., a trace below the line   .[, specks   20]....[, traces at letter-top level; perhaps the top of an upright followed by a gently descending low stroke with a trace at letter-top level above its right-hand end: perhaps κ; perhaps o; two uprights, the second perhaps joined from the left low in the line   [.], possibly a blank space, but ink may have been lost to abrasion   ν[, the junction of the first upright and oblique and two further traces to the right: apparently N rather than м   21]..[, traces on a narrow strip of cross-fibres   22]...., a stroke ascending from left to right; perhaps the turn-up of ∈ or c; high and mid-level traces; a low trace 23 .., a dot on the line close to the tail of ʌ; two low specks   .[, perhaps the lower left-hand part of c   ]., specks   24 ..[, the lower part of a short upright; a high speck on the edge of the upper layer   27 .[, a trace on the line   ].[, a tall upright   28 ....., the top of ∈ or c; a high speck on the edge; perhaps the top of o or c; the base of ∈ or c; again the base of ∈ or c, with a higher trace belonging to its left-hand side   ν, the upper parts   ., the top of an upright followed by the edge of the top of an upright, perhaps a narrow N   ...[above the line, rubbed traces, the third perhaps ∈ or c   29 τ, the left-hand end of the cross-bar and the foot   ..., the edge of the lower right-hand arc of a circle; traces suggesting both feet and the upper left-hand corner of м, of which the last (together with the preceding trace) is on a piece displaced to the right; perhaps the lower left-hand corner and the edge of the right-hand side of ω   30 ., specks   31 .[, part of an upright   ., a flat trace on the line close to o   32 ν, the upper left-hand corner   π, the upper right-hand corner   .., specks; above letter-top level, perhaps the upper left-hand corner of γ   .[, the lower part of an upright   35 The final ν is written on γ   ˙36 just above δ, of which the middle part is abraded, a short cross-stroke extending to the right-hand side of the letter 40 ọ, traces suiting the lower right-hand arc of a circle   o[, the upper left-hand arc and part of the top: not ω   ]., a high trace on the edge

'. . . with reference to (?) (the phrase?) "(that?) those who wish take up". (?)

'"And Nicias is of the Aegeis". For Nicias son of Niceratus (belonged to the tribe) Aegeis. Seleucus raises a problem . . . ally . . . [13] . . . to the market-place . . . coming in here towards . . . female innkeeper . . . incident: . . . shepherd . . . goatherd . . . represents . . . boiling . . . lately . . . hints that . . . has had intercourse with the female innkeeper; he calls (?) . . . "disturb" (?) . . . because of . . . in the deed . . . pot(s) . . . untoward fortunes . . . to the goatherd . . . Atreus . . . his own (?) . . . [ii 3] to nothing (?) . . . (in) Arist— . . . home . . . untoward fortunes" is Euripidean . . . that is (?) . . . (of the?) goatherd, as Dionysius says . . . Arche—'s (?) . . . not (?) . . . has been turned (?) . . . not (?)

. . . and quickly (or: perhaps) . . . left behind (?): and (he) ridicules him (or: them) . . . for softness . . . [25] (in) Aristophanes' (writings): for they say "about . . ."; in Callistratus': . . . is "that of short . . ."; in Aristarchus': in place of "about (him)self," i.e. "not for another". Aristomenes' *Dionysus in Training*: "this encomium, O Satyrs, (is) about the knuckle or about (our)selves". Because they use "himself" in place of "yourself". Aeschylus' *Danaids*: "you are detested . . . such . . ."'

Col. i

2–3 Even if correctly restored, the lines are multiply ambiguous. If a quotation, ἀναλα[βεῖν] τοὺς βουλομένους may belong to a passage in iambic trimeters or trochaic tetrameters catalectic.

4 Νικ]ίας τ' Αἰγηΐδός ἐστιν. The first two metra of a trochaic tetrameter catalectic. Nicias is fairly frequently mentioned in comedy: Eupolis fr. 193, Ar. *Eq.* 358 (in which play his name is also given to the second slave), *Av.* 363, 639, fr. 102, Phrynichus fr. 62, Teleclides fr. 44. In view of the prominence of a goatherd in what follows, there is no doubt a pun here on αἴξ.

5–6 Perhaps τῆ]ς γὰρ Αἰγηΐδ[ος φυλῆς | ἦν].

13 βο]ύλεται, φ]υλέται (cf. 4–6)?

14–15 δεῦρ' εἰσιών" πρὸς [τὴν πα]νδοκεύτριαν? Or possibly δεῦρ' εἰσιὼν πρός[ελθε πα]νδοκεύτριαν, an iambic trimeter. Eupolis fr. 9 (from the *Goats*) mentions a πανδοκεύτρια: see on ii 12 below.

19 ἕψων: cf. 29 χύτρας. ἑφητοί appears twice in Eupolis' *Goats* (frr. 5, 16).

20 ἀρτίως or ἄρτι seems likely.

22 Presumably said with reference to a passage in the text under discussion.

23 αἰπό]λος does not seem excluded.

24–5 Perhaps καλεῖ (or καλεῖ[ται) . . . κινῆσαι, if μέ[μ]εικται (23) is used of sexual intercourse.

27–8 Perhaps διὰ τό followed by a weak aorist infinitive active ending in -ςαι.

30 ἀνα]ρςίοις τύχαις restored from ii 7.

32 Atreus may have been named in the original context of the Euripidean phrase ἀναρςίοις τύχαις (ii 7–8).

Col. ii

3–4 Perhaps ἐν] δὲ τοῖς Ἀρις[ταρχείοις: cf. 29–30. Ἀρις[τοφανείοις would be slightly too long: cf. 25, where τοῖς Ἀριστοφαν[είοις is a complete line. But these are not the only possibilities.

6 δόμων will belong to a poetic quotation, whether from the text under discussion or a parallel passage.

7–8 ἀναρςίοις τύχ[αις Εὐρι]πίδε[ι]όν ἐστι[. ἀνάρςιος is found infrequently in tragedy (Aesch. *Ag.* 511, Soph. *Trach.* 640, 853), but does not seem to be attested elsewhere for Euripides. He has a similar expression at *Hel.* 1142–3 ἀντιλόγοις (ἀμφι- Dobree) πηδῶντ' ἀνελπίστοις τύχαις. Eupolis uses Euripidean language most clearly in fr. 99 at 102 (= Eur. fr. 507) and 35 (cf. Eur. fr. 558).

10 τουτέστιν seems acceptable.

11–12 Διονύ]ςιος: note references to scholars of this name in the scholia to Aristophanes at *Av.* 1297–9 (Δ. . . . . ὁ Ζώπυρος) and *Plut.* 322. There is a short blank space after this word, perhaps meant as punctuation.

12 Ἀρχε[. The only κωμωιδούμενοι known from Eupolis whose names begin thus are Archedemus (fr. 80) and Archestratus (fr. 298). Ἀρχε[στράτου would extend to the margin and leave no room for the beginning of the word that ends λακην in the next line. If Ἀρχε[δήμου is accepted, there will be room for one or perhaps two more letters, and φυ]λακήν may be a possibility, though its reference will be unclear. If neither of these names is correct, παλ]λακήν may also be considered. μα]λακήν may be a further possibility (cf. 19), but an adjective would not be easy to accommodate here.

It has been argued that Eupolis fr. 9 τὴν πανδοκεύτριαν γὰρ ὁ γλάμων ἔχει (from the *Goats*) is a second reference in this poet to Archedemus, to whom the same adjective is applied by Aristophanes at *Ran.* 588: see Storey, *Eupolis* 73–4 (doubting the connection). If this identification is correct, the references to a πανδοκεύτρια in the previous column (15, 24) may be relevant.

13–14 (-)τέ]τραπται rather than (-)ἐc]τραπται since the combination cτ is not divided at line-end at 29–30.

17 ἀ]πο-, ὑ]πο-. The participle in whatever case may refer to the same person or persons as αὐτο.[in the next line.

17–19 κωμ]ωιδεῖ δ’ αὐτο.[. . . . . . .]c εἰc μαλα[κίαν. Cf. for the construction e.g. sch. in Ar. *Pac.* 803 ὁ δὲ Μελάνθιοc κωμωιδεῖται εἰc μαλακίαν καὶ ὀψοφαγίαν. καὶ πολὺ μᾶλλον ἐν τοῖc Κόλαξιν Εὔπολιc (fr. 178) ὡc κίναιδον αὐτὸν διαβάλλει καὶ κόλακα.

18 αὐτόν [(perhaps referring to Arche— (12)), or αὐτού[c.

18–19 Εὔ|πολι]c?

23 -κται τῆc?

24 The division at the start is uncertain. At the end, ἐν or ἐν δέ.

24 ff. The explanation found in Aristophanes of Byzantium is followed by those of his pupils Callistratus and Aristarchus.

26 Perhaps περ[ὶ αὐτοῦ: cf. 31.

28–9 τὴν cυντόμων: ω is not certain, but ο was not written. The phrase may be an explanation of a feminine accusative singular that stood in the poetic text (added above the line for clarification?). Before, ὅ ἐcτιν may be possible (cf. 31) but fails to account for the preceding trace. Perhaps that trace is associated with the supralinear addition rather than the main text, and the scribe left a short gap: cf. 12 above.

34–6 τουτὶ τοὐγκώμιον, ὦ [C]άτυρο[ι], περὶ κονδύλ[ο]υ ἢ περ[ὶ] αὐτῶν. An anapaestic te-trameter catalectic. Little is known of this play, to which Aristomenes frr. 11–13 belong. To judge from the line quoted, the chorus will have been Satyrs, as in Cratinus’ *Dionysalexander* and plays entitled *Satyrs* by Ecphantides, Callias, Cratinus, and Phrynichus. A chorus of Satyrs boasts of its prowess in boxing at Soph. fr. **1130.11 (VIII **1083** fr. 1.11).

36 If the sign over the initial letter is a paragraphus, as seems likely, it is out of place. Perhaps it should have been placed under the line, to mark the end of the quotation.

37–8 Cf. Antiatt. *AB* I 77.7 αὐτοῦ: ἀντὶ τοῦ cαυτοῦ. For examples of this usage, familiar from Aeschylus and other authors, see e.g. LSJ s.v. ἑαυτοῦ II.

40 cτυγῆι δὲ τοιουτο[.] : at the end, -ο[υ]c seems possible. -ου is perhaps not excluded, but would be rather generously spaced: contrast the end of 38.

Presumably these words began an iambic trimeter and the whole line was quoted. It is not otherwise known. As it is given as an example of αὐτοῦ used in place of cαυτοῦ, the subject will be second person singular, and cτυγῆι will be indicative passive rather than subjunctive active.

W. B. HENRY / S. TROJAHN

5161–3. GRAECO-LATIN GLOSSARIES

We present here parts of three glossaries on papyrus. Each is of a type familiar from the Hermeneumata Pseudo-Dositheana: **5161** is an alphabetical glossary of conjugated verbs, while **5162** and **5163** are lists of nouns arranged under subject headings. Published bilingual glossaries from papyri have been collected in C. Gloss. Biling. The various versions of the Hermeneumata are cited as A (Amploniana), Mp (Montepessulana), B (Bruxellensis), S (Stephanus), L (Leidensia), M (Monacensia), E (Einsidlensia), Vat (Vaticana), and C (Celtis). Most of the relevant material is included in CGL III and cited by Goetz's page and line, but for L we have used the continuous numeration of G. Flammini, *Hermeneumata Pseudodositheana Leidensia* (2004), and for Vat that of G. Brugnoli and M. Buonocore, *Hermeneumata Vaticana* (2002). The thematic glossary of C (Vindob. suppl. gr. 43) is published in photographic form at http://data.onb.ac.at/rec/AL00147700, and an edition is being prepared by Professor Rolando Ferri, who has kindly made his draft available to us; see in general Ferri, '*Hermeneumata Celtis*: The Making of a Late-Antique Bilingual Glossary', in id. (ed.), *The Latin of Roman Lexicography* (2011) 141–69. In citations from this glossary, Roman numerals refer to sections and Arabic numerals to items within a section. For the table of contents, see A. C. Dionisotti, *JRS* 72 (1982) 92–3; sections i–v, which are of particular relevance to **5162**, have been edited by J. Kramer as P. Paramone 5. The alphabetical glossary of B, not included in CGL, was edited from Brux. 1828–30 (*Br*) by J. Gessler, *RBPh* 16 (1937) 169–78, and from Angers 477 (*A*) by H. Omont, *Bibliothèque de l'École des chartes* 59 (1898) 676 (penult. gloss)–9; another manuscript, Heidelberg, Salem IX.39 (*H*), is published in photographic form at http://digi.ub.uni-heidelberg.de/diglit/salIX39. There is no standard numeration, but entries are easily located in the alphabetical sequence. A fuller version of B forms the basis of the alphabetical glossary in Leid. Voss. Lat. F. 26 (Vo), printed in CGL III 398–421, which preserves, for items beginning with each letter of the Latin alphabet, the original order of the entries in B; the end of this glossary, missing from the Leiden manuscript, can be restored from the fragment in Angers 477 (*A*, published by Omont, as above, 671–6). For general accounts of the Hermeneumata, cf. A. C. Dionisotti, 'From Ausonius' Schooldays?', *JRS* 72 (1982) 83–125; ead., 'Greek Grammars and Dictionaries in Carolingian Europe', in M. W. Herren and S. A. Brown (edd.), *The Sacred Nectar of the Greeks* (1988) 1–56, esp. 26–31, including a table setting out the contents of each of the versions (26–8). A stemma of B is given by Dionisotti, 'From Stephanus to Du Cange: Glossary Stories', *RHT* 14–15 (1984–5) 303–36 (312).

5161. Graeco-Latin Alphabetical Glossary of Conjugated Verbs

7 1B.5/F(b)   11.7 × 20 cm   Third/fourth century
                                                                            Plate VI

Written across the fibres, a fragment of a Greek–Latin alphabetical list of verbs conjugated in the present indicative active, in the first, second, and third persons singular. The upper margin and upper parts of four columns are preserved, containing Greek verbs starting with ρ, ς, τ, υ, and φ, alongside their Latin equivalents. The other side was used for a private letter in Greek, **5182**, of which the address is written downwards along the fibres between cols. i and ii of the glossary.

The Greek is written in an informal, medium-sized round hand, with some ligatures. Bilinearity is respected only to a limited extent, being violated especially by ϕ, ρ, ι (often in ligature with ε), and the enlarged form of γ that may be used in initial position (iii 14–21), and sometimes by the long tail of λ (e.g. at iii 1–3). The uprights of π, τ, ι, and н tend to have curves on the base line. The mid-stroke of ε usually protrudes and connects with the following letter. ε is sometimes written in one movement (e.g. at i 23). The cap of c is regularly flat and in final position extends well into the narrow intercolumnium. γ is often looped at the base (e.g. i 22, iii 4). н tends to have a high cross-bar. N usually has its oblique and second upright made separately but also appears in a cursive form, looped at the upper right (both forms occur side by side at i 25). θ narrows to a point at the bottom, and its cross-bar protrudes from its body to connect with the following letter. There is a correction, executed by the scribe himself, at iii 21. The only diacritic mark in the Greek part of the glossary is the diaeresis inconsistently applied to initial υ (iii 4, etc.). Long paragraphi separate the five alphabetical sections. Iota adscript is not written. The script resembles that of the glossary's closest parallel, P. Strasb. inv. g 1175 (C. Gloss. Biling. II 3; iii/iv), which may suggest a dating in the third or fourth century.

The quality of the Latin script indicates that the scribe was a Greek speaker. There are two cases of character switching (on which see J. N. Adams, *Bilingualism and the Latin Language* (2003) 46): the scribe wrote ηγ for *eg* at ii 25 (though he corrected the γ to g), and η for *e* again at iv 6. Other corrections are found at ii 5 and iv 8–9. The influence of the Greek script also appears in the formation and ductus of several Latin letters (e.g. *x, t, a, e*): on this phenomenon, see e.g. M. Norsa, 'Analogie e coincidenze tra scritture greche e latine nei papiri,' in *Miscellanea Giovanni Mercati* vi (1946) 105–21; B. Rochette, *Le Latin dans le monde grecque* (1997) 204–6; id., 'Écrire en deux langues: Remarques sur le mixage des écritures grecque et latine d'après les papyrus littéraires bilingues d'auteurs classiques', *Scriptorium* 53 (1999) 325–34. There appear to be fewer ligatures in the Latin than in the Greek, which again suggests that the scribe was more experienced in Greek. The scribe tends to lengthen considerably the oblique of *s* and the cross-bar of *t* in inflectional endings, while *l* and *r* descend well under the base line.

Only the sections containing verbs starting with c and υ are preserved complete. Each of these consists of six verbs and occupies eighteen lines. Assuming that the alphabetical sections were all of the same length, we may estimate the original number of lines to a column. The τ section begins at i 31 and ends at iii 3. Thus col. i will have been 45 lines long. On the basis of the same assumption of six verbs (eighteen lines) per alphabetic section, the list will have contained 144 Greek verbs, i.e. 432 conjugated Greek verb forms with their Latin equivalents (another 432 items). It will have occupied approximately twenty columns.

Dr Henry notes that the use of the vertical fibres for this text, which must have been copied before the letter on the back, suggests that the preserved fragment is from the final leaf of a codex which had horizontal fibres on the outside:

such codices, including the bilingual Virgil glossary P. Ryl. III 478+ (M–P³ 2940), are listed by Turner, *The Typology of the Early Codex* 66–7 (Table 11). If col. i was the first column of the page, the alphabetical sequence may have been completed on the same page at col. vii/viii.3. A pair of columns (Greek + Latin) takes up a space 5.75 cm wide. The width of the written area (8 columns) will then have been about 23 cm. 30 lines of text occupy a space about 18 cm high; a 45-line column will then have been about 27 cm high. The upper margin (preserved to its original height, to judge by the horizontal edge above cols. iii–iv) is 1.4 cm high; with a lower margin a little deeper, the page will have been 30.5–31 cm tall. The codex may then have belonged in Turner's 'nearly square' category (*Typology* 15). About 6½ columns of Greek and the same number of Latin, a total of 12 columns and two more half-filled, would be required for the lost beginning of the glossary, up to the top of col. i of the fragment. The glossary is thus unlikely to have been the only work contained in the codex.

The verbs are not alphabetized beyond the initial letter. The observance of alphabetical order within the ϲ section may be accidental. The ρ section is not complete: three conjugated verbs came before ῥάπτω, but it seems unlikely that all of them preceded it alphabetically. In this respect, the glossary follows the general tendency observed by M. Naoumides, 'The Fragments of Greek Lexicography in the Papyri', in *Classical Studies Presented to Ben Edwin Perry* (1969) 181–202 at 188: 'it seems that as a rule there was a certain relation between the size of a dictionary and the degree of strictness of its alphabetical arrangement.' Because of the relatively limited number of verbs found under each letter, strict alphabetical arrangement was not necessary; the same applies to the shorter alphabetical glossaries XLIX **3452** (C. Gloss. Biling. II 7) and P. Strasb. inv. g 1175 (C. Gloss. Biling. II 3).

The closest parallel to this text among the papyri is the codex P. Strasb. inv. g 1175 (C. Gloss. Biling. II 3), the remains of a list of conjugated Greek verbs organized alphabetically (α–γ) together with their Latin equivalents. But in that papyrus the present indicative forms (first, second, and third persons singular) are given in reverse order, beginning with the third person and ending with the first, and the Latin verbs are transcribed in Greek script. Conjugated verbs are found in two further glossaries preserved in papyri. P. Berol. 21246 (C. Gloss. Biling. I 1; I BC), apart from proverbs and sentence models, contains conjugated forms of ἀποδίδωμι *reddo* (5–14), κρατέω *teneo* (23–28), ἔρχομαι *venio* (48–57), and possibly a fourth verb pair (29–35). However, there the verbs are conjugated in different tenses, moods, and voices; the Latin equivalents are transcribed in Greek script. P. Sorb. inv. 2069 (III; new edition: E. Dickey and R. Ferri, *ZPE* 175 (2010) 177–87), a Latin-Greek alphabetic glossary of homonyms with additional grammatical information, also contains conjugated Latin verbs with their Greek equivalents (3–5, 16, 109–10, 129–34); on the sphere of application and the origin of this papyrus see E. Dickey, *ZPE* 175 (2010) 188–208.

All but one of the word pairs in **5161** are attested in the Hermeneumata. One Greek verb (i 25–7) does not occur with its Latin equivalent as given in the papyrus either in the Hermeneumata or in the glossaries of CGL II. Dr Henry notes that the best parallel for the form and content of the text is the alphabetical glossary of B. There, as here, Greek verbs alphabetized by first letter only are conjugated in the first three persons singular (given in order from first to third), and accompanied by Latin translations. B has fewer verbs for each Greek letter, but where we can check, all of its verbs also come up in the present glossary, and in two cases, it shares with **5161** verbs not found in the other alphabetical glossaries among the Hermeneumata (i–ii 13–15, 28–30; cf. 25–7 n.). If we take into account also the fuller form of B quarried by Vo, it shares nearly all the verbs found in the papyrus (exceptions: i–ii 10–12, 16–18 (but see n.), iii–iv 19–21). M also has many of the same verbs conjugated; like Vo, it generally gives more forms than **5161** and B.

On the basis of the script and high number of divergences from classical Latin, the papyrus seems to be a study aid for a Greek speaker learning Latin, perhaps at school. The material could help with language acquisition in two different respects: it was useful for learning new vocabulary and helped with the practising of the conjugation in the simple present.

cols. i–ii

	[-ω	-o]
	-ε]ι[c	-s]
	-]ει [	-]t
	ραπτω	c[onsuo]
5	ραπτεις	[c]onsuis
	ρ]απτει	consit
	ρ]ενω	sparge[o]
	ρ]ενε[ι]c	spargis
	ρενει	spargit
10	ριπτω	precio
	ριπτεις	precis
	ριπτει	precit
	cαλευω	mobeo
	c]αλευεις	mobis
15	c]αλευει	mobit
	c]ηθω	cernio
	c]ηθεις	cernis
	cηθει	cernit
	cιωπω	tacio
20	cιωπας	tacis

cols. iii–iv

	ταραccω	turbo
	ταραccεις	turbas
	ταραccει	turbat
	ὑφενω	texio
5	ὑφενεις	texis
	ὑφενει	tηxit
	ὑποδηννω	calcio
	υποδηννεις	calcis^a
	ὑποδηννει	calcit^a
10	ὑπηρετω	minist[ro
	ὑπηρετεις	minist[ras
	ὑπηρετει	ministr[at
	ὑπαγω	bado
	υπαγεις	badis
15	υπαγει	badet
	υπολυω	exculci[o
	υπολυεις	exculci[as
	υπολυει	exculci[at
	ὑποφερω	suffer[o
20	υποφερεις	sufferi[s

	ςιωπα	tacit		υποφερει	sufferi[t
	ςυρω	trago		φιλω	amo
	ςυρεις	tragis		φιλεις	amas
	ςυρει	tragit		φ[ιλει]	amat
25	ςυννευω	accęngo	25	[φυςω]	s[u]fflo
	ςυννευεις	accęgis		[φυςας	sufflas]
	ςυννευει	accęgit		[φυςα	sufflat]
	ςυντηρω	conserbo		*18 lines lost*	
	ςυντηρεις	conserbas			
30	ςυντηρει	conserbat			
	τηρω	serbiio			
	[τηρεις	serbis]			
	[τηρει	serbit]			

12 lines lost

'. . . I sew together, you sew together, he/she sews together; I sprinkle, you sprinkle, he/she sprinkles; I throw, you throw, he/she throws; I move, you move, he/she moves; I sift, you sift, he/she sifts; I keep silence, you keep silence, he/she keeps silence; I drag, you drag, he/she drags; I agree, you agree, he/she agrees; I protect, you protect, he/she protects; I watch over, you watch over, he/she watches over; . . . I trouble, you trouble, he/she troubles; I weave, you weave, he/she weaves; I put on shoes, you put on shoes, he/she puts on shoes; I do service, you do service, he/she does service; I go, you go, he/she goes; I take off my shoes, you take off your shoes, he/she takes off his/her shoes; I endure, you endure, he/she endures; I love, you love, he/she loves; I blow, you blow, he/she blows; . . .'

cols. i–ii

1–3 A verb with initial ρ is to be restored on the Greek side. [Dr Henry suggests ῥήϲϲω] -ε]ι̣[ϲ -]ει *allido] -is] -i]t*, which fits traces and spaces on both sides. This is one of the verbs conjugated in the ρ section of B (cf. also Vo 399.71–7), together with ῥιγῶ, ῥαίνω, and ῥάπτω. As the verbs found in B all come up in the papyrus wherever it is possible to check, we should expect ῥήϲϲω and ῥιγῶ to have been two of the remaining three verbs in the ρ section of the papyrus text, and the latter will not fit here (note 3 -]ει). Cf. for the pair also L 236, A 79.3, Gloss. Steph. CGL III 439.20.]

4–6 The word pair recurs in B (cf. also Vo 402.7–14). The verb *consuo* also appears as *cuso* (cf. L 237, Gloss. Steph. 444.75–6, Gloss. Lois. CGL III 475.42, 44) or as *cossuo* (so cod. *Br* in B; cf. Gloss. Steph. 444.27). In A 78.70 and M 157.25–8 the Greek verb is glossed by forms of *sarcio*.

4 *c[onsuo]*: the spelling is uncertain: cf. 5–6.

5 *[c]onsii̲s*: l. *consuis*. The final *s* is corrected from *o*.

6 *con̲sit*: l. *consuit*. See C. Battisti, *Avviamento allo studio del latino volgare* (1949) 142.

7–9 -ε- is written for -αι-: see Gignac, *Grammar* i 191–2. The pair recurs in B (cf. Vo 417.44–9); cf. also L 235, A 79.9–10 (*reni aspargo*; *ranon asparge*), M 157.14–18, Gloss. Steph. 464.22, Gloss. Bern. CGL III 503.12, CGL II 427.22.

7 *sparge[o]*: l. *spargo*. The incorrect verb form *spargeo* illustrates the hesitation in the conjugation of the verb classes *-ĕre* and *-ēre* which was characteristic of Vulgar Latin (cf. V. Väänänen, *Introduction au latin vulgaire* (³1981) 136), and of which several examples are present in the papyrus.

10–12 *preci̲o preci̲s preci̲t*: l. *proicio proicis proicit*. -oi- here was pronounced as a diphthong. Monophthongization produced a closed *e*: see Väänänen, *Introduction* 38. B and Vo do not have this pair, but cf. L 233, A 79.8, M 157.20–24, Gloss. Steph. 461.21, CGL II 428.23 Ριπτω επιακοντιου *iacio iaculor proicio*.

13–15 *mo̱beo mo̱bis mo̱bit*: l. *moveo moves movet*. For the spelling with *-b-*, see TLL VIII 1538.21–4; Väänänen, *Introduction* 50; J. G. F. Powell in R. Ferri (ed.), *The Latin of Roman Lexicography* (2011) 113–14. For *-is -it* in this verb, cf. TLL VIII 1538.36–8; 7 n. The word pair is found in B (cf. Vo 411.28–31), and in Gloss. Steph. 456.74, CGL II 131.2 *Movet* κεινει, cαλευει, 429.38 Cαλευω *moveo commoveo agito*.

16–18 For the word pair, cf. L 244 cη̑cον *cerne*, A 79.23, M 158.12–15, Gloss. Steph. 441.60 *cerne*, cη̑cον, Gloss. Lois. 475.46 *cerne* cη̑cον, CGL II 99.51 *Cernit* οραι, cηθει. This Greek verb is not found in B, and in Vo its place in the c section is taken by the synonymous cινιάζω, with the same Latin gloss (402.15–18).

16 *ce̱rnio*: l. *cerno*. The verb form *cernio* seems to follow the analogy of the type *capio*: cf. iv 4.

19–21 *ta̱cio ta̱cis ta̱cit*: l. *taceo taces tacet*. Because of the phonetic alternation of *-eo* and *-io* (Väänänen, *Introduction* 45), some verbs with the infinitive *-ēre* tended to be conjugated as *-īre* verbs in Vulgar Latin; see Väänänen, *Introduction* 135. The word pair is found in B (cf. Vo 419.37–42); cf. L 243 cιώπα *tace*, A 79.20, M 158.4–11, Mp 339.74–6, Gloss. Steph. 465.12 *taceo*, cιωπω̑, cιγω̑, Gloss. Bern. 503.56, CGL II 432.25 Cιωπω *taceo obticeo sileo conticuo*.

22–4 *tra̱go tra̱gis tra̱git*: l. *traho trahis trahit*. The form *trago* for *traho* is found in a ninth-century manuscript of the pseudo-Eusebian collection of Gallican sermons (A. Souter, *JThS* 41 (1940) 48). *h* was not pronounced in this intervocalic position (see Väänänen, *Introduction* 55), and *g* was not pronounced between such back vowels as *a* and *o* (cf. e.g. CIL II 5728 *Austo = Agusto*) or even between palatal vowels in some instances (cf. e.g. CIL III 14730 *maester = magister*): see Väänänen, *Introduction* 58. This may explain the use of *g* instead of *h* in this position. The change may also be motivated by the fact that γ before a front vowel was regularly pronounced as fricative [j], which was in some cases omitted in writing or conversely inserted: see Gignac i 71–2. Thus a scribe more familiar with Greek than Latin could easily use the grapheme *g* in this verb paradigm, especially in the forms *trahis*, *trahit*, and then analogically in *traho* as well. The word pair is not found in B but is present in Vo 419.43–54; cf. L 248 cυ̑ρον *trahe*, Gloss. Steph. 465.51 *trahe*, cυ̑ρον, CGL II 200.9 *Trahit* cυρει, 449.2 Cυρω *traho*.

25–7 cυννεύω is not found in the Hermeneumata nor in the glossaries of CGL II. The Latin equivalent is also problematic. On the basis of Vulgar Latin phonology, one may consider *accedo*, *attingo*, and *accingo* as possible candidates. *Accedo* could be paired with cυννεύω as both mean, among other things, 'agree' (LSJ s.v. II.3; OLD s.v. 8). There are sporadic examples of the interchange of *d* and *g* before the front vowel *i* in Vulgar Latin, e.g. *fastigium* for *fastidium*, *corridiae* for *corrigiae*, *Remidium* for *Remigium*; cf. Battisti, *Avviamento* 147. It is also possible that *-go -gis -git* is due to the influence of 22–4. [Dr Henry compares for the confusion the spellings of *allido -is -it* glossing ρή̑ccω -εic -ει in B (cf. 1–3 n. for the suggestion that this verb was present in those lines of the papyrus): *H* has *d* throughout, but *Br* gives *alligo alligis allidet*, and *A alligo allidis allidit*. He notes that the interpretation of the Latin in the papyrus as representing *accedo -is -it* is supported by B, where in manuscripts *A* and *Br*, the c section curiously includes πληcιάζω -εic -ει (with Greek transliterated and misspelt) glossed as *accedo -is -it*. (In manuscript *H*, the verb has been moved to the end of the π section, but this is certainly a later development: for re-alphabetization in *H*, see A. C. Dionisotti, *RHT* 14–15 (1984–5) 312.) This is one of only five items in the B verb-list not taken over into Vo (noted by Dionisotti 306 n. 6). The papyrus suggests an explanation. Perhaps the Greek, as given in the papyrus, had dropped out at an early stage through damage to a common archetype and was missing from the fuller form of B used for Vo. The verb was useless without a Greek equivalent and so was omitted from Vo. At a later stage, the gap was conjecturally filled by forms of πληcιάζω (*A Br*), shown by the 'wrong' initial letter to be no more than a guess. Finally, these were moved to the 'correct' place in the alphabetical sequence (*H*). Gloss. Steph. 438.5 is the only other example of the pair *accedo*, πληcιάζω indexed at CGL VI 12; Stephanus's source for the entry is likely to have been his manuscript of B (cf. Dionisotti 313–17 with stemma at 317).]

25 *acçṇgo*: the scribe originally wrote ηγ. He corrected the γ to Latin *g*, but left the η unchanged: cf. iv 6.

28–30 For -*b*- replacing -*v*-, cf. 13–15 n. The word pair is found in B (cf. Vo 402.19–24); cf. also Gloss. Steph. 443.44, CGL II 112.19 *Conservat* cυντηρει, cωζει, διατηρει, 448.21.

31 *serbiio*: l. *servo*. For -*b*- replacing -*v*-, cf. 13–15 n. *servo* has been confused with *servio*. Its compound in *con*- has the correct terminations at 28–30, but in that case there is no corresponding compound of *servio* to generate confusion. The word pair is not found in B but is present in Vo 417.50–58; cf. L 259 τηρεῖ *servat*, A 79.47, M 159.58–65, Gloss. Steph. 463.52 *servat*, τηρεῖ, CGL II 455.16.

32–3 Restored on the basis of 31.

cols. iii–iv

1–3 The word pair is found in B (cf. also Vo 419.63–5, where forms of *turbulento* have taken the place of those of *turbo*); cf. M 160.8–11, Gloss. Steph. 465.69, Gloss. Bern. 504.11, CGL II 451.48.

4–6 -ε- is written for -αι-: cf. i–ii 7–9 n. The word pair is found in B (cf. Vo 419.67–75); cf. also L 279 ὑφαίνουcιν *texent*, A 80.6, M 161.27–9, E 270.22, Gloss. Steph. 465.34, Gloss. Bern. 505.36, CGL II 198.11 *Texit* υφαινει, 468.57.

4 *texio*: l. *texo*. Cf. i–ii 16 n.

6 *tṇxit*: l. *texit*. Cf. i–ii 25 n.

7–9 -η- is written for -ε-: cf. Gignac i 246. ὑποδέννω is a late Greek form of ὑποδέω; see LSJ s.v. ὑποδέω. The pair is not in B, but is in Vo 402.39–50; cf. L 281 ὑπόδηcον *calcia*, M 161.12–16, CGL II 465.51 Υποδεομω *calcio*, 466.5 Υποδηcον *calcia*, Dosith. *Ars gramm.* 77.3 Tolkiehn.

8–9 The -*io* ending was at first associated with the paradigm -*is*, -*it* (though a correction has been carried out). The verb class in -*āre* was the most resistant to changes in Vulgar Latin; see Battisti, *Avviamento* 244.

10–12 The word pair is in B (cf. also Vo 411.32–9); cf. L 280 ὑπηρετοῦcιν *ministrant*, A 80.3, M 161.17–20, CGL II 465.19 Υπηρετω *ministro obsequor*.

13–15 For the spelling with *b*- instead of *v*-, cf. i–ii 13–15 n. The word pair is in B (cf. cod. *A* of the Vo glossary, p. 675 Omont); cf. also M 161.56–8, Gloss. Steph. 465.77, Gloss. Bern. 505.43, CGL II 463.8 Υπαγω αντιτουπορευομαι *vado*. There are also other equivalents for the Greek verb ὑπάγω in the tradition, cf. L 275 ὕπαγε *duc te*, A 80.1 *ypago eo*.

15 For -*et* instead of -*it*, cf. i–ii 7 n.; Väänänen, *Introduction* 30 (confusion of the graphemes *E* and *I*).

16–18 For the Latin endings, cf. 8–9 n. -*culc*- and -*calc*- are both found in this and related words, but -*culc*- (as here) is perhaps to be preferred: cf. TLL V.1 1274.68–80. The pair is not found in B, but is in Vo 405.68–72; cf. L 282 ὑπόλυcον *exculcia*, Gloss. Steph. 447.43 *excalcia*, ὑπόλυcον. For the Greek verb with other Latin equivalents, cf. M 161.6–12 *ypoluo discultio* etc., CGL II 466.53–55 Υπολυομαι *disculcior excalcior*; Υπολυcον *excalcia*; Υπολυω *decalcio*.

19–21 Cf. L 291, A 79.74, M 160.65–7, Gloss. Steph. 464.68, CGL II 468.29 Υποφερω *perfero subfero*. The pair is not found in B or Vo.

20–21 *sufferi[s] sufferi[t]*: l. *suffers suffert*. On the normalization processes applying to irregular verbs, see Väänänen, *Introduction* 136.

21 ει is corrected from ω.

22–4 The pair is in B (cf. Vo 400.4–15); cf. also L 296 φιλεῖ *amat*, A 80.28, M 162.32–8, Gloss. Steph. 439.29 *amat*, φιλεῖ, Gloss. Bern. 495.2, CGL II 472.6 Φιλω *amo adamo*.

25–7 The pair is in B (*Br H*; cf. Vo 417.75–418.2); cf. also L 303 φυcᾷ *sufflat*, A 80.31, M 162.58–9, Gloss. Steph. 464.69, Gloss. Bern. 495.3, CGL II 474.12 Φυcω *flo sufflo*; CGL VII 313.

ZS. ÖTVÖS

5162. Graeco-Latin Thematic Glossary

100/34(a)　　　　　　　　　　12.5 × 29.1 cm　　　　　　　　First/second century
　　　　　　　　　　　　　　　　　　　　　　　　　　　　　　　　　Plate VII

The papyrus contains parts of three columns. Of the first, some Latin word-ends are preserved, while the second and third, of which only the latter is preserved to its full height, give the remains of 42 lines of Greek lemmata and their Latin equivalents. The column height is 23.6 cm, the lower margin is 4.2 cm deep (probably its original depth), and the upper margin was at least 1.2 cm high. The intercolumnium is about 1.9 cm at its narrowest. On the back, upside down in relation to the text of the glossary, are remains of two columns of Greek medical prose, which will be published in a forthcoming volume.

The glossary is written entirely in the Greek alphabet with the Latin transliterated. This suggests that it was primarily intended for Greek speakers learning Latin; cf. A. Bataille, *RechPap* 4 (1967) 165–6. The text is written in an informal round hand. Letters are sometimes joined with ligatures, and there are some cursive tendencies. There is some resemblance to the hands of II **225** (pl. v; Cavallo–Maehler, *Hellenistic Bookhands* 91; 1) and XVIII **2161** (pl. iii; *GMAW*² 24; ii). The majority of the letters are bilinear, with only ϕ, ẏ, ρ, and at times ι violating bilinearity. Uprights and obliques are often slightly curved. The cross-stroke of ε is usually slightly detached and extends beyond its body. It is often connected to the following letter. γ is normally V-shaped and looped at the base, but it is y-shaped in iii 37 (first) and iii 40 (first). λ has a rounded bowl, while μ has a low round saddle and legs curving out at the bottom. c may have an almost flat top and is written in two movements, with the cap sometimes separated; ο can be quite small, floating between the lines. There are no diacritical marks except for internal diaeresis in ii 13 and rough breathing where needed in the Latin (iii 5). Long ι is regularly spelt ει. Corrections are present at i 5 and iii 20 and 27. Both Greek headings in col. ii are placed in *ekthesis*, as is the first of the Latin headings in col. iii (6). There is a serious corruption in the Latin at iii 11–12 (see commentary), not corrected in what is preserved. Other errors in the Latin (not including mere orthographical variants) are found at iii 23, 25, 28, 34, 38, and 40: those at 23 and 34 at least are visual corruptions.

The lemmata are organized thematically under headings, three of which can be recognized (i 14: *On the sky*; ii/iii 6: *On stars*; and ii/iii 32: *On winds*). The first section (i 1–13) is fragmentary, but probably lists the names of goddesses. The closest parallel among papyri of bilingual glossaries is XLVI **3315** (i/ii; C. Gloss. Biling. I 8), which gives parts of two thematic groups. One column is partially preserved, with Latin written in the Greek alphabet. **3315** presents the last five of the signs of the zodiac, given in the correct order: Scorpio, Sagittarius, Capricorn, Aquarius,

Pisces. (In our papyrus at ii/iii 27–31, a different order is found.) The names given under the heading *On winds* in **3315** recur in our papyrus, with one exception: *Volturnus* is only given in **3315** 12. There are slight differences in the orthography of the wind names in the two lists. The order of names is identical, except that **3315** omits *Eurus* after *Africus*, and has *Volturnus* (not present in **5162**) after *Favonius*; it breaks off after *Subsolanus*. Differences in the Greek–Latin equivalences cannot be detected, since the Greek of **3315** is missing.

If the reconstruction adopted here is correct, the first thematic group in the papyrus (names of goddesses) is paralleled by P. Mich. inv. 2458 (II/III; N. E. Priest, *ZPE* 27 (1977) 193–200; C. Gloss. Biling. I 12). There a series of names of gods (i/ii 1–11) is followed by a list of names of goddesses (i/ii 13–28), introduced by a heading (i/ii 12). Again, the Latin is written in the Greek alphabet.

There are numerous papyri containing similar thematic lists of names (e.g. fish in C. Gloss. Biling. I 5; fish and vegetables in C. Gloss. Biling. I 6 and 7 (XXXIII **2660** and **2660a**); months in C. Gloss. Biling. I 11): see C. Gloss. Biling. II p. 26.

The lemmata in the glossary are well attested in the Hermeneumata. The order of the sections in our papyrus is closely matched by M (167.25–   ) and C. In each of these, the first five sections of the thematic glossary (omitting minor divergences in the wording of the titles) are (in Latin) *deorum nomina, dearum nomina, de caelo, de signis caelestibus*, and *de XII signis*. The last four of these are found in the same order in the papyrus (although *de XII signis* is attached to the preceding section without a separate heading). Other thematic glossaries in the Hermeneumata also begin with *deorum nomina, dearum nomina, de caelo* (L 391–513, A 82.51–83.46) or *deorum nomina, dearum nomina* (E 236.21–237.9, Mp 289.41–291.53) before diverging (I have not distinguished cases where goddesses follow gods in a single list). Only in B (followed by S) are *deorum nomina* and *dearum nomina* in second and third place, after *de caelo* (393.28–394.10, 348.8–49). Dr Henry suggests that the papyrus text also began with a list of names of gods and that the preserved section listing names of goddesses was the second (cf. for this part of the sequence also C. Gloss. Biling. I 12, mentioned above): in that case, to judge by M, in which the first two sections extend from 167.25 to 168.57, two pairs of columns might suffice to contain the material lost at the start.

As in our papyrus (ii/iii 2–5), the seasons are often listed under the heading περὶ οὐρανοῦ *de caelo* (L 484, M 168.58, S 347.27, C iii). In Mp, the relevant heading is περι κεμωνων *de tempestatibus* (293.65), while in E, they are listed under the heading περὶ χρόνου *de temporibus* (242.25), and in Vat they appear under the heading περὶ γῆϲ *de terra* (399). In A, they are attached to the list of goddesses' names, but *perioyranu de caelo* is the next section (83.34).

The section *de caelo* is followed by *de signis caelestibus* in M and C (see above) and in E (241.17, 35) and effectively in Vat (265 *de caelo*, 278–9 *nomina stellarum*), while in Mp the sections on stars immediately precede *de tempestatibus*. The papyrus includes the signs of the zodiac at the end of the section περὶ ἄςτρων, while in the thematic glossaries found in the Hermeneumata they have a separate heading, whether they stand alone (L 1703 (cf. A 82.49–50), Mp 291.54, Vo 405.24) or with other stars (M 170.16, C v, E 241.67, Vat 291–2). (There is another list in L at 72.34–45, without separate heading, but this is not part of the thematic glossary.) The signs of the zodiac are given in the correct order in the Hermeneumata and in **3315** where preserved, as mentioned above. In our papyrus they appear in a different order, though the first two and last are correctly placed.

The list of wind names appears in the Hermeneumata at L 599–610, A 84.50–64, M 172.5–28, E 245.30–50, Mp 295.10–28, S 354.6–29, B 395.66–396.6, Vat 380–98, C xlviii. In **3315**, as in **5162**, the wind names come immediately after the signs of the zodiac. This sequence of these two elements is found in the Hermeneumata only in the fuller version of B used in Vo, with a book division before *de ventis* (Dionisotti, *RHT* 14–15 (1984–5) 306–7 with 307 n. 1).

col. i　　　　　　　　　　　cols. ii–iii

	col. i		cols. ii	col. iii
	]τας		[ ]	ν[
	].		[εαρ]	ου[ηρ
	].α		[θερος]	α[ι]ςτ[ας
	]ξ		[φθινοπωρον]	αυτο[υμνουc
5	κονκο]ρδ⟦έ⟧ια	5	χειμων	ἱεμψ[
	]		περι αστρω[ν]	δη cε[ιδεριβουc
	]ωραι		αστρα	cειδ[ερα
	]		αστερες	cτηλ[λαι
	]		εςπερος	ουεςπ[ερ
10	]	10	φωςφορο[ς]	λουκι[φερ
	]τια		αρκτος	ουεργ[ιλια
	].		πλειας	φειδικ[ουλα
	ιουου]εντους		οϊςτος	cαγιτα
	δη κα]ιλω		κυων	κανιc
15	καιλο]υμ	15	λυρα	φηδικου[λα
	]		ειρις	αρκουc
	]ουμ		δελφειν	δελφεινου[c
	]		cτεφ[α]νος	κορωνα
	]τους		ιππο[ς]	εκουc
20	]c	20	κρειος	αρ⟦έ⟧ηνc
	]ατ		ταυρος	ταυρουc
	]		λεων	λεο
	].		ζυγον	λιβολ
	]		παρθενος	ουιργο

25	]μ	25	αιγοκερως	καπριοκ[ορνους
	]		διδυμοι	γεμεινει
	]		υδροχοος	ακ⟦ο⟧υαριου[ϲ
	]		τοξοτηϲ	ταγιταρ[ιους
	].α		ϲκορπιος	ϲκορπιο
30	]	30	κανκινος	κανκρου[ϲ
	]		ιχθυϲ	πιϲκε̣[ι]ϲ̣
	]		περι ανεμων	δη ο̣[υεντεις
	]α̣		α̣νεμος	ουεν[τους
	]		β]ορεας	ακοιλε
35	]	35	νοτος	αυϲτερ
	. . . .		λ]ειψ	αφρικους
			ευρος	ευρους
			ζεφυρος	φαωνικους
			α]παρκιας	ϲεπτεντριο
		40	α]πηλιωτης	ϲουβ[ϲ]ωλανιους̣
			χ]ωρος	τερεϲτρις
			κ]αικιας	καικιας

'. . . , Concordia, . . . , Horae (?), . . . , Iuventus.

'On the sky: sky, . . . , spring, summer, autumn, winter.

'On stars: stars, stars, Evening Star, Morning Star, Ursa Major, Pleiad, Sagitta, Sirius/Canis Major, Lyra, rainbow, Dolphin, Corona, Equus, Aries, Taurus, Leo, Libra, Virgo, Capricorn, Gemini, Aquarius, Sagittarius, Scorpio, Cancer, Pisces.

'On winds: wind, north wind, south wind, south-west wind, east wind, west wind (zephyr), north wind, east wind, north-west wind, north-east wind.'

col. i

The upper margin is not preserved, but to judge from col. iii, no lines are lost at the top of the column.

1 The first trace is an upright. If it represents τ, suitable names of goddesses (cf. 5 n.) with approximately five letters before the ending *-tas* are *felicitas* (L 457, Mp 291.25, B 394.6 (S 348.45), C ii.40–41), *dignitas* (L 475), *libertas* (M 168.17, C ii.56), *castitas* (M 168.36, C ii.83), *voluptas* (Mp 291.43, C ii.112).

2 The upper arc of a circle and a trace on the line, perhaps ϲ.

3]., a speck at mid-line level. Naturally, there are many names of goddesses (cf. 5 n.) ending with *a* and having approximately six letters before this ending, e.g. *minerva* (L 434, A 83.14, etc.), *fortuna* (L 437, C ii.47, etc.), *bellona* (M 168.43, C ii.44, etc.), *victoria* (M 168.48, C ii.48).

4 Since there is space for about five letters, the name of a goddess (cf. 5 n.) to be supplied is probably *ultrix* (C. Gloss. Biling. I 12 ii 21; M 168.21, Mp 291.40, C ii.23).

5 The ε is deleted by dots above and below, and a short cancel stroke is squeezed in between it and the preceding δ. As the name of a goddess, *concordia* occurs frequently in the Hermeneumata in CGL III with its Greek equivalent ὁμόνοια: L 458, M 168.28, Mp 291.15, B 393.54 (S 348.34). It also appears in C ii.38, where it is immediately followed by *discordia* (ii.39), which does not appear as the

name of a goddess in the Hermeneumata in CGL III. For the placing of goddesses' names here in the sequence of topics, see the introduction.

7 Of ω, a trace suiting the right-hand side. With the ending -ραι we find only one goddess name: *horae* (A 83.33, M 168.46, C ii.59). But by itself this would not extend so far to the right. [Dr Henry suggests that the entry in the preceding line, only about four letters long to judge by 5, was ωραι, and that line 7 contained αυρ]ωραι, a corruption (for *aurora*) due to the influence of the preceding line: cf. on ii–iii 38, 40 for corruption in the Latin possibly due to the influence of earlier entries. For the sequence, cf. M 168.45–6, where *aurora* immediately precedes *horae*; for Ἥὼϲ Aurora in lists of goddesses, cf. also L 447, 477, Mp 290.70, C ii.24.]

11 The most likely goddess name with approximately eight letters before the ending -*tia* is *providentia* (L 476, C ii.66, etc.) or *clementia* (Mp 291.53). C, however, contains further possible items (e.g. *indulgentia* ii.98, *experientia* ii.100, *immetuentia* ii.109) which usually do not occur in other Hermeneumata.

12]. : the lower part of an oblique descending from left to right.

13 For the goddess Iuventus, cf. OLD s.v. 3. The name appears in C ii.61 as the equivalent of the Greek Ἥβη; cf. *Iuventas* in L 478.

14 Of]ι, the edge of an upright. For parallels for the order of topics, see the introduction.

15 For the assumed pattern, with *caelum* immediately following the heading *de caelo*, cf. L 485, M 168.59, E 241.18, Vat 266, S 347.2, 28, and comparable sequences below at ii/iii.6–7, 32–3; for *caelum*, also P. Lond. II 481 (C. Gloss. Biling. I 13) 8 (κηλωϲ), C iii.6.

17 Possible meteorological terms with approximately five letters before the preserved ending include *nubilum* (L 489, C iii.45, etc.), *serenum* (L 490, C iii.47, etc.), *tonitrum* (L 508, written as *tonitruum*, A 83.35), etc.

19 Possibilities found under this heading include *aestus* (L 499, A 83.43, C iii.71, etc.), *hiatus* (C iii.50), *crepitus* (C iii.82), *tumultus* (C iii.89), etc. Since only *aestus* is preserved in more than one source and its length also matches the size of the lacuna, it is the most likely.

20 Possibilities include *nubes* (L 488, C iii.44, etc.), *ros* (L 492, C iii.63, etc.), *frigus* (L 498, C iii.142, etc.). As the lacuna is short, *ros* is the most probable.

21 Possibilities of about the right length include *rorat* (M 169.5, C iii.66, etc.) and *tonat* (M 169.16, C iii.102, etc.). [Dr Henry notes that the sequence favours the former: cf. M 169.3–5, E 244.52–4, Mp 294.38–9, C iii.63–6.]

23 A spot of ink on the edge.

25 Cf. 17 n. for possible supplements.

29]. : an upright, perhaps ι. A possibility is *pluvia* (L 493, M 169.7, C iii.55, etc.).

33 Meteorological terms with approximately four or five letters before the ending -*a* include *nebula* (L 491, C iii.96, etc.), *nubila* (B 393.7 (S 347.4)), *stilla* (C iii.69), *umbra* (C iii.90, etc.).

There is space for nine more lines at the foot of the column below line 35.

cols. ii–iii

1 In the Hermeneumata, the Latin word beginning with *n* that appears closest to *ver* is most often *nix* (L 496, M 169.9, Mp 294.43, S 347.43), but the two never occur one after the other.

2–5 In the Hermeneumata, we find the names of the four seasons one after the other five times: three times in the same order as in the papyrus (L 500–503, A 83.27–30, C iii.34–37), and twice in a different order (S 347.49–52: winter, spring, summer, autumn; Vat 436–8: summer, spring, autumn, winter). In other versions, the names do not form a single block: M 168.65, 169.27–9; E 242.42, 44, 46–7; Mp 293.72, 294.32, 46, 51.

2 Restored on the basis of the presence at 3–5 of the other three seasons.

3 α[ι]ϲτ[αϲ: or -[ουϲ. Both forms appear in this word pair in the Hermeneumata. Cf. L 501, A 83.28, M 169.27, E 242.46, Mp 294.32, S 347.51, Vat 436, C iii.35, CGL II 327.64.

4 On the basis of the Latin, a Greek word meaning 'autumn' is to be restored, either φθινόπωρον or μετόπωρον. φθινόπωρον is more probable, since all of the Hermeneumata use it: L 502, A 83.29, M 169.29, Mp 294.51, S 347.52, C iii.36. E 242.47 has both terms. In CGL II we find μετόπωρον as the Greek equivalent of *autumnus* three times (27.36, 366.27, 542.14), and φθινόπωρον occurs similarly three times (470.52, 491.4, 514.34).

5 The word-initial iota seems to be written with an L-shaped rough breathing. For the word pair, cf. L 503, A 83.30, M 168.65, E 242.42, Mp 293.72, S 347.49, Vat 438, C iii.37, CGL II 68.41, 476.20, 495.72, 540.51, 553.12. In the majority of these entries (all except E 242.42, C iii.37, and CGL II 540.51), the word is spelt with -*ps* as here. See in general on the spelling with *ps* TLL VI.3 2773.64 ff.

6 The thematic title under which the names of stars are grouped is not found in this form in the Hermeneumata, which instead attest a longer form: περὶ τῶν οὐρανίων ἄστρων (or περὶ ἄστρων οὐρανίων) *de signis caelestibus*: cf. M 169.63, E 241.35, Mp 292.55. In C iv the title appears as *de signis caelestibus* περὶ ἄστρων ζωδίων οὐρανοῦ (but in the table of contents (5) the Greek is περὶ ἄστρων οὐρανίων). On the basis of the Hermeneumata, δη cε[ιγνειc would also be possible. The translation of αcτρα in the next line lends some support to the supplement printed, but the inconsistency is not impossible: M has the same in the first entry of the section.

7 For the word pair, cf. M 169.64, E 241.36 (in the singular and with the Latin equivalents *signum, astrum, sidus*), Mp 293.10 (in the singular), Vat 277, CGL II 183.39, 42 (in the singular), and 248.50 (in the singular).

8 For the word pair, cf. P. Lond. II 481 (C. Gloss. Biling. I 13) 6, L 486, M 168.63, E 242.9 (in the singular), S 347.32, 48 (in the singular), B 393.6 (S 347.3), Vo 417.70, CGL II 188.15 and 248.36 (both in the singular).

9 For the word pair, cf. M 170.15, Gloss. Bern. CGL III 492.77, CGL II 315.23; also C iv.6 (Lat. *vesperugo*), Vat 280–81.

10 For the word pair, cf. M 169.65, E 242.21/2, Mp 293.44, Vat 282, C iv.5, CGL II 124.36 and 474.26.

11 ουεργ[ιλια glosses πλειάc (ii 12): at some stage in the transmission, a scribe accidentally skipped the Latin equivalent of ἄρκτοc and copied the Latin equivalent from the next line instead. Cf. M 169.66 *arctos septentrio*, E 241.29 ὁ ἄρκτοc *septentrio*, 241.60 ἡ ἄρκτοc *ursa*, Mp 293.14–15 αρκτοc ελικη *septentrio maior*, αρκτοc κυνοcορα *septentrio minor*, Vat 286 αρκτοc *septentrio*, C iv.1 *ursae* ἄρκτοι, CGL II 244.53 αρκτοc η εν τω ουρανω *hic septentrio*.

12 πλειαc. The Greek word otherwise occurs in bilingual lists in the plural, with Latin *vergiliae* (11 n.): cf. M 170.2, E 241.63 (Lat. *pliades, vergiliae*), Mp 293.18, Vat 284, CGL II 206.34 and 409.11.

φειδικ[ουλα: i.e. *fidicula*. The usual transcription of Latin *i* would be ι or ε; see Gignac, *Grammar* i 254–6. φειδικ[ουλα may have come in, after the presence of an omission (cf. 11 n.) had been detected, from an unrelated marginal addition meant as a correction for φηδικου[λα (15). The correct Latin equivalent of the Greek πλειάc is found in the previous line.

13 cαγιτα: i.e. *sagitta*; for the simplification of the geminate, cf. 28, 41; V. Väänänen, *Introduction au latin vulgaire* (³1981) 58. For the word pair in astronomical context, cf. M 170.6, E 241.47, Mp 293.35, C iv.16.

14 For the word pair, cf. M 169.67, E 241.56, Mp 293.28 (Lat. *canicula*), S 348.4 (Lat. *canicula*), C iv.20, CGL II 97.5 and 357.22.

15 For the transcription of Latin *i* as η, see Gignac, *Grammar* i 239. For the word pair, cf. M 170.5, C iv.18, E 241.42 (both *fidicula* and *lyra*). Mp 293.33 has only *lyra* as the Latin equivalent. Cf. also 12 n. above.

16 ειρις: l. ἶρις. Cf. 17, 20, 36; Gignac, *Grammar* i 189–91. For the pair, cf. M 170.4, S 348.6, Vat 285, C iv.17, CGL II 333.10. Mp has *plaga* for ἶρις (292.64) and *arcus* as the equivalent of ζώνη (292.65), apparently as a result of transposition.

17 δελφειν: l. δελφίν, a later form of δελφίς; see LSJ s.v. For the pair, cf. E 241.49, Mp 293.36, C iv.22, CGL II 42.4, 268.2.

18 Cf. M 170.14, E 241.40, Mp 293.21, S 348.5, C iv.24, CGL II 116.55 and 437.38.

19 Cf. Mp 293.32, C iv.25, CGL II 62.27 and 332.56; C. Gloss. Biling. I 9.5 αικους with n.

20 κρειος: l. κριός.

αρ[[ε]]ίηνς: for the correction, cf. i 5. The reverse insertion of the nasal is the result of the corresponding loss of nasals in speech; see Gignac, *Grammar* i 119. In Latin, this phenomenon is particularly characteristic of the consonant cluster -ns-; see Väänänen, *Introduction* 64. Starting from this line, the twelve signs of the zodiac are listed without an introductory title. For the word pair, cf. L 1704, 72.34, M 170.17, E 241.68, Mp 291.56, Vat 295, C v.2 (starting after this entry, we find the symbols of the signs of the zodiac instead of their Latin names), CGL II 355.26.

21 For the word pair, cf. L 1705, 72.35, M 170.18, E 241.69, Mp 291.60, Vat 295, Vo 420.25, CGL II 452.4.

22 λεο: o for final -o in the nominative, as regularly in this papyrus (24, 29, 34 (corrupt: see n.), 39), implies the colloquial pronunciation -ŏ: cf. e.g. R. G. G. Coleman, in J. N. Adams and R. G. Mayer (edd.), *Aspects of the Language of Latin Poetry* (1999) 38. For the word pair, cf. L 1708, 72.38, M 170.21, E 241.72, Mp 292.5, Vat 298, Vo 409.71, CGL II 360.7.

23 λιβολ written in error for *libra* (λίβρα): perhaps the upright of ρ and a part of α were not easily recognizable in the exemplar. For the word pair, cf. L 1710, 72.40, M 170.23, E 242.2, Mp 292.12, Vat 300. The Hermeneumata (including C v.8) have ζυγός instead of ζυγόν.

24 ουιργο: for the final -o, cf. 22 n. For the word pair, cf. L 1709, 72.39, M 170.22, E 242.1, Mp 292.8, Vat 299, CGL II 209.19.

25 καπριοκ[ορνους: i.e. *capricornus* (καπρικορνους). For the word pair, cf. L 1713 (contaminated with the word pair τοξοτης *sagittarius*), 72.43, M 170.26, E 242.5, Mp 292.27, Vat 303, Vo 403.62, CGL II 97.23 and 220.10.

26 γεμεινει: for ει corresponding to short Latin *i*, cf. 12 n.; Γέμεινος is common in the name. For the word pair, cf. L 1706, 72.36, M 170.19, E 241.70, Mp 291.65, Vat 296, CGL II 32.40.

27 ακ[[ο]]υαριου[ς: the correction was carried out with a cancel stroke touching the right-hand side of ο. For variations in representation of Latin *qu*, see Gignac, *Grammar* i 225–6. For the word pair, cf. L 1714, 72.44, M 170.27, E 242.6, Mp 292.30, Vat 304, Vo 400.53.

28 ταγιταρ[ιους: τ is written for ς at the start, perhaps the result of a visual corruption (cf. 23 above), ς having been written with a pronounced angle at the top left. For the simplification of the geminate *tt*, cf. 13 n. For the word pair, cf. L 1712 (cf. 25 n.), 72.42, M 170.25, E 242.4, Mp 292.20, Vat 302, Vo 418.49, CGL II 177.10 and 457.14.

29 σκορπιο: for the final -o, cf. 22 n. For the word pair, cf. L 1711, 72.41, M 170.24, E 242.3, Mp 292.15, Vat 301, Vo 418.48, CGL II 433.58.

30 κανκινος: l. καρκίνος. For the interchange of liquids and nasals see Gignac, *Grammar* i 109–10. [Dr Henry notes that κανκ- shows the influence of the Latin, suggesting that the two columns were copied together at some stage.]

κανκρου[ς: i.e. *cancer*. The false ending (cf. TLL III 228.32–4) may be due to the Vulgar Latin process whereby nouns of the second declension ending in *-er* tend to adopt the more transparent *-us* ending of masculine nouns, for which a standard example is provided in *Appendix Probi* 139 *aper non aprus*; cf. J. G. F. Powell in R. Ferri (ed.), *The Latin of Roman Lexicography* (2011) 117–18. For the word pair, cf. L 1707, 72.37, M 170.20, E 241.71, Mp 292.2, Vat 297, CGL II 97.10 and 338.57.

31 ιχθυς πισκε[ι]ς. The Greek name of the constellation Pisces is plural (cf. L 1715, 72.45, E 242.7, C v.13, CGL II 151.15); but in three Hermeneumata it occurs as here in the singular (M 170.28, Mp 292.36, Vat 305). For -ει- representing -*i*-, cf. 12 n.

32 The thematic title is found in L 599, A 84.50, M 172.5, E 245.30, Mp 295.10, S 354.6, B

395.66 (Vo 405.25), C xlviii (Greek only, but cf. the table of contents, 56), and **3315** 6. A different thematic title is found in Vat 380–81: τωυ αυεμωυ τα ουοματα *ventorum nomina*.

33 With one exception (A), all the thematic lists of names of winds (including that in **3315**) start with this word pair (for the Vo glossary, cf. *A* p. 675 Omont). It also appears in the glossaries of CGL II (206.10, 225.49); cf. also P. Lond. II 481 (C. Gloss. Biling. I 13) 11.

34 ακοιλε: i.e. *aquilo*. ε will be a visual corruption of the expected *o* (cf. 22 n.). The normative transcription of the Latin word *Aquilo* would be ακουιλω; cf. **3315** 8. According to Gignac, *Grammar* i 225–6, the similar word *Aquila* never appears as Ἀκοιλ-, only Ἀκυλ- or rarely Ἀκουλ-, but κο for *qu* is well attested in the name *Quintus*. For the word pair, cf. L 602, A 84.57, M 172.8, Mp 295.13, S 354.15, B 395.69 (Vo 400.57), Vat 384, C xlviii.10, CGL II 258.47.

35 The Latin wind name is present in **3315** 9. For the word pair, cf. L 604, Mp 295.20, S 354.13, B 395.70 (Vo 400.56), Vat 385, C xlviii.11, CGL II 27.33 and 377.12. In other versions of the Hermeneumata, υότος has different Latin equivalents: A 84.62 and M 172.9 *africus*, E 245.42 *notus*.

36 λ]ευψ: l. λύψ. The Latin wind name is present in **3315** 10. For the word pair, cf. L 603, E 245.44, Mp 295.19, S 354.16, B 395.71 (Vo 400.59), C xlviii.13. A 84.64 has *auster* as the Latin equivalent (cf. previous n.).

37 For the word pair, cf. A 84.54, M 172.12/13 (owing to the omission of a Latin equivalent in this thematic group, several Greek lemmata have their Latin equivalents in the preceding line), E 245.35, S 354.29, B 395.72, C xlviii.6, CGL II 319.22. Another Latin equivalent appears with εὖρος in Mp 295.22 (*chorus*), 23 (*terrester*), S 354.12 (*vulturnus*; cf. CGL II 212.42, Gloss. Steph. CGL III 474.48, L 607 (cj.)).

38 The normative Latin transcription would be φαουωυιους as in **3315** 11. The omission of the semivowel *v* as elsewhere in this word (TLL VI.1 382.34–7) is characteristic of Vulgar Latin: see Väänänen, *Introduction* 51. There are several examples in the *Appendix Probi* (e.g. 29 *avus non aus*, 62 *flavus non flaus*, 176 *pavor non paor*); cf. Powell (30 n.) 114. The superfluous κ may be due to the influence of 36 αφρικους. For the word pair, cf. M 172.10/11, Mp 295.21, S 354.14, B 396.1 (Vo 406.70), Vat 389, C xlviii.17, CGL II 71.10 and 322.8. The Greek word appears with a different Latin equivalent in E 245.37 (*zephyrus*).

39 a]παρκιας: for the spelling, see CGL Index s.vv. Aparcias, Septemtrio; LSJ and Rev. Suppl. s.v. ἀπαρκτίας.

cεπτευτριο: present in **3315** 13. For the final -*o*, cf. 22 n. For the word pair, cf. L 605, A 84.58, M 172.11/12, Mp 295.18, S 354.24, B 395.74, Vat 388, C xlviii.16, CGL II 182.29 and 233.23. The Greek word has a different Latin equivalent in E 245.39 (*aquilo*), while Vo 418.51 has *septentrio arctos* (shown by the sequence to be the wind, but cf. 11 n. above).

40 couβ[c]ωλανιους: l. couβcωλανους; the superfluous ι may be due to the influence of 27–8 above. For the word pair, cf. M 172.14/15, E 245.33, Mp 295.25, S 354.25, B 395.73 (Vo 418.50), Vat 387, CGL II 253.1. The Greek word has a different Latin equivalent, *desolanus* (-*rius*), in L 608, C xlviii.15 (cf. Vo 405.26).

41–2 There is casual ink (a large blot) to the left of the initial letters of col. iii.

41 τερεcτρις: i.e. *terrestris*; for the simplification of the geminate, cf. 13 n. The meaning 'northwest wind' is not given in OLD or Lewis and Short. The word pair only occurs in C xlviii.18 (Lat. *terrester*), but in Mp 295.22–3, *chorus* and *terrester* appear in successive lines each as a translation of εuρος. The Greek word appears with different Latin equivalents: L 609 *aequalis*, A 84.60 *corus*, S 354.27 *equalis*, B 396.2 (cf. the Vo glossary, *A* p. 675 Omont) and Vat 390 *vulturnus*. Likewise, *terrestris* (-*ter*) appears with different Greek equivalents, ἀπόγειος (S 354.17, Vat 397, CGL II 197.38, 235.59) and *epigios* (Vo 420.26).

42 The word pair is attested only once in the Hermeneumata, at E 245.34.

ZS. ÖTVÖS

5163. Graeco-Latin Thematic Glossary

74/7(a)   fr. 1 16.3 × 22.9 cm   First/second century

Two fragments of a roll, blank on the back, the larger (fr. 1) with upper margin, preserved to its original height of 3.6 cm, and remains of two columns, broken at the foot. Parts of the first 23 lines of col. i and of the first 13 lines of the following column are present, together with a narrow intercolumnium (0.9 cm wide at its narrowest). (Not included below are two unplaced fragments, of which one is blank and the other has no decipherable letters except a single x.)

The text (Greek and transliterated Latin in the Greek alphabet) is written in a medium-sized informal upright round hand. ᴀ is broad with a triangular loop, narrowing to a sharp point, which may extend well below the line underneath the preceding letter. ʙ (fr. 1 i 2) has a flat base with the loops added in a sinusoid not touching the upright. The right-hand sides of ʜ and ᴨ may be curved (e.g. i 13), or virtually upright (e.g. i 14). Serifs are sometimes added, but not consistently: note especially ᴋ with exaggerated left-pointing serifs at top and bottom, as at i 6, 9, 20, ii 2. The hand of III **466** (directions for wrestling), placed by the editors in the second century but by Cavallo (Pap. Flor. XXXVI [2005] 228) in the first, has many similar features. A comparable dated hand is that of LVIII **3917** (early ɪɪ); cf. also LXV **4453** with the editor's introduction.

The text is copied without the use of lection signs. A break between two thematic divisions at i 3 is marked by an ornamental divider extending as far right as the longer of the two preceding lines (1) and beginning slightly to the left of the preceding line-beginnings. Then the Greek title of the new section stands in ἔκθεϲιϲ. Outward-pointing obliques set off the Greek title to the right and were probably balanced by symmetrically placed obliques to the left, where the papyrus is lost. Following the long Greek title, the Latin equivalent necessarily begins further to the right than the Latin glosses at the top of the column, but it stands slightly in ἔκθεϲιϲ in relation to the Latin glosses below, just as the Greek title stands in ἔκθεϲιϲ in relation to the lines that follow. The scribe does not take the trouble to match the alignment of the Greek entries following the title precisely to that of the entries preceding the break, but begins instead slightly further to the left. The initial letter of the first entry of the new section (i 5) is enlarged. It is likely that the scribe copied each Latin gloss together with the corresponding Greek entry, as expected. If he had copied all the Greek entries for the column before he began adding the Latin glosses, he would no doubt have avoided placing the glosses for the first two lines on an alignment too far to the left to be maintained in what follows.

The orthography is generally good. There are itacistic spellings at i 6 and 22 (?), a minor error at i 20, and possibly a more serious corruption in the Latin at i 9.

The text is of value as treating subjects not hitherto represented in thematic

glossaries on papyrus: insects (i 1–2, but the original heading is lost: see n.), furniture (i 4–ii 13), and perhaps iron objects (fr. 2). As was to be expected, the entries
and their organization correspond fairly closely to those of the Hermeneumata.
While they do not match precisely any single version, there are several striking
unique correspondences to Mp: see on fr. 1 i 1–2, 16, 22, ii 5, 10–11. There are also
a few more or less noteworthy novelties: see e.g. on fr. 1 i 7, 9, 19, 20, 22, ii 2.

fr. 1

col. i   col. ii

```
      ]   μυρμηξ      φορμικα                   τρ[υτ]ανη [
      ]   cιλφη       βλαττα                    κλ[ι]μαξ [
    ]\\\\\\\\\\\\\\\\\\\\\\\\\              λυ̣[χν]ο̣c   [
    ]περιεν̣[δ]ο̣μενειαc/ δηcουπελλεκτιλε        ολ̣[μ]ο̣c  [
  5   ]  ενδ[ομ]ενεια    \ cουπελλεξ       5    υπ[ε]ρον [
      ]  κλει[νη]           λεκτουc            κ[οc]κινο[ν
      ]  ενη[λατ]α̣         cπονδαι            εν[
        ......]ο̣ν           φουλκρουμ          λικ[νον
        .......].           κοντιναι           μα[κτρα
 10               ] λεκτικα                10   cκα[φ
                  ] .α̣...ουμ                    cκα[φ
     πυργιcκο]c̣    αρμαριουμ                    cφ.[
     cκευο]θηκη    ουαcαρ̣ιουμ                   .[
     τρα]πεζα      μηνcα̣
 15  τρι]πουc      τριπη[c]
     κιc]τ̣η        κιcτ̣[α ]
       ...]ρ̣ον      cου[
       ....].       c̣ε̣[
     κα]μπτρα       α̣[
 20  γλω]cοκομον    α̣[
     μ]ο̣διοc        μο̣[διουc
       ...].ικιον   λε[
       ....]c̣        [
```

'ant, cockroach.
'On furniture: furniture, couch, frame of a couch, back of a couch, . . . , litter, footstool (?),
cupboard, chest, table, three-legged table, box, bench (?), seat (?), case, casket, 1-*modius* vessel, 1-*choenix*
vessel (?), . . . balance, ladder, lamp, mortar, pestle, sieve, . . . , winnowing-fan, kneading-trough,
trough, small trough (?), basket (?), . . .'

col. i

1–2 These pairs are commonly attested. C includes both in section xliv, περὶ θηρίων (43 (*formica μοξος*), 94), and the second again in section xlv, περὶ ἑρπετῶν (11). Otherwise, those thematic glossaries that include both pairs place cίλφη *blatta* with birds and μύρμηξ *formica* with quadrupeds (L 1006, 1060; M 188.51, 189.52) or beasts (Vat 1069, 762). The sequence of topics found here is paralleled in Mp, where cίλφη *platta* stands at 320.53 towards the end of a list of quadrupeds (320.1–60) which immediately precedes the furniture section.

4–7 κλίνη *lectus* is regularly the first entry in such lists after ἐνδομένεια *supellex* itself. In three cases (L 1147–50, A 92.8–11, C xxiv; cf. S 365.76–9, where the list proper begins instead with *supellex lignea* ἐνδομενία ξυλίνη), it is followed immediately by ἐνήλατον *sponda*, of which we find here the plural (see 7 n.); Mp 320.61–3, M 196.65–7, and E 269.28–30 diverge after κλίνη *lectus*.

7 We should have expected the singular *sponda* on the Latin side. Other thematic glossaries have the singular in both languages (L 1150, A 92.11, S 365.79, Mp 321.2–3, M 197.11, C xxiv.3; E 269.32 ἐνήλατον *sponda lecti*). The plural (Ενηλατα *sponde*) is found at CGL II 299.1.

8 Various forms of the Greek are attested in thematic glossaries: C xxiv.5 has *fulcrum* ἀνάκλιτον, Mp 321.1 ανακλιθρον *fulcrum* (ἀνάκλιντρον Boucherie), M 197.12 *ancaliton fluctum*, and E 269.33 ἀγκαλητον (with no Latin). CGL II 74.8 gives *Fulcrum* ανακλειτον (ἀνάκλιτον e), and ανακλιτον is among the glosses for *Pluteum* at CGL II 152.33; CGL II 526.24 gives *Fulcrum . anacliter .* (ἀνάκλιτον e). To judge by the space available, [ανακλιτ]ον as in C may be the likeliest here. See further C. A. Lobeck, *Phrynichi Eclogae* (1820) 131–2; also LXIII **4389** 2 n.

9 κοντιναι is puzzling. CGL II 521.53 gives *Contila . mesaulion .*, in which *contila* has been thought to stand for *cortina*, and *cortinae* in the late sense 'curtains' would be fairly suitable, but seems not to be paralleled in lists of this kind, and we would expect an item of wooden furniture. ν for ρ is not found often in Greek documents (Gignac, *Grammar* i 109). The high flat trace at letter-top level on the Greek side appears to be too far to the right to be part of αὐλαῖαι, which would be expected as the Greek equivalent of *cortinae* (cf. TLL IV 1072.15–21); παραπετάсματα, glossed elsewhere by *aulaea* (CGL VI 115), would extend well to the right of the trace, but it is possible that the end of the word has been lost through abrasion.

10 Greek φορειον (CGL VI 632).

11 cκαβελλουμ (*scabellum*) seems suitable. If it is correct, ὑποπόδιον will probably have stood on the Greek side (CGL VII 236).

12 πυργιcκο]c: cf. XLIX **3452** i 16 (C. Gloss. Biling. II 7.16). The standard gloss (CGL VI 95).

13 For parallels, cf. Mp 322.27, S 366.57; CGL VII 394.

14 A common pair (CGL VI 691; cf. C. Gloss. Biling. I 15.7).

15 Cf. Mp 321.25, S 366.11, Vo 420.23 *tripedem tripoda*; C xxiv.143 *tripes* τρίπους, πυρίcτατον; CGL VII 367.

16 Not a common pair in such lists, but cf. Mp 321.19; CGL VI 216.

17 Perhaps διεδ]ρον cου[βcελλιουμ: cf. S 366.12, C xxiv.26; CGL VII 308. In CGL II 255.21, *subsellium* is the last gloss for Βαθρον.

18 Perhaps διφρο]c cε[λλα (CGL VII 252; add C. Gloss. Biling. I 14.21 *sela sifrin* (= διφρί(ο)ν?)). cε[διλε is also possible on the Latin side (CGL VII 250).

19 The regular gloss for κάμπτρα is *capsa* (CGL VI 179), but that does not seem to suit the trace. καμπτρα is among the glosses for *Arca et arcla* at CGL II 24.49, and one of those may have stood here.

20 γλω]cοκομον: i.e. γλωccόκομον. There does not seem to be room for a second c. The same spelling is found in papyri in the letter P. Tebt. II 414.21 (II) and the list P. Berl. Sarisch. 21.35, 50 (v/ vi); cf. LXXIV **4979** 3 n. We expect *locellus* or *loculus* on the Latin side (CGL VI 652–3), but the trace seems unsuitable. Perhaps a[ρκα or a[ρκλα was written, as in the previous line.

21 μο[διουμ is also possible on the Latin side (CGL VI 705).

22 χοι]νικιον λε[ιβραλε (i.e. *librale*)? For the sequence, cf. Mp 322.19–21, where μοδιος *modium*

was originally followed by χοινιχ *librale*, but the second hand added ἡμιμοδιυμ *semodium* (20) between them. (C xxiv.151 and xxiii.3 has *modius* χοῖνιξ.) For χοινίκιον used of a measure, cf. P. Fouad 49.13 (100) χοινικείωι, CPR I 31.17 (153) χοινι[κε]ίω[ν] (BL I 117); P. Fouad 43.48 (189–90) μέτρῳ χο(ινικίῳ) (BL III 61). At Phld. *Ind. Sto.* col. 5.4, cited by LSJ s.v. 1, it is a false reading for φοινίκι[α (T. Dorandi, *Filodemo: Storia dei filosofi: La stoà da Zenone a Panezio* (PHerc. *1018*) (1994)). CGL II 122.56 offers instead *Librale* χοινικις.

col. ii

1 Lat. *trutina* (E 270.1, Mp 321.28, C xvi.71; CGL VII 371).

2 Lat. *scala* (CGL VII 237); not otherwise found in lists of furniture. The sense here will no doubt be 'ladder' rather than 'staircase.'

3 Lat. *lucerna* (CGL VI 656), a common item in thematic glossaries, where it appears four times in the furniture section (M 197.55, E 270.32, Mp 322.16, C xxiv.56), though it is also found in other sections. Cf. also for this pair C. Gloss. Biling. I 15.12, 38; II 8.4.

4 Lat. probably *pila* (CGL VII 88), as in all the parallel lists of furniture except E, where ὅλμος is the last in a long series of words glossed by *mortarium* (270.8).

5 ὕπερον follows ὅλμος in Mp 321.43–4, where it is glossed first as *pisabulum*, then as *pilum*; cf. C xxiv.40 *pilus* ὕπερον υνιοιcoc. In E 270.9, it is again the last in a list of Greek terms, all glossed as *pistillum*.

6 Lat. *cribrum* (CGL VI 287): so all the other lists of furniture, except that the Latin has dropped out in L 1171, while E includes the entry not in the furniture section but under the heading περὶ τῶν ἐργαλείων *de ferramentis* (263.8).

7 Cf. perhaps M 197.49 *ensistron cerniclum*, E 269.61 ἔνδειcτρον *ceruiculum*, C xxiv.59–60 *cerniculum* ενcειcιηριον, *incerniculum* ενcειτρον; TLL III 863.59–67.

8 Lat. *uannus* (CGL VII 393): cf. C xxiv.51 *uannus* λιcμος cκαφιcτήριον; E 263.6 (under the heading περὶ τῶν ἐργαλείων *de ferramentis*), where the gloss is shared with βραcτήρ in the previous line. The alternative interpretation 'cradle' is not suited to the context and does not seem to be paralleled in the thematic glossaries.

9 Cf. Mp 321.37–9 (Lat. *matra, magis, firmentatorium*), S 366.16 (*magidem* μάκτραν), C xxiv.92 *magis* μάκτρα.

10–11 Cf. especially Mp 321.40–41 (after the entries for μάκτρα): cκαφη *alueum*, cκαφιδιον *scafisterium*. In other thematic glossaries, cκάφη stands alone, glossed by *alueus* (A 92.25, S 366.49) or *alueum* (L 1164, M 197.50); cf. C xxiv.52 *alueus* cκάφιον.

12 Perhaps cφυ[ρις (= cπυρίς) glossed as *sporta*, a regular component of such lists of furniture (CGL VII 288). For the variation in the spelling of this word, see LSJ + Rev. Suppl. s.v. cπυρίς.

fr. 2

```
           ·    ·
        α[
        μ[
        ψα . [
        κρ . . [
    5   κη . [
        . . [
        . [
```

3–4 ψα is an uncommon word-beginning (cf. CGL VII 684). The word here is likely to be ψαλ[ιδες (Lat. *forfices*), 'scissors' (CGL VI 462). This entry is found under the heading περὶ cιδηρέων *de ferreis* in L 1310, M 204.48, and Mp 325.45. If that is the context here, κρ . . [may represent κρεα[γρα (Lat. *carnarium*: CGL VI 183), 'flesh-hook,' which occurs under the same heading at L 1338 and M 204.58. Cf. C xxv (περὶ ἐργαλείων).68 *forfex* ψαλίc λαυτον, 80 *arpago* κρεάγρα.

W. B. HENRY

V. DOCUMENTARY TEXTS

5164. Receipt for Delivery of Oil

34 4B.72/H(1–4)c   7.5 × 15 cm   30 July 26 bc or 31 January 25 bc?

Asclepiades, the father of an overseer of the temples of the Oxyrhynchite and Cynopolite nomes, acknowledges receipt of oil from Patoiphis, an oil-worker. The oil is said to 'fall to' Patoiphis for Year 4 of Augustus. In XII **1453** = Sel. Pap. II 327 (30/29 bc), four lamplighters declare on oath to two overseers of the temples of the Oxyrhynchite and Cynopolite nomes that they will service the lamps and provide oil to two temples of Oxyrhynchus in Year 1. One of the lamplighters is Thonis alias Patoiphis, later simply called Patoiphis. If he is to be identified with the oil-worker named in this receipt (see below, 4 n.), and Asclepiades is acting on behalf of his son or in a similar capacity, **1453** may provide the context for the delivery mentioned in **5164**. However, it is also possible that the transaction was private in nature (cf. below, 8 n.).

The back is blank.

$$
\begin{aligned}
&\ \textit{Ἀσκληπιάδης ὃς καὶ} \\
&\ \textit{Ἀπίων ὁ πατὴρ Πτολ(εμαίου)} \\
&\ \textit{τοῦ ἐπὶ τῶν ἱερῶν τοῦ} \\
&\ \textit{Ὀξυ(ρυγχίτου) καὶ Κυνο(πολίτου) Πατοίφει} \\
5 &\ \textit{ἐλαιουργῶι χαί(ρειν). ἀπέχω} \\
&\ \textit{παρὰ σοῦ τοὺς ἐπιβάλλον(τάς)} \\
&\ \textit{σοι τοῦ τετάρτου ἔτους} \\
&\ \textit{Καίσαρος ἐλαίου κνηκίν(ου)} \\
&\ \textit{μετρη(τὰς) δύο, (γίνονται) ἐλ(αίου) κνη(κίνου) μ(ετρηταὶ) β,} \\
10 &\ \textit{καὶ οὐδέν σοι περὶ τούτων ἐγκαλῶ.} \\
&\quad\ \textit{(ἔτους) . Καίσαρ(ος), Με( ) ε.}
\end{aligned}
$$

η β   2 πτο λ   4 οξ υ   κυ ο   5 χ7   6 επιβαλλο ν   8 κνηκι η   9 μετρ η | ε λ
κν μ   10 ουδεν: υ may be a correction   εγκαλ ω   11 L   καιcρ α

'Asclepiades alias Apion, the father of Ptolemaeus, the overseer of the temples of the Oxyrhynchite and Cynopolite (nomes), to Patoiphis, oil-worker, greetings. I am in receipt from you of the two *metretai* of safflower oil that fall to you for the fourth year of Caesar, total 2 *metretai* of safflower oil, and I have no claims against you about these matters.

'Year . . . of Caesar, Mesore (or Mecheir) 5.'

1 *Ἀσκληπιάδης*. The name occurs also in **5165** 1, a papyrus of about this date found close to **5164**: could it be that both texts refer to the same person?

3–4 τοῦ ἐπὶ τῶν ἱερῶν τοῦ Ὀξυ(ρυγχίτου) καὶ Κυνο(πολίτου). Cf. XII **1453** 13–14 τοῖς ἐπὶ τῶν ἱερῶν κτλ., the only other attestation of this title for these nomes. In **1453** 13 n. it is suggested that it is 'a variant for ἐπιστάτης τῶν ἱερῶν', a function attested in the Ptolemaic period (see P. Gen. III 135 introd.; P. Paramone 7.8–9 n.).

4 Πατοίφει. For the name, see LXXI **4822** 9 n. In view of its rarity, it is worth considering the possibility that this person is to be identified with the Patoiphis attested in **1453**, who is called Thonis alias Patoiphis when described as a lamplighter of the temple of Sarapis and Isis (2–5), but simply Patoiphis when mentioned as the father of another lamplighter (7). It is conceivable that an ἐλαιουργός could serve as a λυχνάπτης, a function that required the provision of oil. P. IFAO I 13.29 (23 BC), in which a man named Patoiphis subscribes to a marriage contract, may refer to the same person.

8 ἐλαίου κνηκίν(ου). See D. B. Sandy, *The Production and Use of Vegetable Oils in Ptolemaic Egypt* (1989) 83–7, 116–18. If the oil was used for lamp-lighting, it should be noted that there appears to be no evidence in the papyri for such a use of safflower oil; see M. Mossakowska, *JJP* 24 (1994) 109–31.

9 μετρη(τάς). These will have been 'Attic' *metretai*, whose capacity was 39.1 litres; see N. Kruit, K. A. Worp, *APF* 45 (1999) 102.

11 (ἔτους) Καίσαρος Με( ) ε̄. The year figure ought to be δ or ε, since the oil is supplied on account of Year 4. Neither letter can be confirmed, though δ would be more difficult to fit in the space. There is also no palaeographical basis for deciding between Με(σορη) and Με(χειρ). Mesore is the last month of the year, and it is possible that the oil for Year 4 was delivered at the end of the year, in which case the date Mesore 5, Year 4, would correspond to 30 July 26 BC. Compare **1453**, where the period for the maintenance of lamps and supply of oil to temples at Oxyrhynchus runs from Thoth 1 to Mesore 7 (see BL VIII 246) of Year 1 of Augustus (= 30/29 BC). (Whether Mesore 5 fell at the very end of the year need not concern us here; on the dating system used at the time, see C. Bennett, *ZPE* 142 (2003) 221–40, esp. 230; for a different view, see E. Grzybek in Y. Perrin (ed.), *Neronia VII: Rome, l'Italie et la Grèce* (2007) 145–57, with Bennett's response at http://www.tyndalehouse.com/Egypt/ptolemies/chron/roman/chron_rom_anl_frame_026.htm.) The other possible date is Mecheir 5, Year 5, which converts to 31 January 25 BC.

L. CAPPONI

5165. ORDER TO A BANKER

34 4B.74/D(1–2)b   9.8 × 9.8 cm   27 January 24 BC

Miccalus, the agent of a certain Asclepiades, orders the banker Apollophanes to pay three hundred silver drachmas to Myrmex. The reason for the payment is not specified.

This is the earliest order to pay of the Roman period addressed to a banker. In terms of format and wording it is comparable to a group of Heracleopolite bank orders of 87–82 BC, namely BGU XIV 2401–16, 2416A, and especially SB XIV 11309–28. The paucity of information given may indicate that it is not itself a cheque but rather an instruction to a banker to honour a cheque that has been issued; see R. Bogaert, *AncSoc* 31 (2001) 209–11.

The writing runs along the fibres. There are several traces on the back, perhaps the remains of a docket.

Μίκκαλος *vac.* ὁ πα[ρ’ Ἀ]ϲκληπιάδῃ Ἀπολλοφάνει τραπεζ(ίτῃ) χα(ίρειν). χρημάτιϲον Μύρμηκι
ἀφ’ οὗ ἔχειϲ μου ἐπιϲτάλματοϲ ἀργυρίου τριακ(οϲίαϲ),
(γίνονται) (δραχμαὶ) τ. (ἔτουϲ) ϛ Καίϲαροϲ, Μεχειρ β̄.

2 τραπεζ ᾳ χ χρ^η *vac.* ματιϲον   3 τριακ̄   4 / ʃ   L

'Miccalus, the agent of Asclepiades, to Apollophanes, banker, greetings. Pay to Myrmex, from the instruction of mine that you have, three hundred (drachmas) of silver, total 300 dr. Year 6 of Caesar, Mecheir 2.'

1 ὁ πα[ρ’ Ἀ]ϲκληπιάδῃ. The use of the dative instead of the genitive in this construction is only sporadic; see Mayser, *Grammatik* ii.2 370.

A banker called Asclepiades is attested in IV **806** = SB XIV 11884 (42 or 20 BC). This may then be a note sent by (the agent of) one banker to another; on collaboration between banks, which may have required bankers to hold accounts with other bankers, see Bogaert, *Trapezitica Aegyptiaca* 102, 250–52. On Asclepiades see also **5164** 1 n.

1–2 Ἀπολλοφάνει τραπεζ(ίτῃ). This is no doubt the Apollophanes named at **5166** 1, who was to receive the tax on the sale of a slave. He is not given a title in **5166**, but the inventory numbers of **5165** and **5166** indicate that the two papyri were found close together, and the name has not occurred in any other Oxyrhynchite documents of this date.

Apollophanes was probably a private banker, in which case this would be the earliest reference to a private bank in Roman Egypt; see Bogaert, *ZPE* 109 (1995) 153. A private bank in Oxyrhynchus is attested as early as 73 or 44 BC (XIV **1639**).

2 Μύρμηκι. This name is otherwise attested in the papyri only in the Zenon archive, though see N. Gonis, *CE* 75 (2000) 130.

3 ἀφ’ οὗ ἔχειϲ μου ἐπιϲτάλματοϲ. This expression is novel, but recalls formulas found in orders for transfer of credit in grain, especially XLIX **3486** 2–4 (41/2?) διάϲτιλον ἀφ’ οὗ ἔχειϲ μου μετρή-ματοϲ (more often, ἔχειϲ μου ἐν θέματι). μέτρημα there refers to the result of the action of 'measuring in' or depositing grain, and hence to the deposit itself. It corresponds to ἐπίϲταλμα here. This is one of the terms used for orders for payment addressed to bankers in the Roman period, though we do not have any such examples from before the second century; see Bogaert, *Trapezitica Aegyptiaca* 238, 240–43 (= *AncSoc* 6 (1975) 100, 103–6). This ἐπίϲταλμα is said to be with Apollophanes (ἔχειϲ), and the payment to Myrmex is to be taken from the ἐπίϲταλμα. The ἐπίϲταλμα in question may be a cheque given to Apollophanes to cover (at least) the amount due to Myrmex. Bogaert notes that 'the deposit from which the payment is to be made is mentioned only once in the Roman orders': P. Fay. 100.14–15 (99) (χρημάτιϲον . . .) ἃϲ ἔχιϲ μου ἐν θέματι ἀργυρίου δραχμὰϲ κτλ.

L. CAPPONI

5166. Instruction to Receive Tax on Sale of Slave

34 4B.73/H(3–5)a   10.4 × 14.5 cm   *c.*20s BC
                                                              Plates VIII–IX

Mnesitheus, possibly a tax-farmer, instructs Apollophanes, probably the banker of **5165**, to receive from Philiscus son of Tryphon, a Macedonian ἱππάρχης ἐπ' ἀνδρῶν (see 3 n.), the tax on the sale of Thermuthion, a runaway slave whom Philiscus had bought from Lucius Rutilius Philomusus. On the back a second hand wrote two lines concerning a payment of twelve drachmas to a certain Nicolaus, probably a clerk in the bank. The persons involved are not given any titles, perhaps an indication that this is a piece of internal correspondence. The date is damaged, but the hand and prosopography (see 1 n.) point to the late first century BC.

In its structure **5166** resembles two later documents. In I **185** = SB XX 14395 (181), two contractors for the tax on sales (ἐγκύκλιον) write to the public bankers of Oxyrhynchus ordering them to receive from a woman the τέλ(ος) δούλ(ων) on a female slave and her son, bought through the office of the agoranomus. Cf. also I **96** (180). On this type of document, see A. Martin and J. Straus, *CE* 64 (1989) 254–5.

5166 offers a clear indication that the tax on the sale of the slave was just under 20% of the sale price; see further 8 n.

The text of the letter is written along the fibres.

> Μνηcίθεοc Ἀπολλοφάνει χαίρειν.
> δέξαι παρὰ Φιλίcκου τοῦ Τρύφωνος
> Μακεδόνος ἱππάρχου ἐπ' ἀνδρῶν
> τέλος δούλης Θερμουθίου ὡc (ἐτῶν) λ
> 5 οὔcης ἐν δρασμῶι, ἣν ἀναζητήcας
> ὁ Φιλ[ί]cκος ἑαυτῶι ἀνάξει, ἧς ἐπρία(το)
> παρὰ Λουκίου Ῥοτιλίου Φιλομούcου
> χαλκοῦ (ταλάντων) ι Ῥ, χ[α(λκοῦ) π]ρὸς ἀργ(ύριον) (τάλαντα) β χϙγ γ ∠.
> (*vac.*) ἔρρω[co]. (ἔτους) [*c.*5]ικ—

Back, across the fibres:

> 10 (*m.*2) Νικολάῳ· coὶ ἀπὸ τοῦ τέλους
> παρέξ( ) (δραχμὰς) δεκαδύο, (γίνονται) (δραχμαὶ) ιβ.

4, 9 L   6 ηc corr. from ηε   επρι^a   7 l. Ῥουτιλίου   8 ⊼ (*bis*)   αρ͞γ
11 ∫ (*bis*) |

'Mnesitheus to Apollophanes, greetings. Receive from Philiscus the son of Tryphon, a Macedonian, cavalry-commander over men, the tax on the slave Thermuthion, about 30 years old, a runaway, whom Philiscus will track down and bring back for himself, whom he purchased from Lucius Rutilius Philomusus for 10 talents 3,000 (drachmas) in bronze, 2 talents 693 (drachmas) 3½ (obols) in bronze (converted) to silver.

'Farewell. Year . . .'

Back: (2nd hand) 'To Nicolaus; . . . will pay you twelve drachmas out of the tax (money), total 12 dr.'

1 Μνηcίθεοc. Nearly all occurrences of this name in papyri are from Oxyrhynchus. In XX **2277** 17 (13) we find a landholder of this name; cf. also II **296** 5. A Mnesitheus features in the

documents from the archive of Comon (XXXVIII **2834–46**) as the husband of Aline, daughter of Comon I and mother of Comon III; that Mnesitheus died in 50 (**2837**).

Ἀπολλοφάνει. Presumably to be identified with the banker of this name in **5165** 1–2 (24 BC).

3 Μακεδόνος. For a list of early Roman references to 'Macedonians', see O. Montevecchi, *Pap. Congr. XXI* (1997) 724 n. 23 = *Scripta selecta* (1998) 398 n. 23. Cf. **5168** 3.

ἱππάρχου ἐπ' ἀνδρῶν. The title originally indicated a type of officer in the Ptolemaic army, but survived into the first century AD. Its exact meaning is difficult to establish. In II **277** (19 BC) a land-holder and his tenant describe themselves as Macedonians and ἱππάρχαι ἐπ' ἀνδρῶν. Grenfell and Hunt thought that this was an honorary title that descended from the Ptolemaic period and indicated cavalry officers who were not in active service. E. van't Dack, *JJP* 19 (1983) 84, suggested that the title indicated cavalry officers of the Ptolemaic army who were in office after 55 BC and survived for a decade or so after the Roman conquest. It is possible that some cavalry contingents of Macedonians were still used in Augustan Egypt as the *auxilia* of the Roman army. A different interpretation was put forward by B. E. Nielsen and K. A. Worp, *ZPE* 136 (2001) 135–6 = P. NYU II 16.4–5 n., who articu-lated ἐπάνδρων, 'manly'; but the absence of the article before the alleged adjective in P. Tebt. I 54.2–3, ἱππάρχηι ἐπ' ἀνδρῶν κατοίκων ἱππέων, makes this less likely. Besides, P. W. Pestman, in P. Tor. Cho-ach. p. 123 n. 3, suggests an equivalence with inverse word-order between the Greek *commander* + ἐπ' ἀνδρῶν and the Demotic *soldier* + ḥn nꜣ rmt.w n ('one of the men of') + *commander*, which would make ἐπ' ἀνδρῶν a technical term, used to designate the eponymous commander.

4 τέλος δούλης. This must be the tax on sales (ἐγκύκλιον) that was levied under both Ptolemaic and Roman rule as a percentage of the market price; see P. Coll. Youtie II 126 introd., and Straus, *L'Achat* 71–7, esp. 72–5, where the various ways in which this tax is referred to in connection with slave sales are listed and discussed. Other occurrences of the phrase τέλος δούλου for the sales tax are listed in Straus, *L'Achat* 74 n. 265.

4–6 On runaway slaves in Graeco-Roman Egypt, see LI **3616** introd.; Y. Rivière, 'Recherche et identification des esclaves fugitifs dans l'Empire romain', in J. Andreau and C. Virlouvet (edd.), *L'Information et la mer dans le monde antique* (2002) 117, 150–52, 166–78, 182–3.

7 Λουκίου Ῥοτιλίου Φιλομούσου. A certain Philomusus is expected to come from Alexandria to Oxyrhynchus on a business trip in XII **1479** 8, assigned to the late first century BC. In the early first century AD, the bronze tablet SB I 4226 refers to the estate of Agrippina the elder and Rutilius, which was probably acquired later by a Julio-Claudian emperor; see G. M. Parássoglou, *Imperial Estates in Roman Egypt* (1978) 18 and n. 23. The spelling Ῥοτιλίου is attested in O. Claud. I 156.5 (II); the note ad loc. refers to further instances of the name in two unpublished ostraca with lists of soldiers. Cf. T. Eckinger, *Die Orthographie lateinischer Wörter in griechischen Inschriften* (1892) 63.

8 χαλκοῦ (ταλάντων) ι 'Γ. This is the nominal price at which the slave was bought: 10 talents 3,000 drachmas represent a fossilized sum and not necessarily the actual amount paid; see P. Col. VIII 222 introd., and A. Benaissa, *ZPE* 177 (2011) 225–6. This document and the agoranomic notices III **581** (ed. *ZPE* 170 (2009) 178–9), LXXV **5051**, and LXXVIII **5176** are unique in not citing a silver price, though the sale document itself would have mentioned it.

χ[α(λκοῦ) π]ρὸς ἀργ(ύριον) (τάλαντα) β χϟγ γ δ´. Cf. **5176** fr. 2.9–10. This sum is the τέλος to be received by Apollophanes. For similar cases in which the sum of the *enkyklion* is preceded by χαλκοῦ πρὸς ἀργύριον, cf. II **333** 12–13 (ed. *ZPE* 170 (2009) 178), **242** 34, and **243** 47–9. Dr Benaissa observes that the tax is *c.*20% of the price, not 10% as has sometimes been assumed on the analogy of the rate on other sales (rightly questioned by S. L. Wallace, *Taxation in Egypt from Augustus to Diocletian* (1938) 230, and Straus, *L'Achat* 76–7). For examples of 20% sales tax on slaves from the early Ptolemaic period, see C. Ptol. Sklav. I 5 (198/197 BC) and 9 (197 BC), and p. 62. The phrase χαλκοῦ πρὸς ἀργύριον, 'bronze against silver', indicates that the tax payment was in bronze coinage (including the conversion fee); Maresch, *Bronze und Silber* 93–5.

9 The year figure is lost. The last two letters seem to be ι and κ. The day is thus likely to be the twentieth, and the month name probably ended with ι: either *Παυν*]ι or *Φαωφ*]ι would fit the space.

10 ἀπὸ τοῦ τέλους. The mention of τέλους without further specification and with the article suggests that this is a note to be understood with reference to the text on the front.

11 Read παρέξ(ω), παρέξ(ομεν), or παρέξ(ει), depending on who the payer would be: the staff of the bank or Philiscus.

(δραχμὰς) δεκαδύο. If the sum of 10 talents 3,000 bronze drachmas is equivalent to 600–900 silver drachmas, as is usual in slave sales and manumissions (see P. Col. VIII 222 introd.; Maresch, *Bronze und Silber* 119), 12 drachmas was 1.33—2% of the price of the slave—if 10 tal. 3,000 dr. is a real amount, actually paid. It is possible that this referred to one of the many taxes on sales, such as πεντηκοστή (2%), ἑκατοστή (1%), τέλος ἀγορανομίας, or ἀγορανομία ὠνίων; see Wallace, *Taxation* 224–32, 270, 303. On the other hand, if the 12 drachmas derive from the tax on the sale (see above, 10 n.), this sum would be 6.5–10% of the tax amount. We have considered whether it is a conversion fee, but this percentage is not attested for the *enkyklion*; see Maresch, *Bronze und Silber* 214.

L. CAPPONI

5167. RECEIPT FOR PIG-TAX

102/123(c)   7.3 × 8.8 cm   12 March 20 BC
                                                                     Plate IV

This receipt offers the earliest reference to the pig-tax (ὑϊκή) in the Roman period (see L. Capponi, *Augustan Egypt* (2005) 151, where this text is mentioned), as well as the earliest attestation of an urban district (Τεμγενούθεως) in an administrative context. The Roman pig-tax was one of the capitation taxes (including poll- and dike-tax; see **5172** 3 n.) newly introduced to Egypt; the division of an Egyptian metropolis into administrative districts only appeared after the Roman conquest (see J. Krüger, *Oxyrhynchos in der Kaiserzeit* (1990) 77–80; S. Daris, *ZPE* 132 (2000) 211 n. 4). The fact that both novelties are attested here for the early Augustan period seems to support the suggestion that there is an institutional correlation between them; see R. Alston, *The City in Roman and Byzantine Egypt* (2002) 138–9, who relies on the evidence of poll-tax and the discussion in A. K. Bowman and D. W. Rathbone, *JRS* 82 (1992) 112–13, 120. In Oxyrhynchus at the very beginning of Roman rule, a new way of registering the urban population by residence in different quarters is likely to have been required for a rational imposition of the new capitation taxes. The same association of urban subdivision and taxation by person is found in contemporary ostraca from Coptus, mostly poll-tax receipts; see O. Leid. pp. 74–5.

The amount paid is 2 drachmas; see 3 n. The payment is counted for the district of Temgenouthis, presumably the registered place of residence of the taxpayer. Except for II **313** descr. (= SB X 10242), **389** descr., and XII **1518**, where no names of districts have been read, all published papyri from Oxyrhynchus recording payments for pig-tax refer to city districts. **5167** and LXXV **5053** (149) are the only receipts that do not combine the pig-tax with other taxes. For the pig-tax in general and a list of Oxyrhynchite receipts attesting it, see **5053** introd.

The formula used in **5167** is noteworthy in that it places the date at the end instead of the beginning of the text. This is not paralleled by any other receipt for capitation taxes from Oxyrhynchus, but is common e.g. in ostraca from Upper Egypt.

The writing runs along the fibres. The back is blank.

διαγέγρα(φεν) Ἄφυγχιϲ
ναυτικὸϲ ὑϊκῆϲ
Τεμ(γενούθεωϲ) δύο το.( ) ..( ) Τεμ(γενούθεωϲ).
(vac.) (ἔτουϲ) ι Καίϲαροϲ, Φαμ(ενωθ) ιϛ.

1 διαγεγρ́   3 τε̅μ́   το.)   τε̅μ́   4 L   φα̅μ́

'Aphynchis, sailor, has paid for pig-tax for Temgenouthis two (drachmas) . . . of Temgenouthis. Year 10 of Caesar, Phamenoth 16.'

1–2 Ἄφυγχιϲ ναυτικόϲ. Previously unknown.

3 Τεμ(γενούθεωϲ). Mu is raised and simplified into a downward-turned arc. The abbreviation can be compared with CPR V 1.4 (= Taf. 1); see also note ad loc. The alternative reading τέλ(ουϲ) would entail an abnormal word order. On this district of Oxyrhynchus, see S. Daris, *ZPE* 132 (2000) 220–21 = *Diz. geogr.* Suppl. III 102, 147, Suppl. IV 99, 129. The second earliest mention of the district of Temgenouthis comes in II **253** 3 (19).

This is the earliest reference to an urban district in Oxyrhynchus and the Egyptian *chora* in general, predating Ἑρμαίου in **5172** 3 and the district Φοινικῶνοϲ Φρούριον of Coptus in O. Leid. 170 (14 BC).

δύο, sc. δραχμάϲ. This is presumably the annual amount due for pig-tax. The same rate is probably attested in III **574** 4 (11): inspection of the original suggests reading (δραχμὴ) α (τετρώβολον) (ἡμιωβέλιον), προϲδ(ιαγραφομένων) (ὀβολὸϲ) (ἡμιωβέλιον) (the second (ἡμιωβέλιον) not in the first edition). Two other rates are known for Oxyrhynchus in the first century AD: 2 dr. 1½ ob., recorded in II **288** (22–5), **311** = SB X 10223 (23) and SB XX 14665 (30); and 1 dr. 4½ ob., recorded in II **313** = SB X 10242 (47), **308** = SB X 10243 (50), **289** (83), P. Oxy. Hels. 12 (99). The latter amount may also occur in XII **1520** 7 (102): as already suspected by S. L. Wallace, *Taxation* (1938) 145, a photograph indicates that it is possible to read (δρ.) μίαν (τετρώβολον?) [(ἡμιωβέλιον)], (γίνονται) α (τετρώβολον) (ἡμιωβέλιον) instead of the original editors' (δρ.) μίαν (τετρώβολον?), (γίνονται) α (τετρώβολον). From the reign of Hadrian onwards, the rate of 1 dr. 5½ ob. occurs in P. NYU II 41 (131/2), IV **733** (147) and LXXV **5053** (149; cf. 4 n.), with a minor variation of 1 dr. 5½ ob. 1–2 ch. in SB I 5677 = XXIV 15968 (223) (in line 18, read (πεντώβολον) instead of (τετρώβολον)). Although these variable amounts stand in contrast to the stable rate for pig-tax in the Arsinoite nome (see Wallace, *Taxation* 144–5, 328; P. Col. V pp. 301–2), they need not imply that the Oxyrhynchite pig-tax was not a capitation tax: they may be due to tariff fluctuation over time. Furthermore, as the first three amounts mentioned (2 dr.; 2 dr. 1½ ob.; 1 dr. 4½ ob.) present a ratio of 8:9:7, it is tempting to see in them some arithmetic involving supplementary payments (implicit or explicit as in **574** 4, depending on scribal practice), and to take 1 dr. 4½ ob. as the base rate.

το.( ). The year for which the payment was counted is expected here, but this cannot be read.

I have not found a satisfactory reading. If the right-turned curve after omicron is part of an ill-formed kappa, we may read τοκ(άδων) (not τοκ(αδείας), a capitation tax typical of the Mendesian nome; see P. Thmouis I pp. 38–9), implying ὑπέρ and meaning 'for breeding sows'. This would indicate that the Roman pig-tax still referred in some way to pig-rearing; see Wallace, *Taxation* 145, Capponi, *Augustan Egypt* 151–2, and **5053** introd. However, the only attestation of breeding sows in a fiscal context comes from the early Ptolemaic period, viz. SB III 7202.32–3 (227 BC).

. . ( ) *Τεμ*(γενούθεως). The two unread letters stand one above the other, and resemble two curves pointing to each other. The letter at the top may be kappa or, less likely, upsilon or alpha. The letter under it may be epsilon, while lambda and rho cannot be excluded. One possibility is ἐκ( ), but it does not make good sense here. I have also considered λα(ύρας) and ῥύ(μης). The rho may seem too short and slanted when compared to those in lines 1 and 4, but the form can be accounted for by its initial position and the fact that there is an abbreviation. *Τεμγενούθεως* is coupled with λαύρα in SB XXIV 16186.3–4 (70), but not found elsewhere with ῥύμη. The collocation ῥύμη *Τεμγενούθεως* would not, however, be implausible; cf. SB XXIV 16011.7 (11/12?) ῥύμη Μυροβαλάνου (known otherwise as an ἄμφοδον), with R. Duttenhöfer, *BASP* 34 (1997) 59, and Daris, *ZPE* 132 (2000) 211 and n. 3. In any case, it is not clear why the name of the district is repeated, nor why, after mentioning it for the first time, the scribe described the district as λαύρα or ῥύμη, if this can be read.

R.-L. CHANG

5168–5170. Collection of Documents

29 4B.63/C(12)a   25.5 × 15.9 cm

Three sheets of papyrus, each containing a separate document, assembled in a τόμος ϲυγκολλήϲιμοϲ. The lower parts are missing. Only the second document retains both left and right margins, with a sheet-join in the middle. The first two documents seem to have been written by the same scribe on the same day. It is not clear why they were joined with the third document (**5170**), which is of a very different kind. τόμοι ϲυγκολλήϲιμοι containing documents of different types are uncommon: see W. Clarysse in M. Brosius (ed.), *Ancient Archives and Archival Traditions* (2003) 344–59, at 355. A parallel for the combination of **5168** and **5169** is given by BGU IV 1153 (14 BC), which consists of a nursing contract and a document relating to παραμονή.

The writing runs along the fibres in all three documents. The back is blank except for some traces of ink.

5168. Wet-Nurse Contract

29 4B.63/C(12)a, col. i   10 October 18(?) BC

Apollonia agrees to become wet-nurse to a foundling whom Sarapion, a 'Macedonian', had collected from a dung heap and probably intended to keep or sell as a slave. Wet-nurse contracts are discussed and re-edited by M. Manca Masciadri and O. Montevecchi in C. Pap. Gr. I; cf. also Z. Tawfik, *Pap. Congr. XXI* (1997)

939–53, and J. Bingen, *CE* 81 (2006) 208–11. See in general on wet-nurses C. Laes, *Children in the Roman Empire* (2011) 69–77. To judge by certain supplements (e.g. at 5, 7–9), the original line-length was approximately 12 cm.

ἔτους τρεισκαιδεκάτου(?) Καίϲαροϲ, Φαω]φι ι̅β̅, (vac.) ἐν Ὀξυρύγχων πόλει.
ὁμολογεῖ Ἀπολλωνία *c*.6 -δ]ώρου Περϲείνη μετὰ κυρίου
τοῦ ἑαυτῆϲ πατρὸϲ Ϲαραπίων]ι Διδύμου Μακεδόνι παρει-
ληφέναι παρ’ αὐτοῦ ὃ ἀνήρηται ὁ Ϲαραπί]ων ἀπὸ κοπρίαϲ ἀρϲενι-

5   κὸν ϲωμάτιον ᾧ ἐπέθηκεν ὄνο]μα Ἔρωϲ, ὃ καὶ ἐπάναγκον θηλά-
ϲει καὶ θρέψει τῷ ἰδίῳ αὐτῆϲ γάλα]κτι καὶ τιθηνήϲει ἐπὶ χρόνον μῆναϲ δεκαοκτ]ὼ ἀπὸ τῆϲ ἐνεϲτώϲηϲ ἡμέραϲ λαμ-
βάνουϲα παρὰ τοῦ Ϲα]ραπίωνοϲ κατὰ μῆνα εἰϲ τὰ τροφῆα καὶ
ἱματιϲμὸν καὶ τὴ]ν ἄλλην δαπάνην πᾶϲαν ἀργυρίου δρα-

10   χμὰϲ ὀκτώ(?), καὶ ἀπέχ]ειν τὴν Ἀπολλωνίαν παρὰ τοῦ Ϲαραπίωνοϲ τῶν πρώτων μ]ηνῶν τριῶν ἀργυρίου δραχμὰϲ εἴκοϲι
καὶ τέϲϲαραϲ(?)· τούτων δ]ὲ πληρωθέντων χορηγήϲιν τὸν
Ϲαραπίωνα τῇ Ἀπολλω]νίᾳ [κατ]ὰ [μῆ]να τὸν [ἐϲ]ταμένον α-
    c.9   , μὴ οὔϲηϲ] τῇ Ἀπολλωνίᾳ ἐξουϲίαϲ προϲρεί-

15   πτειν τῷ Ϲαραπ]ί[ω]ν[ι τ]ὸν παῖδα μέχρι τοῦ τοὺϲ δεκαοκτὼ μῆναϲ πληρωθῆνα]ι, τῇ δ’ Ἀπολλωνίᾳ μηδ’ ἀνδροκοιτήϲιν ἐπι
    c.6   πρὸϲ τὸ μὴ δ]ιαφθαρῆναι τὸ ἑατῆϲ γάλα. τὴν δὲ
πᾶϲαν προϲτ]αϲίαν καὶ ἐπιμέληαν ποιήϲθω καὶ μετὰ
τὸν χρόνον παραδότ]ω αὐτῷ τεθραμμένον καὶ τετευχότα

20   *c*.17   ἐὰν μ]ή τι πάθῃ ἀνθρώπινον, ὃ καὶ
ϲυμφανὲϲ   *c*.9   καταϲτ]ήϲει. γενομένου δέ τινοϲ
       c.25   ]όνου, ἐπάναγκον ἕτε-
ρον   *c*.21   π]αρὰ τοῦ Ϲαραπίωνοϲ
       c.24   ε]ἰϲ τοὺϲ δεκαοκτὼ μῆ-

25   ναϲ   *c*.21   ἐὰν(?)] δὲ ἡ Ἀπ[ολλ]ωνία μὴ
                                  ]. . . .

. . . .

2 l. Περϲίνη   8 l. τροφεῖα   12 θεντων corr. from θεντωγ   l. χορηγήϲειν
13 τον corr. from τοϲ?   14 απ corr.   14–15 l. προϲρίπτειν   16 l. ἀνδροκοιτήϲειν
17 l. ἑαυτῆϲ   18 l. ἐπιμέλειαν ποιείϲθω   19 τεθρ- corr. from θεθρ-

'Year thirteen(?) of Caesar, Phaophi 12, in the city of Oxyrhynchi. Apollonia daughter of —dorus, Persian, having her own father with her as guardian, acknowledges to Sarapion son of Didymus, a Macedonian, that she has received from him the male child whom Sarapion has pulled out from a dunghill, to whom he gave the name Eros, whom she will perforce breast-feed and nourish with her own milk and tend as his nurse for a period of eighteen months counting from the present day, receiving monthly from Sarapion eight(?) silver drachmas for fostering and clothing and all the other expenses; and that Apollonia is in receipt of twenty-four(?) silver drachmas from Sarapion for the first three months, and that when these (months) have been completed, Sarapion will provide Apollonia each month with the agreed (wage), with Apollonia not being permitted to hand the baby over to Sarapion until the eighteen months have been completed, nor to have a male bed-mate . . . , so that her milk is not spoilt. Let her give all attention and care, and after the period (of the contract), let her hand (the child) over to him nursed and fully cared for(?), unless it suffers some mortal event, which she shall make clear(?). If something . . . happens . . . , of necessity . . . another . . . from Sarapion . . . the eighteen months . . . If Apollonia does not . . .'

1 The day of the month is the same as in **5169**, hence the supplement ἔτους τρεισκαιδεκάτου, though it seems slightly too long for the space.

3 [τοῦ ἑαυτῆς πατρός]. If Apollonia's guardian were her husband or other relative, his name would be given, but there is no room for it unless ἑαυτῆς is omitted. The name of her father has already been given in 2, and there is no need to repeat it here.

Cαραπίων]ι Διδύμου. A Sarapion son of Didymus is found at **5171** 20–21 (6 BC), but both names are common.

Μακεδόνι. Cf. **5166** 3 n.

Before παρει[ληφέναι, we expect ἐν ἀγυιᾷ. Cf. the omission of τῆς Θηβαΐδος in 2.

7 μῆνας δεκαοκτ]ώ. Cf. 15–16, 24. The term of service of eighteen months is in line with those known from other documents; see e.g. C. Pap. Gr. I 5.8 (Alex., 13 BC).

10 For the monthly salary, see 11–12 n.

11–12 There is not enough room for διὰ χειρὸς ἐξ οἴκου. Three months' salary being 24 drachmas, Apollonia was paid 8 drachmas a month (10).

12 πληρωθέντων. After the rho, there is an unfinished omega, followed by a space about 0.5 cm wide left blank (perhaps due to the unevenness of the surface) and then a fresh omega.

13–14 ἀ|[πότακτον μισθόν, as conjecturally supplied in C. Pap. Gr. I 16.10, would be unparalleled and too long if the supplement printed at 14 is correct.

14 Cf. for the genitive absolute C. Pap. Gr. I 31.319–20 μὴ οὔσης τῇ Ἡρῷ ἐξουσίας [. . . -ρῖ]ψαι τοῖς γονεῦσι τὸ παιδίον μηδὲ παρα[. Both προς- (C. Pap. Gr. I 24.7) and ἀπορρίπτειν (C. Pap. Gr. I 28.18, 24(?)) are found in such phrases, and it is not certain which is to be preferred at C. Pap. Gr. I 29.3, 31.319–20.

16 πληρωθῆνα]ι. Cf. II **275** = W. Chr. 324 = Sel. Pap. I 15.24–5 (66); XIV **1641** 8 (68) μέχρι τοῦ τὸν χρόνον πληρωθῆναι.

For τῇ δ᾽ Ἀπολλωνίᾳ μηδ᾽ we expect simply μηδ᾽ (cf. C. Pap. Gr. I 28.19 μηδὲ παραθηλάσειν). Apparently the scribe has inserted τῇ δ᾽ Ἀπολλωνίᾳ for the sake of clarity (cf. τὴν Ἀπολλωνίαν at 10).

μηδ᾽ ἀνδροκοιτήσιν ἐπι. μηδ᾽ ἀνδροκοιτοῦσαν μηδ᾽ ἐπικυοῦσαν is a standard pair; cf. also C. Pap. Gr. I 14.18–19 καὶ [μὴ] ἀνδροκοιτεῖν πρὸς τὸ μὴ διαφθαρῆναι [τὸ γάλα μηδὲ ἐπι]κυεῖν. If we restore ἐπι|[κυής(ε)ιν, it will be necessary to assume that μηδ᾽ has dropped out between the infinitives.

The future infinitive here provides an interesting parallel to C. Pap. Gr. I 26.26 (110) μὴ ἀνδροκοιτήσιν, but the construction there is uncertain and apparently confused; for discussion, see J. Bingen, CE 81 (2006) 216–17.

18 πᾶσαν προστ]αcίαν is paralleled by C. Pap. Gr. I 14.17, but seems short for the space.

20 At the start, πάσης ἐπιμελείας alone (cf. C. Pap. Gr. I 35.20, 36.20) may be a little too short: perhaps it had the article, as in the similar phrase above (17–18).

20–21 C. Pap. Gr. I 14.21 ἐὰν μή τι πάθῃ ἀνθρώπινον, ὃ καὶ cυνφανὲ[c γέν]ηται gives the general sense expected. Here we may have had, e.g., ὃ καὶ [cυμφανὲς ἐπάναγκον καταcτ]ήcει: cf. P. Köln III 147.5–7 (Augustan) πλὴν ἐὰν μή τι βίαιον ἐκ θεοῦ γ[έ]νη[τ]αι . . . ὃ κα[ὶ] cυμφανὲς καταcτήcω.

(In the light of that passage, the ἐὰν μή clauses in both wet-nurse contracts are to be taken with what precedes: the wet-nurse must return her charge unless she can prove that it has died.)

21–2 γενομένου δέ τινος probably refers to an eventuality such as that implied in ἐὰν μ]ή τι πάθῃ ἀνθρώπινον. The clause may have ended with ἐντὸς τοῦ χρ]όνου in 22. Cf. SPP XXII 36.14 (145) ἐὰν δὲ πάθῃ [τ]ι ἀνθρώπινον ἐντὸς τοῦ χρό[νου], ἐ[πάναγκο]ν κτλ. See further 22–5 n.

22–5 This clause specifies what should happen if Eros dies: ἕτε[|[ρον (22) was probably followed by παιδίον or παῖδα (cf. 15). The phrase π]αρὰ τοῦ Cαραπίωνος, not paralleled in this context, may suggest that Apollonia will have to accept a substitute 'from Sarapion' (cf. C. Pap. Gr. I 14.21–5); in other cases, it was the wet-nurse herself who had to find a replacement (cf. C. Pap. Gr. I 4.19–26, 5.20–26, 9.11a–12a).

25 ἐπὶ τοῖς προκειμένοις would fit the space available after μῆ]|[νας; cf. C. Pap. Gr. I 14.23–4.

ἐὰν(?)] δὲ ἡ Ἀπ[ολλ]ωνία μὴ may have been followed in the next line by βούληται τοῦτο ποιῆσαι; cf. C. Pap. Gr. I 14.24.

5169. REPAYMENT OF LOAN

29 4B.63/C(12)a, col. ii   10 October 18 BC

Arsinoe acknowledges the return of money that she had lent to Petosiris and his two sons, both named Herceus. She had made the loan on condition that Petosiris' daughter, Senerceus, serve her for two years. The document is not complete: of the subscription, only the subscriber's name, Ἀρςιν[όη, survives.

On contracts involving *paramone*, see W. L. Westermann, *JJP* 2 (1948) 9–50; B. Adams, *Paramone und verwandte Texte* (1964); A. E. Samuel, *JJP* 15 (1965) 304–5; J. Hengstl, *Private Arbeitsverhältnisse freier Personen in den hellenistischen Papyri bis Diokletian* (1972) 9–34; A. Jördens, P. Heid. V pp. 284–95. Parallels for the vicissitudes suffered by Senerceus are found in other contracts of service, most of which probably originated from private debts. We find another *paramone* involving a daughter forced to work outside her family in order to repay a debt in BGU IV 1139 (5 BC), reedited by O. Montevecchi, *BASP* 22 (1985) 231–41 = *Scripta selecta* (1998) 345–54. BGU IV 1153 ii (14 BC) and 1154 (10 BC) are two contracts of *paramone* and repayment of apparently interest-free loans of 300 and 100 drachmas respectively. See also C. Pap. Gr. I 8 (7/6 BC), the cancellation of a contract according to which a woman called Philotera was acting as wet-nurse for her own child in order to repay a debt; BGU IV 1126 (9 BC), a contract for services in return for a loan of one hundred drachmas; PSI X 1120 (1 BC or AD), a *paramone* for one year involving a certain Heraclius (the debtor) and two creditors called Gaius and Lucius; P. Mich. V 241.24–38 (16), a contract of service in a pottery of a certain Patynis and his son Aunes, who received a loan of 40 drachmas from the owner of the pottery; P. Diog. 16 (207).

The personal names in this document show that the servant came from a native Egyptian background, while her employer belonged to the Hellenized upper class. A further point of interest is that the contract offers an early mention of the archive (ἀρχεῖον) of the record office (γραφεῖον) of Oxyrhynchus, where the τόμος was probably deposited.

ἔτου[c] τρειϲκαιδ[ε]κάτου Καί[ϲα]ροϲ, Φαῶφι ι̅β̅, (vac.) ἐν Ὀξυρύγχων πόλει τῆϲ
Θηβαΐδοϲ. ὁμολογεῖ Ἀρϲινόη Ἀρ[ί]ϲτωνοϲ μετὰ κυρίου τοῦ ἑατῆϲ ἀ-
δελφοῦ Ἀπίωνο[ϲ] τοῦ Ἀρίϲτωνοϲ Ἑρκεῖ πρεζβυτέρῳ Πετοϲίριοϲ
οἱ τρεῖϲ ἐν ἀγυ[ι]ᾶι ἀπέχειν παρὰ τοῦ αὐτοῦ καὶ τοῦ νεωτέρου αὐτοῦ
5   ἀδελφοῦ Ἑρκέουϲ ἔτι δὲ καὶ [τ]οῦ ἀμφοτέρων πατρὸϲ Πετοϲίριοϲ
τοῦ Βενιαιοϲ ὄντων ἀποδήμων ἀργυρίου νομίϲματοϲ δραχμὰϲ ἑκατὸν [. .] αν κεφαλαίου, αἷϲ οὐδὲν προϲήχθη, ἃϲ ἐδά-
νειϲεν αὐτοῖϲ ἡ Ἀρϲινόη κατὰ ϲυγγραφὴν τὴν τελιωθῆϲαν
διὰ τοῦ ἐν Ὀξυρύγχων π[ό]λει ἀρχήου τοῦ γραφίου ἐν τῷ δεκάτῳ
10 ἔτει Καίϲαροϲ Φαμενωθ ἐπὶ παραμονῇ τῆϲ τοῦ Πετοϲίριοϲ
θυγατρὸϲ τῶν δ' ἄλλων ἀδελφῆϲ Ϲενερκεὺϲ οὐδέπω οὔϲηϲ
ἐν ἡλικίᾳ ἐπ' ἔτη δύο ἀκολούθωϲ ταῖϲ δι' αὐτῆϲ ϲημανθείϲαιϲ
διαϲτολαῖϲ, καὶ μηθὲν ἐνκαλεῖν μηδ' ἐνκαλέϲιν μηδ' ἐπελεύ-
ϲαϲθαι Ἀρϲινόην μηδ' ἄλλον ὑπὲρ αὐτῆϲ τοῖϲ προγεγραμ-
15 μένοιϲ μ[η]δὲ τοῖϲ παρ' αὐτῶν περὶ μηδενὸϲ ἁπλῶϲ τῶν κατὰ τὴν δηλουμένην τῆϲ παραμονῆϲ [ϲ]υγγραφὴν ἢ χωρὶϲ
τοῦ τὴν ἐϲομένην ἔφοδον ἄκυρον εἶναι καὶ προϲαποτίνιν
Ἀρϲινόην ἢ τὸν ὑπὲρ αὐτῆϲ ἐπελευϲόμενον τοῖϲ προγεγραμμέ-
νοιϲ ἢ τοῖϲ παρ' αὐτῶν καθ' ἑκάϲτην ἔφοδον τό τε βλάβοϲ καὶ ἐ-
20 πίτιμον ἀργυρίου δραχμὰϲ τριακοϲίαϲ καὶ εἰϲ τὸ δημόϲιον
τὰϲ ἴϲαϲ καὶ μηθὲν ἧϲϲον. κυρία ἡ ϲυγγραφή.

⌒

(vac.)

Ἀρϲιν[όη

. . . .

2 l. ἑαυτῆϲ   3 l. πρεϲβυτέρῳ, some correction on β   5 l. Ἑρκέωϲ   6 απο (vac.) δημων   8 αρϲινοη: some correction on ν; ο is squeezed in   l. τελειωθεῖϲαν   9 l. ἀρχείου, γραφείου   11 l. Ϲενερκέωϲ   13 l. ἐγκαλεῖν, ἐγκαλέϲειν   13–14 l. ἐπελεύϲεϲθαι   17 l. προϲαποτίνειν

'Year thirteen of Caesar, Phaophi 12, in the city of Oxyrhynchi in the Thebaid. Arsinoe daughter of Ariston, having with her as guardian her brother Apion son of Ariston, acknowledges to Herceus the elder, son of Petosiris, the three of them in the street, that she is in receipt from the said (man) and from his younger brother Herceus, and, in their absence, also from their father Petosiris son of Beniaeus(?), of (the sum of?) one hundred drachmas in silver currency, as principal to which nothing was added, which Arsinoe lent them in accordance with a contract concluded through the bureau of the record-office in the city of Oxyrhynchi, in the tenth year of Caesar in Phamenoth, in consideration of the service of the daughter of Petosiris and sister of the others, (namely) Senerceus, not yet of age, for two years, in accordance with the guidelines notified through it; and that Arsinoe will bring no claim now or in the future, nor take proceedings, nor will another on her behalf, against the afore-mentioned, nor against their agents, concerning any provision whatever of the contract of service here made known: otherwise, apart from any future claim being invalid, Arsinoe or the person who will take proceedings on her behalf will also pay in addition, to the afore-mentioned or their agents, in respect of each claim, both the damages and a fine of three-hundred drachmas of silver, and an equal number to the treasury and no less. The contract is binding.'

'Arsinoe . . .'

2–3 ἀ|δελφοῦ. The reading is unclear. There may be faint traces at the end of line 2, making ἀν|εψιοῦ a possibility, though it would be incorrectly divided.

3 Ἑρκεῖ πρεζβυτέρῳ. Ἑρκεύς is probably a variant of the common name Ἑριεύς, which is often spelled Ἑργεύς; for Oxyrhynchites called Herieus, see B. W. Jones and J. E. G. Whitehorne, *Register of Oxyrhynchites 30 B.C. – A.D. 96* (1983) 116 (nos. 2260–67). In P. Wash. Univ. I 50 (Oxy.; late I bc), we find Ἑρ( ) νεώτ[ε]ρ[ος (23) and two lines later a name beginning Ἑρ- (25).

6 τοῦ Βενιαιος. The form in the nominative is unclear. The name may be attested also in the Arsinoite VI **918** iii 11 Βενια[ ]ος (genitive, restored from an entry in the unpublished col. iv). Grenfell and Hunt noted that 'Βενιά[μιος is not improbable' but dismissed the possibility of a connection between this name and Βενιαμιν, since this person's father and grandfather had an Egyptian name. It is probably not related to the Roman name Benius (one Γάιος Βένιος Κέλερ appears in I. Koptos 52, engraved under Domitian).

7 [. .]. αν: presumably [τὸ] πᾶν, though there is no exact parallel. (There are some instances of the collocation πᾶν κεφάλαιον.)

κεφαλαίου, αἷς οὐδὲν προσήχθη. The aorist προσήχθη, 'was added', in the repayment corresponds to the perfect προσῆκται, 'has been added', in the formula commonly appended to the capital in loan contracts; cf. **5173** 6–7 (25–6) κεφαλαίο[υ], αἷς οὐδὲν τῶι καθόλου προσῆκται with n. (τῶι καθόλου is occasionally omitted.) The *paramone* clause is often found in loans apparently free of interest: in such cases, the interest was probably paid off by the obligation for service. This may have been the case in BGU IV 1153 ii (14 bc) and 1154 (10 bc). The presence of the *paramone* clause in a loan contract may also indicate that the service was the repayment for both the capital and the interest, as was suggested by A. E. Samuel, *JJP* 15 (1965) 304–5.

9 διὰ τοῦ ἐν Ὀξυρύγχων π[ό]λει ἀρχήου τοῦ γραφίου. This is the only passage in which ἀρχεῖον and γραφεῖον appear together. On γραφεῖα, see W. E. H. Cockle, *JEA* 70 (1984) 112; Straus, *L'Achat* 57–8. **5169** is the earliest certain reference to an ἀρχεῖον at Oxyrhynchus (the provenance of P. Ryl. II 65.4 (?67 bc) is uncertain). An ἀρχεῖον τῶν μνημόνων is attested in LV **3777** 13 of 57 bc.

9–10 Phamenoth, Year 10 Augustus = 25 February – 26 March 20 bc.

11 Cενερκεύς. This name is not otherwise attested in this form, but Cενεριεύς (Tc-) is familiar. For the spelling with kappa, see above, 3 n.

11–12 οὐδέπω οὔcης ἐν ἡλικίᾳ. This formula was used to indicate minors in wills and property declarations; see e.g. P. Fouad 35.6–7 (48), in which a woman appoints her husband as her guardian, and the cession of land II **273** = M. *Chr.* 221.13–14 (95), both from Oxyrhynchus.

12–13 ἀκολούθως ταῖς δι' αὐτῆς cημανθείcαις διαcτολαῖς. This phrase has no exact parallel, though cf. P. Tebt. I 24.44–5 (117 bc) ἀκολούθως ταῖς δεδομέναι⟨c⟩ δι' α[ὐ]τῶν διαcτολα⟨ῖ⟩c, or P. Flor. I 86 = M. *Chr.* 247.26 (*post* 25.vii.86) ἀκολούθω[c] ταῖς διὰ τῶν [cυν]γραφῶν δηλωθείcαις διαcτολαῖς.

15–16 The only Oxyrhynchite parallel for this expression is XIV **1644** 16–18 (63/62 bc) μηδὲ περὶ ἄλλου μηδενὸς ἁπλῶς τῶν κατὰ τὴν δηλουμένην τοῦ δανείου cυγγραφήν.

22 Ἀρcιν[όη. The name of one of the parties opens the subscription, the rest of which is lost.

5170. Notice to an Agoranomus

29 4B.63/C(12)a, col. iii   Late first century BC

What little survives seems to establish that this papyrus belongs to the category of notices to agoranomi (2 ἀνάγραψον); it probably deals with mortgaged property (land). This type of document is well attested in the Oxyrhynchite nome in the later first century AD, but nowhere else and at no other time. The text is therefore of some importance, since it would seem to prove that the practice was known at Oxyrhynchus from the very beginning of the Roman period. See further **5176** introd.

The text is written in a larger and more cursive hand than **5168–9**.

Θέων (vac.) [1?] . [

ἀνάγραψον [

Παύσιος τ[οῦ

ευν[ ]υφις η[

5   ἐπὶ νότον . [

πῆχυν ε . [

κ̣α̣ὶ τῆς εἰ̣[c

τῶν ὄντω[ν

ἐν τῶι α . [

.   .   .

'Theon . . . Register . . . of Paysis son of . . . Eunouphis(?) . . . towards the south . . . cubit . . . and the . . . that are . . . in the . . .'

1 Θέων. In notices to agoranomi, the sender may be an official 'not precisely specified or his agent', perhaps the farmer of the ἐγκύκλιον, the tax on sales; see Straus, *L'Achat* 49–50, and Benaissa, *ZPE* 170 (2009) 171.

At the end of the line, probably τῷ ἀγορανόμῳ χαίρειν.

2 ἀνάγραψον. The verbs ἀναγράφειν and καταγράφειν are technical terms for the action of registering conveyances of property or drawing up a contract; see Straus, *L'Achat* 44–52, and Benaissa (1 n.) 170–71. The use of ἀνάγραψον places this text in Benaissa's category IIB, which consists of orders to register loans and mortgages; for references to such texts see LXXIV **4984** introd.

At the end of the line, perhaps restore δανείου cυγγραφήν or cυγγραφὴν ὑποθήκης.

3 Παύσιος. The name Παῦcιc is attested at Oxyrhynchus in the early Roman period; see Jones and Whitehorne, *Register* 161–2 (nos. 3266–7).

4 ευν[ ]υφις: Εὔν[ο]υφις? The name in this form is not attested elsewhere, but cf. Αὔνουφιc, Ἔνουπιc, Ἔνουφ, and Ἔνουφιc, all variants of the name Ἄνουφιc.

5 ἐπὶ νότον. Cf. II **243** = M. *Chr.* 182.21 (79). Cardinal points are normally mentioned in the topographical description of the boundaries of a property.

6 At the end, εν[(ἔν[α?) or ει[.

7–8 Perhaps restore something on the lines of e.g. XLI **2972** 15–16 (72) καὶ τῆς εἰc αὐτὸ εἰcόδου καὶ ἐξόδου καὶ τῶν cυνκυρόντων | τῶν ὄντων κτλ. The phrase has hitherto occurred only in sales of real property, though cf. II **241** 19–22 (98), from a registration of a mortgage.

9 ἐν τῶι α.[. The letter on the edge is more likely to be gamma than pi.

L. CAPPONI

5171. Report from a *Topogrammateus*

105/220(a) 15 × 28 cm 6 BC

Arius, *topogrammateus* of the Middle toparchy, reports a rescinded sale of land, which no doubt originated from unproductive properties put on public sale, as the references to 'bought land' (4) and *paradeixis* (3–4) imply. The sale contravened the rulings of the prefect Gaius Turranius, pronounced during the audit that he held on the matter of revenues collected in the Hermopolite nome for 8/7 BC; this probably happened in the early months of 6 BC (see below, 6–7 n.). Arius quotes the prefect's rulings (8–16), which prohibited all officials in the *chora* from purchasing land. A list of properties thus repossessed by the government is added (19–22). The recipient of this report is not specified; it may have been a copy or draft of a report from the *topogrammateus* to his superior, perhaps the *basilikos grammateus*. Cf. P. Oxy. Hels. 9 (26), a report of a toparch which likewise has no addressee.

The text contains the earliest clear reference to public sale of land, and offers the second earliest attestation of 'bought land' as a land category, which began to develop in Egypt under Augustus; see below, 4 n. Turranius' rulings, though fragmentary and only partially intelligible, apparently belong to the same judicial tradition as the *Gnomon of the Idios Logos* §70, transmitted by BGU V 1210.174–80 (after 149) and already in force in P. Mil. Vogl. II 98 (138/9?; BL V 71). On this regulation, which forbids any official or liturgist to engage in purchases and loans within the territory of his office, see S. Riccobono, *Il gnomon dell'idios logos* (1950) 210–22, where the previous studies are summarized, especially Th. Reinach, *Un code fiscal de l'Égypte romaine* (1920–21) 152–7, and W. Graf Uxkull-Gyllenband, BGU V.2 (1934) 70–77. See also A. Jördens, *Statthalterliche Verwaltung in der römischen Kaiserzeit* (2009) 478–9.

The *kleroi* of Diognetus, of Socindrus and Demetrius, and of Demetrius (19–21) are new.

The text lacks its right-hand and lower left-hand parts. What remains is broken into an upper and a lower fragment, which almost join. The extent of the loss on the right can be deduced from supplements in 2–8. The writing runs along the fibres. The back is blank.

The edition has benefited from the advice and criticism of Andrea Jördens and J. David Thomas. Paul Heilporn, Dominic Rathbone and Jane Rowlandson have also provided helpful comments.

παρ' Ἀρείου τοπογραμματέως τῆς μέϲης τοπαρχί[αϲ.   *c*.5

ἀναλημφθῆναι τὰϲ ὑπὸ Φαμούνιοϲ κωμ[ο]γρ[αμματέωϲ

Τᾳνᾴεωϲ καὶ τοῦ Ἴϲτρου ἐποικίου κατὰ πίϲτι[ν παραδε-

δειγμέναϲ εἰϲ ἐωνημένην τ...δι( ) τοῖϲ ὑπο..[*c*.7

5   υἱοῖϲ παρὰ τὰ ὑπὸ Γαΐου Τυρρανίου τοῦ ἡ[γεμόνοϲ *c*.4

κεκριμένα ἐπὶ τοῦ γενομένου διᾳ[λο]γ[ιϲμοῦ   *c*.6

ἀργυρικῶν τοῦ κγ (ἔτουϲ) Καίϲαροϲ τοῦ Ἑρμο[πολίτου νομοῦ

ἐφ' ὧν (*vac*.) μ[ηδέ]να τῶν κατὰ τὴν χώραν π[ραγματικῶν

ὠνεῖϲθ[αι..]ι.τ( ), τοὺϲ δὲ γράφ[ο]νταϲ τὴν [*c*.6 ἀκρι-

10   βέϲτᾳ[τα] ἐπὶ πάντων λ[α]μβάνειν [*c*.10

δικ[αϲτ]ὰϲ μήτε πραγματικοῖϲ ὠνεῖϲθαι [*c*.7

     c.7]ϲιν εἰϲ τὰϲ τούτων γυναῖκαϲ ε[*c*.7

     c.6]τε Ῥωμαῖοϲ τὸ ὑπὸ [τῶ]ν ϲημαινομέ[νων *c*.5

     c.6]ου ὠνημένου ε[ἴ]δουϲ ιδ..[*c*.6

15   *c*.6]. ἄλλου τοιούτου [τ]ὸ(?) ἐπὶ τοῦ νο[*c*.10

     c.6]..( ) (*vac*.) τ[..]..ουτ..[

         ]. κδ (ἔτουϲ) Κᾳ[ί]ϲαροϲ

         ] νθ( )

        ] καὶ Διδύμῳ ἀμφο(τέροιϲ) Διδ(ύμου) ἐκ (τοῦ) Διογνή(του) ε [

20 Ϲα]ραπίωνι Διδ(ύμου) ἐκ (τοῦ) Ϲωκίνδ(ρου) καὶ Δημη(τρίου) α.[

      ] Ϲαραπίωνι Διδ(ύμου) ἐκ (τοῦ) Δημη(τρίου) ε ∠ d (*vac*.) [

      ].. (*vac*.) (γίνονται) ιϲ .. (*vac*.) [

      ]μωι ἀδελφῷ[ι

3 l. Τανάεωϲ   4 τ...δῑ   7, 17 ∠   13 ϲημαινομε[νων: a corr.   18].$\frac{\theta}{\nu}$

19 αμφ°διδε°διογν^η   20 διδε°ϲωκιν^δ δημ^η   21 διδε°δημ^η   22 /

'From Arius, *topogrammateus* of the Middle toparchy. . . . (that) the (arouras) be repossessed that were verified in good faith by Phamounis, *komogrammateus* of Tanais and of the hamlet of Istrou, as belonging to (the category of) bought land . . . , and assigned to the . . . sons . . . , contrary to the rulings of the prefect Gaius Turranius . . . during the past audit of the cash revenues(?) of the 23rd year of Caesar of the Hermopolite nome, in respect of which none of the officials in the *chora* should purchase . . . , and those who record . . . are to take . . . most accurately on all points . . . judges, and not . . . officials . . . purchase . . . (in the names of) the wives of these men . . . nor(?) any Roman . . . the . . . by the indicated officials(?) . . . of the category of bought land . . . or of something(?) else of this kind . . . over the nome(?) . . . , . . .

'. . . 24th year of Caesar

'. . .

'To(?) . . . and Didymus, both of them sons of Didymus, from the (allotment) of Diognetus, 5 . . . (arouras) . . .

'. . . to(?) Sarapion son of Didymus, from the (allotment) of Socindrus and Demetrius, 1 . . . (arouras) . . .

'. . . to(?) Sarapion son of Didymus, from the (allotment) of Demetrius, 5¾ (arouras) . . .

'. . . total 16 (arouras) . . .

'to . . . the brother . . .'

1 Ἀρείου τοπογραμματέωϲ. Previously unknown.

There seems to be no room for an addressee at the end of the line. There may have been a verb governing ἀναλημφθῆναι (2) or a preposition followed by τὸ (ἀναλημφθῆναι), meaning 'as for' (e.g., περὶ τοῦ) or 'because of'.

2–4 τὰϲ ὑπὸ . . . κωμ[ο]γρ[αμματέωϲ . . . παραδε]δειγμέναϲ, sc. ἀρούραϲ. Cf. IV **718** 26–7 (179–81; see J. D. Thomas, *Epistrategos* ii (1982) 189) τ]ὰ[ϲ] ὑπὸ τοῦ κωμογραμματέωϲ προϲφωνηθείϲαϲ [ἀρούραϲ. παραδε]δειγμέναϲ suits the context better than ἀποδε]δειγμέναϲ, which is not attested as a technical term in sales of land by the state. παράδειξιϲ was the final step in a successful public sale of unproductive land (at fixed price), before the payment of the buyer. It was carried out by *komogrammateis*: with the help of on-site γεωμέτραι, they authenticated the description of the public property on sale given in the offer of purchase, and made a report to *basilikoi grammateis* either directly or through *topogrammateis*. See P. Petaus 17.3 n.; P. Thomas 12 introd.; Th. Kruse, *Der königliche Schreiber und die Gauverwaltung* (2002) 508–14, 517–18; S. Alessandrì, *Le vendite fiscali nell'Egitto romano* i (2005) 50–91, 190–200, and esp. 218–19.

2 Φαμούνιοϲ κωμ[ο]γρ[αμματέωϲ. Previously unknown. This variant of the name Pamounis is not common and appears more frequently in the Ptolemaic period. It is attested for the Oxyrhynchite nome only in BGU X 1943 (215/214 BC); cf. also P. Leit. 1 = SB VIII 10192.8 (*c.*160) Φαμουνίου.

3 Τανάιεωϲ καὶ τοῦ Ἴϲτρου ἐποικίου. These are the earliest mentions of the two localities, situated in the Middle toparchy. There is no other evidence that they were joined in a single *komogrammateia*, though they are mentioned side by side in other texts; see A. Benaissa, *Rural Settlements of the Oxyrhynchite Nome* (²2012) s.vv. It is suggested in LVIII **3918** 16 n. that the place names 'reflect the presence of Thracian immigrants in the area', but Dr Dan Dana has kindly pointed out to me that this is not very likely: (1) it would be arbitrary to conflate the supposedly Scythian settlements on the Tanais (river Don) and the Greek city of Istros (by the Danubian delta) into a single Thracian framework; (2) Istros, rather than referring to the Danube or the Greek city, may have been the name of the founder of the hamlet; (3) most of the Thracian cleruchs in Egypt did not originate from the Danubian region.

Τανάιεωϲ. This spelling of the genitive of Τάναϊϲ with a redundant iota is also found in XXXVIII **2874** 3 (108) and XXII **2351** 8, 46 (112).

κατὰ πίϲτι[ν. Perhaps equivalent to (καλῇ) πίϲτει, *bona fide*. Cf. SB XX 14339.16–17 (III), where a prefect is reported to have said that he acted κατὰ πίϲτιν in wrongly assigning a liturgy; see J. Maspero, *BIFAO* 10 (1912) 156. Both this prefect and the village scribe in **5171**, though acting 'in good faith', may have been in the wrong; see A. Berger, *EDRL* s.v. *error facti*. Phamounis may have carried out the παράδειξιϲ before C. Turranius issued his rulings.

4 ἐωνημένην, sc. γῆν. This is the first contemporary reference to this land category, though P. Oxy. Hels. 9.6 (AD 26) indicates that it already existed by 16/15 BC. It was formed from unproductive land put on public sale at fixed prices and was created as a distinct category in the very early years of Roman rule; see J. Rowlandson, *Landowners and Tenants in Roman Egypt* (1996) 48–54; Alessandrì, *Le vendite fiscali* 205–6; Jördens, *Statthalterliche Verwaltung* 486, with further references.

Public sales of land were previously not mentioned in any document earlier than XX **2277** of AD 13. Cf. also IV **721** (13/14), IX **1188** (13).

τ. . . δι( ). It may be possible to read τῆϲ ἰδι(ωτικῆϲ?), but the wording would be clumsy. See also 8–9 n., 14 n.

4–5 τοῖϲ ὑπο. . [*c.*7 | υἱοῖϲ. After ὑπο there is a trace that looks like the top of an upright, followed by the upper part of an oblique rising from left to right, and then perhaps the upper part of an upright. If we read τοῖϲ ὑποκε[ιμένοιϲ] υἱοῖϲ, the implication would be that the name of the father of the 'sons', i.e. Διδύμου (see 19–21), has been omitted: Didymus' sons presumably acted as front men for the fraudulent purchase (cf. below, 11–12 n.). Another possibility would be to restore ὑπὸ χε[ῖρα/ χε[ιρὶ αὐτοῦ or ὑποχε[ιρίοιϲ, which would imply that these were Phamounis' sons under his tutelage, for whom he illegally bought the properties and to whom he transferred them; however, unless we reckon with the implicit use of a double name, it would be impossible to explain why the name of their father is given as Διδύμου.

5 Γαΐου Τυρρανίου τοῦ ἡ[γεμόνοϲ. C. Turranius is the fifth prefect of Egypt known to us, attested in office between 10 March 7 BC and 5 June 4 BC. For a list of texts mentioning him, see P. Bureth, *ANRW* II 10.1, 475; G. Bastianini, *ANRW* II 10.1, 504; add BGU XVI 2605.1, CPR XV 15.1. His career was first reconstructed by A. Stein, *Die Präfekten von Ägypten* (1950) 19–20, with I. Philae II 142 (= SB V 8420 = IGR I 1295) of 8 March 7 BC as the earliest attestation. In this inscribed epigram, Catilius alias Nicanor writes of his travel from Alexandria to Philae and his inscription there and mentions the name of the prefect, C. Turranius. As the prefect would have travelled up the Nile some time between January and April (see 6–7 n.), Catilius' journey must have coincided with the *conventus*, that is, he must have joined Turranius' retinue at the beginning of 7 BC, as É. Bernand suspects (I. Philae II 142.6 n., pp. 82–3). It is highly likely that Turranius was in office already by the end of 8 BC.

6–7 δια[λο]γ[ιϲμοῦ c.6] ἀργυρικῶν τοῦ κγ (ἔτουϲ) κτλ. There is not enough room at the end of 6 for ϲιτικῶν καί. φόρων may be considered as a stopgap.

If διαλογιϲμόϲ here refers to the prefect's *conventus*, as seems likely, it is its earliest attestation in this sense, the next earliest being M. *Chr.* 68 (before 30 June 15). Alternatively, it may have the more general sense 'audit,' as in several Ptolemaic papyri.

This audit of the revenues from the Hermopolite nome for Year 23 (8/7 BC) must have been carried out in Year 24 (7/6 BC); cf. below, 17. The fact that this nome was singled out may suggest that the audit was performed during the assizes held for Middle and Lower Egypt, which should have taken place some time between January and April (6 BC); see R. Haensch, *Pap. Congr.* XXI 329–32.

8 ἐφ' ὧν. ὧν presumably refers to κεκριμένα. For ἐπί + gen. meaning 'in respect of which', similar to ἐπί + dat., see perhaps Mayser, *Grammatik* ii.2 469–70, 473. Cf. the fragmentary P. Lips. II 124.61–2 τὰ προϲταχθέντα | ἐφ' ὧν.

8–12 This passage, after ἐφ' ὧν, consists of three infinitive clauses which may have depended on a finite verb now lost. One possibility is προϲήκει, perhaps to be restored at the end of 11. However, a finite verb may not be required for infinitives expressing orders. Besides, the second and third infinitives seem to form a unity, with τοὺϲ . . . γράφ[ο]ντας (9) as the subject; see 9–11 n. and 11–12 n.

8–9 μ[ηδέ]να τῶν κατὰ τὴν χώραν π[ραγματικῶν] | ὠνεῖϲθ[αι ﹍]ι﹍τ( ). This regulation is reminiscent of Dig. XVIII 1.62 *qui officii causa in provincia agit vel militat, praedia comparare in eadem provincia non potest, praeterquam si paterna eius a fisco distrahantur.* The unread part may be the equivalent to *praedia*, and ἰδ]ιωτ(ικ-) may be a possibility; cf. 4 n., 14 n. Cf. also Dig. XVIII 1.46, XLIX 14.46.2, C. Th. VIII 15.1.

8 π[ραγματικῶν]. Cf. 11, where the word survives in full. This is the earliest attestation of the term in papyri of the Roman period. It refers to minor officials, very often *komogrammateis*, and probably does not include liturgists, as in later times (there is no proof that the Roman liturgical system had been introduced at such an early date). This specific meaning of the term can also be deduced from the edict of Ti. Iulius Alexander (68) 21 ἢι ϲτρατηγοῖϲ ἢι πραγματικοῖϲ ἢι ἄλλοιϲ τῶν προϲοφειληκότων [τῶι δημοϲίωι λόγωι. Turranius' ruling thus seems to have a less extended application than *Gnomon* §70, which concerns liturgists as well; see BGU V.2 pp. 72–4. For πραγματικοί as 'subordinate officials', see also VI **899** 17 n.; G. Chalon, *L'Édit de Tiberius Julius Alexander* (1964) 126 n. 12; CPR XXIII 17.8 n.; Kruse, *Der königliche Schreiber* 1103 n. 220.

9–11 τοὺϲ δὲ γράφ[ο]ντας τὴν . . . δικ[αϲτ]άϲ. The subject of λ[α]μβάνειν ought to be τοὺϲ . . . γράφ[ο]ντας, perhaps secretaries in charge of the registration of sales of land; the object will then begin with τήν, e.g., τὴν [γνώμην ('the secretaries are required to take good notice of the prefect's judgement').

9–10 ἀκρι]∥βέϲτα[τα]: not εὐϲεβέϲτατα, which is used exclusively for honorific titles in the papyri, and not attested before the third century. It should be specified that there is not enough room to restore -τά[την].

11 δικ[αϲτ]άϲ: ἀρχι]∥δικ[αϲτ]άϲ?

11–12 μήτε πραγματικοῖϲ ὠνεῖϲθαι [c.7] | [c.7]ϲιν εἰϲ τὰϲ τούτων γυναῖκαϲ. This is the third infinitive proposition, which prohibits illegal purchase by functionaries through front men. The gap at the end of 11 or even 12 will have held an infinitive meaning 'allow' or similar to account for the dative. Cf. Dig. XVIII 1.46 *non licet ex officio, quod administrat quis, emere quid vel per se vel per aliam personam*; XLIX 14.46.2 *quod a praeside seu procuratore vel quolibet alio in ea provincia, in qua administrat, licet per suppositam personam comparatum est, infirmato contractu vindicatur.* Compare also P. Mil. Vogl. II 98 (138–9?), where a village scribe is accused of fraudulent purchase of land: 9–10 τὴ[ν καταγρ]αφὴν π[ε]ποιῆϲθαι εἰϲ ὄνομα τῆϲ πενθερᾶϲ αὐτοῦ Ἰϲαρίου, 27–8 ἐνκεκτῆϲτε (l. -θαι) ἐπ' [ὀ]νόματοϲ τῆϲ Ἰϲαρί[ου]. For the interchange between the expressions εἰϲ ὄνομα τοῦ δεῖνοϲ and εἰϲ τὸν δεῖνα, frequently attested in tax and land registers, see F. Preisigke, *Girowesen* (1910) 149–50; P. Ryl. II 202a.8ff. n.

12–13 ε[. . .]τε Ῥωμαῖοϲ. Perhaps read ἐ[πεὶ οὔτε | ἀϲτὸϲ οὔ]τε Ῥωμαῖοϲ, with two groups of people of special civil status standing in opposition to 'the officials in the *chora*' (8), though it would be unusual if ἀϲτόϲ preceded Ῥωμαῖοϲ. This regulation, which presumably runs down to the beginning of 16, does not correspond to any Roman legislation of which we are aware.

14]ου ὠνημένου ε[ἴ]δουϲ ιδ . [. At the start, τ]ού? At the end, before the break, the edge of a high semi-circle, followed by a speck on the edge. ἰδιω(τικ-) may be considered, though the form of the omega would be irregular. If correct, it would offer the earliest record of 'bought land' being treated as a sub-category of private land. Cf. also above, 4 n. and 8–9 n.

ὠνημένου. For the perfect forms of ὠνοῦμαι without reduplication, see F. T. Gignac, *Grammar* ii 227.

15 Perhaps restore ἤ τινο]ϲ ἄλλου τοιούτου and ἐπὶ τοῦ νο[μοῦ.

16 The first letter on the edge looks like mu, topped by an L-shaped alpha. τ[. .] . ουτ . . [. Perhaps τ[οὖ]το or τ[αὖ]τα οὕτωϲ though it is hard to read sigma.

17–23 The structure of the text here differs from that of the preceding lines; this, as well as the smaller hand, makes it difficult to estimate the number of letters lost to the left.

17] . κδ (ἔτουϲ) Κα[ί]ϲαροϲ. Not το]ῦ: the short horizontal before κδ can hardly belong to upsilon.

18] . νθ( ). Of the uncertain letter, which must be a vowel, there are traces belonging to the upper and lower right-hand corners. The only available choices are epsilon and eta, and] ἐνθ(άδε) or ἔνθ(α) may be considered (referring to the village and farmstead mentioned at 3).

19 In the break at the beginning of the line perhaps restore [Ϲαραπίωνι] (cf. 20–21), though we do not know whether Didymus had more than two sons.

ἐκ (τοῦ) Διογνή(του). This *kleros* was previously unknown. The name is rarely attested in Egypt after the Ptolemaic period. The original holder may or may not be related to Bilis son of Diognetus, an (ὀγδοηκοντάρουροϲ) κλ(ηροῦχοϲ) in P. Tebt. III.2 830.4 (II BC; κλ(ῆροϲ) ed. pr., but cf. e.g. P. Enteux. 8.1).

20–21 The same Sarapion son of Didymus is probably meant in both lines. Cf. **5168** 3 n.

20 ἐκ (τοῦ) Ϲωκίνδ(ρου) καὶ Δημη(τρίου). This *kleros* too was not attested previously. The name Ϲώκινδροϲ has appeared only in O. Edfou III 371 1.41, 2.2, 3.6, 3.9 (49 BC?). No etymology has been offered.

21 ἐκ (τοῦ) Δημη(τρίου). This *kleros* too appears to be new. Several *kleroi* 'of Demetrius' have been attested in the Oxyrhynchite nome, but none in the Middle toparchy; see P. Pruneti, *Aegyptus* 55 (1975) 172–3.

22 This line may have started with ἄλλαι, introducing another amount of arouras. What comes after ιϛ looks like the siglum for (πυροῦ) or (ἀρτάβαι), but this is not expected here. The final traces may be read as alpha or lambda, or as a word abbreviated at the second letter, which would be a simplified and raised alpha.

23 Διδύ]μωι ἀδελφῶ[ι? In this line the hand is larger than that in 19–22, and looks more like that in 1–18. This, as well as the fact that this name follows the sum total of illegally bought arouras in 22, suggests that this line is not part of the list. Thus we cannot tell with certainty whether this person is the Didymus son of Didymus named in 19, the brother of the Sarapion mentioned in 20–21.

This was the last line of the column. It is not clear whether the report abruptly ended here, or was carried on in a lost second column.

R.-L. CHANG

5172. RECEIPT FOR DIKE-TAX

103/124(b)   8.3 × 12.2 cm   30 July 7

This is the earliest receipt for dike-tax from the Roman period so far published, taking the place of O. Petr. 79 (15). The closest parallel is CPR V 1 (66), which has the same arrangement: date of payment, verb of paying, names of private banking agents, year for which the tax was due, district for which the tax was counted, name of tax-payer, amount paid; see R. Bogaert, *AncSoc* 31 (2001) 250 (formula 1), and below, 3 n. Another point of interest is the mention of the city quarter of Hermaion, the earliest to date; see 3 n.

The papyrus is complete except for a small loss at the lower right. This is not likely to have contained a signature, also absent from CPR V 1 and II **312** descr. = SB X 10237. A *kollesis* is visible 3.2 cm from the left edge. The writing runs along the fibres. The back is blank.

> ἔτους λϛ Καίϲαροϲ,
> Μ[ε]ϲ(ορη) ϛ̄. διαγέγρ(αφε)
> διὰ Ὡρ( ) τρα(πεζίτου) χω(ματικοῦ) λβ (ἔτουϲ) Ἑρμα(ίου)
> Ὠρίων Πλουτάρχ(ου)
> 5   (δραχμὰϲ) πέντε (πεντώβολον), (γίνονται) ε (πεντώβολον).

3 ωρ̄τρ⌐χʷλβ∟ερμᵃ   4 πλουταρχˣ   5 ʃ ₣ | ₣

'Year 36 of Caesar, Mesore 6. Horion son of Plutarchus has paid through Hor—(?), banker, for dike-tax for the 32nd year, for (the district of) Hermaion, five drachmas 5 obols, total 5 (dr.) 5 ob.'

2 διαγέγρ(αφε). The expansion in the active voice is suggested by the use of the nominative for the name of the tax-payer (4). We should therefore resolve διαγέγρ(αφε) instead of διαγέγρα(πται) in II **288** 1, 7, 12, 17, 21, 25, 30, 32, and **289** i 2, ii 2, 4; these two texts should be classified under formula 1 of bank receipts in R. Bogaert, *AncSoc* 31 (2001) 250. (Bogaert's formula 2 with διαγέγραπται seems to be characteristic of tax receipts from Philadelphia; see A. E. Hanson, *BASP* 19 (1982) 54–5.)

3 Ὡρ( ): not Ὡρ(ου), as the type of the abbreviation indicates. Ϲαρ( ) is not excluded, but the putative alpha would have an abnormally flat bottom; cf. Καίϲαροϲ in 1. In any case, this banker is not otherwise known.

τρα(πεζίτου). The absence of the article (τῆϲ) before the banker's name tells against resolving the abbreviation as τρα(πέζηϲ), which is what earlier editions have (contrast CPR V 1.4): see **288** 8 *et passim*, **289** 2 *et passim*, SB X 10221 iii 3, iv 2, 10223, 10237, 10242.3, 10243 i 3, ii 2; in all these passages the expansion τρα(πεζίτου) should be preferred. Thus there is no distinction to be drawn so far as this point is concerned between the examples cited by Bogaert (2 n.) for his formula 1 and for his formula 2. Indeed Bogaert already includes **288** in his second category, with τραπεζίτου rather than τραπέζηϲ.

For private banks in Roman Oxyrhynchus, see Bogaert, *ZPE* 109 (1995) 151–7.

χω(ματικοῦ). For Roman dike-tax as a capitation tax, see P. Brookl. 45 introd.; P. Köln III 138.3 n., IX 376 introd. (p. 143); K. Maresch, *Bronze und Silber* (1996) 164–72; Bogaert, *AncSoc* 30 (2000) 148–9; P. Heilporn, *Thèbes et ses taxes* = O. Stras. II (2009) 25 n. 91, 94–7. It is first recorded in BGU IV 1198 (Heracl.; 5/4 BC), a petition to the prefect from four priests who complained of being subject to poll- and dike-tax. There are seventeen published Oxyrhynchite papyri attesting this tax, excluding P. Köln III 138 and XII **1438**, which are of uncertain provenance. Except for P. Princ. II 46 (II) and XLIII **3107** (238), they are all from the first century; see the list in Maresch, *Bronze und Silber* 232–3, 235, to which add SB XX 14665 (30), SB X 10236 = II **322** descr. (36), P. Oxy. Hels. 29 (54), and XLI **2971** (66). Apart from the last three documents, which are contracts of apprenticeship, they are largely cumulative receipts and tax accounts, in which the dike-tax is often connected with other charges, especially poll- and pig-tax. The poll-, pig- and dike-taxes were the main taxes levied on persons in Oxyrhynchus from the reign of Augustus to the end of the first century (or later); see II **389** descr. (early I), SB XX 14665, P. Oxy. Hels. 29.30–31, **2971** 19–20, P. Oxy. Hels. 12 (99).

Ἑρμα(ίου). This is the earliest attestation of this district, on which see S. Daris, *ZPE* 132 (2000) 215–16 = Calderini, *Diz. geogr.* Suppl. III 99–100; see also Suppl. III 36, Suppl. V 32, 73.

5 (δραχμὰϲ) πέντε (πεντώβολον). This same amount paid for dike-tax, including *prosdiagraphomena* and other taxes, is recorded in some Theban ostraca of the late first century; see Maresch, *Bronze und Silber* 223. The standard rate for dike-tax in the first and second centuries was 6 drachmas 4 obols, attested as early as AD 15 in Upper Egypt (O. Petr. 79) and 18 in Oxyrhynchus (II **309** descr. = SB X 10221 iv). *Prosdiagraphomena* and other additional payments were included in the sums collected elsewhere in Egypt, but such payments are not recorded in any Oxyrhynchite document relative to the dike-tax, and thus can hardly account for the difference between the standard rate and the payment of 5 dr. 5 ob. in **5172**. Whether this amount indicates a different rate or partial payment, we cannot tell; cf. the instalments recorded in II **308** descr. = SB X 10243 ii 5–6 (3 dr. 4½ ob. + 2 dr. 5½ ob. paid for 46/7), and possibly in II **312** descr. = SB X 10237 (3 dr. 4½ ob. paid for 35/6), or **288** 20 (6 dr. paid for 23/4).

R.-L. CHANG

5173. LOAN OF MONEY

104/178(a)   13 × 12 cm   29 August 25 – 3 February 26

Anteis son of Titan, previously known from LVIII **3915** (30), acknowledges receipt of a loan of 100 silver drachmas through a private bank at the Serapeum of Oxyrhynchus. What remains is paralleled by SB XVI 12700A (end of reign of Augustus; see R. Bogaert, *ZPE* 109 (1995) 154), SB X 10222.1–12 (20), 10238.1–10

(37), 10246.1–11 (55), and II **269** 1–8 (57). The lost part will have contained the penalties in case of default, the *kyria*-clause, the signature of an amanuensis (Anteis was illiterate; see **3915** 27–9) with the date, and the notification of payment through the bank. Cf. also P. IFAO III 30 (early 1), P. Yale I 60 (6/5 BC), XLVII **3351** (34), and XLIX **3490** (140/41) (the last two did not require the involvement of a bank).

The text offers the earliest dated instance of the expression 'imperial and Ptolemaic silver coinage'; see below, 4–5 n.

The papyrus was rolled up from the right and crushed; the leftmost panel was tucked in prior to the endorsement. The strip was then folded horizontally at least twice. A *kollesis* is visible 5.2 cm from the left. The text runs along the fibres.

Ἀντεῖϲ Τιτᾶνοϲ Πέρϲηϲ τῆϲ ἐπιγονῆϲ
Ζωΐλωι Θέωνοϲ χαίρειν. ὁμολογῶι ἔχειν παρὰ ϲοῦ ἐπὶ τοῦ πρὸϲ Ὀξυρύγχων πόλει Ϲαραπείου
διὰ τῆϲ Ἱέρακοϲ τοῦ Πτολεμαίου τραπέζηϲ ἀργυ-
5 ρίου Ϲεβαϲτοῦ καὶ Πτολεμαϊκοῦ νομίϲματοϲ δρα-
χμὰϲ ἑκατόν, (γίνονται) ἀργ(υρίου) (δραχμαὶ) ρ κεφαλαίο[υ], αἷϲ οὐδὲν τῶι καθόλου προϲῆκται, ἃϲ κ[α]ὶ ἀποδόϲω ϲοι τῆι δεκά-
τη]ι τοῦ Με[χ]ειρ [τοῦ ἐν]εϲτῶτοϲ δωδεκάτου
ἔτ]ουϲ Τιβερίου Κα[ίϲα]ροϲ Ϲεβαϲτοῦ χωρὶϲ πά-
10 ϲηϲ ὑ]περθέϲεω[ϲ c.4]................[..]....
  ]..[c.7   ]..[

.   .   .   .

Back, downwards, along the fibres
(*m.2?*) Ἑρμαίου [..]....[

  2 l. ὁμολογῶ   6 /αργ͞ρ͞   7 l. ἀποδώϲω   8 δωδεκατου -   9 πα -

'Anteis son of Titan, Persian by descent, to Zoilus son of Theon, greetings. I acknowledge that I am in receipt from you, at the Serapeum in the city of Oxyrhynchi through the bank of Hierax, son of Ptolemaeus, of one hundred silver drachmas of imperial and Ptolemaic coinage, in total 100 silver drachmas as principal, to which nothing has been added at all, and which I will return to you on the tenth of Mecheir of the present twelfth year of Tiberius Caesar Augustus, without any delay. If I fail to refund you according to the set conditions(?) . . .'

Back: 'Of Hermaeus . . .'

1 Ἀντεῖϲ. This confirms the reading of the name in LVIII **3915** 23.

Πέρϲηϲ τῆϲ ἐπιγονῆϲ. Anteis is not called a 'Persian by descent' in **3915**, where he is the seller of a camel; this is further evidence that this designation was legal fiction at that time and applied to debtors. This situation is paralleled e.g. by P. Mich. V 332 = PSI VIII 910 (47/8), where a certain Orseus is or is not described as 'Persian by descent' depending on whether he is a borrower or vendor; see P. Merton I 10.4 n.

2 Ζωΐλωι Θέωνοϲ. A person of this name is attested in X **1316** 4–5 of 57 (we have seen a pho-

tograph). Zoilus son of Theon in II **265** 41, 42 (81–95) and LXXV **5051** 7 is probably a namesake, since he was alive some time in the reign of Domitian; cf. also P. Eirene I 5 = SB XXIV 16093.2 (1), though the patronymic is only tentatively restored.

3–4 ἐπὶ τοῦ πρὸς Ὀξυρύγχων πόλει Cαραπείου διὰ τῆς Ἱέρακος τοῦ Πτολεμαίου τραπέζης. The banker Hierax son of Ptolemaeus was not known previously. R. Bogaert, *ZPE* 109 (1995) 155–6, argues that there were two private banks operating at the Oxyrhynchite Serapeum at least from AD 30 to 74, one of which, unlike the bank mentioned here, included the Serapeum in its name: **3915** 13–14 διὰ τῆς ἐπὶ τοῦ πρὸς Ὀξυρύγχων [πόλει Cαρα]πιείου Cαραπίωνος τοῦ Ζωίλου τραπέζ(ης) would be a reference to the other bank. To Bogaert's list of documents mentioning the bank(s) at the Serapeum add now also LXXV **5052** 30–31 (86/7) and P. Sijp. 49.7–10 (II, but not later than 153/4: this bank was confiscated by the state and was farmed out regularly from 153/4 onwards; see Bogaert 156).

4–5 ἀργυρίου Cεβαστοῦ καὶ Πτολεμαϊκοῦ νομίσματος. This expression reflects the simultaneous use of the old Ptolemaic coinage and the new billon tetradrachm, first minted in 20/21; see E. Christiansen, *ZPE* 54 (1984) 292–6. **5173** offers its earliest attestation, followed by SB XVI 12609 = ChLA XLV 1340 = C. Epist. Lat. I 13 (27). (The reference to such coinage in SB XX 15028 allows us to narrow down the possible range of dates for that document from 14–37 to 20–37.)

6–7 κεφαλαίο[υ], αἷς οὐδὲν τῶι καθόλου προσῆκται. This formula is characteristic of Oxyrhynchite loans of money from AD 20 to 85; see F. Lerouxel, *ZPE* 181 (2012) 165–8, who argues that the usual rate of 12% p. a. lies behind the lack of a reference to interest. Cf. now **5169** 7 (18 BC) with n.

7–9 Mecheir 10, Year 12 Tiberius = 4 February 26. The form of words may suggest that Mecheir had not yet begun.

10 After ὑ]περθέcεω[c, parallels suggest reading ἐὰν δ]ὲ μὴ ἀποδῶ καθὰ γέγραπται.

12 The purpose of this line, much too damaged and containing a name which does not occur on the front so far as it is preserved, is unclear. The endorsements of other Oxyrhynchite loan contracts of this period (P. Yale I 60.19–20 (6/5 BC), XLIX **3485** 38–40 (38), P. Genova II 62.49 (98), etc.) are of no help.

R.-L. CHANG

5174. LETTER TO APELLES, STRATEGUS

58/B(37)a   15.5 × 16 cm   28 October – 26 November 26

A fragment from the end of a letter addressed on the back to Apelles, a strategus of the Panopolite nome not known previously. A further point of interest is the reference to an unnumbered 'August day' (see 10 n.).

The letter is written along the fibres on a sheet that seems to have belonged to a composite roll: there is a three-layer sheet-join close to the right-hand edge, and a four-layer one 2.3 cm from the left-hand edge, while the sheet attached at left is of finer quality and lighter in colour than that at right.

  .   .   .   .

                                       ] . ιωι

  .....] .... [c.20   ]το

  ....]λιον τουτ[c.20   ] .ων

  ε.[..]. οὖν ἤγηcα.[c.20   ] ἐκ-

5   π[έ]μψαι μοι αὐτ . [*c.*20   ] ὧν

      ἐ[ὰ]ν αἱρῆι γράφε κ[*c.*20   ]ωι.

      πρὸ δὲ πάντω(ν) ϲεα(υτοῦ) ἐπ[ιμέλου ἵν' ὑγιαίνηιϲ.

                    ἔρρωϲο.

            (ἔτουϲ) ιγ Τιβερίου Καίϲαροϲ Ϲεβαϲτοῦ, μηνὶ Νέωι

10   Ϲεβαϲτῶι, Ϲεβαϲτῆι.

Back, downwards, along the fibres:

      ] (*vac.*) Ἀπελλεῖ ϲτρατηγῶι Πανοπολ(ίτου)

4 two horizontals over υ and νη: perhaps only accident   7 πανϊϲεᾱ   9 L
10 short oblique stroke over η of ϲεβαϲτηι   11 πανοπό^λ

'. . . therefore if(?) you(?) have considered . . . send me . . . Write about whatever you choose . . . Before everything, take care of yourself so that you are healthy. Farewell.

      'Year 13 of Tiberius Caesar Augustus, in the month of Neos Sebastos, August day.

      Back: '. . . to Apelles, strategus of the Panopolite nome.'

4 Perhaps read εἰ [μὲ]ν οὖν ἥγηϲαι, though iota does not reach below the baseline elsewhere in the text.

      5 αὐτ . [: αὐτη[(αὐτή[ν?) or αὐτι[(αὐτί[κα would go well with ἐκπ[έ]μψαι).

      5–6] ὧν ἐ[ὰ]ν αἱρῆι γράφε. In the break restore περί, as in P. Lips. I 104.13–14 (95/62 BC), SB XVIII 13273.10–11 (Ptolemaic), etc.; or ὑπέρ, as in IV **787** (16).

      10 Ϲεβαϲτῆι. Cf. **5176** fr. 2.7. There is one other instance of an unnumbered ἡμέρα Ϲεβαϲτή in the month of Neos Sebastos from the reign of Tiberius, viz. O. Stras. I 54 (15); there may be another from the fourth year of Gaius (39/40), if the name of the month is correctly read (O. Wilck. 385, with BL II.1 58; a different reading is proposed in O. Bodl. II 429 introd. = BL VIII 539 [BL slightly misrepresents this as a correction to the suggestion in BL II.1]). It is possible that such unnumbered days indicate the birthday of the ruling emperor, but Snyder has pointed out that this is not likely to apply to Tiberius. There are grounds to believe that from the reign of Tiberius onwards the day intended under this name was the first of each month. See generally W. F. Snyder, *Aegyptus* 18 (1938) 227–32 and 44 (1964) 162–4, and more recently the discussion by C. Bennett at http://www.tyndalehouse.com/Egypt/ptolemies/chron/egyptian/chron_eg_anl_augustus.htm.

      11 Ἀπελλεῖ ϲτρατηγῶι Πανοπολ(ίτου). No other strategus of the Panopolite nome is known for the early Roman period. As often, he may have been an Oxyrhynchite who came back to Oxyrhynchus with his papers, though the name Apelles is not attested in this region before the second century.

      The inventory number of **5174** (58/B(37)a) is adjacent to that of LV **3807** (58/B(36)a), a letter apparently sent from an official, perhaps a royal scribe, to another notable some time between years 12 and 15 of Tiberius. **3807** mentions affairs in Diospolis, probably one of the two cities of this name in Upper Egypt ('Parva' or 'Magna'), to the south of and not too far away from Panopolis. The names of the sender and addressee are lost. One may wish to associate the two letters, but it should be noted that the addressee of **3807** was probably not a strategus when that letter was written (see **3807** 24–6).

                                                        N. GONIS

5175. Petition to the Prefect

57/102(a)   14 × 9 cm   c.49

Only the top of the document survives. It appears to be a duplicate of I **38** = M. *Chr.* 58 = M. V. Biscottini, *Aegyptus* 46 (1966) 237–8 (no. 24), a petition of the weaver Tryphon to the prefect, written some time after 29 March 49. **5175** is not written by the same hand as **38**, and has a number of spellings of its own (1, 3, 4); see also 5–6 n.

For bibliography on the archive of Tryphon see M. Piccolo, *Aegyptus* 83 (2003) 197 n. 1; add now P. J. Parsons, *City of the Sharp-Nosed Fish* (2007) 211–14, and B. Kelly, *Petitions, Litigation, and Social Control in Roman Egypt* (2011) 131–3, 312–16. I **39** = II **317** (52) is another duplicate in the archive.

The back is blank.

$$\Gamma\nu\alpha\acute{\iota}\omega\iota\ O\mathring{v}\epsilon\rho\gamma\iota\lambda\acute{\iota}\omega\iota\ K\alpha\pi\acute{\iota}\tau[\omega]\nu\iota$$
$$\pi\alpha\rho\grave{\alpha}\ T\rho\acute{v}\phi\omega\nu o\varsigma\ \tau o[\mathring{v}]\ \varDelta\iota o\nu\nu\sigma\acute{\iota}o\nu$$
$$\tau\tilde{\omega}\nu\ \mathring{a}\pi\grave{o}\ `O\xi\nu\rho\acute{v}\nu\chi\omega[\nu\ \pi]\acute{o}\lambda\epsilon\omega\varsigma.\ C\tilde{v}[\rho o\varsigma$$
$$C[\acute{v}\rho]o\nu\ \mathring{\epsilon}\nu\alpha\iota\chi\epsilon\acute{\iota}\rho\iota\varsigma\epsilon\nu\ \tau[\tilde{\eta}]\iota\ \gamma\nu\nu\alpha[\iota\kappa\acute{\iota}\ \mu o\nu$$
5      $$C[\alpha]\rho[\alpha\epsilon\tilde{v}]\tau\iota\ `A\pi\acute{\iota}\omega\nu o\varsigma\ \tau\tilde{\omega}\iota\ ..[$$
$$\quad c.6 \quad \delta\iota^{'}]\ \mathring{\epsilon}\nu\gamma\acute{v}o\nu\ [\mathring{\epsilon}]\mu[o\tilde{v}$$

.   .   .   .

3 l. Ὀξυρύγχων   4 l. ἐνεχείρισεν   6 l. ἐγγύου

'To Gnaeus Vergilius Capito from Tryphon son of Dionysius, (one) of those from the city of Oxyrhynchi. Syrus son of Syrus handed over to my wife Saraёus daughter of Apion, in the (seventh?) year, on my security . . .'

1 Cn. Vergilius Capito was prefect of Egypt from *c.*47 to 52. His *nomen* is spelt Οὐεργελίωι in **38** 1.
2 το[ῦ]. Dr Henry observes that the article is present also in **38** 2, but omitted by editors.
5–6 Perhaps τῶι ϛβ[δό]∥[μωι ἔτει]; I **38** 4–6 run τῶι ζ (ἔτει) Τιβερίου Κλαυδίου Καίσαρος Σεβαστοῦ Γερμανικοῦ Αὐτοκράτορος δι' ἐνγύου ἐμοῦ ὃ ἀνείρηται. This Year 7 = 46/7.

N. GONIS

5176. Notice to an Agoranomus

9 1B.172/A (fr. 1)   11.7 × 8 cm   23 June 52
9 1B.172/E (fr. 2)   12.2 × 16.5 cm

Fr. 2 is the lower part of a document whose top (fr. 1) was previously published as LXXIV **4985**. Fr. 1 preserves the beginning of a letter from Heraclides and Ammonius authorizing an agoranomus to register the sale of house property. Fr. 2

provides the foot of the document, and contains the end of the dating clause, the signature of Heraclides with a repetition of the date, and a note to the agoranomus from a banker and his associates confirming their receipt of the requisite tax, a sum of 2 talents and 1500 drachmas in bronze (see 6–10 n.). The two fragments do not appear to join and little is left of the first hand in fr. 2.1–2; but the continuity of a sheet-join *c*.5 cm from the left-hand edge and the alignment of the vertical folds guarantee that the fragments belong to the same document.

This type of document, in which officials of unspecified function either authorize agoranomi to register the sale or mortgage of house property or a slave, or order them to grant the manumission of a slave, is represented by some two dozen examples and is peculiar to Oxyrhynchus; for a discussion and list of the relevant papyri, see M. G. Raschke, *BASP* 13 (1976) 17–29, and A. Benaissa, *ZPE* 170 (2009) 157–85, to which add now LXXIV **4984**, LXXV **5051**, and very probably **5170** in this volume. The exact function of the senders of these letters is uncertain, but they are most commonly identified with the supervisors of the sales-tax (ἐπιτηρηταὶ ἐγκυκλίου); see J. A. Straus, *L'Achat et la vente des esclaves dans l'Égypte romaine* (2004) 49–50, and cf. *ZPE* 170 (2009) 171.

Virtually all published letters of this kind date from the last three decades of the first century AD, probably because a batch of documents was cleared from the office of the agoranomi at the end of this period. Since the vast majority were published or described in P. Oxy. I–II, they were no doubt excavated together during Grenfell and Hunt's first season at Oxyrhynchus (1897). **5170** of the late first century BC and this letter, both likewise found in the first season, are the first specimens outside this date range, a proof (if one was needed) that the chronological concentration of the other letters is the result of ancient archival and disposal history rather than of a short-lived administrative practice.

The writing runs along the fibres and the back is blank. Fr. 2 preserves a generous lower margin (7 cm).

Fr. 1

Ἡρακλείδης καὶ Ἀμμώνιος τῶι
ἀγορανόμωι χ(αίρειν). κατάγραψον
ὠνὴν Διοκλεῖ Πτολεμαίου τοῦ
ἐπιβάλλοντος τῶι διατιθεμένωι
5   μέρους οἰκίας καὶ αὐλῆς καὶ τῆς εἰς ταύτ(ας)
εἰσόδου καὶ ἐξ[ό]δου καὶ τῶν cυνκυρόντων
κοινῶν [καὶ] ἀδιαιρέτων πρὸς τούς τε
α[ὐ]τοῦ ἀδε[λ(φοὺς) κατ]ὰ πατέρα καὶ τοὺς . . . . ε
α̣ . [*c*.12   ]εντω . . . . . [. .] . χω( )

Fr. 2

. . . .

.[*c*.8].[. . .].[. . .].[. . . . . .].

(*vac.*) [ ] ὀγδόῃ καὶ εἰκάδι κ̄η̄.

(*m.*2) Ἡρ̣ακλε[ίδηϲ] χρη(μάτιϲον). (ἔτουϲ) ιβ Τιβερίου Κλαυδίου

Κα̣ίϲαροϲ [Cεβα]ϲ̣τοῦ Γερμανικοῦ Αὐτοκράτοροϲ,

(*vac.*) Παυνι κ̄η̄.

(*m.*3) Πολέμων καὶ οἱ μέτοχ(οι) τῶι ἀγορα(νόμωι) χαίρε(ιν).

τῇ κ̄θ̄ Cεβαϲτῆι {Cεβαϲτῆι} τοῦ Παυνι

τοῦ ἐν⟨ε⟩ϲτῶτο(ϲ) ἔτουϲ καθ' ἣ(ν) ἔχε(ι) διαγρα(φὴν)

χα(λκοῦ) πρὸ(ϲ) ἀργ(ύριον) (τάλαντα) δύο χιλίαϲ πεντακο(ϲίαϲ),

(γίνονται) χ̣α̣(λκοῦ πρὸϲ ἀργύριον) (τάλαντα) β̣ 'Αφ. (*vac.*) ἔρρω(ϲο).

Fr. 1

2 χ̄ʃ 3 υ of -μαιου corr. 5 ταυ$^{\tau}$ 6 l. ϲυγκυρόντων 9].χ̣$^{\omega}$

Fr. 2

3 χρ$^{\eta}$ ∟ 6 μετο$^{\chi}$ αγορ^{o}χαιρ$^{\epsilon}$ 7 η of second ϲεβαϲτηι corr. το̆ 8 ενϲτωτ^{o} καθ$^{\eta}$εχ$^{\epsilon}$διαγρ$^{\phi}$ 9 χ^{ʹ}πρ^{o}αργ$^{\upsilon}$⸆ πεντακ^{o} 10 = χ̣^{ʹ}⸆β'Αφ ερρ$^{\omega}$

(Fr. 1) 'Heraclides and Ammonius to the agoranomus, greetings. Register a sale for Diocles son of Ptolemaeus of the share that falls to the one disposing of it, of a house and courtyard and the entrance and exit to these and the appurtenances, (being) common and indivisible with his brothers on his father's side and . . .'

(Fr. 2) '. . . twenty-eighth, 28.'

(2nd hand) 'Heraclides: register (it). Year 12 of Tiberius Claudius Caesar Augustus Germanicus Imperator, 28 Pauni.'

(3rd hand) 'Polemon and associates to the agoranomus, greetings. On 29 Pauni, August day, of the present year, (N.N. has paid,) in accordance with the bank draft in his possession, two talents and one thousand five hundred (drachmas) of bronze (converted) to silver, total 2 tal. 1500 (dr.) of bronze (converted to silver). Farewell.'

Fr. 1

7–8 τούϲ τε | α[ὐ]τοῦ ἀδε[λ(φοὺϲ) κατ]ὰ̣ π̣ατ̣έρα καὶ τοὺϲ̣ . . . .ε: τοὺϲ ἑ|αυτοῦ . . [. . . .] . . . .ερα καὶ το . [. . . .] . ε *ed. pr.* (ἀ̣δ̣[ελ(φοὺϲ) and π̣α̣τέρα suggested in 7–8 n.). I am grateful to R.-L. Chang for restoration work on these lines and the recovery of further text.

9 α̣ . [*c*.12]ε̣ν̣τω̣ . . . . . . [. .] . χ̣ω( ): [*c*.14]ε̣ν̣τω̣ . . . [. . . . .] . *ed. pr.*

Fr. 2

3 Ἡρ̣ακλε[ίδηϲ] χρη(μάτιϲον). Letters to agoranomi authorizing the registration of sales or mortgages or ordering the manumission of slaves typically contain the 'signature' N.N. χρημάτιϲον in the sender's own hand; for a list of instances, see *ZPE* 170 (2009) 170 n. 32, to which add I **48** 21, **49** 14. In the other examples, the signer does not repeat the date as here. In **48** 22 (see BL VII 126) Φαω(φι) ιθ belongs to the bankers' subscription (checked on a photograph). **49** 15–18 contains after the signature a subscription specifying the month, the day, and a sum, but not in the hand of the signer.

The editors assign this subscription to the first hand, but a photograph shows clearly that it is due to a third hand; note also that the subscription is dated a day later than the main letter, suggesting that it was made by bankers to confirm the payment of the requisite sum (see below, 6–10 n., and cf. the identical amount in **I 50**, a bankers' notice to agoranomi).

6–10 In this note bankers confirm that they have received from the purchaser the sales-tax (ἐγκύκλιον), payment of which was presumably a prerequisite to the agoranomic registration of the sale. Although the tax is not explicitly named, cf. the parallel subscriptions in **II 242** 31–4, **243** 45–9, **333** 12–13 (fully published in *ZPE* 170 (2009) 177–8), all of which confirm explicitly the payment of the ἐγκύκλιον; cf. also the self-standing notice **I 50** (with BL VII 126), acknowledging the receipt of the προπρατικόν tax for a manumission. **I 48** 22–4 (BL VII 126) preserves the beginning of a similar note following a letter to an agoranomus ordering him to manumit a slave; see also above, 3 n., on **I 49**.

The formulation of this notice is more compressed than that of **50**, **242** 31–4, and **243** 45–9: it omits the main verb τέτακται, the name of the payer (as subject), and the name of the tax, but adds an otiose τοῦ ἐν⟨ε⟩στῶτο⟨ς⟩ ἔτους. **333** 12–13 follows an altogether different and even more abbreviated format: διαγραφὴ *date* ἐγκυκλίου *sum*. **49** 15–18 (see above, 3 n.) is reduced further to simply *date* + *sum*.

6 Πολέμων καὶ οἱ μέτοχ(οι). Polemon is probably the banker named in **XXXIV 2720** 2 (41–54) τραπέ[ζης ἐφ' ἧς .] . λέμων κα[ὶ μέτοχοι. The editor notes ad loc.: 'presumably *Π*]ολέμων (though *Τ*]ελέμων is not palaeographically excluded)'; but the former is surely the likelier restoration: the form Τελέμων is not attested as a variant of the name Τηλέμων, and the latter name is itself very rare; cf. also R. Bogaert, *ZPE* 109 (1995) 152.

7 τῇ κ̄θ̄ Σεβαστῆι {Σεβαστῆι} τοῦ Παῦνι. The bankers' note to the agoranomus is dated to the day after that of the main letter, as in **49** 15–16 (see above, 3 n.) and **242** 32. In **243** the letter is dated generally to Phamenoth (43), without specification of a day, while the bankers' notice is dated to the 28th of the same month (46). In **333** 10, 12, the main letter and the bankers' note date from the same day; cf. also **48** 22.

For the 29th as a ἡμέρα Σεβαστή, which probably commemorates the birthday of Germanicus, see W. F. Snyder, *Aegyptus* 18 (1938) 218–21, and 44 (1964) 146–7, 159. **I 39** 4 (see BL I 312) and its duplicate **II 317** provide another instance from the same year in the month of Pharmouthi.

A. BENAISSA

5177. LETTER OF DIOGENES, STRATEGUS, TO HERACLIDES

47 5B.43/F(4–6)a　　　　　9 × 14.5 cm　　　　　27 November – 26 December 132

The left-hand side of a letter from Diogenes, strategus, to Heraclides, a sitologus or another strategus (see 3 n., 16 n.). The papyrus was found together with **5178**, a letter from Heraclides to the strategus Claudius Diogenes, and it is reasonable to assume that these are the same people. The letter seems to have been sent to acknowledge receipt of official correspondence from Heraclides. Possibly orders or decisions taken by the central administration were being sent around as a circular from nome to nome; cf. P. Ryl. II 78 (157). The official nature of the letter is confirmed by the file number added in the top margin.

Diogenes added the closing greeting in a fast and abbreviated cursive, while the hand responsible for the main body of the text is that of a professional scribe. A third hand wrote the file number at the top and what may be a docket at the foot.

The presence of vertical folds suggests that the letter was rolled up and squashed flat before being sent. Staining on the back may suggest that a seal was placed there, but it seems more likely that it is subsequent to the opening of the letter.

The writing runs along the fibres.

(*m.3?*)   ⟦ν⟧ϲζ′
                     (*vac.*)

(*m.1*)   Διογένης ϲτρατ[ηγὸς *name of nome*(?)
              Ἡρακλε[ίδ]ηι ϲ.[
              τῶι φ[ι]λ[τ]ά[τωι χαίρειν.
    5   ἃϲ ἔπε[μ]ψ[α]ϲ ἐπιϲτ[ολὰϲ
              θωϲη περὶ τῆϲ .[
              αὐτῶν ἐπιϲτολ.[
              κεχρονιϲμέν[
              τ[ο]ῦ ιζ (ἔτουϲ) Ἀδριαν[οῦ τοῦ κυρίου
    10   ἐκομιϲάμην .[
              ἵν' ε[ἰδ]ῆϲ, [φ]ίλτατ[ε.
(*m.2*)   ἐρρῶ[ϲ]θαί [ϲ]ε εὔχομ(αι) διὰ παν[τόϲ.
                     (*vac.*)

(*m.1*)   (ἔτουϲ) ιζ Αὐτοκράτοροϲ Καίϲαροϲ Τρ[αϊανοῦ
                     Ἀδριανοῦ Ϲεβαϲτοῦ, Ἀδρια[νοῦ *n.*
    15   (*m.3?*)   (. .ου. . . . .)

Back, downwards, along the fibres:
(*m.1*)   Ἡρακλείδηι (*vac.?*) . . . . . (*vac.?*) .[

        9 ιζ⌠   12 ευχ°̄   13 L

(3rd hand?) '207.'
(1st hand) 'Diogenes, strategus (of the . . . nome?), to Heraclides, . . . , his dearest friend, greetings.

"The letters you sent . . . concerning the . . . of them . . . letter . . . dated (. . .) to the 17th year of Hadrianus the lord, I received . . . so that you may know, my dearest friend.'
(2nd hand) 'I pray for your continual good health.'
(1st hand) 'Year 17 of Imperator Caesar Traianus Hadrianus Augustus, (in the month of) Hadrianus *n.*'
Back: (1st hand) 'To Heraclides, . . .'

1 ⟦ν⟧ϲζ′. The number indicates that this document is part of an archive of official correspondence. It may have been filed by means of a *tomos synkollesimos*, although there is no sign of a join on the left. The position of the number suggests that the letter is preserved to just over half its original width, and this is confirmed by the formulaic supplement at 13. The non-indented lines will then have contained about 22 letters.

2 Διογένης στρατ[ηγός. No Diogenes was previously attested as strategus of any nome in 132, but we do not know who the Oxyrhynchite strategus was at that time; see J. Whitehorne, *Strategi and Royal Scribes of Roman Egypt*² (2006) 96.

3 Ἡρακλε[ίδ]ηι ϲ [. After sigma there is an upright, with the surface stripped above; if this was tau, its crossbar will have been lost. ϲι[τολόγωι would suit the indications that in **5178** the strategus Diogenes is Heraclides' superior, as well as the subject matter of that letter. On the other hand, φ[ι]λ[τ]ά[τωι in 4 would suit a letter from a strategus to a strategus (see 4 n.) but would be unparalleled among communications from strategi to sitologi; but see **5178** 2 n. If the papyrus had ϲτ[ρατηγῶι, it should be noted that no Heraclides is attested as strategus of any nome in 132. See also 16 n.

4 φ[ι]λ[τ]ά[τωι is confirmed by [φ]ίλτατ[ε in 11. For the use of this superlative, confined to correspondence between social equals, see Th. Kruse, *Der königliche Schreiber und die Gauverwaltung* (2002) 884–90.

5 ἃϲ ἔπε[μ]ψ[α]ϲ ἐπιϲτ[ολάϲ. Cf. P. Brem. 16.3 (*c*.117). ἔπε[μ]ψ[ε]ν and ἔγρ[α]ψ[α]ϲ are not possible readings.

5–6 E.g. κα]θὼϲ ἥ. Not ἀκολού]θωϲ ᾗ, since what follows is not a verb; contrast e.g. XLVII **3345** 58–9 (209) ἀκολούθωϲ ᾗ ἔγραψεν ἐπιϲτολῇ κεχρονιϲμένῃ | εἰϲ τὸ ιϛ (ἔτοϲ).

6 [: ᴧ or λ, less likely χ.

7 ἐπιϲτολ [: e.g. ἐπιϲτολή[(if ἥ is right at 6), ἐπιϲτολῇ[ϲ (with 6 περὶ τῆϲ); apparently not ἐπιϲτολά[ϲ (with 5 ἃϲ ἔπε[μ]ψ[α]ϲ), to judge by the final trace.

8 κεχρονιϲμέν[: κεχρονιϲμέν[αϲ, of the letters mentioned in 5, which seem to have prompted this letter, rather than κεχρονιϲμέν[η or -ηϲ, of the letter mentioned in 7. After κεχρονιϲμέν- we expect εἰϲ (+ acc.) or ἐπί (+ gen.) and a year date (exceptional simple dative in XII **1451** 22, if correctly supplemented), which may or may not have been followed by a month date; the year may be accompanied by ἐνεϲτόϲ or διελθόν/διεληλυθόϲ (accusative or genitive). τ[ο]ῦ ιζ (ἔτουϲ) in 9 suggests that the participle may have been followed by εἰϲ with a month date and then a year date, but this would be against the norm; otherwise restore ἐπὶ | τ[ο]ῦ ιζ (ἔτουϲ), but this would result in a very short line.

10 E.g. κ[αὶ γέγραφά (or ἔγραψά) ϲοι], ἔ[γραψα οὖν ϲοι], γ[έγραφα οὖν ϲοι], δ[ιὸ γράφω ϲοι].

13–14 These lines may have been written by the first hand though in a more cursive style than the body of the letter.

14 Ἀδρια[νοῦ. This month corresponds to Choiak.

15 The text is badly damaged and largely illegible. The brackets may indicate cancellation.

16 The function of Heraclides is elusive. After a space blank except for traces of the lower part of a descending oblique, perhaps remnants of the common saltire pattern, ϲιτολο may be possible: after the putative sigma there is an upright descending well below the line; then a long horizontal at letter-top level with traces suggesting a semi-circle directly under its right-hand part, followed by the feet of one ascending and one descending oblique, and further traces at mid-line and letter-foot level. ϲτρατ is more difficult to read: the crossbar of the first tau would extend too far to the right, rho would be oddly placed, and alpha though possible is less likely than lambda. Following a patch on which no traces are visible, before the break, there may be the right-hand half of eta or the junction of a crossbar with the left-hand side of omega (τω); pi (π[αρὰ) is less likely. Alternatively, Dr Chang suggests that the first set of traces may represent [ϲτρ]\ ἐρ̄ πο[λ], i.e., [ϲτρ]α(τηγῷ) Ἑρμ(ο)πο[λ(ίτου)]. (There is a gap in our evidence on Hermopolite strategi between mid 130 and early 133; see Whitehorne, *Strategi and Royal Scribes* 67.)

M. MALOUTA

5178. Letter of Heraclides to Claudius Diogenes, Strategus

47 5B.43/F(1–3)a   12 × 22 cm   Early second century
                                                                    Plates X–XI

This letter, complete except for some loss at the right-hand edge, refers to the transportation of wheat on river boats in mid-June of an unstated year. At this time the harvest was still ongoing, and the Nile at low water. The large shiploads mentioned and the fact that a strategus was concerned with the matter suggest that this was tax grain destined for Alexandria.

The inventory number indicates that **5178** was found with **5177**, a letter from Diogenes, strategus, to Heraclides, dated to 132. Though **5178** is not exactly dated, it is probable that we are dealing with the same persons and that the two letters are contemporary. The apparent reference to the day of the Sabbath would be remarkable in the wake of the crushing of the Jewish revolt of 115–17; see below, 14 n.

The script is large and rounded, comparable to PSI V 446 (G. Cavallo et al., *Scrivere libri e documenti nel mondo antico* pl. cxi), dated to 133–7; and to two copies of the Ninus romance, PSI XIII 1305 (pl. v), assigned to the first century; and P. Berol. 6926 (*GLH* 11a), also dated to the first century (before 100–101).

The column of text is preserved to nearly its original width. There seems to be no complete letter lost at 6 or 13. Several vertical folds are discernible. To judge from the placing of the address at the very top of the back, corresponding to the left-hand edge of the front, it seems that the regular process of folding was followed (cf. LIX **3989**), but that the left edge of the papyrus was not tucked in for protection. It is not likely that there was another flap that was tucked in and then broke off, as the surviving edge of the papyrus is damaged, and the resulting left-hand margin would have been unusually wide.

The writing runs along the fibres.

  Ἡρακλείδης Διο[γένει
   τῶι δεσπότηι χαίρειν.
  τὸ πλοῖον Πάπου Νικοστρατει[
  ἀπέσχεν τὸν γόμον (ἀρταβῶν) ᾽γτ[
5 καὶ τὸ Ἀλεξᾶτος Θεοφιλε[
  ἀγωγῆς (ἀρταβῶν) ᾽στξβ ἤδη ἐνε-[
  βάλετο (ἀρτάβας) ᾽εψμβ. τὰ[ς δὲ
  λοιπὰς ἀπὸ γῆς τῆς [
  βάθρας τεθείκαμεν [
10 εἰς δὲ τὸ ἄλλο πλοῖ[ον
  Ἀλεξάνδρου Ἀλεξανδρ[
  ἐνεβάλοντο ἀπὸ τ[ῆς

ἐκθὲς (ἀρτάβας) ᾱς. τῶι δὲ [

Cαμβάθωι τὸ ἐν ἑτο[ίμωι

15   ἦρται εἰς θησαυρόν. [

ἐρρῶcθαί cε εὔχομα[ι.

Παυνι ιϛ.

Back, downwards, along the fibres:

Κλαυδίωι Διογέν(ει) (design) cτρατηγῶι [

1 ηρακλειδης   4, 6, 7, 13 ᵒ̄   13 l. ἐχθέc   18 διογεν

'Heraclides to Diogenes, his master, greetings.

'The boat of Papus of the Nikostratean deme(?) received its load of 3,300(+) artabas, and that of Alexas of the Theophilean deme(?), with a capacity of 6,362 artabas, has loaded 5,742 artabas so far. The rest we have placed (away) from the ground of the gangway. And since yesterday, they loaded 1,200 artabas onto the other boat, of Alexander the Alexandrian(?). But(?) on the Sabbath(?) what was ready has been taken into the granary.

'I pray for your good health.

'Pauni 16.'

Back: 'To Claudius Diogenes, strategus.'

1 Ἡρακλείδηc. See introd.

Διο[γένει. Cf. the address on the back (18), which gives him the *gentilicium* Claudius and specifies that he is a strategus. See **5177** 2 n.

2 τῶι δεcπότηι. This is among the earliest instances of δεcπότηι in the opening greeting of a letter. Cf. P. Sarap. 21 (126), where a ζευγηλάτηc writes to his employer using a similar formula: he states his own name first, and uses κυρίωι δεcπ[ότηι of his employer. δεcπότηc in this context is virtually equivalent to κύριοc, which it supplanted in late antiquity. In general on the use of δέcποτα, see E. Dickey, *Greek Forms of Address* (1996) 95–8. The fact that Heraclides places his name before that of Diogenes suggests that there was no vast difference of status between them, though cf. W. *Chr.* 481 = P. Giss. I 17 = Sel. Pap. I 115 = P. Giss. Apoll. 13 (113–20), where the sender, who states her name first, is presumed to have been a slave of the recipient, but one who had a very close relationship with the addressee and his family. In that letter κυρίωι occupies the place δεcπότηι has here. Several other letters to the strategus Apollonius, mostly from professionals who worked for him (e.g. P. Brem. 15–16), display the same type of prescript and address. We may posit a close professional relationship between Heraclides and Diogenes the strategus here. Contrast **5177**, which shows the typical formula of one official transmitting information to another.

3 Νικοcτρατει[: apparently Νικοcτρατεί[ου. (There is a short semi-sinusoid over the epsilon; its purpose is unclear, but its position speaks against an abbreviation.) Cf. 5 Θεοφιλε[, presumably Θεοφιλε[ίου. Rather than the names of the men's fathers, these may be Alexandrian demotics. These particular demotics are not attested, but the organization of demes and phylae was a very fluid affair; see D. Delia, *Alexandrian Citizenship During the Roman Principate* (1991) 63. We might also consider the possibility that these are the names of the boats, but the forms are not suitable: see P. Heilporn in P. Bingen, pp. 343–4. See also below, 11 n.

4 γόμον. This is the technical term for tonnage, and denotes the sum total of the cargo on board a ship.

5 Θεοφιλε[: see 3 n.

6 ἀγωγῆς. This is the technical term for capacity. The figures given here and at 4 indicate that these were large ships (I. J. Poll, *APF* 42 (1996) 128; for various kinds of ships, see P. Heilporn in P. Bingen, pp. 339–59). The capacity is given with greater precision than usual; according to Poll, such numbers are always rounded, and where the figure is 1200 or more, it is given in hundreds. See also the table in E. Börner, *Die staatliche Korntransport* (1939) 28–9: even in cases where the load (γόμος) is given precisely, the capacity (ἀγωγή) is not, though admittedly in different kinds of documents. To judge by the stated figure, the ship's storage capacity was about 250 m³ (cf. Poll 131). If we assume that the storage space was about 1 m high (though this may be on the high side: cf. Poll 132) and apply the formulas used by Poll 131–2 in the case of BGU VII 1663, the storage space will have been about 9.4 m wide and 26.5 m long, and the ship will have been roughly 12.5 m wide and 38 m long.

6–7 ἐνε|βάλετο. Cf. 12. It is unusual to have the ship as the subject of this verb. A person would be expected.

8–9 [ ]|βάθρας. The word is not attested in papyri without a prefix. ἀπο- occurs regularly in literary sources, which gloss both ἀποβάθρα and διαβάθρα with κλῖμαξ νεώς (Hesych. α 50) and Latin *scala* (Pollux 1.93). Greek and Roman boats of a certain size normally carried such 'gangplanks' or 'landing ladders'; see L. Casson, *Ships and Seamanship in the Ancient World* (1995) 251. References to δια-βάθρα in papyri include P. Cair. Zen. IV 59542 and PSI V 543 (in the context of horse-travel); ἐπι- is found in the accounts of a river-journey, P. Cair. Zen. IV 59753. The word could also refer to a (fixed) pier (see CPR XXX 16.10 and n.), and that is a possible sense here.

10 This line extends slightly into the left-hand margin and has an enlarged initial letter. This presumably indicates the start of a new sense unit.

11 Ἀλέξανδρ[. If there are Alexandrian demotics in 3 and 5, this may be another, viz. Ἀλέξ-ανδρ[είου (for the uncertain demotic Ἀλεξάνδρειος, see Fraser, *Ptolemaic Alexandria* ii 125–6 n. 77). Other possibilities include Ἀλεξανδρ[έως and even Ἀλέξανδρ[ου (patronymic). Note that in XLIII **3111** 2–3 (257) a ship-owner is described principally by means of his name and origin: πλοίου σκαφοπάκτωνος Διονυσάμμωνος Ἀλεξαν|δρέως λινοκαταγωγέως καὶ ὡς χρημ(ατίζει).

14 Σαμβάθωι. A σάμβαθον was an earthenware jar and the corresponding liquid measure, between 14 and 22 *sextarii* (P. Mayerson, *IEJ* 46 (1996) 258–61; *BASP* 35 (1998) 215–18; *BASP* 36 (1999) 83–6; N. Kruit, K. A. Worp, *BASP* 38 (2001) 79–87). However, as the word appears here in the singular and in a context where thousands of artabas are mentioned, this sense is unsuitable. It is more likely that σάμβαθον has to be understood as a spelling of σάββατον/-α, 'Sabbath', as in VI **903** 19 = C. Pap. Jud. III 457d (IV); see also the earlier P. Cair. Zen. IV 59762 = C. Pap. Jud. I 10.6, and H. C. Youtie, *Scriptiunculae* ii 803–4. This would suit the context, especially since it seems that a contrast is intended between the words ἐχθές and τῶι . . . σαμβάθωι. A more remote possibility is that this is a personal name, as occasionally elsewhere (SB IV 7291.1 (I BC) Σαββ-; O. Stras. I 590 = C. Pap. Jud. I 115.4 (II BC) Σάμβαθον, though this may be a version of the common Σαμβαθίων), but in that case the use of the article would be unexpected.

If the reference is to the Sabbath, it is conceivable that Heraclides and Diogenes were Jewish or, less likely, pagans who acknowledged the Sabbath (cf. W. Clarysse, S. Remijsen, M. Depauw, *SCI* 29 (2010) 51–7, at 52). On the assumption that **5177** and **5178** refer to the same persons and are contemporary, the notion of Jewish strategi in Egypt not long after the end of the Jewish revolt of 115/16–17 would be highly problematic, unless some members of the Jewish elite succeeded in escaping the fate of the majority and retained their status in society. But there is nothing in our sources to support this scenario. (On the aftermath of the revolt in Egypt, see M. Pucci Ben Zeev, *Diaspora Judaism in Turmoil, 116/117 CE* (2005) 186–90.) An alternative interpretation, put forward by Professor Parsons, takes the problem away from the elite: 'Heraclides and his staff (= "we", 9) organize the arrival of the grain, and the ships' crews ("they", 12) load it. In 7–9 "we" have put the unloaded remains of the cargo at the landward end of the gangway, from where the crew will carry it across. These two boats belong to proper Alexandrian citizens (demotics). The third boat (11) belongs to someone who comes from Alexandria but is not a citizen (no demotic: a Jew on the outside?). His crew is Jewish, and they do not work on the Sabbath; so what was ready to be loaded (i.e. on the river bank) has been taken (back) to the granary (for safe-keeping).'

τὸ ἐν ἑτο[ίμωι. The space seems tight, but see 3 n.

15 εἰc θηcαυρόν. The granary is the last place where grain was deposited before it was loaded onto ships. It was kept there until all the relevant administrative steps had been taken to give it clearance for further transportation; see A. J. M. Meyer-Termeer, *Die Haftung der Schiffer im griechischen und römischen Recht* (1978) 5–6.

17 Pauni 16 = June 10.

18 Διογέν(ει). There is no mark of abbreviation, unless it is concealed by the common saltire pattern, the tops of which survive. The sender's name may have been given at the end of the line, now lost, but the spacing would be tight. If there is room for another word, it may have been the name of the nome after cτρατηγῶι.

M. MALOUTA

5179. LETTER TO ATTIUS

46 5B.49/H(1–7)c   8.5 × 6 cm   Second century

This letter to Attius, secretary of the 1% and 2% levy at Ptolemais Hormou, is not dated, but is in a neat hand typical of the second century; see e.g. BGU I 73 (135) and BGU V 1210 (post-149), partially reproduced in W. Schubart, *Griechische Paläographie*, Abb. 35 and 36. It looks like the work of a professional scribe.

The text offers the first indication, albeit indirect, of a customs post at Ptolemais Hormou (Lahun), which was the sole port of the Arsinoite nome on an external waterway (the Bahr Yusuf) and must have been a busy transit point; see further 12 n.

There is a sheet join 3 cm from the left edge. The letter was rolled up from right to left, and the address was written on the top exterior panel with a 1-cm space in the middle for a binding.

Ἀττίωι.
Ἡλιόδωρος ὁ φίλος παρακαλεῖ cε
διαπέμψαcθαι αὐτῷ τὰ ἐπιμήνια ἑαυτοῦ, ἐπεὶ μὴ τῷ πενθερῷ
5 αὐτοῦ διεπέμψω. (vac.) εἰ οὖν ὡc γρά-
φει μήπω τῷ πενθερῷ αὐτοῦ
ἀπεcτάλη, εὐθέωc τῷ Ἡλιοδώρῳ
πέμψον αὐτὰ εἰc Ἀλεξάνδρειαν.
ἐὰν δὲ τοῖc ἡμετέροιc ἀποκατα-
10 cταθῇ, ἐκεῖνοι αὐτὰ ἀποδώcουcι.
ἔρρωcο.

Back, downwards, along the fibres:

Ἀττίωι γρ(αμματεῖ) (vac.) ρ̄ καὶ ν̄ Πτο(λεμαΐδος) Ὅρμ(ου)

5, 9 tail of final alpha extended as line-filler   6 αυτου —   12 ρ̄   πτ° ορμ

'To Attius.

'Our friend Heliodorus asks you to have his monthly allowance sent on to him, since you have not had it sent on to his father-in-law. So if, as he writes, it has not yet been dispatched to his father-in-law, send it immediately to Heliodorus in Alexandria. If it is delivered to our people, they will hand it over.

'Farewell.'

Back: 'To Attius, secretary of the 1% and 2% at Ptolemais Hormou.'

1 Ἀττίωι. The name Attius is rare in the papyri. The only other second-century attestation is in LXII **4335** (128), a receipt to Attius son of Attius alias Apollonius, of Oxyrhynchus, for payment of the cash rent on half of a 50-aroura plot. The decent socio-economic status of this person accords with the possible identification of him—or, less likely, his father—with the Attius of this letter, which would also explain how it ended up in the refuse of Oxyrhynchus.

2 παρακαλεῖ ϲε. The phrase also occurs in SB X 10240.3 (41) and XIV 11900.15 (11), in both cases of a request from a third party transmitted through the writer.

3–4 ἐπιμήνια can be a monthly allowance in cash or kind (Preisigke, *WB* s.v.; O. Berenike I pp. 21–2).

12 γρ(αμματεῖ) ρ̄ καὶ ν̄ Πτο(λεμαΐδος) Ὅρμ(ου). On the Arsinoite village of Ptolemais Hormou see the references collected in P. Narm. 2006, p. 43 n. 12. The ρ̄ καὶ ν̄ levy and its collection are discussed by S. L. Wallace, *Taxation in Egypt from Augustus to Diocletian* (1938) 268–70; P. J. Sijpesteijn, *Customs Duties in Graeco-Roman Egypt* (1987) 19–20, 23–5, 91–7; F. Reiter, *Die Nomarchen des Arsinoites* (2004) 236–59. It was a 3% (1% + 2%) levy on certain goods imported to and exported from the Arsinoite nome, which was collected, alongside the levies for the 'Memphis harbour' (λιμὴν Μέμφεωϲ) and the 'desert guard' (ἐρημοφυλακία), at customs posts (πύλαι, 'gates') in border villages. It was particular to the Arsinoite nome, at least in its name, and was collected by the nomarch, a private tax-contractor also unique to this nome. For Attius' title of γραμματεὺϲ ρ̄ καὶ ν̄ we can compare Phanias 'secretary of the Memphis harbour tax' (gate not specified) to whom the letter P. Coll. Youtie I 54 (II/III) is addressed, and the anonymous 'secretary of the gate of Theogonis' (levy not specified) mentioned in the account P. Gen. I² 71.16 (early III). The content of this letter implies that the γραμματεὺϲ ρ̄ καὶ ν̄ had a managerial role superior to the collectors of the levy, who were either employees, with various titles, of the nomarch or liturgic 'inspectors' (ἐπιτηρηταί) appointed by the strategus of the nome. The specification of Attius' remit as the ρ̄ καὶ ν̄, comparing the different remit of Phanias, supports Reiter's view that this levy was administered separately from the Memphis harbour and desert-guard levies. His subordinate Heliodorus was probably one of the nomarchy's collectors, in which case this would be the first direct evidence that the post was salaried. Alternatively, Heliodorus may have been an 'arab-archer' (ἀραβοτοξότηϲ), a sort of state policeman stationed at each gate whose salary was paid by the nomarchy. The curt address and farewell of the letter, the use of a professional scribe and his anonymity suggest that the sender was much superior to Attius, perhaps the nomarch himself. He writes, apparently, from Alexandria, where he has staff ('our people') to whom Attius is to transmit Heliodorus' 'monthly allowance' or salary. [*Professor D. W. Rathbone kindly contributed this note.*]

S. RISHØJ CHRISTENSEN

5180. Letter to Isidorus and Tyrannus

| 20 3B.37/J(1–4)b | 12.7 × 9.9 cm | Second/third century |

The letter deals primarily with two business matters. The nature of the one, however, is obscured by a lacuna in line 2, and the other is only alluded to. The sender does not identify himself in the address. The addressees may be employees of the sender, since he reprimands them for not having done what they were told. The tone of the letter is rather harsh: there is not even the greeting at the beginning or a salutation at the end. For such omissions in a letter of similar tone, cf. P. Tebt. II 424 (III). A point of interest is the use of the rare word ἀδεξίαϲτοϲ (6).

The hand is similar to that of the final lines of P. Hamb. I 39 xvi (179); cf. also P. Mert. II 84 (201), or P. Vind. Tand. 23 (225).

The letter is written across the fibres. The vertical breaks in the papyrus and the damage on the left part of the sheet suggest that the letter was rolled from right to left and then flattened. Since the left margin is preserved, this part was probably tucked in for protection afterwards. The back is blank.

```
    Ἰϲιδώρῳ (vac.) [κ]αὶ Τυράννῳ. (vac.)
    τὸν ἕνα .[..]. ἀπὸ τῶν δύο ὧν εἴχαμεν
    ἔπεμψα ὑμ[ε]ῖν διὰ τ[ο]ῦ ἀναδιδόντοϲ
    ὑμεῖν τὰ γρά[μ]ματα, [1–2] τοϲ ἀπὸ Ϲε[ρ]ύφεωϲ,
 5  οὗ ἐνετειλάμεθα τὰ κτήνη τὰ τρία ἀνεῖναι.
    εἰ δὲ μέλλομεν ἤδη ἀδεξίαϲτοι εἶναι, οὐ κα-
    λῶϲ γείνεται. (vac.) περὶ γὰρ τῶν ἄλλων ὧν
    κατ' ὄψιν ὑμεῖν ἐνετειλάμεθα, τὰ ἐναν-
    τία ἐπράξατε, καὶ μέλλει ἤδη τὸ πρᾶγμα
10  ἀργεῖν.
```

| 3, 4, 8 l. ὑμῖν | 7 l. γίνεται |

'To Isidorus and Tyrannus.
'Of the two that we had, the one . . . I have sent to you through the person delivering you the letter, . . . from Seryphis, whom we instructed to send up the three beasts. If we are now going to be untrustworthy, it is not a good situation. For concerning the other instructions which we gave you in person, you did the opposite, and the matter is now going to be cancelled.'

2 .[..]. At the beginning, the lower part of a left-facing curve; at the end, part of a horizontal, probably of a final N, since the missing word must be in the accusative. We might consider β[οῦ]ν or ὄ[νο]ν.

ἀπὸ τῶν δύο. For a similar example of the use of the preposition instead of the partitive genitive, see e.g. XXXI **2583** 10.

εἴχαμεν. It is not clear whether the plural represents the sender alone (ἔπεμψα is used in the next line) or other persons are included; cf. E. Mayser, *Grammatik* ii.1 40 ff. For the form see B. G. Mandilaras, *The Verb* 127–8 (§ 279), and F. T. Gignac, *Grammar* ii 332.

4 [1–2] ̣τος: probably the name of the deliverer of the letter in the genitive (apparently not [ὄ]ντος).

Cϵ[ρ]ύφεως. This village lay 6.4 km southeast of Oxyrhynchus, in the Western toparchy; see A. Benaissa, *Rural Settlements of the Oxyrhynchite Nome* s.v.

5 οὖ: either 'whom' (for the attraction of the relative pronoun cf. 2, 7) or 'where'. The former seems more likely. In the latter case the sender would have given the order in Seryphis.

ἀνεῖναι: ἀνά is used for the movement from village to city, from valley to desert or up the Nile, κατά for the opposite.

6 ἀδεξίαστοι. Cf. Ptol. *Tetr.* 3.14.35, 1416–17 Hübner (in a long list of qualities) ψεύςτας, διαβόλους, ἐπιόρκους, βαθυπονήρους, ἐπιβουλευτικούς, ἀςυνθέτους, ἀδεξιάςτους. The sense is 'unreliable' (Robbins; LSJ Rev. Suppl. offers instead 'not to be trusted in an engagement'): cf. LSJ s.vv. δεξιά 2, δεξιάζω. The opposite is found at Ptol. *Tetr.* 3.14.31, 1385–6 Hübner πρὸς τοὺς ὁμοίους εὐςυνθέτους καὶ εὐςυνδεξιάςτους.

οὐ καλῶς γείνεται. See LSJ s.v. γίγνομαι II 2. Cf. the similar usage of these words in contracts, in the formula περὶ δὲ τοῦ ταῦτα οὕτως ὀρθῶς καλῶς γεγονέναι ἐπερωτηθέντες ὑπὸ ςοῦ ὡμολογήςαμεν; see D. Simon, *Studien zur Praxis der Stipulationsklausel* 47–8.

8–9 τὰ ἐναντία ἐπράξατε. Cf. P. Sakaon 48.6 (343) τοὐναντία διεπράξατο.

10 ἀργεῖν. For the sense of the verb see LSJ Rev. Suppl. s.v.: 'to be nullified, cancelled'; cf. E. A. Sophocles, *Lexicon* s.v. 3.

PH. SCHMITZ

5181. FOOT OF PRIVATE LETTER

70/77(b)   10.3 × 18 cm   Third century

The papyrus contains the lower half of a letter with salutations. The text consists mainly of personal names in the accusative indicating people who are greeted. The hand is upright, large and clear, but not very practised. A date in the third century would suit.

To judge from the folds, the damage, and the position of the address on the back, the papyrus was rolled up from the right to the left, squashed flat and folded in two (between lines 2 and 3); the address, of which only the last four letters remain, was written on one side of the package.

The text is written along the fibres of a thick piece of papyrus.

      .   .   .   .
     *c.*11   ] ̣ ̣α
    *c.*6   ]ν αὐτοῦ καὶ
    τὴν μητέρα μου Θάη-
    ϲιν καὶ τὴν μητέρα
5   μου Κοπροῦν καὶ Ἀπολ-
    λώνιον καὶ Ῥωμαῖν

καὶ Ὠριγένην καὶ Μῶ-
ρον καὶ Διογένην καὶ
Πτολεμαῖον τὸν ἀ-
10 δελφόν cου καὶ Δι-
μιτρίαν τὴν γυναῖκα
αὐτοῦ καὶ Διονύcιον
τὸν υἱὸν αὐτοῦ καὶ
Κορνήλιον καὶ Ἡρα-
15 κλῆν καὶ Cαραπιάδα.
ἐρῶcθαι ὑμᾶc βούλομαι.

Back, downwards along the fibres:

]ωνοc

2 αυτο⟦ν⟧ʹυʹ 3 See comm. 6 l. Ῥωμαῖον 7 μω: ω corr. from ο 10 after
δι, a smudge or cancelled letter 10–11 l. Δημητρίαν 11 γυναικα corr. from γυνακα
12 -ιον: ο corr. from ν 13 υἱον 16 l. ἐρρῶcθαι

'. . . his . . . and my mother Thaesis and my mother Coprous and Apollonius and Romaeus and
Horigenes and Morus and Diogenes and your brother Ptolemaeus and his wife Demetria and his son
Dionysius and Cornelius and Heracles and Sarapias. I want you to be healthy.'

1–2 It is tempting to restore τ]ὸν ἀ|[δελφὸ]ν αὐτοῦ (RLC); cf. 9–10 τὸν ἀδελφόν cου, 13 τὸν υἱὸν
αὐτοῦ.

3–5 τὴν μητέρα μου Θάηcιν καὶ τὴν μητέρα μου Κοπροῦν. For this 'extended' use of μήτηρ, see
E. Dickey, *Mnemosyne* 57 (2004) 131–76, esp. 165. The addition of the women's names strongly suggests
that these are 'older women with a close connection to the writer', and that neither is his mother.
When the term is used in this way, it is often applied to more than one woman: cf. e.g. X **1296** (8–9,
15–16), XIV **1678** (20, 23), LVI **3859** (34, 41), P. Ammon I 3 (vi 12–13, 19–20).

3 μητέρα. There is a short vertical stroke after ε and another after α. The first is slightly below
the line and most likely only a slip of the pen, but the latter could almost be interpreted as ι, though
the combination αι is written differently everywhere else in the letter.

16 ἐρῶcθαι ὑμᾶc βούλομαι. βούλομαι is far less frequent in this phrase than εὔχομαι.

17]ωνοc. This ought to be the end of the sender's name.

M. VIERROS

5182. LETTER OF CHENTHONIS TO PETOSIRIS

7 1B.5/F(b)   11.7 × 20 cm   Early fourth century
                                Plate XII

This letter is written on the back of a piece of a Graeco-Latin glossary (**5161**).
Chenthonis, possibly a Christian (see below, 4–5 n.), complains to Petosiris about
the offensive behaviour of his father and brother, who have come to the house with

a group of government agents and demanded sixty-five talents in taxes (*canonica*) on a plot of land. The sum mentioned may suit a date in the 330s or 340s (14–15 n.; cf. 11–12 n.). The address on the other side identifies the sender as 'Theon, son', presumably of Petosiris. He may have taken the letter down from Chenthonis' dictation; see further 24 n.

It is unclear how Chenthonis was related to Petosiris, especially since the relevant part of the opening salutation is lost (1). There are two main pieces of evidence: Petosiris' children were with her (8–9; cf. 22, and the use of the first person plural in 12–13); and she is referred to by Petosiris' brother Sarapion as 'the one who holds everything of our brother's' (19–20). If 'our brother' refers to Petosiris himself, Chenthonis will have been his wife: in her husband's absence, she is forced to pay the taxes in his stead. Alternatively, one may conjecture that she had inherited the property of a deceased brother of Petosiris and Sarapion; perhaps she was his widow. On the latter hypothesis, Petosiris' wife will not be mentioned in the letter, except perhaps in the lacunose final line (23).

The hand is not particularly practised. The text is written along the fibres. To judge by the five vertical folds, the letter was rolled up from left to right. After the roll was pressed flat, the address was added in the space between two columns of the glossary on the other side.

```
        κυρίῳ μου (vac.)  [
        Χένθωνις (vac.)  Πετοσίρι
           (vac.)   χαίρειν. (vac.)
        πρὸ μὲν πάντων εὔχομαι τῷ
   5    κυρίῳ θεῷ ἀπολαβεῖν ϲε μετὰ
        ὑγιείαϲ καὶ ὁλοκληρίαϲ ϲὺν τοῖϲ
        παιδίοιϲ ϲου. θέλω ϲε δὲ γνῶναι τὰ πέ-
        πονθα ὑπὸ τοῦ πατρόϲ ϲου μετὰ τῶν
        παιδίων ϲου ἔνεκεν τῶν δύο ἀρου-
  10    ρῶν· ἐνέγκαϲ πρὸ θυρῶν τὸν κομ.-
        ϲτην μετὰ τῶν φρουρῶν τοῦ ἐξάκτο-
        ροϲ καὶ ἀπήτηϲαι ἡμᾶϲ τοὺϲ φό-
        ρουϲ καὶ ἀπαιτήθημεν μετὰ
        ὕβρεων ἐξήκοντα πέντε τάλαν-
  15    τα ὑπὲρ τῶν κανωνικῶν εἰδῶν.
        ἐϲτάθη μοι γὰρ ὁ πατήρ ϲου καὶ Ϲαρα-
        πίων ὁ ἀδελφόϲ ϲου ὅτι ϲοὶ ὑπὲρ
        αὐτοῦ δειδιϲ τὰ πάντα ἐκ πλήροιϲ,
        ἐπειδὴ .ιει ἡ ἔχουϲα τὰ πάντα τοῦ ἀδελ-
  20    φοῦ ἡμῶν. [ἀϲ]πάζεταί ϲε Ϲαραπο-
```

c.9   πάν]τες κατ' ὄνομα

c.13   ]‸ιν σε τὰ παιδία cου

c.11   ] cύμβιος.

Back, downwards along the fibres:

ἀπό]δος Πετοcίρι παρὰ   (vac.)   Θέωνος (vac.) υἱοῦ

2, 24 l. Πετοcίρει   7 l. ἅ   12 l. ἀπήτηcε   13 l. ἀπῃτήθημεν   15 l. κανονικῶν
16 και: κ corrected from cα   17 cοι: l. cύ   18 l. πλήρους   21 κατο νο μα: spaces left
blank because of defects on the surface?   23 cυμβιος: υ corrected

'To my lord . . . , Chenthonis to Petosiris, greetings. Before all I pray to the lord god that I find
you in good health and well-being, together with your children. I want you to know what I have suffered at the hands of your father with your children because of the two arouras. Having brought before our (house) doors the conveyer(?) with the guards of the *exactor*, he exacted the taxes from us, and
we had sixty-five talents exacted from us with insults, on account of the levies for the *canon*; for your
father and your brother Sarapion (?)came upon(?) me (saying), "you ought to hand over everything in
full for him, since you are(?) the one who holds everything of our brother's". Sarapo— greets you . . .
everyone by name . . . you . . . your children . . . wife.'

Back: 'Deliver to Petosiris, from Theon, (his) son.'

1 Petosiris would have been addressed as cυμβίῳ or ἀδελφῷ; see introd.

2 Χένθωνις. The name is not attested elsewhere, though for the formation cf. Θένθωνις, Cένθω-
νις, Τcένθωνις. On female Egyptian names with the prefix Χεν-, 'daughter of', followed by a personal
name, see J. Bingen, *CE* 63 (1988) 167–72 = *Pages d'épigraphie grecque* ii (2005) 103–11.

The word order is unusual; we would expect τῷ κυρίῳ μου [. . .] | Πετοcίρι Χένθωνις.

4–5 εὔχομαι τῷ κυρίῳ θεῷ. This prayer may be an indicator of Christianity, though this
assumption is not inescapable; see M. Naldini, *Il Cristianesimo in Egitto* (²1998) 10–12; M. Choat, A.
Nobbs, *JGRChrJ* 2 (2001–5) 40–51; M. Choat, *Belief and Cult in Fourth-Century Papyri* (2006) 108–12.

5–6 On the health wish formula, common in third- and fourth-century letters, see J. L. White,
The Form and Function of the Body of the Greek Letter (1972) 8 n. 4; G. Tibiletti, *Le lettere private nei papiri
greci del III e IV secolo d.C.* (1979) 47–52. The formula used here is unique in that μετά with substantives
denoting health is employed instead of the usual adjectives or participles, though μετὰ ὁλοκληρίας
is similarly used in XIV **1682** (= Naldini, *Cristianesimo* no. 52) 6–8 ἡ μὲν τοῦ θεοῦ πρόνοια παρέξει τὸ
μετὰ ὁλοκληρίας cε τὰ οἰκεῖα ἀπολαβεῖν.

6–7 cὺν τοῖς παιδίοις cου. This phrase is used rather loosely: Petosiris is not 'with' the children,
who are with Chenthonis herself (8–9, cf. 22). Apparently she intends merely to pray for their good
health as well as his. It is considerably less likely that the phrase is to be taken with the more distant
εὔχομαι (4; 'I pray that I find you well—and your children join me in the prayer') or ἀπολαβεῖν (5;
'I pray that I as well as your children find you well').

Chenthonis may be the mother of the children, although she writes τοῖς παιδίοις cου; 'in letters
between spouses, the couple's children are sometimes referred to with a possessive that includes only
one parent' (E. Dickey, *Mnemosyne* 57 (2004) 167).

7 θέλω cε δέ. The particle follows an enclitic and occupies third place in the sentence also at
16 ἐcτάθη μοι γάρ.

τά, l. ἅ. See F. T. Gignac, *Grammar* ii 179.

10–12 ἐνέγκαϲ . . . καὶ ἀπήτηϲαι (l. ἀπήτηϲε). καί appears to be connective, as though a finite verb rather than a participle preceded; cf. Mayser, *Grammatik* ii.1 343–4.

10–11 κομ ϲτην. After μ, we could read two letters instead of one, but in that case only -οϲ- would be possible, which would not produce any viable word. κομηϲτήν, l. -ιϲτήν, is the less unsatisfactory reading. Although not a known title of a municipal official and not found in any published papyrus or ostracon, κομιϲτήϲ may be compared to the term ἀνακομιϲτήϲ used in XLIII **3124** 9 (Lyc.; *c*.322?) of a conveyer for military *annona*, on which see F. Mitthof, *Annona militaris* (2001) 123. A money-conveyor may have been required for this exaction. Mitthof suggests that ἀνακομιϲτήϲ is an alternative designation of the ἐπιμελητήϲ, and the same may apply to κομιϲτήϲ here (or the offices may have had similar functions); cf. XXXVI **2766** 5 (305) ἐπιμελητοῦ ϲιτοκρίθου ἀνακομιζομένου.

11–12 τῶν φρουρῶν τοῦ ἐξάκτοροϲ. That guards were attached to the bureau of *exactor civitatis* was known for Hermopolis from P. Stras. IV 197 (with BL VIII 415), in which a φρουρὸϲ ἐξακτορίαϲ was sent to assist *praepositi pagi* in summoning tax collectors; they were an inheritance from the office of the strategus (LXI **4116**).

On the office of *exactor* in Egypt, see Mitthof, *Annona militaris* 143–4, 184; A. Laniado, *Recherches sur les notables municipaux dans l'Empire protobyzantin* (2002) 113. Although *exactores* replaced the strategi about 309, they were still frequently, especially in the area of Oxyrhynchus, referred to as strategi; see J. D. Thomas, *CE* 70 (1995) 237–9.

13–14 ἀπαιτήθημεν (l. ἀπη-) μετὰ ὕβρεων. The same phrase with the order reversed occurs in XLVIII **3393** 12 (365). ὕβρειϲ seems to refer to insults rather than physical attacks; see e.g. VI **903** 1, P. Select. 18.10–11, SB I 5235.12–13, and generally Preisigke, *WB* s.v., *BDAG* s.v. 2.

14–15 ἑξήκοντα πέντε τάλαντα. The figure given is for tax exacted on two arouras (9–10). R. S. Bagnall, *TAPhA* 115 (1985) 305, suggests that 'at least from the time of Diocletian and Constantine to that of Justinian, the total taxation on arable land seems to have been roughly constant at a level equivalent to about 2²/₃ artabas per aroura'. In our case, the figure for 2 arouras would then be *c*.5¹/₃ artabas; if this were paid in money rather than kind, and 65 talents were not an extortionate sum, their market value would not have been much higher than *c*.5¹/₃ artabas of wheat (12–13 tal./art.). On the other hand, assuming that in the fourth century the taxes in kind may have amounted to ²/₃–³/₄ of the total tax burden (see Bagnall, loc. cit. 304; J.-M. Carrié in *L''inflazione' nel quarto secolo d.C.* (1993) 137), 65 talents would not be worth less than ²/₃–1 art.: in the early part of the fourth century, private land in Oxyrhynchus was taxed at 1 art./ar. (Bagnall, loc. cit. 300), which means that the correlated tax burden in money may be equivalent in value to ¹/₃–¹/₂ art./ar. The price of wheat (per artaba) was *c*.3 tal. in 327 (PSI IV 309, in a *coemptio*, with the market price no doubt higher), 14 tal. in 335 (P. Lond. VI 1914), 24 tal. in 338 (I **85**), 50 tal. in the 340s (P. Abinn. 68 of *c*.348–51), and rose to much higher levels in the 350s (334 tal. in P. Princ. III 183v of *c*.353); see Bagnall, *Currency and Inflation in Fourth Century Egypt* (*BASP* Suppl. 5: 1985) 64, and P. Kell. IV p. 226. Thus a date in the 330s or even 340s for this letter would suit.

15 κανωνικῶν (l. κανο-) εἰδῶν. κανονικὰ εἴδη are no doubt equivalent to κανονικοὶ φόροι, attested in I **71** ii 6–7 (Ars.; 303) and SB XX 14657.24 (Herm.; *c*.300–310); 'εἴδη is a general designation for all taxes whether in money or in kind' (P. Cair. Isid. 51.2 n.). The term may refer generally to regular taxes in kind and money, excluding levies for military use: in **71** κανονικοὶ φόροι are distinguished from ϲτρατιωτικαὶ εὐθένειαι, i.e., the *annona militaris*, levied in kind (see Mitthof, *Annona militaris* 8–9). The *canonica* were part of the *canon*, 'fixed tax schedule', but the *canon* was not limited to them; see L. Wenger, *Canon in den römischen Rechtsquellen und in den Papyri* (SAWW 220/2: 1942) 31.

16–17 ἐϲτάθη μοι . . . ὅτι. The construction is unclear. If ἐϲτάθη is simply 'he stood', the dative pronoun is hard to account for. Perhaps the sense is rather 'he came upon', 'he accosted', with a dative like that found with ἐφίϲτημι (LSJ s.v. B.III.2; cf. also s.v. ἐνίϲτημι B.III.1, 'threaten', and IV.1, 'stand in the way', also with a dative). Then a *verbum dicendi* can be understood with ὅτι κτλ. from the main verb; cf. Mayser, *Grammatik* ii.3 4–5. ἐϲτάθη may have the same construction at SB XVIII 13867.24–5 (II) ἐϲτάθη μοι, λέ[γω]ν ὅτι (followed by direct speech), where the editors take the dative with the participle. This construction is reflected in the translation above, which assumes that the singular subject (ὁ πατήρ ϲου) was expanded by the addition of καὶ Ϲαραπίων ὁ ἀδελφόϲ ϲου; Sarapion is the speaker in the sentence introduced by ὅτι. The alternative is to dissociate Ϲαραπίων from ἐϲτάθη and make him the subject of a *verbum dicendi* that has been left out.

17 ϲοί (for ϲύ) refers to Chenthonis, not Petosiris: we are in direct speech here after ὅτι. For ὅτι introducing direct speech (*recitativum*), see LVI **3855** 7 n.

17–18 ὑπὲρ αὐτοῦ. αὐτοῦ refers to Petosiris ('our brother' in 19–20).

18 δειδιϲ. The injunctive function of this verbal form will remain the same, whether it is understood as jussive subjunctive διδοῖϲ or δίδῃϲ, or indicative διδοῖϲ or δίδειϲ, or even optative διδοίηϲ, διδοῖϲ, or δίδοιϲ. For the present system of δίδωμι in papyri, see Gignac, *Grammar* ii 382–4.

19 ̣ιει. We expect ϲὺ εἶ ἡ ἔχουϲα; cf. P. Köln IV 199.4–5 (*c.*311?) ϲὺ εἶ ὁ ἔχων τὸν ϲῖτον. It is tempting to read ϲοί (for ϲύ; cf. 17) εἶ, with sigma ligatured to a tiny omicron, but we would have to reckon with a sigma with an unusually short cap, and a ϲο ligature that is very different from that used in ϲου (7–9, 16, 17, 22). The first letter would be easier to read as omicron, but this would lead to impasse.

19–20 ἡ ἔχουϲα τὰ πάντα τοῦ ἀδελφοῦ ἡμῶν. See introd.

20 Ϲαραπο-. The right-hand leg of pi is extended to the right and then hooked upwards, and omicron is written above it. This probably does not indicate an abbreviation, unexpected in this text.

20–21 Perhaps restore Ϲαραπο|[δῶρα or Ϲαραπό|[δωροϲ καὶ πάν]τεϲ; there is no room for οἱ ϲοί before πάν]τεϲ (cf. BGU II 615.14), still less for οἱ ἐμοί (cf. e.g. P. Thomas 14.17). P. Merton II 82.16–19 ἄϲπα[ϲαι] . . . καὶ πάνταϲ κατ᾽ ὄνομα may offer a parallel for καὶ πάν]τεϲ, even if in that text 'everyone' receives and does not send greetings. Closer perhaps is LVI **3855** 23–4 (*c.*280/81) ἀϲπάζο[ντέ ϲε] πάντεϲ κατ᾽ ἄν[δρ]α.

22–3] ̣ιν looks like the end of an infinitive with itacistic spelling. Of the unread letter only a trace under iota remains, which suggests chi or xi. We expect a farewell formula at this point, and we may consider supplying e.g.] ̣ιν ϲε τὰ παιδία ϲου | [εὔχονται καὶ ἡ] ϲύμβιοϲ, but this sequence is without parallel.

24 It is curious that the letter is said to be from Theon rather than from the author, Chenthonis (2), but cf. LXV **4493**, LXVII **4627**, and P. Grenf. I 53 = W. *Chr.* 131 = Naldini, *Cristianesimo* no. 56 (IV). The last is a double letter: the author encloses in her letter to her husband Theodorus a message that she asks him to show to another person. The whole letter is in the same hand, probably that of Theodorus' son, who endorsed it. In **5182** also, the letter and the address on the back appear to be in the same hand, and it is highly likely that Chenthonis dictated the letter to Theon.

The long gap following παρά is at approximately half-height, and may have been intended to accommodate a binding.

R.-L. CHANG

INDEXES

Figures in raised type refer to fragments, small roman numerals to columns. Square brackets indicate that a word is wholly or substantially restored by conjecture or from other sources, round brackets that it is expanded from an abbreviation or a symbol. Greek words not recorded in LSJ or its Revised Supplement and previously unattested names and places are asterisked. The article and (in the documentary sections) καί are not indexed.

I. NEW LITERARY TEXTS

ἀεικέλιος **5131** ii 14
Ἀθάμας **5131** ii 8 mg.
ἀλγεινός **5131** ii 9
Ἀλκιδάμας **5130** ¹ ii 26
ἀλλά **5130** ² 3 (?)
ἄλλος **5131** ii 3
ἀναιρεῖν **5130** ² 6
ἀνθρώπειος **5130** ¹ ii 18
ἀνόςιος [**5131** ii 17]
ἀποδοκιμάζειν [**5130** ³⁺⁴ 3]
ἄτοπος **5130** ¹ ii 13
αὔξειν **5130** ³⁺⁴ 5
ἄχθος **5131** ii 9

βάλλειν [**5131** ii 13]
βαρυδαίμων **5131** ii 5
βία **5130** ¹ ii 7 (?)
βοηθεῖν **5130** ¹ ii 17–18

γάρ **5131** ii 4
γενεά **5131** ii 6
γυμνοῦν **5131** ii 10

δέ **5130** ¹ ii 5 (?), 6 (?), 7 (?), 12, 16, 19 [**5131** ii 9]
δεικνύναι **5131** ii 10
δεςπόςυνος **5131** ii 7
διατρίβειν **5130** ¹ ii 21
διαφθείρειν [**5130** ¹ ii 11]
δουλεύειν **5130** ¹ ii 22–3
δυςπείςτως **5130** ¹ ii 19–20
δύςτηνος **5131** ii 15, 19
δῶμα **5131** ii 7, [8]

ἐάν [**5130** ² 6]
ἐγκώμιον **5130** ¹ ii 27
ἐγώ **5130** ¹ ii 17 [**5131** ii 9]
εἰ **5130** ¹ ii 19
εἰς **5131** ii 10
ἐκ **5130** ¹ ii 26

ἐκεῖνος **5130** ¹ ii 16
ἐν **5131** ii 11
ἐπαινεῖν **5130** ¹ ii 14
επτε.[**5131** ii 1
ἔχειν **5130** ¹ ii 20

ἥκειν **5131** ii 4
ἡςύχως [**5131** ii 8]

θήρα [**5131** ii 5]

ἱερός [**5130** ² 4]
ἱκανῶς **5130** ¹ ii 17
ἵνα [**5130** ² 3]
Ἰνώ [**5131** ii 12 mg. (?)]
ἴςος **5130** ¹ ii 20

Κάδμος **5131** ii 6
καί **5130** ¹ ii 21 **5131** ii 11
κάμαξ [**5131** ii 13 (?)]
καταφρονεῖν **5130** ¹ ii 15
κρίςις **5130** ¹ ii 23–4

λανθάνω **5131** ii 11
λίθος **5131** ii 16 (?)
λόγος **5130** ¹ ii 21

μάλιστα **5130** ¹ ii 14–15
μέν **5130** ¹ ii 13, 17, ² 7 **5131** ii 9
μή **5130** ¹ ii 16 **5131** ii 11
μικρός **5131** ii 9
μοχθ[**5131** ii 12

νιν [**5131** ii 8]

ὅδε **5131** ii 4
ὅμοιος **5130** ¹ ii 16
ὅς **5130** ¹ ii 21
οὐκ **5130** ¹ ii 12
οὖν **5130** ¹ ii 17, ² 7
οὕτω **5130** ¹ ii 23

παλαιός [**5130** ¹ ii 13]
παραςκευ[**5130** ¹ ii 3
πέλας **5131** ii 8
πενία **5130** ¹ ii 27
πέπλος **5131** ii 11
πλάνη **5130** ¹ ii 18–19
πλοῦτος **5130** ¹ ii 8, 14, ² 5
πο[**5131** ii 10
ποιεῖν **5130** ¹ ii 23
πρό **5131** ii 8
πρός **5131** ii 7
πῶς [**5130** ¹ ii 12]

(-)ςτροφή [**5131** ii 22 (?)]
ςυγκυρεῖν [**5131** ii 3 (?)]
ςυμβαίνειν [**5131** ii 3 (?)]
ςυνήθεια **5130** ¹ ii 22

ταλαπείριος [**5131** ii 14]
τιθέναι **5131** ii 8
τις **5130** ¹ ii 19
τλῆναι **5131** ii 24 (?)
(-)τροπος **5130** ³⁺⁴ 2
(-)τροφή [**5131** ii 22 (?)]

ὑμεῖς **5131** ii 9

φάος **5131** ii 10
φέρειν **5131** ii 7
φοράδην **5131** ii 5
φρονεῖν **5130** ¹ ii 16

χαῦνος **5131** ii 2
χρῆμα [**5130** ¹ ii 10 (?)]
χρόνος **5130** ¹ ii 20

ψυχή **5131** ii 12

ὦ **5131** ii 14 (?), 24 (?)

II. SUBLITERARY TEXTS

(a) Chapter on Tetrasyllabic Feet (**5159**)

(b) Commentary on Eupolis, *Goats* (?) (**5160**)

Cάτυρος ii 35
cεαυτοῦ ii 38
Cέλευκος i 7
cτρα- ii 24 (?)
cτυγεῖν ii 40
cύμμαχος i 8
cύντομος ii 28–9
cυντυχία i 16

τάχα ii 15

τε i 4
τοιοῦτος ii 40
τουτέςτι ii 10 (?)
τρα- ii 24 (?)
(-)τρέπω ii 13–14
τύχη i 30, ii 7

ὑπέρ ii 32
ὑπολείπειν [ii 17 (?)]

φάναι ii 11
φυλακή [ii 12–13 (?)]
φυλέτης [i 13 (?)]
φυλή [i 5]

χρῆςθαι ii 37–8
χύτρα i 29

ὦ ii 35
ὡς ii 11

(c) Graeco-Latin Glossaries (**5161–3**)

(i) Greek

αἰγόκερως **5162** ii 25
ἀνάκλιτον [**5163** [1] i 8]
ἄνεμος **5162** ii 32, 33
ἀπαρκίας **5162** ii 39
ἀπηλιώτης **5162** ii 40
ἄρκτος **5162** ii 11
ἀcτήρ **5162** ii 8
ἄcτρον **5162** ii 6, 7

Βορέας **5162** ii 34

γλωccόκομον **5163** [1] i 20

δελφίν **5162** ii 17
δίδυμος **5162** ii 26
δίεδρον [**5163** [1] i 17]
δίφρος [**5163** [1] i 18]

ἔαρ [**5162** ii 2]
εν[**5163** [1] ii 7
ἐνδομενία **5163** [1] i 4, 5
ἐνήλατον **5163** [1] i 7
ἔcπερος **5162** ii 9
εὖρος **5162** ii 37

ζέφυρος **5162** ii 38
ζυγόν **5162** ii 23

θέρος [**5162** ii 3]

ἵππος **5162** ii 19
ἶρις **5162** ii 16
ἰχθῦς **5162** ii 31

καικίας **5162** ii 42
κάμπτρα **5163** [1] i 19
καρκίνος **5162** ii 30

κίcτη [**5163** [1] i 16]
κλῖμαξ **5163** [1] ii 2
κλίνη **5163** [1] i 6
κόcκινον **5163** [1] ii 6
κρεάγρα [**5163** [2] 4]
κριός **5162** ii 20
κύων **5162** ii 14

λέων **5162** ii 22
λίκνον **5163** [1] ii 8
λίψ **5162** ii 36
λύρα **5162** ii 15
λύχνος **5163** [1] ii 3

μάκτρα [**5163** [1] ii 9]
μόδιος **5163** [1] i 21
μύρμηξ **5163** [1] i 1

νότος **5162** ii 35

ὀιcτός **5162** ii 13
ὅλμος **5163** [1] ii 4

παρθένος **5162** ii 24
περί **5162** ii 6, 32 **5163** [1] i 4
Πλειάς **5162** ii 12
πυργίςκος [**5163** [1] i 12]

ῥαίνειν **5161** i 7–9
ῥάπτειν **5161** i 4–6
ῥήccειν [**5161** i 1–3]
ῥίπτειν **5161** i 10–12

cαλεύειν **5161** i 13–15
cήθειν **5161** i 16–18
cίλφη **5163** [1] i 2
cιωπᾶν **5161** i 19–21

cκάφη [**5163** [1] ii 10 (?), 11 (?)]
cκαφίδιον [**5163** [1] ii 10 (?), 11 (?)]
cκευοθήκη [**5163** [1] i 13]
cκόρπιος **5162** ii 29
cτέφανος **5162** ii 18
cυννεύειν **5161** i 25–7
cυντηρεῖν **5161** i 28–30
cύρειν **5161** i 22–4
cφυρίς [**5163** [1] ii 12]

ταράccειν **5161** iii 1–3
ταῦρος **5162** ii 21
τηρεῖν **5161** i 31–3
τοξότης **5162** ii 28
τράπεζα **5163** [1] i 14
τρίπους **5163** [1] i 15
τρυτάνη **5163** [1] ii 1

ὑδροχόος **5162** ii 27
ὑπάγειν **5161** iii 13–15
ὕπερον **5163** [1] ii 5
ὑπηρετεῖν **5161** iii 10–12
ὑποδέννειν **5161** iii 7–9
ὑπολύειν **5161** iii 16–18
ὑποφέρειν **5161** iii 19–21
ὑφαίνειν **5161** iii 4–6

φθινόπωρον [**5162** ii 4]
φιλεῖν **5161** iii 22–4
φυcᾶν [**5161** iii 25–7]
φωcφόρος **5162** ii 10

χειμών **5162** ii 5
χοινίκιον [**5163** [1] i 22]
χῶρος **5162** ii 41

ψαλίς [**5163** [2] 3]

(ii) Latin

III. RULERS AND REGNAL YEARS

Augustus

Tiberius

Claudius

HADRIAN

Ἀδριανὸς ὁ κύριος **[5177** 9] (year 17)
Αὐτοκράτωρ Καῖσαρ Τραϊανὸς Ἀδριανὸς Cεβαστός **5177** 13–14 (year 17)

IV. MONTHS AND DAYS

(a) Months

Φαωφι **[5166** 9 (?) **5168** 1] **5169** 1
Νέος Cεβαστός **5174** 9–10
Ἀδριανός **5177** 14

Μεχειρ (**5164** 11) (?) **5165** 4 **5173** 8
Φαμενωθ (**5167** 4) **5169** 10

Παυνι **[5166** 9 (?)] **5176** ² 5, 7 **5178** 17
Μεσορη (**5164** 11) (?) (**5172** 2)

(b) Days

Cάμβαθον **5178** 14

Cεβαστή **5174** 10 **5176** ² 7

V. DATES

30 July 26 BC or 31 January 25 BC **5164** 11
27 January 24 BC **5165** 4
25 February – 26 March 20 BC **5169** 9–10
12 March 20 BC **5167** 4
10 October 18 BC **5169** 1

10 October 18 (?) BC **[5168** 1]
30 July 7 **5172** 1–2
4 February 26 **5173** 8–9
28 October – 26 November 26 **5174** 9–10
22 June 52 **5176** ² [2], 3–5
23 June 52 **5176** ² 7–8

27 November – 26 December 132 **5177** 13–14
10 June (no year given) **5178** 17
14 June or 17 or 18 October (year lost) **[5166** 9]

VI. PERSONAL NAMES

Ἀδριανός *see* Index III s.v. Hadrian; Index IV (a)
Ἀλέξανδρος, boat-owner **5178** 11
Ἀλεξᾶς, boat-owner **5178** 5
Ἀμμώνιος **5176** ¹ 1
Ἀντεῖς, s. of Titan **5173** 1
Ἀπελλῆς, strategus of the Panopolite **5174** 11
Ἀπίων, f. of Saraeus **5175** 5
Ἀπίων, s. of Ariston, br. of Arsinoe **5169** 3
Ἀπίων, Asclepiades alias **5164** 2 **5166** 1
Ἀπολλοφάνης, banker **5165** 1–2 **5166** 1
Ἀπολλωνία, d. of —dorus **5168** [2], 10, [13], 14, 16, [25]
Ἀπολλώνιος **5181** 5–6
Ἄρειος, *topogrammateus* of the Middle toparchy **5171** 1
Ἀρίστων, f. of Arsinoe and Apion **5169** 2, 3
Ἀρσινόη, d. of Ariston, sis. of Apion **5169** 2, 8, 14, 18, 22

Ἀσκληπιάδης, alias Apion, f. of Ptolemaeus **5164** 1
Ἀσκληπιάδης, banker (?) **5165** 1
Ἄττιος, secretary of the 1% and 2% levy at Ptolemais Hormou **5179** 1, 12
Ἀφυγχις, sailor **5167** 1

*Βενιαιος, f. of Petosiris, gf. of Herceus sr, Herceus jr, and Senerceus **5169** 6

Γάϊος Τυρράνιος, *praefectus Aegypti* **5171** 5
Γναῖος Οὐεργίλιος Καπίτων, *praefectus Aegypti* **5175** 1

Δημητρία, w. of Ptolemaeus **5181** 10–11
Δημήτριος *see* Index VII
Δίδυμος, f. of Sarapion **5168** 3
Δίδυμος, f. of Sarapion and Didymus **5171** (19), (20), (21)

Δίδυμος, s. of Didymus, br. of Sarapion **5171** 19, [23 (?)]
Διογένης **5181** 8
Διογένης *see* Κλαύδιος Διογένης
Διόγνητος *see* Index VII
Διοκλῆς, s. of Ptolemaeus **5176** ¹ 3
Διονύσιος, f. of Tryphon **5175** 2
Διονύσιος, s. of Ptolemaeus **5181** 12

*Ἑρκεύς sr, s. of Petosiris, gs. of Beniaios, br. of Herceus jr and Senerceus **5169** 3
*Ἑρκεύς jr, s. of Petosiris, gs. of Beniaios, br. of Herceus sr and Senerceus **5169** 5
Ἑρμαῖος **5173** 12
Ἔρως, foundling **5168** 5
*Εὔνουφις **5170** 4

Ζωΐλος, s. of Theon **5173** 2

Ἡλιόδωρος **5179** 2, 7

VII. GEOGRAPHICAL

Cέρυφιϲ **5180** 4

*Cωκίνδρου καὶ Δημητρίου (κλῆροϲ) (**5171** 20)

Τάναϊϲ **5171** 3
Τεμγενούθεωϲ (**5167** 3) (*bis*)

VIII. RELIGION

θεόϲ **5182** 5

ἱερόν **5164** 3
κύριοϲ **5182** 5

Cαραπεῖον **5173** 3

IX. OFFICIAL AND MILITARY TERMS AND TITLES

ἀγορανόμοϲ [**5170** 1] **5176** [1] 2, ([2] 6)
ἀρχεῖον **5169** 9
ἀρχιδικαϲτήϲ [**5171** 10–11 (?)]

γραμματεύϲ (ρ̄ καὶ ν̄) (**5179** 12)
γραφεῖον **5169** 9

δημόϲιον **5169** 20
διαλογιϲμόϲ **5171** 6
δικαϲτήϲ **5171** 11 (?)

ἐξάκτωρ **5182** 11–12

ἡγεμών [**5171** 5]

θηϲαυρόϲ **5178** 15

ἱππάρχηϲ ἐπ' ἀνδρῶν **5166** 3

κομιϲτήϲ **5182** 10–11 (?)
κωμογραμματεύϲ [**5171** 2]

πραγματικόϲ **5171** [8], 11

ϲιτολόγοϲ **5177** [3 (?)], 16 (?)
ϲτρατηγόϲ **5174** 11 **5177** [2], [3 (?)] **5178** 18

τοπογραμματεύϲ **5171** 1

φρουρόϲ **5182** 11

X. PROFESSIONS, TRADES, AND OCCUPATIONS

ἐλαιουργόϲ **5164** 5

ναυτικόϲ **5167** 2

τραπεζίτηϲ (**5165** 2) **5172** 3

XI. MEASURES

(*a*) Weights and Measures

ἄρουρα **5182** 9–10
(ἀρτάβη) **5178** 4, 6, 7, 13

(μετρητήϲ) **5164** 9 (*bis*)

πῆχυϲ **5170** 6

(*b*) Money

δραχμή (**5165** 4) (**5166** 11) (*bis*) **5168** [9–10], 11 **5169** 6–7, 20 (**5172** 5) **5173** 5–6, (6)

νόμιϲμα **5169** 6 **5173** 5 (Cεβαϲτὸν καὶ Πτολεμαϊκόν)
(πεντώβολον) **5172** 5 (*bis*)

τάλαντον (**5166** 8) (*bis*) **5176** [2] (9), (10) **5182** 14–15

XII. TAXES

ἀργυρικόϲ **5171** 7

εἶδοϲ *see* κανονικὸν εἶδοϲ
ἑκατοϲτὴ καὶ πεντηκοϲτή (ρ̄ καὶ ν̄) **5179** 12

κανονικὸν εἶδοϲ **5182** 15

πεντηκοϲτή *see* ἑκατοϲτὴ καὶ π.
τέλοϲ **5166** 4 (δούληϲ), 10

ὑϊκή **5167** 2

φόροϲ [**5171** 6 (?)] **5182** 12–13
χωματικόν (**5172** 3)

XIII. GENERAL INDEX OF WORDS

πᾶϲ **5168** 9, [18, 20] **5169** 7 (?) **5171** 10 **5173** 9–10 (**5174** 7) **5177** 12 **5182** 4, 18, 19, [21]

πάϲχειν **5168** 20 **5182** 7–8

πατήρ **5164** 2 [**5168** 3] **5169** 5 **5176** ¹ 8 **5182** 8, 16

πέμπειν **5177** 5 **5179** 8 **5180** 3

πενθερόϲ **5179** 4, 6

πεντακόϲιοι (**5176** ² 9)

πέντε **5172** 5 **5182** 14

πεντηκοϲτή *see* Index XII s.v. ἑκατοϲτὴ καὶ π.

πεντώβολον *see* Index XI (b)

περί **5164** 10 **5169** 15 [**5174** 5 (?)] **5177** 6 **5180** 7

πῆχυϲ *see* Index XI (a)

πίϲτιϲ **5171** 3

πλήρηϲ **5182** 18

πληροῦν **5168** 12, [16]

πλοῖον **5178** 3, 10

ποιεῖν **5168** 18, [26]

πόλιϲ *see* Index VII s.v. Ὀξυρύγχων π.

πρᾶγμα **5180** 9

πραγματικόϲ *see* Index IX

πράϲϲειν **5180** 9

πρεϲβύτεροϲ **5169** 3

πρίαϲθαι (**5166** 6)

πρό **5174** 7 **5182** 4, 10

προγράφειν **5169** 14–15, 18–19

προκεῖϲθαι [**5168** 25]

πρόϲ **5166** 8 [**5168** 17] **5173** 3 **5176** ¹ 7, ² (9), (10)

προϲάγειν **5169** 7 **5173** 7

προϲαποτίνειν **5169** 17

προϲρίπτειν [**5168** 14–15]

προϲταϲία [**5168** 18]

πρῶτοϲ [**5168** 11]

ῥύμη (**5167** 3) (?)

ῥωννύναι **5166** 9 **5174** 8 (**5176** ²

10) **5177** 12 **5178** 16 **5179** 11 **5181** 16

Ϲάββατον *see* Index IV (b) s.v. Ϲάμβαθον

ϲεαυτοῦ (**5174** 7)

ϲεβαϲτόϲ *see* Index III s.vv. Tiberius, Claudius, Hadrian; Index IV (a) s.v. Νέοϲ Ϲεβαϲτόϲ; Index IV (b); Index XI (b) s.v. νόμιϲμα

ϲημαίνειν **5169** 12 **5171** 13

ϲιτολόγοϲ *see* Index IX

ϲτρατηγόϲ *see* Index IX

ϲύ **5164** 6, 7, 10 **5166** 10 **5173** 3, 7, [10, 12] **5178** 16 **5179** 2 **5181** 10 **5182** 5, 7 (*bis*), 8, 9, 16, 17 (*bis*), 19, 20, 22 (*bis*)

ϲυγγραφή **5169** 8, 16, 21 [**5170** 2]

ϲυγκύρειν [**5170** 7] **5176** ¹ 6

ϲύμβιοϲ **5182** 23

ϲυμφανήϲ [**5168** 21]

ϲύν **5182** 6

ϲωμάτιον [**5168** 5]

τάλαντον *see* Index XI (b)

τε **5169** 19 **5176** ¹ 7

τελειοῦν **5169** 8

τέλοϲ *see* Index XII

τέϲϲαρεϲ [**5168** 12 (?)]

τέταρτοϲ **5164** 7

τιθέναι **5178** 9

τιθηνεῖν **5168** 6

τιϲ **5168** 20, 21

τοιοῦτοϲ **5171** 15

τοκάϲ (**5167** 3) (?)

τοπαρχία *see* Index VII s.v. μέϲη τοπαρχία

τοπογραμματεύϲ *see* Index IX

τράπεζα **5173** 4

τραπεζίτηϲ *see* Index X

τρεῖϲ **5168** 11 **5169** 4 **5180** 5

τρειϲκαιδέκατοϲ [**5168** 1 (?)] **5169** 1

τρέφειν **5168** [6], 19

τριακόϲιοι (**5165** 3) **5169** 20

τροφεῖον **5168** 8

τυγχάνειν **5168** 19

ὕβριϲ **5182** 14

ὑγιαίνειν [**5174** 7]

ὑγίεια **5182** 6

ὑϊκή *see* Index XII

υἱόϲ **5171** 5 **5181** 13 **5182** 24

ὑμεῖϲ **5180** 3, 4, 8 **5181** 16

ὑπέρ **5169** 14, 18 [**5174** 5 (?)] **5182** 15, 17

ὑπέρθεϲιϲ **5173** 10

ὑπό **5171** 2, 5, 13 **5182** 8

ὑποθήκη [**5170** 2 (?)]

ὑποκεῖϲθαι [**5171** 4]

φέρειν **5182** 10

φίλοϲ **5177** [4], 11 **5179** 2

φόροϲ *see* Index XII

φρουρόϲ *see* Index IX

χαίρειν (**5164** 5) (**5165** 2) **5166** 1 [**5170** 1] **5173** 2 **5176** (¹ 2), (² 6) [**5177** 4] **5178** 2 **5182** 3

χαλκόϲ **5166** 8 **5176** ² (9), (10)

χίλιοι **5176** ² 9

χορηγεῖν **5168** 12

χρηματίζειν **5165** 2 (**5176** ² 3)

χρονίζειν **5177** 8

χρόνοϲ **5168** 6–7, [19, 22]

χωματικόν *see* Index XII

χώρα **5171** 8

χωρίϲ **5169** 16 **5173** 9

ὠνεῖϲθαι **5171** 4, 9, 11, 14

ὠνή **5176** ¹ 3

ὡϲ **5166** 4 **5179** 5

XIV. CORRECTIONS TO PUBLISHED TEXTS

PLATE I

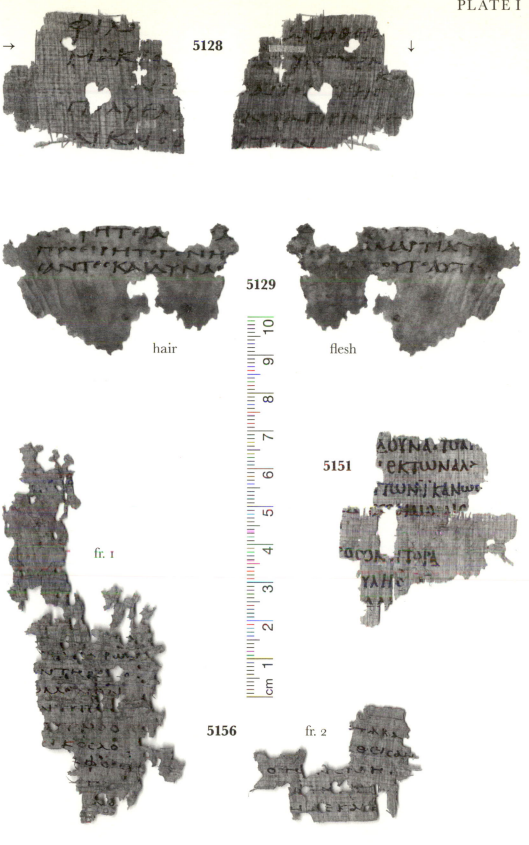

5128

5129

hair

flesh

5151

fr. 1

5156

fr. 2

PLATE II

5130

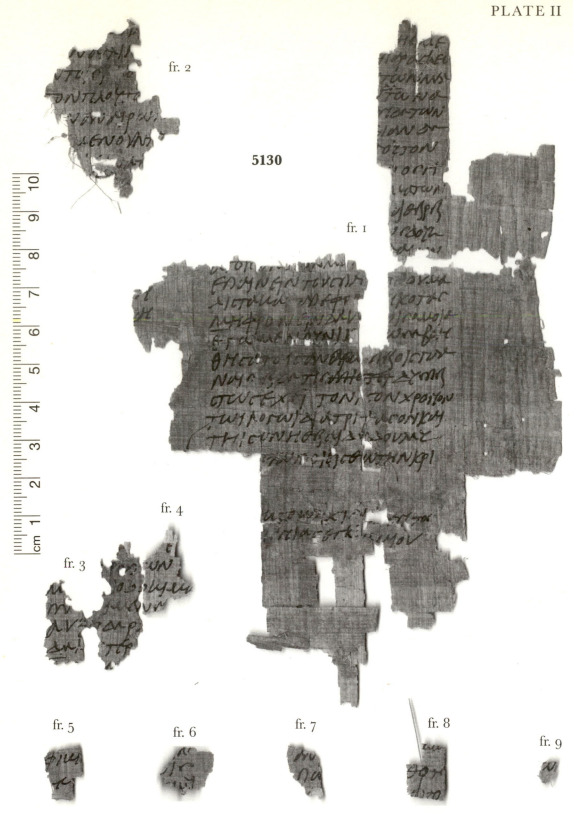

fr. 2

fr. 1

fr. 4

fr. 3

fr. 5

fr. 6

fr. 7

fr. 8

fr. 9

PLATE III

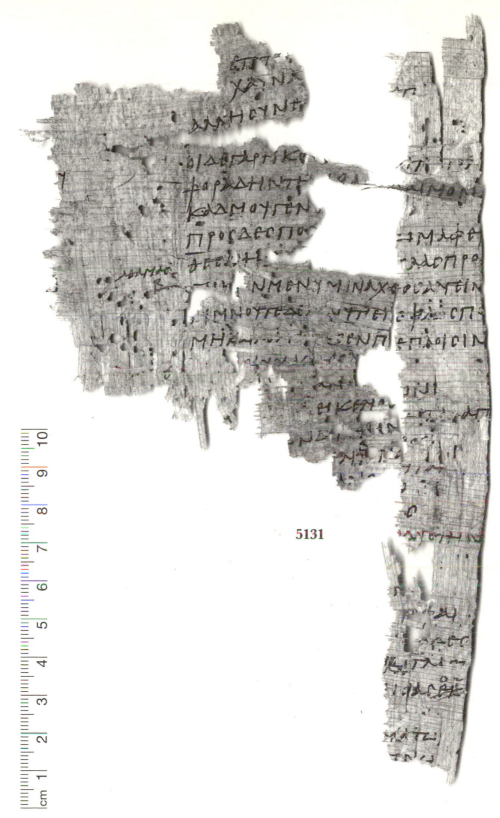

5131

PLATE IV

5153

5157

5167

PLATE V

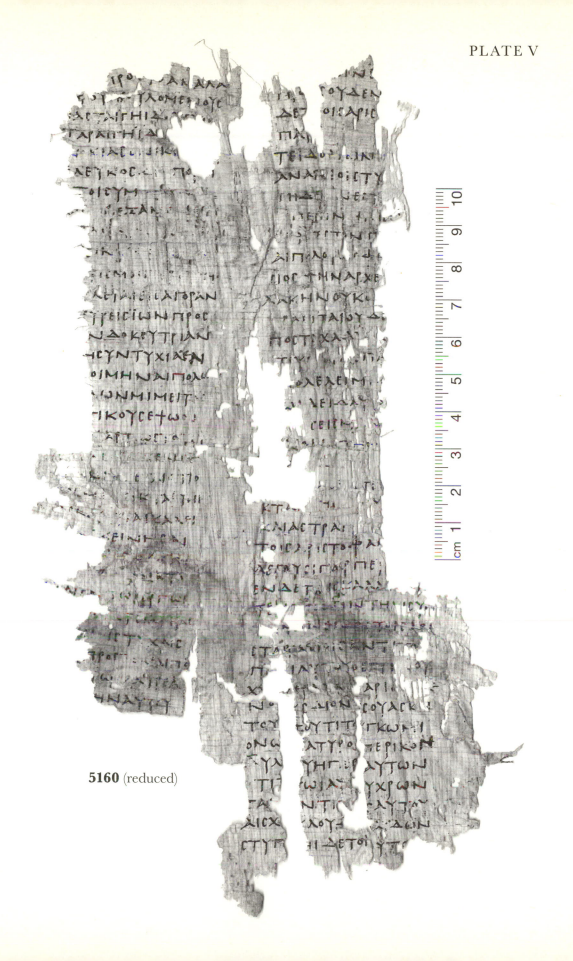

5160 (reduced)

PLATE VI

5161

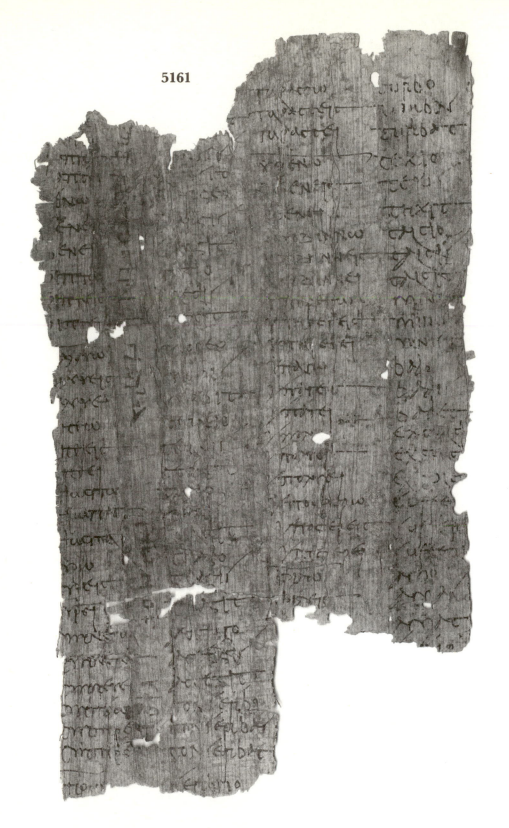

PLATE VII

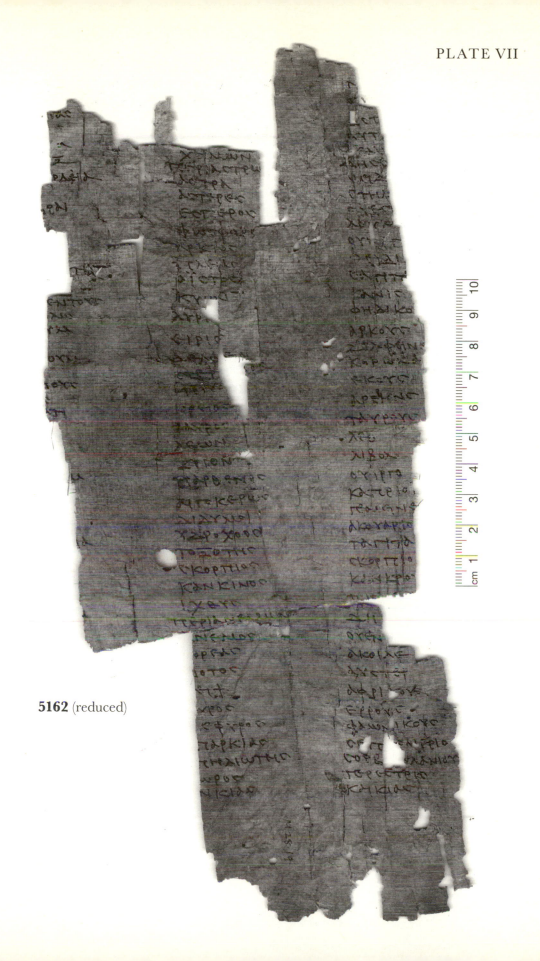

5162 (reduced)

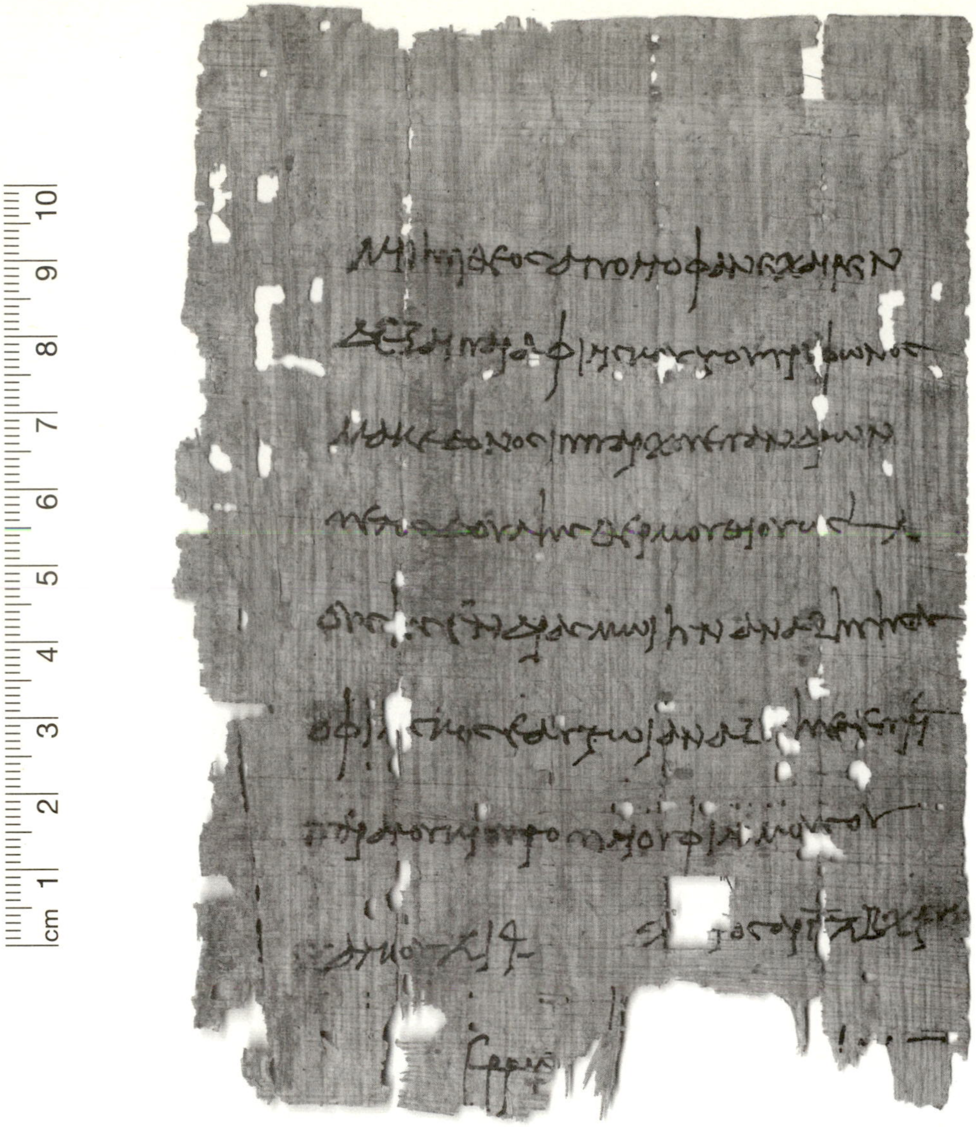

PLATE VIII

5166 front

PLATE IX

5166 back

PLATE X

PLATE XI

5178 back

PLATE XII

5182

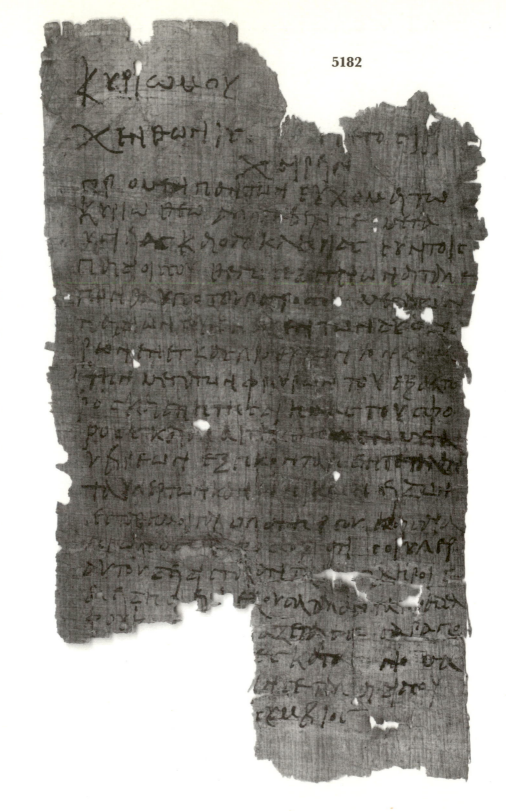